Feminisms and Internationalism

Feminisms and Internationalism

Edited by
Mrinalini Sinha, Donna Guy and Angela Woollacott

BLACKWELL
Publishers

ISBN: 0-631-20919-0

First published in 1999

Blackwell Publishers Ltd
108 Cowley Road, Oxford OX4 1JF, UK

and
350 Main Street
Malden, MA 02148, USA

British Library Cataloguing in Publication Data
A catalogue record for this book is available
from the British Library

Library of Congress Cataloging-in-Publication Data
Applied for

Printed in Great Britain by MPG Books Ltd, Bodmin, Cornwall
This book is printed on acid-free paper

Feminisms and Internationalism

edited by Mrinalini Sinha, Donna Guy and Angela Woollacott

CONTENTS

Forum

Forum Respondents

Review Essays

Notes on Contributors

Index

ABSTRACTS

An Alternative Imperialism: Isabella Tod, Internationalist and 'Good Liberal Unionist'

HELOISE BROWN

This paper argues that a discourse of conservative Imperialism was present during the Irish Home Rule debate of 1886. The arguments of Isabella Tod (1836–96), a feminist who took a conservative imperialist approach, are examined to show how an alternative role was envisioned for Britain within its empire. Her critiques of imperial expansion are contrasted with her support for the maintenance of the Union between Ireland and Britain. It is argued that existing discourses of nationalism and imperialism are insufficient in explaining Tod's identity, and that a re-evaluation of these discourses is necessary in order to accommodate such marginalised perspectives.

'The New Women's Movement' in 1920s Korea: Rethinking the Relationship Between Imperialism and Women

INSOOK KWON

Recently, some feminist scholars' analyses of imperialism have focused on illustrating imperial power as a multi-dimensional hegemonic domination process established by a variety of forms of authority, knowledge and power. However, the perspective focusing on Western hegemonic domination can destroy criteria for evaluating the colonised women's movements which are not closely related to the nationalistic movement and cannot embrace diverse women's interests. In this essay, I attempt to rethink the gendered impact of imperialism by challenging the criteria based on an 'all powerful' Western hegemony and disclosing a more complicated relationship between colonised women and imperialism in the case of the Korean New Women's movement in the 1920s. Korea's New Women were a group of women who challenged the moral system of Confucian patriarchy, on the basis of a new self-identity acquired through modern education, and comprised the first feminist generation in Korea. Through examining the dynamics of how and why the New Women chose certain types of Western feminism, I try to build up new criteria which can inclusively represent diverse women's interests in the colonial or post-colonial context.

Madrinas and Missionaries: Uruguay and the Pan-American Women's Movement

CHRISTINE EHRICK

Despite the rhetoric of internationalism, liberal feminists in the Americas were heavily grounded in their own particular national contexts. Uruguayan liberal feminists, for example, were as concerned about Argentine designs on their movement as they were with US feminists' attempts to dominate Pan-American women's networks. Correspondence between Uruguayan liberal feminist leader Paulina Luisi and her counterparts in Latin America tells the history of Pan-American women's networks from the Latin American perspective, and documents the impact of growing nationalism in the 1920s on liberal feminism in the Pan-American context.

Inventing Commonwealth and Pan-Pacific Feminisms: Australian Women's Internationalist Activism in the 1920s–30s

ANGELA WOOLLACOTT

Australian feminists, through the British Commonwealth League founded in London in 1925, forged a Commonwealth feminism that was both more inclusive than and a reconstitution of late nineteenth- and early twentieth-century imperial feminism. At the same time, Australian women's involvement within the Pan-Pacific Women's Association, whose first conference was held in Honolulu in 1928, signalled a geopolitically different field of vision. Based on conference programmes and feminists' writings, my aims in this essay include outlining Australian women's activism in both these organisations in the interwar period, assessing the global politics involved, considering their stances as white British dominion women in international contexts and in terms of Australia's colonisation of Aboriginal people, and historicising their activism in the broader picture of feminist internationalism.

The Politics of Pan-American Cooperation: Maternalist Feminism and the Child Rights Movement, 1913–1960

DONNA J. GUY

Maternalist feminists, those interested in promoting mother–child issues as part of their efforts to expand the rights of women, influenced the Pan-American child welfare movement. Latin American women began in Buenos Aires, Argentina, in 1913. No US women attended these early meetings, and efforts from 1916 to 1927 by the US Women's Auxiliary Committee to the Second Pan-American Scientific Congress (WAC) created more antagonisms than it promoted Pan-American efforts. In 1927 the Instituto Internacional Interamericano del Niño (International Inter-American Child Institute, IIAPI), founded and controlled by male physicians, took over the Pan-American Child Congresses. The second phase of the child welfare movement took place from 1927 until 1960. During this era, IIAPI physicians initially refused to cooperate with feminists, but they reversed this policy after meeting feminist US Children's Bureau social workers in the 1920s. Katherine Lenroot, a key US delegate, Chief of the Children's Bureau from 1934 to 1951, served as a catalyst to promote broader mother and child welfare programmes in the Americas by focusing on child rights rather than state intervention. She also helped bring Latin American feminists back into the Pan-American child rights movement.

Jie Gui – Connecting the Tracks: Chinese Women's Activism Surrounding the 1995 World Conference on Women in Beijing
PING-CHUN HSIUNG AND YUK-LIN RENITA WONG

This paper examines Chinese women's activism surrounding the 1995 United Nations World Conference on Women in Beijing. We show that while women activists in China wanted the Conference to begin to connect local initiatives with global feminist activism, their hopes were compromised by heated exchanges between the CCP state and Western feminist and human rights groups. In effect, the voices of women activists in China were suppressed and marginalised. To uncover and acknowledge Chinese women's agency and subjectivity, we examine Chinese women activists' gender and national identities in the historical context of their liberation. We find that the gender identity of Chinese women activists is not in opposition to their national identity, but, rather, intertwined with it. This finding calls for a conceptualisation of collective selves in the theorisation of agency and subjectivity. It challenges the confrontational paradigm projected in the NGO model that has been advocated by Western feminist/activist groups. It also demands a dialectical approach to the analysis of the relations between the CCP state and Chinese women. On the one hand, our analysis is derived from, and seeks to contribute to, the feminist debate about the way Sinologists present and re-present Chinese women. On the other hand, we seek to shed light on the tension between global and local feminist activism. Our sources are Internet discussion groups and world wide web homepages on the Conference, the CCP's statements and other official documents, and published books and articles.

Unifying Women: Feminist Pasts and Presents in Yemen
MARGOT BADRAN

This article argues that women's cohesive gender activism is a major force in consolidating the unification of the Republic of Yemen, formed out of the former North and South Yemens. Acting as feminists, women contest re/assertions of patri-archal excesses that threaten the new national unity and the equality of citizens fundamental to its declared democratic project. The paper focuses on two recent events: the high-profile parliamentary elections of 1997 and the simultaneous, hidden attempt to impose a reactionary personal status law. The latter politicised women who rallied together across the political and ideological spectrum to protect their rights and to establish the linkage between the private and public as together constitutive of citizenship and the equal rights for all that this implies.

Some Trajectories of 'Feminism' and 'Imperialism'

ANTOINETTE BURTON

This essay surveys some of the intellectual and institutional contexts out of which scholarly work on women, feminism, and imperialism has been produced in the last two decades. The call to reconstitute both feminist histories and the practices of feminist historiography that was issued largely by women of colour in the 1980s has made new landscapes visible, even as it has raised important and unresolved questions about the subjects of feminism and the availability of 'the nation' as the ground of critically engaged feminist scholarship. Focusing equally on the ways in which recent research has transformed our understanding of colonial *and* metropolitan histories, this review of recent literature tracks some of the trajectories of 'feminism' and 'imperialism' and suggests possible avenues of future inquiry.

Feminisms and Transnationalism

FRANCESCA MILLER

The essay considers new work by feminist scholars addressing the history of women's transnational organising, gender and international relations, and the complex nature of transnational feminist interactions that are at once local and global in the late 1990s. Drawing specific examples from work on women of the Americas, the essay explores the ways in which increasingly subtle understandings of gender inform the new literature, concluding that the wealth of information emerging from the presses of women's documentation centres constitutes a politics of information, creating a new historical record. The need for historical context and analysis is critical to this effort.

Feminisms and International Relations

V. SPIKE PETERSON

A bastion of male practitioners, masculine activities and androcentric constructs, the discipline of International Relations (IR) guards itself well against feminist theory/practice. In the past decade, however, a small but rapidly expanding community of feminists has 'made a difference' in IR. Four of the most widely read books are reviewed here, to suggest both the historical development and transborder range of this scholarship.

Feminisms and Development

VALENTINE M. MOGHADAM

The article examines the evolution of the field of women-in-development, and discusses the body of knowledge and field of research currently known as gender and development (GAD). Key works are cited as representing and contributing to the assumptions, concepts, and methods that constitute the GAD framework. Some studies document the effects of various development processes on women. Others focus on gender roles, gender relations, and gender ideologies to reveal their influence on economic policy and development outcomes. Finally, I draw attention to the contradictions of globalisation and to the increasing visibility of women's movements and transnational feminist networks.

Introduction: Why Feminisms and Internationalism?

MRINALINI SINHA, DONNA J. GUY AND ANGELA WOOLLACOTT

We arrived at the theme for this special issue on 'Feminisms and Internationalism' from a desire to think together, on the one hand, the wide range of different feminisms and women's movements as they have emerged in historically specific sociopolitical contexts,[1] and, on the other, the universalist ideals that have been claimed historically on behalf of feminism.[2] These ideals appear in some contexts as mere ideology and in others as valuable utopian goals to a better political practice. In either case, moreover, such ideals have had international and transnational implications. The choice of Feminisms and Internationalism, therefore, reflects our own attempt to acknowledge, and to work through, the productive tension between the centrifugal force of discrepant feminist histories and the promising potential of political organising across cultural boundaries. Our approach to the special-issue topic has been informed by the contribution of some recent feminist scholarship that has raised new questions about the relation between the local and the global contexts of women's movements and feminisms world-wide.

We identify several strands of this scholarship as pertinent to our project. Our thinking has been informed, for example, by the valuable critiques that several feminist scholars have made of the use, as if they were self-evident, of such concepts as 'universal sisterhood' and 'global feminism', positing thereby either a bodily identity or a common experience of oppression supposedly shared by women all over the world.[3] These claims of universalism on behalf of an international feminist solidarity have been shown, in fact, to rest on an unreflective equation of the 'provincial'[4] or parochial experience of certain dominant versions of feminism in Western Europe and North America as the paradigmatic form of feminism per se. Thus such paradigms of 'universal sisterhood' inevitably run afoul of the many divisions between women along the lines of class, race, sexuality, ethnicity, nationality, First World/Third World, and so on. At the same time, however, we have also learned from a feminist scholarship that has warned against the easy alternative of merely positing a plurality of feminisms organised around some absolute conception of national and/or cultural difference over and against the universalist project of feminism. For, as Rey Chow cautions:

> The attempt to deconstruct the hegemony of *patriarchal* discourses through feminism is itself foreclosed by the emphasis on 'Chinese' as a mark of absolute difference. To my mind, it is when the West's 'other women' are prescribed their 'own' national and ethnic identity in this way that they are most excluded from having a claim to the reality of their existence.[5]

What is becoming clear is that 'woman' needs to be disarticulated from its function as the designated embodiment of culture and that cultures themselves need to be recognised not as fixed products but in terms of historical processes.[6] The retreat into discrete national or cultural feminisms, moreover, forecloses the analysis of the co-implication of these multiple feminisms in a shared history of the combined, but uneven, evolution of a system whose economic, political and ideological reach has in fact been world-wide for several centuries.

We arrive at the theme for the special issue, therefore, via a recognition that the real challenge for feminisms and internationalism today lies in a historical critique both of a *false* universalism that would subsume the diversity of feminisms within an elite or 'provincial' understanding of feminism and of a relativism that would abandon any universalist claim for feminism in obeisance to reified and absolute conceptions of difference.[7] Such a project requires both the uncovering of alternative feminist histories that challenge the selective memory of a parochial and univocal history *and* the recognition of the necessary imbrication of such alternative histories in a world-wide social formation fashioned by imperialism and colonialism.

Finally, in choosing this particular theme for the special issue, we have been inspired by the growing examples of the contemporary mobilisations of women and feminists in various women's movements and the new social movements around common 'global' problems. Many of these movements, as Peter Waterman has suggested, are 'less interested in relations between nations than in global problems'; and, as such, they 'tend to "cross borders" in their analyses and demands, whether these borders are those of gender, race, class, or a territorial understanding of the region or world'.[8] We refer here to such examples as the following: the common bond being forged between women workers in countries of both the North and the South as a result of a growing shift towards more flexible forms of production and structural adjustments associated with a post-Fordist global economy; the growing emphasis in women's movements and the new social movements on problems created by ecological and environmental degradation; the broad alliance of women against various religious chauvinisms and fundamentalisms; and international feminist campaigns for the recognition of women's rights as human rights. These examples of 'globalisation from below',[9] indeed, reveal existing potential for a new phase in the history of feminisms

and internationalism and for imagining alternative forms of feminist internationalism. It is against this background of both feminist scholarship and
practice that we decided to undertake this project of thinking together
both the diverse histories of feminisms and the potential for cross-cultural
alliances.

We see this special issue as a ground-clearing project for understanding
both the problems and the potential of feminist internationalism. The
necessary first step in this direction is to explore the subject of feminisms and
internationalism historically. Our call for papers thus invited contributions
that addressed the theme of the history of internationalism in feminist theory
and praxis, possibly including the following topics: the ways in which 'internationalism' has been conceived historically within feminism and women's
movements; the nature of and historical shifts within 'imperial' feminisms;
changes in the meaning of feminist internationalism both preceding and
following the end of most formal empires in the twentieth century; the
challenges to, and reformulations of, internationalism within feminism
by women of colour and by women from colonised or formerly colonised
countries; the fragmentation of internationalism in response to a growing
emphasis on local over global contexts of struggle as well as on a variety
of different feminisms instead of a singular feminism; and the context for
the re-emergence of internationalism within feminisms and women's movements as a result of the new modes of globalisation in the late twentieth
century. The contributions chosen for this volume provide a rich inventory
of the differing contexts for the connections between feminisms and internationalism historically.

Connecting women and feminisms in different parts of the world means
comparing histories, at least implicitly, and in the process identifying a
variety of global power dynamics in historical profile. At its broadest, the
history of feminisms and internationalism is a lens through which we can
view modern world history. Through narratives of women's international
organising we can see, for example, the trajectory of the abolitionist movement of the eighteenth and early nineteenth centuries: its eventual absorption,
that is, within the imperatives of 'free-trade imperialism' and the emerging
science of 'race'. We can see also the ascendancy of European and other
empires from the late nineteenth century, and with it Western feminism's
imperial roots. We can see the emergence of anti-colonial movements, and
with them nationalist feminisms in the twentieth century. We can observe
the creation of a self-consciously international women's movement within
international socialism; we can trace the growth of the international ideal
and international feminism's powerful links first to the League of Nations
and then to its successor, the United Nations; and, alongside these
developments, we can observe the shift to the more decentred global
structures of transnational capitalism. The history of internationalist feminist organising reflects other global dynamics as well: the waning of British
power; the emergence of the United States as a superpower with hegemonic

claims to hemispheric 'spheres of influence'; the rise and fall of international socialism; and the massive disruptiveness and destruction wrought
by the world wars, which both provoked and curtailed international feminist pacifism. It is possible, moreover, to identify decolonising impulses in
the emergence of such regional feminist networks as the following: the
Asian and Pan-American women's conferences; Latin American feminist
and Pan-Pacific women's networking in the interwar decades; and the later
twentieth-century growth of African women's movements for political
stability, economic possibilities, and appropriate development assistance.
Indeed, women's regional and global networking from the middle decades
of the twentieth century needs to be linked to geopolitical realignments
during and following the crumbling of European empires. Such are the
contexts and ramifications of exploring feminist international histories.

Given the complexities of, and obstacles to, international feminist organising, it is worth asking what impulses have driven women for over a century
determinedly to build international channels and bodies. The essays in
this issue, as well as any perusal of international feminist conference programmes, testify to the list of causes that have connected women both
through time and across racial, cultural, religious, class, national, linguistic
and other barriers. The list of shared issues reveals the global resonance of
concern about education for girls and women; about women's access to,
and rights at, work; about marriage and divorce laws; about married women's
citizenship laws; and about a spectrum of health issues, including reproductive
rights. The growth of socialism and the emergence of a strong feminist
movement within international socialism provided one framework for the
development of an international women's movement in the early parts of
this century. The International Proletarian Women's Day, authorised by the
international socialist women's conference in 1910, became the inspiration
for the International Women's Day in March that is celebrated well into our
own times.[10] Pacifism drove women to protest war and militarism, from the
historic 1915 conference at the Hague, which led to the foundation of
the Women's International League for Peace and Freedom; to innumerable
resolutions taken at international women's conferences for disarmament in
the 1920s and against rearmament in the 1930s; to international anti-
nuclear movements in the 1970s and 1980s; to international support for
the Mothers of the Plaza de Mayo in Argentina; and to African women's
shared concerns about civil wars on that continent in recent decades.
Religion and related social reform work have also provided the basis for
cross-cultural women's networks from nineteenth-century Christian
temperance reforms to such current coalitions as the international network
Women Living Under Muslim Laws, which is based in France.

Women's suffrage was a critical motive for international networking from
the middle decades of the nineteenth century onwards, with international
agitation often seen as a crucial strategy for moving recalcitrant national
governments. Since the gradual achievement of women's right to vote in

democratic countries through the early and middle twentieth century, women's access to political office, as well as women's representation at, first, the League of Nations and then the United Nations, have become common issues. Prostitution, and the kidnapping of women into prostitution, have been perennial issues on international feminist agendas since the late nineteenth century.[11] Given the international scale of the continuing trade in women and children in many parts of the world, international feminist efforts have been crucial in calling attention to the problem. Institutionalising internationalism itself has been both an issue and a goal, from the moves to found the first international feminist organisations in the 1870s to the United Nations Decade for Women beginning in 1975.[12] With the recent appropriation of various local feminist platforms by international donor agencies and the World Bank, scholars and activists have also begun to raise questions about the corporate agendas being served by the incorporation of feminisms within the institutions of international finance.[13]

It might be argued that, at the end of the twentieth century, the stakes for feminist internationalism have been increased considerably because of the very conditions of contemporary globality in which the tightly integrated nature of the world economy coexists with increasing cultural fragmentation. Both the difficulties in, and the importance of, building broad alliances of progressive forces internationally have been addressed by Algerian feminist-activist Marie-Aimée Helie-Lucas:

> I think we should work with Left people and with women, wherever they are. And if we are not satisfied with what they think, we can explain, instead of attacking them, because we don't identify the principal enemy by doing so. We destroy our own possibilities and forces, in the long run.[14]

We suggest that understanding the history of feminisms and internationalism has important implications for building the kinds of international alliances that have become so crucial today.

What distinguishes this collection on Feminisms and Internationalism is the attempt to examine the history of feminists' long engagement with internationalism from within a global framework. We have assembled together in this volume the histories of a broad array of feminist episodes and movements that were integrally internationalist. When taken together, these contributions serve to defamiliarise the received history of feminisms and internationalism by manifesting the multiple contexts from which feminists have initiated engagements with internationalism. As such, therefore, this volume is different from other works in the field in two ways. First, this volume extends the discussion of the international women's movement beyond the more familiar histories of the dominant international women's networks. Much of the literature on the international women's movement has focused on these dominant Euro-American women's organisations from the 1880s to 1940. Even here, however, there has been more work available on liberal-feminist international organisations than on the socialist-feminist international women's movement.[15] The picture of an international women's movement that has emerged has mainly focused on the experiences of those women's groups that were dominant in the movement. The current volume, however, includes the stories of feminist organisations and individual women from several different countries who forged international links beyond the operation of the dominant international networks. This collection, therefore, by retrieving for historical memory the existence of rival international women's networks and their engagement with internationalism, rounds out the picture of internationalism in women's movements.

Second, even though the essays in this collection deal with different region- and country-specific women's movements, they all engage either explicitly or implicitly with their relation to international feminism.[16] This makes this collection different from several others that include diverse histories of women's movements around the world but do not focus steadily on issues of internationalism. The objective of this collection, therefore, has not been to strive for exhaustive 'representation' in, for example, ethnic or national terms. Its objective, instead, has been to uncover the multiplicity of locations from which a writing of the histories of feminist engagements with internationalism must proceed. The contribution of this collection, therefore, lies in a broader refocusing of the lens through which the discussion on feminisms and internationalism has hitherto been framed.

This shift in perspective has several implications for the existing scholarship on organised feminisms. It was held, on the basis of the history of European and North American feminist histories, that organised activism ground to a halt with World War I and tailed off soon thereafter. In powerful contrast to that paradigm, several essays in this volume reveal the decades between the world wars as a crucial and consolidating period of feminist international activism in diverse arenas around the world. Francesca Miller notes in her review essay that, while World War II all but extinguished international feminist organising in Europe, in the Americas it actually spurred feminist activism. The inclusion of other locations in constructing histories of feminist internationalism may, indeed, call not just for different periodisations but also for different paradigms for understanding this history.

This defamiliarisation of the history of feminisms and internationalism also raises new questions about the complex dynamics between local, national, regional and international feminist organising. It has often been assumed that even though national and international consciousness coexisted within the international networks of the women's movement, the important precondition for internationalism lay in the existence of a strong and secure national consciousness. This was, indeed, true of the women's organisations in Western and Northern Europe and North America that held the leadership positions in the dominant international organisations. However, the interaction between national and international consciousness was in reality far more complex. Leila Rupp in her contribution to this collection suggests that the perspectives of women from Latin America, Asia, the Middle East and Africa have historically challenged the notion that nationalism and internationalism were complete opposites. And the essays by Angela Woollacott and Christine Ehrick, for example, suggest that the rival international organisations in the interwar period pioneered by women from Australia and New Zealand as well as from Uruguay and other countries in South America could be seen in terms of national and regional self-assertion. These organisations identified themselves, whether explicitly or implicitly, against the national domination enjoyed by Britain and the United States in the most influential international women's organisations of the time. When extended to other examples, such as the All-Asian Women's Conference held in Lahore in 1931 that Mary E. John refers to in her contribution to this collection, it would seem that a relatively embattled and precarious national consciousness – no less than a more self-confident one – has galvanised the drive toward internationalism.

The decentring of the history of feminisms and internationalism that has been attempted in this collection, moreover, also has potential for challenging what Mary E. John identifies as 'the hegemony of the West as our default frame of reference' for internationalism. Taken together, the essays in this collection point in the direction of alternative axes for feminist connections. It has been widely recognised that just as international feminist networks themselves developed out of the initiatives of various national feminist organisations, the development of international networks in turn helped stimulate feminist organising at the local, national and regional levels.[17] The further point that is raised by bringing together the varied engagements of feminisms and internationalism from multiple contexts, however, is the potential and possibilities of different axes of connections for local, national, regional and international feminist organising. The essay by Ping-Chun Hsiung and Yuk-Lin R. Wong on Chinese women's activism and the fourth world women's conference in Beijing and Huairou in 1995, for example, suggests that South–South connections (such as the response of Chinese women activists to the women's organisations in Argentina, the Philippines and Senegal) have as much potential for 'connecting the tracks of Chinese women's movement with the world' as the more familiar Western–non-Western axis. Several of the essays in the volume, indeed, point out the existence of various alternative axes for international connections that go beyond the model of the 'West and the Rest'.

The essays have been organised broadly within a chronological and thematic framework. The first set of essays, by Heloise Brown and Insook Kwon, deal with internationalism in the context of late nineteenth- and early twentieth-century imperialisms and counter-nationalisms. What both of these essays demonstrate, albeit in very different contexts and in very different ways, is that neither feminism nor internationalism could survive unscathed during this period's political upheavals involving imperialism and anti-colonial nationalism. Brown explains the apparent contradictions of Isabella Tod's 'alternative imperialism', her opposition to Britain's imperial wars abroad and her simultaneous support for Britain's 'civilising' presence in Ireland, in terms of her commitment to a liberal feminist and international pacifist politics. Tod's 'alternative imperialism', however, came up against a world in which imperial expansion would become the norm and arguments for deferring the nationalist aspirations of peoples in exchange for the supposed benevolence of a 'civilising' government would become increasingly difficult to sustain. The limits of Tod's 'alternative imperialism', reflected in her marginalisation during and after the bitter controversy over Irish Home Rule in the 1880s, demonstrate the impotence of a liberal internationalism in the face of the very contradictions that imperialism itself had unleashed. Kwon's essay on 'New Women' in 1920s Korea presents an intriguing example of the complex connections between Western culture, feminism and imperialism. The fact that Korea was colonised by Japan, Kwon suggests, meant that Western culture did not always carry the same imperial baggage in Korea as it did elsewhere. Korean 'New Women' encountered internationally circulating feminist thought which they found useful in their own critiques both of the Confucian patriarchalism of Korean society and of their Japanese colonisers. These early feminists, however, lost their struggle in the face of the reformulation of indigenous patriarchy by early Korean nationalists, as well as of an increasingly conservative Japanese imperialism, which began to associate challenges to the traditional order with a threat to its own interests. The story of the 'New Women' in Korea is a stark reminder of the ways in which the forces of imperialism and nationalism, despite their conflict, have often shared an investment in the defence or reconstitution of 'traditional' patriarchal culture.

The second set of essays addresses a different international situation in which the imperial order itself was reconstituted and national assertion had become much more self-confident and pervasive. What these three essays demonstrate, indeed, is that the history of internationalism was not antithetical to challenges to imperial domination or the self-assertion of nationalism. Christine Ehrick's essay discusses the Pan-American women's movement in the first half of the twentieth century from the perspective of liberal feminists in Uruguay who forged international feminist connections within Latin America under the shadow of 'yankee feminist imperialism' from the US as well as of the 'yanquis of the South' in Argentina. The particular national and continental agendas of different Latin American feminists, Ehrick's essay suggests, laid the groundwork for the development of Pan-American liberal feminism in the early decades of the twentieth century. The eventual crisis of interwar Pan-American liberal feminism, according to Ehrick, reflected not just the threat of 'yanqui' domination but also the internal contradictions of liberal feminism's 'class blueprint' that Cuban socialist-feminists, such as Ofelia Dominguez Navarro, had begun to challenge directly.

Angela Woollacott examines the challenge that the interwar feminist internationalism of Australian feminists, who were associated with the British Commonwealth League and the Pan-Pacific Women's Association, posed to existing colonial and racial hierarchies. The new impetus toward internationalism represented by the League of Nations and the shifting relations between Britain and the white-settler dominions provide the background for Woollacott's study. Although the British Commonwealth League was dominated by white dominion women, they were much more attuned to the interests of the women of the 'Empire' and even occasionally provided feminists from the dependent empire, such as India, with more hospitable international platforms. Concurrently, the Pan-Pacific women's conferences represented a significant regional alternative to the dominant European and North American channels of international women's networks. More interestingly, perhaps, organisations such as the British Commonwealth League also provided a platform for progressive Australian feminists to bring national racial and Aboriginal policies in Australia to international attention. Woollacott demonstrates that even as these organisations reproduced many of the colonial and racial hierarchies of their times, they reflected a shifting international situation in which questions about colonial and racial dominance were beginning to transform the networks of international feminism.

Donna Guy's essay, wrapping up the interwar cluster, describes a particular instance of international Pan-American cooperation around the issue of maternalism. Focusing on the contributions of US feminist Katherine Lenroot, Guy suggests that, from the 1930s, maternalist and child-welfare policies became a unique area of Pan-American cooperation. It brought together feminists with their concerns for women's rights, and various social reformers and professionals with their own agendas for building a healthy citizenry into cooperation over maternalist and child welfare policies for governments to follow. Much of the credit for this achievement, according to Guy, belongs to the political strategies and organisational abilities of Lenroot. Lenroot, Guy suggests, was able to coordinate the agendas of feminists and non-feminists alike to enable a hemisphere-wide cooperation on maternal and child-welfare issues. The impact of the rise of socialism, the beginnings of the reconstitution of the old imperial and colonial order, and the emergence of maternalist-welfare policies provide the background for the discussion of internationalist feminism in these three essays.

The final two essays, by Ping-Chun Hsiung and Yuk-Lin R. Wong jointly and by Margot Badran, bring the history of feminisms and internationalism into the present. These essays together demonstrate that globalisation and internationalisation have not automatically created the conditions for feminist internationalism. The task of building feminist networks cross-culturally and internationally still demands painstaking political engagement with local nuances. Hsiung and Wong argue that the controversies between the Chinese Communist Party and Western feminist and human rights groups during the fourth United Nation's World Conference on Women in 1995 show that both fell short of the more nuanced approach adopted by Chinese women activists themselves, who mediated between the Communist Party state and Chinese women's interests, on the one hand, and between the national character of the Chinese women's movement and international feminism, on the other. The essay by Hsiung and Wong suggests that basic questions of representation and translation across cultures and political ideologies continue to plague efforts at connecting feminisms at the national and international levels. Notwithstanding these difficulties, however, the determined efforts of Chinese women activists to negotiatiate a place for themselves simultaneously within both the national framework and the international arena are a testimony to the utopian promise of a feminist internationalism that can bring together the local, the national and the international. Badran's essay on the role of Yemeni women in the struggle to unify the new republic of Yemen after its creation in 1990 from the former Yemen Arab Republic in the north and the People's Democratic Republic of Yemen in the south offers an interesting case study of achieved political unity among women that spanned the divide of 'separate feminist pasts'. The history of the nationalist and socialist states in the north and south respectively, Badran suggests, produced very different feminist legacies in the two halves of the newly formed republic. Yet the controversy over the 1997 Personal Status Law mobilised and politicised women in the north and the south against its conservative gender implications. Yemeni women activists may eschew the label of feminists, but, as Badran suggests, they practise feminism. What Badran's essay emphasises are the pragmatic political practices through which coalitions among women with diverse histories can be built. The importance of working through, rather than ignoring, the diversities of women's histories is, perhaps, one of the key lessons to be learned from a global history of feminisms and internationalism.

Asunción Lavrin's contribution to the forum 'International Feminisms: Latin American Alternatives' serves as the occasion for an exchange on feminisms and internationalism between scholars writing from different contexts and different political perspectives. Lavrin's essay suggests that the long experience with national and international feminisms in Latin America makes the region a particularly useful site from which to raise questions about feminisms and internationalism more generally. Her many questions, indeed, resonate in several contexts, as is testified by the responses to Lavrin's essay. Leila J. Rupp, who describes her own location as 'a ship on the Atlantic', picks up on several of Lavrin's themes. Rupp responds to Lavrin's question about how to conceptualise feminisms globally by arguing for the need to think about feminisms organisationally and tactically as much as ideologically. Mary E. John, writing about India, picks up the themes of pluralism and colonialism as the points of her intersection with and departure from Lavrin's essay. John suggests that internationalism, like feminism, is not singular. She thus questions the disposition to look for internationalism in some directions more than others. Her essay concludes with a discussion of several different examples of what she calls 'newly emergent internationalisms'. Shahnaz Rouse takes up the question of religion that Lavrin does not discuss in her essay as the basis for her own response. Rouse's response draws from examples of countries with majority Muslim populations. The themes of *mestizaje* and motherhood in Lavrin's essay have been picked up and combined in a very different context by Jayne O. Ifekwunigwe in her contribution to the forum. Ifekwunigwe offers the example of 'borderland feminism' as a way of disrupting the dichotomies of Black/White and First World/Third World in feminist discourses.

We conclude this collection with a series of review essays on fields directly related to the historiography of feminisms and internationalism. Antoinette Burton explores the contributions of an interdisciplinary scholarship that has demonstrated how the very category of feminism has emerged from the history of modern European colonialism and anti-colonial struggles. Her review essay raises questions about nation-centred history as an adequate investigative framework for feminisms in the 'West' or in the 'Third World'. Francesca Miller's essay examines the literature on transnational feminist organisations and in the process offers a much more rigorous definition of transnationalism and internationalism. Miller suggests that the contributions of a specifically feminist historiography need to inform the broader scholarship on gender and transnational interactions. V. Spike Peterson focuses on gender in international relations theory and traces the emergence of a 'feminist IR' that has begun to transform the field. The changing focus of the literature on development, from 'Women in Development' to 'Gender and Development', is the focus of Valentine Moghadam's review essay. Moghadam's contribution shows the extent to which the global economy is indeed a gendered economy.

What we have attempted to provide in this collection is the outlines of a global framework for exploring the history of feminisms and internationalism. Our framework has been 'global', first of all in emphasising the multiple sites of feminist histories – a heterogeneity which should render obsolete attempts to universalise any one 'provincial' history. Our framework has been 'global' also, and more crucially, in its attempt to relate the history of feminisms and internationalism to the systemic and structural changes of the developing world system.[18] In providing a global framework for the history of feminisms and internationalism, we have hoped, moreover, to draw attention to the fruitful tension between discrepant feminist histories which have produced very heterogeneous models of feminist practice, and a universalism that nevertheless affirms the promise of common ground, shared understandings, and the hard work of building bridges.

Notes

1. We remain aware, of course, of the controversy surrounding the very term 'feminism', especially when used in a global context. Women activists, whether in the past or in the present, do not always choose to define themselves or their politics as feminist; see in this issue the essays by Ping-Chun Hsiung and Yuk-Lin R. Wong on women activists in China and by Margot Badran on women activists in Yemen.

2. For a provocative argument that historicises the relationship between feminism as a political movement and the conflicting universalisms invoked by the concept of abstract individualism, see Joan Scott, 'Universalism and the History of Feminism', *differences: A Journal of Feminist Cultural Studies,* 7 (1995), pp. 1–14. We read Scott's essay as arguing neither for nor against universalism as strategy or political practice, but for historicising the 'paradox' that is the constitutive condition of feminism as a political movement: 'the need both to accept *and* refuse "sexual difference" as a condition of inclusion in the universal' (p. 7). See also her *'Only Paradoxes to Offer': French Feminists and the Rights of 'Man', 1789–1944* (Harvard University Press, Cambridge, 1996). Where Scott's argument about 'sexual difference' and feminism intersects with our own is in its insistence on historicising feminism and its relationship to universalism.

3. We find especially useful Chandra Talpade Mohanty's argument that concepts such as 'universal sisterhood' have often been predicated upon situating women *outside* of world history. The argument of 'universal sisterhood', therefore, invokes a *transcendence of*, rather than an *engagement with*, history; see Chandra Talpade Mohanty, 'Feminist Encounters: Locating the Politics of Experience', *Copyright,* 1 (1987), pp. 30–44. Also see Antoinette Burton, 'The Feminist Quest for Identity: British Imperial Suffragism and 'Global Sisterhood', 1900–1915', *Journal of Women's History,* 3 (1991), pp. 46–81.

4. We borrow the concept of 'provincialising' European history from Dipesh Chakravarty; see 'Provincializing Europe: Postcoloniality and the Critique of History', *Cultural Studies,* 6 (1992), pp. 337–57; and 'Postcoloniality and the Artifice of History: Who Speaks for the "Indian" Pasts?', *Representations,* 37 (1992), pp. 1–26.

5. Rey Chow, *Women and Chinese Modernity: The Politics of Reading Between East and West,* quoted in Andrew Parker, Mary Russo, Doris Sommer and Patricia Yaeger, *Nationalisms and Sexualities* (Routledge, New York, 1992), Introduction, fn. 6, p. 15.

6. We are drawing here from the following: Valentine M. Moghadam, 'Introduction: Women and Identity Politics in Theoretical and Comparative Perspective', in *Identity Politics and Women: Cultural Assertions and Feminisms in International Perspective,* ed. Moghadam (Westview Press, Boulder, CO, 1994), pp. 3–26; and Avtar Brah, 'Questions of Difference and International Feminism', in *Out of the Margins: Women's Studies in the Nineties,* ed. Jane Aaron and Sylvia Walby (The Falmer Press, London, 1991), pp. 168–76.

7. The above formulation is borrowed from Neil Lazarus, Steven Evans, Anthony Arnove and Anne Menke, 'The Necessity of Universalism', *differences: A Journal of Feminist Cultural Studies,* 7 (1995), pp. 74–145.

8. See Peter Waterman, 'Hidden from Herstory: Women, Feminism and New Global Solidarity', *Economic and Political Weekly,* 28:44 (30 October 1993), WS93.

9. We borrow the phrase from the call for papers for a conference on 'Globalization From Below: Contingency, Conflict, Contestation in Historical Perspective' sponsored by the Graduate Seminar in Interdisciplinary Studies at Duke University, Durham, North Carolina, 5–8 February 1998, *Conference Webpage: http: // jefferson. village. virginia. edu/ ~spoons/global/*

10. Temma Kaplan, 'Commentary On the Socialist Origins of International Women's Day', *Feminist Studies*, 11 (1985), pp. 163–71; and Ellen Carol DuBois, 'Woman Suffrage and the Left: An International Socialist-Feminist Perspective', *New Left Review*, 186 (1991), pp. 20–45.

11. See, for example, Kathleen Barry, Charlotte Bunch and Shirley Castles (eds), *International Feminisms: Networking Against Female Sexual Slavery: Report of the Global Feminist Workshop to Organize Against Traffic in Women, Rotterdam, The Netherlands, April 6–15, 1983* (International Women's Tribune Centre, Inc., New York, 1984).

12. For the history of, and problems within, the UN Decade for Women conferences, see Arvonne S. Fraser, *The U. N. Decade for Women: Documents and Dialogue* (Westview Press, Boulder, CO, 1987).

13. See Mary John, 'Gender and Development: Problems for a History of the Present', *Thamyris,* 4 (1997) pp. 137–54.

14. See Marie-Aimée Helie-Lucas, 'Bound and Gagged by the Family Code', in *Third World–Second Sex*, vol. 2, ed. Miranda Davies (Zed Books, London, 1987), pp. 1–15.

15. See, most notably, Leila J. Rupp, *Worlds of Women: The Making of an International Women's Movement* (Princeton University Press, Princeton, NJ, 1997). For studies of international socialist feminist networks, see Marilyn Boxer and Jean Quataert (eds), *Socialist Women: European Socialist Feminism in the Nineteenth and Early Twentieth Centuries* (Elsevier North-Holland, New York, 1978); and Richard Evans, *Comrades and Sisters: Feminism, Socialism, and Pacifism in Europe, 1870–1945* (St Martin's, New York, 1987).

16. Our central concern with the history of internationalism within feminisms and women's movements, therefore, is somewhat different from the emphasis of such collections as, for example, Amrita Basu (ed.), *The Challenge of Local Feminisms: Women's Movements in Global Perspective* (Westview Press, Boulder, CO, 1995); and Joan W. Scott, Cora Kaplan and Debra Keates, *Transitions, Environments, Translations: Feminisms in International Politics* (Routledge, London, 1997).

17. The 1995 Beijing conference, for example, stimulated the local and regional networks of *dalit* or lower-caste women in India. These women organised at the national level to represent *dalit* women at the conference, independent of the national Indian women's organisations; see Gopal Guru, 'Dalit Women Talk Differently', *Economic and Political Weekly* (14–21 October 1995), pp. 2548–50.

18. We borrow the above formulation for a 'global' analysis from Rosemary Hennessy, *Materialist Feminism and the Politics of Discourse* (Routledge, London, 1993).

An Alternative Imperialism: Isabella Tod, Internationalist and 'Good Liberal Unionist'

HELOISE BROWN

> There was not one [of us] who did not feel the danger of war arising between this country and others, whether with some great military organisation like Russia ... or whether it be one of those wretched little wars, as they were called, in which this country had been often engaged, threatening and overbearing races which we were pleased to think inferior to ourselves.[1]

This paper examines how an alternative imperialist ideology developed through the arguments of Isabella Tod (1836–96), a prominent Irish feminist who envisioned an alternative role for Britain within its empire. Her position as a unionist[2] and an Irishwoman, a conservative imperialist and a feminist, evolved in a period when British feminists increasingly lent their support to the project of imperial expansion abroad. Isabella Tod resisted aggressive imperialism, but the 1886 Home Rule Bill for Ireland forced her to publicly justify her unionist identity and explain her alternative approaches to imperialism, nationalism and internationalism, illustrating how her anti-expansionist principles were consistent with her unionist identity. She clashed with British Liberals and feminists who rejected her claim as an authority on Ireland, and she struggled to assert an identity that could be simultaneously unionist, feminist, pacifist and nationalist. Here it will be argued that while Tod's ideas were consistent in their own terms, they led to her isolation from colleagues and friends precisely because they both challenged accepted definitions of nationalism and epitomised the contradictions implicit in late-Victorian conceptions of empire.

As recent publications, in particular those of Antoinette Burton and Vron Ware, have shown, nineteenth-century British feminism was international in its focus, overwhelmingly imperialist, and in many cases explicitly racist. 'Was it possible', Vron Ware asks, 'to be a feminist and simultaneously to have an alternative view of popular imperialism?'[3] Isabella Tod's views on imperialism offered one such alternative perspective. Antoinette Burton's *Burdens of History* has ably shown how Victorian feminists attempted to claim racial responsibility for the imperial nation-state, in order to legitimise their demands for citizenship in Britain. With relation to India, Burton has provided an extensive and illuminating analysis of how feminist thought in Britain depended for its development upon the imagery of the Indian 'other' woman. Yet while she acknowledges in her introduction that not everyone living in Britain necessarily felt British (and, I would add, many people identified as British who were not resident in England, Scotland or Wales), the main body of her work leaves this subtle distinction absent. Tod, who was simultaneously Irish and British, had a very different relationship to both Britishness and Britain's colonised 'others'. Burton's examination of Victorian feminism as inherently imperialist hinges on the argument that feminists 'ignored the physical force involved in Britain's acquisition and maintenance of imperial possessions'.[4] Isabella Tod was only too aware of how physical force was being used in Britain's empire, but, crucially, in Ireland she saw force in use on both sides. Her project was to manage change in Ireland while minimising the risk of coercion and exploitation of its population, whether unionist or nationalist, Catholic or Protestant. In the process, she argued for an idealised imperialism that respected individual liberty, upheld governmental responsibility and eradicated the compulsion and coercion that Tod believed to be intrinsic to party politics.

With respect to Irish history, Louise Ryan and Margaret Ward, among others, have examined the role that women have played in the construction of Irish nationalism. But while both have produced studies of feminist and nationalist movements within Ireland that have done much to develop the historiography of Irish politics, there has been little work done to advance the place of unionist women within these frameworks.[5] As Louise Ryan has noted, it is very difficult to situate unionist women within public organisations and thus obtain access to their arguments. A more subtle reason is that the theoretical frameworks for understanding these different forms of nationalist and imperialist expression are not yet in place. As Ryan argues, national identity has been defined in terms of an insider/outsider dichotomy, with those representing the nation self-appointed as the 'insiders', and perceived colonial enemies defined as the 'outsiders'.[6] Isabella Tod's situation challenged this approach to some extent. She felt herself to be an insider within Ulster, and yet, as the campaign for Home Rule gathered supporters, she became situated as an outsider within Ireland because she was perceived as the colonial enemy and an outsider within British feminism because she would not retreat into Irish reform circles. This challenged Tod's subject identity and she spent the remainder of her life trying to demonstrate that her choice was a valid one. No single factor defined her position, but rather it was the combination of unionism, liberalism, Irishness, feminism and pacifism which was crucial in the development of her arguments.

Images of the empire and its role were largely absent from Tod's discussions of the need for social reform in Britain and Ireland. In contrast to many feminists, her calls for the suffrage drew no parallels with women in the 'East'. There are no references in the content or structure of her arguments to the colonial 'other' to which Burton refers in such detail. Instead, Tod relied on an internal image of the 'other' – that of the working class, and the need for reform in order to improve their condition. Her analyses of feminist imperialism did utilise the explicit otherising of colonial peoples, as shown in the quote which opens this paper, as part of a conscious effort to provoke considerations of the use of power and the effects of physical force. But she did not employ mainstream feminist images of imperialism in her arguments, and despite deploying the problematic liberal language of 'civilisation' and 'progress', she remained focused upon reform within the United Kingdom, intervening in the imperial domain only to protest against expansion and domination.

Thus, the term 'alternative imperialism' is used here to refer to an ideology that was essentially anti-expansionist and reformist. It was conservative in the sense that it was hostile to rapid change, cautious, moderate, anti-extremist and designed to conserve the empire while subjecting it to a gradual programme of reform. Yet it was also radical in that it argued for moral imperialism to be applied to British subjects, rather than 'other races'. Unlike mainstream moral imperialism, which argued that Britain exerted an essential 'civilising influence' abroad, this conservative imperialism held that Britain itself should also be the subject of 'civilising' reforms. The implications of Tod's 'alternative imperialism' are best seen in the context of the campaigns for Home Rule in Ireland.

The alternative debates on imperialism which are under discussion here originated with women who were active in both the peace movement and the feminist movement, although few were so self-referential as Isabella Tod. The marginalisation of both movements has meant that these ideas were at the time largely ignored, and have proved easily forgotten. An alliance of pacifist critiques of physical force with feminist critiques of male power and domination meant that it was possible for a minority of Victorian feminists to conceive of Britain as an imperial nation which had no business asserting its military and economic strength over 'other' lands. Liberalism, a potent force in both the feminist and pacifist movements of this period, contributed political notions of self-restraint and accountability, which made it a simple task to extend the universalised concepts of the individual and the nation-state to an international context. Arguments of altruism, moral responsibility and justice under the law lent themselves easily to the campaigns against the use of physical force as an expression of power. This is not to imply, however, that liberalism could not also be utilised as a justification for imperial intervention and expansion. During the 1880s and 1890s, popular liberalism became increasingly interventionist in its imperialism, as the Anglo-Boer war of 1899–1902 demonstrated.

At first glance, the most prominent factor in Tod's unionism was her Protestantism. Born in Scotland in 1836 to an Irish mother and a Scottish father, she was raised as a Presbyterian. The family moved to Belfast in the 1860s, and it was there that Tod lived and based her feminist campaigns until her death in 1896. But it is to underestimate Tod's ideas to reduce her opinions to her religious convictions. Her political ideology was founded on 'good Liberal' principles, although she often trod a fine line between Liberal party politics and a feminism that was liberal in its approach.[7] From her first involvement in the women's movement in 1867 until the outbreak of the Home Rule controversy in 1885, Tod was a popular figure. Henrietta Muller wrote of 'her large-heartedness and geniality, her ready sympathy, and ... her rare courage and cheerfulness'.[8] However, as Maria Luddy has argued, her Unionist stance seriously damaged her working relationships with British feminists and she found her contributions increasingly excluded from the British women's movement from 1886 until her death ten years later. During her lifetime she was involved in campaigns for improving women's access to education, the reform of married women's property laws, the repeal of the Contagious Diseases Acts, women's suffrage and temperance. Her work was based almost entirely in Ulster,[9] although she also campaigned in England and Scotland, where she was well known for her work for Irish women. More publicly active and more prolific than her Dublin-based contemporary Anna Haslam, to British feminists Tod was 'the best-known Irish women's activist of her day'.[10] She shared platforms and committee positions with Josephine Butler, Lydia Becker, Frances Power Cobbe and Elizabeth Wolstenholme, among many others. For the Irish middle classes, she fought for women's inclusion in the Queen's Colleges on the grounds that education had a social welfare purpose which could be utilised by women. Middle-class women, she believed, needed and deserved education and enfranchisement so that they would be better qualified to carry out philanthropic work among the working classes. For the working classes themselves she promoted temperance, arguing that drunkenness was the primary cause of their social problems. Her campaign against intemperance was located in the field of rescue and preventive work, rather than in appealing for legislation.[11] As Maria Luddy argues, Tod 'believed in the duty of each individual to practise their own moral judgement and felt that government interference would only coerce people ... "To supersede the conscience," she stated, "is to weaken it."'[12] Private liberty was highly prized by Tod, and her prevailing political focus was always on the rights and duties of the individual rather than the need for protectionist legislation. She extended these views to a deep distrust for political parties. Although Tod gave her support to the Liberal Unionists when they broke away from the Liberal party in 1886, and was influential in setting up a Women's Liberal Unionist Association two years later, she firmly believed that men were too preoccupied with 'mere party politics', and should focus on the 'social and moral questions which ought to be the end for which party politics are only the means'.[13] The study of Tod's unionism offers the cogent reminder that politics took place at local and personal levels, and not only on a party or national level at the London parliament.

Her liberal principles were also the foundation for her stance against war. Tod argued that the national and international use of physical force damaged nations, not only financially but morally and socially. She repeatedly returned to the importance of inculcating in individuals a 'regard for the equal rights of others, and ... unceasing personal self-control over all personal, class, and party impulses'.[14] She attempted to practise what she preached, giving pragmatic economic, social and political reasons for her opposition to Home Rule, and attempting to avoid exacerbating the religious divisions within Ireland. It is a matter of opinion as to whether she succeeded in this. Mary Cullen and Maria Luddy argue that 'the sectarian divide became more entrenched as the result of the activities of people like ... Tod'.[15] Certainly, the Home Rule bill of 1886 was a watershed in Tod's public career. After twenty years of working for change in Britain and Ireland, she suddenly found herself isolated in her opinions and ideology from the majority of her colleagues and friends. Throughout the Home Rule debate she maintained her stance as an opponent of imperialist expansion and physical force, attempting to reconcile her liberal belief in the need to preserve political freedom and local and national democracy with her desire to 'civilise' and 'educate' the Irish people through reform rather than a transfer of constitutional power.[16] She was not against Irish nationalism itself, although she was openly critical of the motivations, as she perceived them, of some nationalists. Nor was she dismissive of Catholicism. Like many Liberal Presbyterians in Ulster, Tod fought against the dominant Protestant ascendancy and the anti-Catholicism of the Orange Order.[17] She worked with nationalists in Ulster for several years, until the Home Rule debate produced social and political divisions which made cooperation impossible. Tod argued that the debate created more sectarian problems than it solved. This was the foundation for her unionism, and rather than supporting the idea of a permanent union with Britain, she viewed it as a temporary but necessary solution to Ireland's problems.

In the speech quoted at the beginning of this paper, Isabella Tod drew on liberal concepts of justice which she applied both nationally and internationally. She developed a critique of war in all its forms, attacking great wars (those which affected the balance of power in Europe or further afield), and 'wretched little wars' alike, and was particularly critical of the role which Britain had played in the latter. Britain's imperial expansion had been based on 'threatening and overbearing' behaviour, or the assumption that 'might was right', rather than on the liberal principles of justice, accountability and responsibility. Its attitude towards other 'races' had been aggressive, supremacist and self-interested: 'we were pleased', she said, 'to think [them] inferior to ourselves'. Read in conjunction with Antoinette Burton's analysis of the various meanings of 'race' in the 1880s, this demonstrates the precarious racial positioning of Celtic identity in the United Kingdom. The colonising and civilising influence was defined by the British as wholly Anglo-Saxon, while the Celtic presence in the empire went 'conveniently unnoticed'.[18] Tod's 'alternative imperialism', of course, bore the marks of this contradiction that was inherent in the late-Victorian conceptions of empire. Her arguments were based on assumptions of racial difference, but primarily designed to counteract arguments of racial superiority. She went on to argue that war was not only damaging to the colonised, or the enemy, but that it also damaged the aggressor. Aside from the economic costs involved, war interrupted social and philanthropic reforms and did long-term moral damage, which was signified by indifference to the deaths of 'others'.

Tod was speaking to the 1885 annual meeting of the International Arbitration and Peace Association (IAPA), a radical organisation which campaigned on many of the grounds Tod described for the introduction of systems of international law and arbitration, in order to prevent the inhumanities of war. She went on to remark that

> People seemed to think that it was a small matter that because persons dressed differently, spoke differently, and who lived differently, were killed and destroyed by thousands ...; it was thought of no moment if half-a-dozen of blacks were killed [sic]. It was a dangerous state for us to relapse into, and if it were for no other purpose than to save ourselves from such dreadful work, everyone in this country ought to do all in their power to stem the tide of such passions for war.[19]

Here, the term 'relapse' is crucial. Like many members of the peace movement, Tod held that the ability to solve disputes without recourse to violence was a direct indication of a society's level of civilisation. The movement towards moral rather than physical force as the organising principle of government was argued to be one of the characteristics of nineteenth-century Britain which qualified it as 'civilised'. Such notions of civilisation and progress are of course deeply problematic, as Burton and Ware, among others, have shown. Yet Tod's reference to the 'small matter' of the mass destruction caused by war was phrased to remind the listener that at the heart of such conflicts were human lives, which were endangered as a direct result of the lack of respect for, and acknowledgement of, racial and cultural difference. In an earlier speech to the IAPA, she had said that 'We have to fight for and protect the interests of the weak, by teaching the strong that they have no rights by virtue of their strength'. I return to the question of what she meant by *protecting* the interests of the weak towards the end of this paper, but the main thrust of her argument functioned to focus attention on 'the strong', those imperial nations who were in a position to force their cultural aims and values on others. Imperialist domination represented the primary expression of rule over the 'weak' by the 'strong', and was unjustifiable in the eyes of those who wanted to bring about more egalitarian international relations.[20]

These critiques of domination and evaluations of racial and cultural difference were central to Isabella Tod's opposition to war, yet they sit uneasily with her unionism, and certainly did not fit easily into existing political paradigms. Studies to date which have focused on anti-imperial struggles have highlighted the contradictions and divisions which exist between feminist and nationalist movements, not least because of national-ist movements' use of 'traditional' imagery of women. But these analyses have no explanations which speak to Tod's experience as a 'coloniser' who took on the cultural identity of the region she colonised. Tod was not an insider in Ulster because she was a Protestant and a unionist who had been raised 'abroad'. She was defined by Liberal and nationalist movements as an outsider, and found only a short-lived sense of belonging and recognition among the minority of Liberals who broke away to Unionism. Her pacifist views on the exploitation that was inherent in imperialism were unpopular among these relatively conservative dissenters. 'Displaced' by the changing political situation, Tod struggled unsuccessfully to re-establish her position as one that was valid and authentic.

Recent Irish historiography has recognised that unionism and national-ism were not monolithic political positions, and that representing Irish/British relations as simply coloniser versus colonised is a false dichotomy.[21] However, the task of interpreting history requires that the dominance of this dichotomy be addressed, given that it tends to dominate the terms of many of the debates which took place and that it continues to exist in popular discourses of Irish/British relations. The representation of unionists in this context as little more than colonisers functions to dismiss their position and render the conflict impossible to resolve. Hence, it is argued that Isabella Tod's dilemma was not unique, and that contradiction is not the only framework by which her politics can be understood. Rather, what is lacking in comprehending her ideas is a fuller understanding of different forms of unionism.

Although Liberal Unionists tended to be 'the more imperialist and Whiggish' of the Liberals, Tod's speeches to the IAPA show that she was not an imperialist in the accepted sense of the word.[22] Her Presbyterianism placed her as a member of the largest Protestant denomination in Ulster, and it was the Ulster Liberal Presbyterians who struggled to convey to Liberals in Britain the fact that unionism was not the stance of the Con-servatives and the Orange Order only.[23] The state of Ireland in the 1880s was such that all parties admitted that land reform was urgently needed, and, like Tod, the majority of Presbyterians in Ireland were in favour of land reform but against Home Rule.[24] The Liberal Unionists represented the main business and financial interests in Ulster, although from 1890 they were eclipsed politically by the Conservatives, the Orange Order and the Church of Ireland, as extreme Protestants and the far right eventually amalgamated under the umbrella of unionism.[25]

A number of studies have been done on individual unionists during this period, notably on Thomas Wallace Russell, James Brown Armour and Thomas Sinclair. Flann Campbell's study of Russell acknowledges his support for social and economic democracy in Ireland and his belief that this could be achieved within the Union, but dismisses his 'contradictory' dislike of landlordism and ascendancy as ambivalence.[26] Again, Russell's support for specific reforms suggests there are alternative frameworks within which his ideas can be situated, and by which his 'contradictions' can be explained. 'Constructive Unionism' is one term that has been applied to those unionists who believed that 'the union remained the best guardian of Irish interests.'[27] The progressive Presbyterian James B. Armour also placed his sympathies with the Liberal Unionists from 1886 until the early 1890s, when he perceived that they were being overpowered by the Conservatives and the Orange Order. He became a prominent and controversial Home Ruler, who continued to argue for 'a Presbyterianism that was tolerant and humane'.[28] Of the three, Thomas Sinclair's approach was perhaps most similar to Isabella Tod's. As Graham Walker's work has shown, Sinclair was keen to refute the claim that unionists merely wanted ascendancy over the Catholic Irish. He emphasised the Liberal Presbyterian history of fighting alongside Catholics for equal rights, and, like Tod, expressed the fear that the Home Rule movement was mainly a bid by Catholic nationalists for the power and privileges which were held by the old ascendancy. Presbyterians, Sinclair believed, would be 'the major potential victims' if Home Rule was brought about before other reforms.[29] It was argued that only under the United Kingdom could Ulster Presbyterians 'feel that their social and economic welfare, cultural vitality and religious liberty would be secure'. Walker's study concludes that Sinclair 'embodied a sense of cultural elitism which characterised much Presbyterian argument'.[30] The conclusion that cultural elitism was the dominant Presbyterian unionist motivation may be convincing, but is difficult to accept with regard to Isabella Tod's convictions, particularly given her attempts to work alongside nationalists and her critiques of ideas of cultural superiority. What the research on Russell, Armour and Sinclair does show is that in 1886, unionist reformists found themselves in a no-win situation. Their acceptance of the need for socio-economic reforms became, with the rise of Irish nationalism, inseparable from the constitutional question. The Liberal Unionist desire for the democratisation of Ireland through the development of a structure of local government was promoted as a means of appeasing the nationalists without severing the union with Britain.[31]

Isabella Tod's reaction to the announcement of the 1886 Bill is in itself enlightening. She was at first shocked that a Liberal government was trying to bring about Home Rule. 'I perceived that [it] would be the stoppage of the whole of the work of social reform for which we had laboured so hard. I saw a large portion of my life work shattered, and another endangered.'[32] The social, economic and political benefits that had been won for women in Ireland (partly by her own efforts) would not, she believed, survive in an Irish state. 'I shrank in horror', she wrote in the *Queen*, 'from the revival of the religious and racial difference which was certain to ensue.'[33] This 'revival of difference', she perceived, would signify a return to the 'dangerous state' of intolerance and division which prevented progress in much the same way as did war. Her recent experience of the nationalist politicians was one of the factors which influenced her conclusions. She described some years later how a number of nationalists had worked with the social reform committees that she had established in Ulster, but suddenly severed their links with these committees during the 1885 general election.

> At that time not one word had been said by us about the Union; and we had worked with and for all women alike, Northerners and Southerners, Protestant and Catholic. We learned indirectly that [the split] was because we were not Home Rulers. Now, what sort of future should *we* have under these men? Englishwomen may take help from them, they are quite safe, but what is our future?
>
>   I suppose Gladstonians think that if by *sheer force* they carried Home Rule, they could compel us to work for the narrow and jealous little legislature they set up. But it cannot be done.[34]

The fears that pervade Tod's writings on Home Rule are essentially focused upon the threat of physical force, and the damage that could be done by an undemocratic and unrepresentative government. She was critical of the effect that the nationalist leadership worked to produce 'on an excitable people', and feared the construction of a Catholic ascendancy which would simply replace the old Protestant ascendancy.[35]

Tod was at pains to emphasise that her stance was not based on 'religious bigotry'.[36] Rather, she outlined objections that were based on the imperfect political infrastructure of 1880s Ireland:

> what we [unionists] dread is the complete dislocation of all society, especially in regard to commercial affairs and to organised freedom of action. [The Government] suppose that Home Rule is a democratic movement and therefore unavoidable … it is needful to point out that the conditions of a free democracy do not exist in Ireland. Before they can exist the two great training influences of widespread education and large local government must have room to be fairly brought into operation.[37]

This demonstrates Irish Presbyterians' two greatest fears: the economic impoverishment and loss of liberty that they believed Home Rule would mean. Tod's remarks can be read as an illustration of the infantilisation of 'other races' that was common among contemporary imperialists, as described by Antoinette Burton. While she did rely on false ideals of civilisation, progress, education and self-government, she was always careful to emphasise that she did not hold Britain up as an example of any of these ideals in practice. Her case against Home Rule implicitly rested on the argument that it would be more productive for Irish reformers to work within an established government than to try to force a new one into existence and work through that. In making a pragmatic case for reform one step at a time, Tod hoped to ensure an informed electorate and a representative government in Ireland. While she repeatedly put forward such arguments, she also introduced the more controversial proposal that Ulster should claim 'a separate jurisdiction' in order to maintain its political freedom and its ability 'to do some good for the rest of Ireland'.[38] This was a possibility which most of her unionist colleagues were not prepared to argue, fearing that their case would be weakened by the admission that a special case should be made of Ulster. Thomas MacKnight, editor of the *Northern Whig* (to which Tod was a frequent contributor), was one of a few who had accepted the idea of a separate solution for Ulster. Another was John Bright, who remarked that Ulster 'may be deemed a nationality differing from the rest of Ireland at least as much as Wales differs from England, but ... is forgotten in the discussion of the Irish question'.[39] Faced with the prospect of Home Rule, for some unionists partition appeared to be the lesser of two evils.

There was always the threat that, as Protestants, the Liberal Unionist Presbyterians would be identified with the Orange Order and the ascendancy, and oppressed by a new Irish government. Indeed, by as early as 1890, Liberal Unionism had become subsumed under the Conservatism of the Orange Order and the old ascendancy. Tod was ever anxious to emphasise that those in Ulster who opposed Home Rule were not those who were 'responsible for old Protestant ascendancy and misgovernment ... The leaders [of Irish Liberal Unionism] are the descendants of those who fought and suffered *for* liberty, and *against* ascendancy.' They have, she said, 'fought for Catholic freedom, but ... will never submit to Catholic ascendancy'.[40] For her, the language of Home Rule was one of force, and political propaganda that demonstrated men's desire for power, with no awareness of the responsibilities that went with that power. Isabella Tod was on many occasions fiercely critical of men's use of political power, as well as their often easy recourse to physical force as a solution for cultural and racial difference. Her opposition to Home Rule was therefore in many ways consistent with her views on the (mis)use of power and coercion.

What, then, were Tod's solutions to the nationalist demands? Despite seriously considering the merits of partition, she ultimately envisioned independence for Ireland within a framework of economic and social improvements which would create a representative government and a responsible democracy. Tod's infantilisation of 'the Irish', by which she meant the majority of working-class, poverty-stricken Irish people, was intended to illustrate that, given the limitations of political and governmental systems, they would be unable to participate in a democratic nation. She envisioned a steady programme of reform under the 'Imperial Parliament', with Home Rule a reality once the required political and educational infrastructure was in place to support a genuinely representative government. The hurried demands for Home Rule in the late nineteenth century would, she believed, lead to disaster if they achieved their objective before Ireland as a whole – as opposed to the nationalist leadership – was ready. 'The hope of Ireland', she told Henrietta Muller in an interview for the *Women's Penny Paper*, 'lies in our being free to develop our energies both in industry and in social reforms, and so help our poorer neighbours in the future as we have in the past'.[41] The transfer of power to Dublin and the nationalists would, she argued, cause the economic, social and financial disintegration of Irish society, and would not of itself create a meaningful democracy. The way forward remained, for the time being, with nationalists, unionists, Liberals and Conservatives 'work[ing] together' to preserve the 'intellectual and social freedom' of Ireland.[42]

Despite the imperialist ideology that was intrinsic to much of Victorian feminism, feminist responses to Isabella Tod's arguments were superficially anti-imperialist. But, in masking their colonialist assumptions and preju- dices, feminists were unsure where to situate Tod. The British feminist response to the Home Rule question largely echoed that of the Gladstonian Liberal Party, as, for the most part, British feminists gave it their support. This underlines Burton's claims that, for dominant Victorian feminist ideology, 'the redemption of colonial peoples was considered to be instrumental to the survival of the nation-in-the-empire'.[43] Particularly when contrasted with Indian nationalism, which was culturally more threatening, Irish claims for self-government appeared politically acceptable. But the separateness of any potential Irish national culture was consistently undermined by British feminists' encroachment upon and appropriation of Irish feminism, as many historians have argued.[44] British women's attempts to 'colonise' the Irish women's movement in the late nineteenth century illustrated their commitment to imperialist feminism, even while they argued for Irish self- government. Unionist feminists' experience of this 'cultural imperialism' was different in content, though not in degree, from that of nationalist feminism. Unionists such as Tod were pressured to prove that their Irish identity was authentic, and had to resist British feminists' attempts to position *them* as the colonising enemy.[45]

British liberal feminists among whom Tod found support for the 'Imperial Parliament' included Priscilla Bright McLaren and Lilias Ashworth Hallett, while in Ireland she had a sound ally in Anna Haslam, a Dublin-based Quaker who shared many of Tod's feminist reform interests, including women's suffrage and the property rights of married women. Like Tod, Haslam feared for the rights of Unionists under an Irish parliament, although the effect of her opinions on her reform career and her relations with British feminists was not so severe. This is possibly because Haslam focused more upon the organisation of political movements, while, as Mary Cullen has argued, Tod as a public speaker and writer had a higher profile in Britain and Ireland. While Haslam saw women as united across political and religious differences, Tod placed the unionist cause above her other reform work.[46] With Millicent Garrett Fawcett, Isabella Tod was instrumental in the formation of the Women's Liberal Unionist Association (WLUA), a break-away movement of unionist women who were dissatisfied with the pro-Home Rule approach of the Women's Liberal Federation.[47] Like their male counterparts the Liberal Unionists, the WLUA gradually drifted into col-laboration with the Conservative party, although this was an uncomfortable alliance, particularly for Tod, who continued to regard herself as a Liberal.[48] She found a prominent ally in Fawcett, despite the fact that she had reached her Unionist opinions by a wholly different route from Tod. Throughout her life, Fawcett placed her faith in the power of Britain's authoritarian empire, believing it 'better to rule Ireland by force than to surrender to force'.[49] The Home Rule issue brought Tod into public conflict with Josephine Butler, who had previously been her colleague in the Contagious Diseases Acts repeal movement. Tod stated in a letter to the *Northern Whig* in 1887 after Butler's adherence to a memorial of sympathy for Parnellite MPs that Butler was representative only of the 'Gladstonian section', who were 'just as intolerant and intolerable' in their philanthropic work as they were in their politics. '[T]hey will not', she concluded, 'succeed in driving us out of the good work in which we have borne our full share.'[50] These open political differences affected the friendships she had built up among British femi-nists, bringing, as Helen Blackburn acknowledged in her obituary of Tod, 'pain and division' to her relationships, although she retained 'her personal affectionate feeling' for such lost friends, 'her one desire being that they should see things as they really were in Ireland'.[51]

The *Women's Penny Paper* became a forum for discussions on Home Rule following an interview with Tod which provoked much correspond-ence and criticism from its readers. In turn, Tod spent some consider-able energy refuting the accusations of bigotry that were made against her. One, for example, came from a correspondent called Miss Chapman, who took issue with Tod's remark that 'All those women who are working for Social Reform are Unionists'. Chapman disputed this claim, taking Britain as her frame of reference and reminding Tod that many reformers were in fact Home Rulers. Tod's reply stated clearly that she had been speaking about workers in Ireland, not in Britain. 'Of course,' she con-tinued, 'I know that plenty of reform workers in England and Scotland are Home Rulers; thanks to the odd mixture of kind intentions, ignor-ance, and impatience, produced by their very recently aroused sympathy with Ireland'.[52] She fell victim as an Irishwoman to British feminists' imperialist ideology and their assumptions of centrality in the debates on Home Rule. Yet this went unrecognised by her critics, if not by Tod, and thus failed to convince them. Chapman and other correspondents re-plied to Tod's arguments against Home Rule, and the debate, char-acterised by misunderstandings and misquotes not unlike those described above, continued back and forth for several weeks.[53] A regular critic,

'Eloisa', declared that, having heard all of Tod's arguments against Home
Rule,

> it [was] completely proved to me that whatever the condition of Ireland ...
> and however completely it might be demonstrated to other people that
> Home Rule would meet many of the needs of Ireland, Miss Tod would
> remain an opponent of Home Rule to the end of the chapter, a conscientious,
> heartsore, impassioned opponent of Home Rule.[54]

Taking the 'moral imperialist' and broadly liberal perspective that
oppressed peoples should be freed as soon as possible, 'Eloisa' argued that
it was in liberating Ireland that its people would 'rise to the measure of
their responsibilities and privileges'. In a final rebuff of Tod's conservative
imperialism, she remarked that 'National development will demand great
faith from us all. I have the faith, and I would say to Ireland I will trust her
though she slay me.'[55] Within the context of British imperialist feminism,
this was a progressive approach. But for a Protestant unionist such as
Isabella Tod, to trust Ireland 'though she slay me' was an infinitely more
demanding and dangerous task, and her detractors must have known this.
The validity of Tod's position was repeatedly denied by British feminists, as
they subsumed her under a British identity and dismissed her Ulster loyalties
and heritage. Challenges such as these epitomised British imperialist feminism, failing as they did to take account of the nuances of different nationalist divisions.

Isabella Tod's most powerful weapon of response to the feminist critics
who had formerly been her allies was to remind them that English men and
women lived in relative ignorance of Ireland. She repeatedly argued that,
compared to the Irish, the correspondents to the *Women's Penny Paper*
lacked expertise.

> ... if anybody has a right to say that they know Ulster, I have. I have relations
> in half its counties, and friends, plenty of them, in all ... I know them [the
> Orange Order] also, with the knowledge of opposition; for, being a good
> Liberal Unionist, I have fought against 'Ascendancy' and Orangeism on the
> one hand, and revolution on the other, all my life, as my ancestors did before
> me.[56]

It was ignorance, she felt, and its consequently misguided good intentions,
that most influenced British supporters of Irish nationalism. She was, it
seems, repeatedly exasperated by their indifference to her point of view. To
her, it was a mixed blessing that 'nothing less than the present agitation
could have compelled English people to study Ireland thoroughly'. She
hoped to make them accept that they were part of her imagined imperial
nation of the United Kingdom, a nation comprised of Britain and Ireland.
The more they understood, she argued, 'the more clearly they will see that

it is their duty to remain in organic union with the poorer country, and not to thrust it away'.[57]

These debates and disagreements illustrate how Isabella Tod felt the harsh reality of what it meant to be an outsider by virtue of living in a small and neglected part of the empire. Any legislative reform had to be done through the 'Imperial Parliament', and those British feminists with whom she worked clearly had only a limited understanding of her situation and background, criticising her for disagreeing when they argued that they knew what was best for her country. Tod's love for her country (Ireland) was explicitly expressed in the long-running debate within the pages of the *Women's Penny Paper*. In another crusade against ignorance, she retorted that her critics liked to believe

> that a visit to Ireland ... can put English visitors on a level as to power of judging the situation with us who live in the country, and who have inherited the habit of loving it and working for it for generations. They also fancy the feelings excited by this superficial knowledge, devoid of all responsibility, are kinder and warmer than those that grow out of long personal work, and that all consideration of unwelcome facts is unkind and cold.[58]

It would take a stern reading not to recognise in these comments the earnest protectiveness that patriotism inspires. Tod was protesting, in her own way, against those who looked from the imperial capital and saw only religious and racial differences in Ireland, or who visited and thought that this limited experience qualified them to judge. She was critical of the imperial attitudes for which the Home Rulers in Britain – such as 'Eloisa' – were so keen to atone by 'handing back' the power of government, and found it politically and morally unjustifiable that her opinion was dismissed because it went against British liberal values of what was perceived to be best for Ireland.[59]

Tod's arguments, of course, were directed mainly at British feminists and the male Irish nationalist leadership. How Irish nationalist-feminists might have complicated her position is beyond the scope of this paper. Rather, the aim here is to problematise relations between Irish unionists and the British. The erasure of British/unionist conflicts from popular understanding has created the myth that these interests were largely synonymous, and it has been left to historians to attempt to dismantle these ideas. In this respect, a study of Isabella Tod's arguments is particularly pertinent. The fact that these disputes were played out within feminism demonstrates that the problem was not only party political, but created personal and political difficulties within the feminist movement that were every bit as divisive as the machinations that went on at Westminster.

Beyond feminist circles, Tod's sphere of power and influence was very narrow. As a poor but middle-class single woman, her arguments counted for little and she enjoyed no special authority other than having her letters published in newspapers and speaking at public meetings. When she recommended patience and improvement for others, she was not dismissing their position but arguing for more equitable and just methods of settling power disputes. She was well versed in the IAPA's arguments for the introduction of courts of arbitration and negotiation as a means of preventing war, and carried this understanding of conflict resolution and power mediation into her feminist and unionist politics. Thus in Tod's reform work in Ulster, she preferred to work with, rather than for, Catholics, although her focus was usually on the poor. While she clearly had blindspots, particularly where class issues were concerned, on the whole she refrained from making exclusionary assumptions. She recognised and understood the populism of Home Rule, and did not oppose it on the grounds that it was a movement made up of uneducated or working-class people. Rather, what concerned her was that once the leading minority of this popular movement reached a position of influence, they would be vindictive and partial in exercising their power. Tod recognised that the movement for self-government had stirred up fresh conflicts and resentments, so if it was successful, the resulting government would almost inevitably carry some of these prejudices within it. Throughout the debate, Tod's points were lost on or misunderstood by the wider British feminist movement, and this served to reconfirm her fears.

Tod's pacifist and internationalist activities provide the link between her position in the Irish Home Rule controversy and her attitude towards imperial expansion abroad. It was during the early 1880s, just a few years before the Home Rule debate reached its height, that Isabella Tod joined the International Arbitration and Peace Association. Founded in 1880 by a group of liberals and radicals, the IAPA aimed to spread the message abroad that international disputes could be resolved without recourse to war. It differed from contemporary British pacifist societies in that it gave tacit support to nationalist revolutions and wars of liberation, arguing that these were, in some instances, necessary before a democratic nation could be established and the commitment be made to abolish war. As its approach to nationalism and democracy was progressive, Tod was in sympathy with many of its ideas. Its members were not required to hold absolutely to its central principles, and thus it did accept members who opposed any use of violence or physical force (absolute pacifists, as they may be called). Although always a small organisation, its membership included many prominent men and women who had an interest in its central principles, and it survived as an active organisation until 1918. Isabella Tod spoke at many of the IAPA's annual meetings until the late 1880s, relinquishing her role as one of its most popular women speakers only as ill health forced her to cut back on her political activities. Here, I examine Tod's arguments regarding the empire and imperialism, and consider the basis of her opposition to the collapse of the 'Imperial Parliament'.

Her earliest objection to imperialism was as part of the Women's Peace and Arbitration Association (WPAA), a body which, from 1882, had been an informal auxiliary of the IAPA. It met in March 1885 to protest against the British government's military interventions in the affairs of the Sudan. Isabella Tod's speech on this occasion criticised the 'war policy' of the government on the grounds that it was 'thoroughly opposed to the spirit of Christ, unjust, contrary to all principles of religious and political liberty and therefore opposed to the truest interests of the community'.[60] The controversy over the Sudan centred upon the British government's indifference to the policy of its representatives there, Governor General Gordon and Sir Garnet (later Lord) Wolseley. The British army occupying Egypt was supporting the Egyptian reconquest of the Sudan, while Gladstone and his cabinet were arguing in the face of criticism that the decisions taken in Egypt were military, rather than political, responsibilities.[61] Vron Ware notes that the occupation of Egypt and the death of Gordon had 'raised imperialist sentiment to a fever pitch', and it was in this context, the immediate aftermath of Gordon's death, that the WPAA protest was held.[62] Tod defined the conflict as war, rather than imperial intervention, and by arguing that Britain's role in the uprisings in Egypt and the Sudan was unchristian, placed the focus on the moral responsibilities of Britain as an imperial nation that liked to call itself 'civilised'. While imperialism was often justified by arguments of Britain's superior level of civilisation, Tod turned the focus back upon Britain's illusions of superiority, to argue that being civilised meant standing back from disputes abroad rather than using the rhetoric of the civilising influence as an excuse for military intervention. Characteristically, Tod also raised the issue of religious as well as political liberty. Her main concern in relation to the conflict in the Sudan was that Britain had no business being involved. The 'truest interests of the community', if the community can be taken to mean an (imagined) international community, did not lie in war or in British domination and oppression. She saw the conflict in the Sudan as an example of British imperialism at its worst, a clear illustration of the 'threatening and overbearing' behaviour that was concerned primarily with trade routes and British economic advantage, rather than the best interests of the people of the Sudan. The obvious absence of any economic or social changes that were in Sudanese interests, rather than British ones, demonstrated to Tod that British behaviour in the region was wholly immoral.

Isabella Tod was not alone in employing these arguments. Other women who publicly criticised British imperialism and its treatment of 'other races' included Florence Balgarnie and Catherine Impey, both of whom feature in Ware's *Beyond the Pale* for their respective roles in the Anti-Lynching Committee and the journal *Anti-Caste*, and Quakers Ellen Robinson and Priscilla Peckover, who were active in the international peace movement.[63] The IAPA and the WPAA included a number of prominent feminists, such as Margaret Bright Lucas, Florence Balgarnie, Laura Ormiston Chant, and Florence Fenwick Miller. And, of course, the IAPA was dominated by radical men, many of whom, like Hodgson Pratt and W. Randall Cremer, propounded anti-imperialist arguments similar to those put forward by Isabella Tod. Here, I am not intending to make a case for the originality or uniqueness of her arguments, but rather to examine how these beliefs intersected with her unionism. How were her opinions regarding the 'truest interests' of an international community to relate to the question of Home Rule for Ireland?

For Tod, her principles directed her arguments. In Britain's relations with North Africa, particularly those countries surrounding the Suez Canal, she saw a preoccupation with trading and economic strength, and indifference to the consequences for those who populated Britain's trade routes and international markets. She saw this indifference to the rights and liberties of the population as characterising an empire that was wholly unacceptable. For her, this type of imperialism was very different to Britain's role in governing Ireland. Britain had emancipated Irish Catholics, begun social reforms, and was increasingly accepting the fact that land reform was necessary. From Tod's perspective, Ireland was 'progressing' gradually to a point when it could become independent of Britain. She did not see the same mercenary and self-interested British policies in force in her home country as she saw in the reports of events in North Africa. Apart from her intervention regarding the Sudan, Tod avoided discussions of specific areas of the empire, preferring to restrict her arguments to theoretical considerations. In some ways, her focus on Ireland led her to represent the rest of the British empire as a homogeneous entity, although this also demonstrates her commitment to refraining from involvement unless she felt she could contribute to an informed discussion. Her experience of British feminists bringing their opinions to bear on Ireland had provided her with first-hand experience of the problems of trying to intervene in affairs of which one had only limited knowledge.

Her liberal approach to international relations reflected her views on the importance of personal liberty. She was conscious of the importance of 'difference' in many of her arguments, recognising that 'It is not, of course, an easy matter for us to lay down rules or suggest plans for those whose lives are different from our own'. Referring to the establishment of French and German branches of the IAPA, she argued that 'if we avail ourselves of every effort we shall clear the way for them'.[64] This is a valuable statement when seen in context with her wider views. She recognised the 'difference' of the French and the Germans, but believed that the British IAPA could be instrumental in their progress. She did not employ her ideas of 'clearing the way' in relation to any imperial project, but, rather, drew a circumspect parallel with other European powers, suggesting that 'clearing the way' referred to a project of international cooperation, rather than a 'white woman's burden'. Tod differed here from many of her feminist contemporaries, for whom the primary 'civilising' force which the British should use abroad was argued to be that of Christianity (Josephine Butler was one prominent example of this 'ethical imperialism').[65] From this perspective, the Christianisation of society was expected to transform it at every level, ending the perceived need for domination and oppression. But for Tod and many pacifist radicals, it was not Christianity per se which would effect change, but the re-education of societies with regard to war. The essential factor in 'clearing the way' for others, Tod argued, was ensuring that 'the rising generation of society round about us feel that war is not the honourable and glorious thing it has been supposed to be'.[66] Many feminists, particularly 'ethical imperialists' such as Butler, argued that this education should be focused on the young, as it corresponded neatly to the perceived responsibilities of moral motherhood and the 'white woman's burden'. Isabella Tod placed her emphasis not only on the young, but on other levels and classes of society. If she had any particular sphere of emphasis, it was on the need to inform and educate politicians to conduct national, imperial and international affairs in more ethical ways.

Tod's distrust of the political system was central to many of her arguments. She believed that it was controlled by men who acted in their own interests with scant concern for the well-being of others. She was hopeful that the IAPA would encourage women 'to take their full share – and that a large and definite share – in enlightening the public mind, and awakening public conscience, not only to the dangers which follow war, but also to those underlying principles of selfishness and tyranny'.[67] The true basis of war, she argued, was the 'selfishness' of political parties and the systems which allowed them to follow their own acquisitive interests. She did not place great faith in political and democratic freedom in itself, arguing that it was how such freedom was used which determined the level of 'civilisation' of any nation and its government. As argued above, this was one of the characteristics of her opposition to Home Rule for Ireland. A government which was established before educational reforms and the introduction of local government would, she believed, be disastrous both in the short and the long term, and lack the means to genuinely improve the condition of its electorate. Tod feared further sectarian division and conflict, and a greater reliance on the use of physical force. She emphasised in a letter to *Concord,* the IAPA journal, in 1891, that democracies 'have not been a whit more placable and reasonable than monarchies'.[68] Rather than relying on government to accurately represent the people, she reminded *Concord*'s readers of the need to educate all classes of people about the importance of peace and arbitration, because democracies were only as peace-loving as the individuals who constituted them. She noted that 'the peoples – meaning by that the larger and poorer portions of every nation – are as easily angered as the richer classes'.[69] The route to peace, and hence civilisation, was education and social reform. Legislation at a parliamentary level was not sufficient.

> Unless every voter in the land learns that it is as much his duty to repress in himself the rash judgement which thinks evil readily, and the temper which

desires to compel and overbear, as it is the duty of the most highly placed statesman, we shall not have a moment's security against either internal or external war. It is the state of mind which is dangerous, not the particular objects affected by it.[70]

This emphasis on internal, as well as external, war suggests that the Home Rule question was to the fore of Tod's mind in relation to this particular point. The 'organised violence', she continued, 'of political parties is simply a survival of the barbaric rules of war'. She was careful not to present Britain as the 'birthplace of modern representative government', implicitly disputing this idea in her writings.[71] Rather than arguing that women's enfranchisement would make a moral difference to government, she held that it would make MPs accountable to women. 'There is no more dis-respect', she wrote, 'in such an assertion than there is in any argument for representation at all. A benevolent despotism is not a safe kind of govern-ment to entrust to average human beings, whether it is a class, or race, or sex, or creed that is ruled.' Instead of relying on arguments of sexual or racial difference, she made her case on the grounds that 'the power of the state' should be placed 'on the broadest possible basis of representation'.[72] Her fears about the lack of self-control that would be exercised by a nationalist leadership which found itself newly empowered within Ireland meant that she preferred to take a long view of progress and reform, envisioning self-government for Ireland when it had the infrastructure to support a government that was genuinely democratic and representative of all the communities within Ireland.

It is argued here that unionist political identity, combined with Isabella Tod's feminist and pacifist ideals, produced a progressive approach to Irish policy. Imperialism was responsible for creating the conditions in which unionist ideas emerged, as generations of colonisers successfully took on identities that were forged from their new geographical locations. Yet the growth of British nationalism and imperialism during this period made it increasingly difficult for ideas of 'Britishness' to accommodate other identities. The combination of Irishness and Britishness that underpinned unionism became marginalised during the Home Rule debate, and it was this process that silenced Isabella Tod. Her critiques of nationalist and imperialist power had only a limited impact upon British feminists, who were more concerned with transferring the power exercised within unionist circles over to the nationalists. Faced with a nationalist movement fighting for change, it was perhaps inevitable that unionism would become more conservative in its desire to preserve the Union with Britain. Caught between the extremes of Irish nationalism and Conservative unionism, it became increasingly difficult for moderate reformists such as Tod to attract political support for their ideas.

The framework of a conservative imperialism that was resistant to change illustrates that, although Tod's principles appear contradictory, they were in many ways consistent. A combination of pacifist and feminist ideas gave her the means to construct a sharp critique of the use of power in international relations. Tod's relevance for a consideration of feminism and internationalism is located not only in her arguments that imperialism amounted to war and that the empire should be managed as sensitively as any international conflict, but also in her difficulties in establishing and validating her identity to her contemporaries. Her conservative definition of imperialism drew it closer towards a framework for managing international relations, but these ideas did not incorporate the power dynamics that were present by definition in discourses of nationalism and imperialism. Given that during this period imperial expansion abroad was increasingly justified, while at the same time nationalist aspirations were gaining wider acceptability, it is no surprise that her ideas were so unpopular. An examination of Tod's conservative imperialism demonstrates the importance of defining the various feminist and imperialist ideologies that were operating in Britain during the late nineteenth century, particularly regarding why disputes over the role of the empire divided the feminist movement. Her position emphasises the inherent contradictions in Victorian conceptions of empire, and the ways in which liberal ideologies could be used to articulate imperialist, or anti-expansionist, or Irish nationalist discourses. Many British feminists of this period were eager to shed the vestiges of imperialism and 'hand back' power and land to colonised peoples. They were therefore unable to engage with Isabella Tod's unionism, and, in turn, Tod was incapable of convincing them that her opinion was valid. As the history of Ireland unfolds, it is clear that popular British (mis)conceptions of unionism have changed little over the century since Tod's death.

Notes

Thanks to Jane Rendall, Ann Kaloski, Trev Broughton and Colin Moran for their comments and support in the writing of this article. This paper is written from a British perspective as a reminder that Britain (as England, Wales and Scotland) needs to foreground the facts of its activities in Ireland and make the resolution of conflict a political priority. A balanced understanding of unionism is essential in reaching any conclusions. Both unionists and nationalists have used armed force where they believed it to be necessary, and, as events have shown, there are no easy solutions. The quotation 'good Liberal Unionist' is from Isabella M. S. Tod in *Women's Penny Paper* (8 December 1888), p. 6.

    1. *Journal of the International Arbitration and Peace Association*, I:13 (31 July 1885), p. 137.

    2. Unionism emerged as a political movement supporting the union of Ireland with Britain, under which Irish MPs sat in the British Parliament. It was in many respects a response to the Irish nationalist movement which, by the mid 1880s, was in a position to demand a parliamentary vote on Home Rule for Ireland, which potentially meant the repeal of the Act of Union. This is, of course, a simplification of the political factors at

work, and accounts of the various perspectives on the Home Rule movement of 1886 can be found in Alan O'Day, *Parnell and the First Home Rule Episode, 1884–7* (Gill and Macmillan, Dublin, 1986); H. C. G. Matthew, *Gladstone, 1875–1898* (Clarendon Press, Oxford, 1995); and Flann Campbell, *The Dissenting Voice: Protestant Democracy in Ulster from Plantation to Partition* (Blackstaff Press, Belfast, 1991).

3. Vron Ware, *Beyond the Pale: White Women, Racism and History* (Verso, London, 1992), p. 162; Antoinette Burton, *Burdens of History: British Feminists, Indian Women, and Imperial Culture, 1865–1915* (University of North Carolina Press, London, 1994).

4. Burton, *Burdens of History*, p. 80.

5. Louise Ryan, 'Traditions and Double Moral Standards: the Irish Suffragists' Critique of Nationalism', *Women's History Review*, 4 (1995), pp. 487–503; Louise Ryan, 'A Question of Loyalty: War, Nation and Feminism in Early Twentieth-Century Ireland', *Women's Studies International Forum*, 20 (1997); Margaret Ward, *Unmanageable Revolutionaries: Women and Irish Nationalism* (Pluto Press, London, 1983); Margaret Ward, 'National Liberation Movements and the Question of Women's Liberation: the Irish Experience', in *Gender and Imperialism*, ed. Clare Midgley (Manchester University Press, Manchester, 1998).

6. Ryan, 'Traditions and Double Moral Standards', p. 501; Ryan, 'A Question of Loyalty', pp. 21–32.

7. Here, I use 'Liberal' to refer to the politics and policies of the Liberal party, and 'liberal' to mean the general ideology of liberalism. The same distinction is used with regard to 'Unionism' and 'unionism'.

8. *Women's Penny Paper* (12 October 1889), p. 2.

9. Ireland was and is still made up of four provinces, Ulster, Leinster, Connacht and Munster. Ulster consists of the area now covered by Northern Ireland, and three counties to its south and west, Donegal, Cavan and Monaghan, which became part of the Republic of Ireland.

10. Maria Luddy, 'Isabella Tod', in *Women, Power and Consciousness in Nineteenth-Century Ireland*, ed. Mary Cullen and Maria Luddy (Attic Press, Dublin, 1995), p. 198.

11. Maria Luddy, *Women and Philanthropy in Nineteenth-Century Ireland* (Cambridge University Press, Cambridge, 1995), pp. 143 and 207.

12. Luddy, *Women and Philanthropy*, p. 207.

13. *Northern Whig* (17 June 1886), in Luddy, 'Isabella Tod,' p. 220.

14. *Concord: Journal of the International Arbitration and Peace Association*, VI:77 (17 March 1891), p. 45.

15. Mary Cullen and Maria Luddy, 'Introduction', in *Women, Power and Consciousness*, ed. Cullen and Luddy, pp. 16–17.

16. Luddy, 'Isabella Tod', pp. 221–5.

17. The ascendancy were those upper-class Protestants who held economic and political power over Ireland. See Campbell, *The Dissenting Voice*.

18. Burton, *Burdens of History*, pp. 37, 84.

19. *Journal*, I:13 (31 July 1885), p. 137.

20. *Journal*, I:2 (1 July 1884), p. 11.

21. For a discussion of revisionism in Irish history, see R. F. Foster, *Paddy and Mr Punch: Connections in Irish and English History* (Allen Lane, London, 1993), and D. George Boyce and Alan O'Day (eds), *The Making of Modern Irish History: Revisionism and the Revisionist Controversy* (Routledge, London, 1996).

22. Campbell, *Dissenting Voice*, p. 311.

23. Campbell, *Dissenting Voice*, table 12, p. 320.

24. However, many Presbyterian farmers cooperated with nationalists against the ascendancy, seeing economic gain in Home Rule. Campbell, *Dissenting Voice*, pp. 282, 293.

25. For a discussion of how the Liberal Unionist alliance with the Conservatives developed, see John D. Fair, 'From Liberal to Conservative: the Flight of the Liberal Unionists after 1886', *Victorian Studies*, 29 (1986), pp. 291–314.

26. Campbell, *Dissenting Voice*, p. 350.

27. Andrew Gailey, *Ireland and the Death of Kindness: The Experience of Constructive Unionism 1890–1905* (Cork University Press, Cork, 1987), p. 4.

28. Campbell, *Dissenting Voice*, pp. 343–7, 350, quote from p. 432; Graham Walker, 'Thomas Sinclair: Presbyterian Liberal Unionist', in *Unionism in Modern Ireland*, ed. Richard English and Graham Walker (Macmillan, London, 1996), p. 20.

29. Walker, 'Thomas Sinclair', pp. 28–9.

30. Walker, 'Thomas Sinclair', pp. 36–7.

31. David Burnett, 'The Modernisation of Unionism, 1892–1914?', in *Unionism*, ed. English and Walker, p. 46.

32. *Women's Penny Paper* (12 October 1889), p. 1.

33. *Queen* (September 1892), in Luddy, 'Isabella Tod', pp. 221–5, quote from p. 221.

34. *Women's Penny Paper* (9 November 1889), p. 35. First emphasis in original; second emphasis mine.

35. *Women's Penny Paper* (7 December 1889), p. 78.

36. Luddy, 'Isabella Tod', p. 221.

37. *Northern Whig* (17 June 1886), in Luddy, 'Isabella Tod', p. 221.

38. *Northern Whig* (17 June 1886), in Luddy, 'Isabella Tod', p. 222.

39. Ian MacBride, 'Ulster and the British Problem', in *Unionism*, ed. English and Walker, p. 7; Walker, 'Thomas Sinclair', p. 26.

40. *Woman's Herald* (21 May 1892), p. 7. Emphasis in original.

41. *Women's Penny Paper* (12 October 1889), pp. 1–2.

42. *Women's Penny Paper* (12 October 1889), pp. 1–2.

43. Burton, *Burdens of History*, p. 60.

44. Ryan, 'Traditions and Double Moral Standards'; Ryan, 'A Question of Loyalty'; Ward, *Unmanageable Revolutionaries*; Ward, 'National Liberation Movements'.

45. Burton, *Burdens of History*, p. 29.

46. Sandra Stanley Holton, *Suffrage Days: Stories from the Women's Suffrage Movement* (Routledge, London, 1996), pp. 71–2; Mary Cullen, 'Anna Maria Haslam', in Cullen and Luddy, *Women, Power and Consciousness*, p. 177.

47. The WLUA remained a much smaller body than the Women's Liberal Federation. David Rubinstein, *Before the Suffragettes: Women's Emancipation in the 1890s*, (Harvester, Brighton, 1986).

48. Martin Pugh, 'The Limits of Liberalism: Liberals and Women's Suffrage, 1867–1914', in *Citizenship and Community: Liberals, Radicals and Collective Identities in the British Isles, 1865–1931*, ed. Eugenio F. Biagini (Cambridge University Press, Cambridge, 1996).

49. David Rubinstein, *A Different World for Women: the Life of Millicent Garrett Fawcett* (Harvester Wheatsheaf, New York, 1991), pp. 115–17. See also Patricia Hollis, *Ladies Elect: Women in English Local Government 1865–1914* (Clarendon, Oxford, 1987), p. 62.

50. Luddy, 'Isabella Tod', p. 223.

51. *Englishwoman's Review* (15 January 1897), pp. 61–2.

52. *Women's Penny Paper* (9 November 1889), p. 35.

53. *Women's Penny Paper* (12 October 1889), p. 1. See also *Women's Penny Paper* (25 October, 9 November, 23 November, 30 November 1889).

54. *Women's Penny Paper* (21 December 1889), p. 103.

55. *Women's Penny Paper* (21 December 1889), p. 103.

56. *Women's Penny Paper* (8 December 1888), p. 6.

57. *Women's Penny Paper* (9 November 1889), p. 35.

58. *Women's Penny Paper* (7 December 1889), p. 78.

59. *Women's Penny Paper* (7 December 1889), p. 78.

60. *Englishwoman's Review* (14 March 1885), p. 135.

61. Matthew, *Gladstone,* pp. 142–9.

62. Patrick Brantlinger, *Rule of Darkness: British Literature and Imperialism, 1830–1914* (Cornell University Press, London, 1988), p. 19 in Ware, *Beyond the Pale*, p. 119.

63. Robinson was active in the Society of Friends' critiques of British atrocities in the Anglo-Boer War of 1899 to 1902, as well as contributing years of work lecturing on peace to women and working men, and strengthening the British peace movements' links with Europe. Priscilla Peckover edited the pacifist journal *Peace and Goodwill: a Sequel to the Olive Leaf* from 1882 to 1931, and was nominated for the Nobel Peace Prize.

64. *Journal*, I:1 (1 July 1884), p. 11.

65. Burton, *Burdens of History*, p. 149; Ware, *Beyond the Pale*, pp. 158–9.

66. *Journal*, I:1 (1 July 1884), p. 11.

67. *Journal*, I:1 (1 July 1884), p. 11.

68. *Concord*, VI:77 (17 March 1891), p. 44.

69. *Concord*, VI:77 (17 March 1891), p. 44.

70. *Concord*, VI:77 (17 March 1891), p. 44.

71. Burton, *Burdens of History*, p. 54.

72. Isabella Tod, 'Women and the new Franchise Bill: a letter to an Ulster Member of Parliament, March 1884', in *Before the Vote Was Won: Arguments For and Against Women's Suffrage*, ed. Jane Lewis (Routledge and Kegan Paul, London, 1987), pp. 398, 401.

'The New Women's Movement' in 1920s Korea: Rethinking the Relationship Between Imperialism and Women

INSOOK KWON

In 'Under Western Eyes', Chandra Talpade Mohanty cautions against the influence of Western feminist hegemonic discourse. She warns that another colonialism exists implicitly in the discourses of Western feminism.[1] Recently, some feminist scholars' analyses of imperialism have focused on revealing how imperial power operates as a multi-dimensional hegemonic domination process established by a variety of forms of authority, knowledge and power. Anne McClintock, for instance, shows how imperialism worked not only through violent occupation but also through the manipulation of personal and communal desire, commodity addiction and the roots of the colonised's culture.[2] Mervat Hatem and Barbara N. Ramusack describe the role of white women and Western feminism in constructing imperial orders that affected colonised peoples and areas.[3] A common objective in this recent feminist research regarding imperialism is to expose the ways that gender-related policies and traditions of colonised peoples were used for rationalising imperial domination in the name of liberating colonised women from traditional practices. This research has been persuasive in demonstrating that virtually everything that happened in the colonised society was tainted to some degree by the working of the imperial hegemonic domination. In fact, within the context of the conflicts and struggles between the coloniser and the colonised, and between the oppressor and the oppressed, a persistent and resistant political critique and detailed analysis of the hegemonic domination of Western over colonised or Third World women remain necessary.

However, that necessary critique is not the whole story of women's strategies and efforts at resistance under the conditions of colonisation. In this essay, I would like to rethink the gendered impact of imperialism by challenging the presumption of an 'all powerful' Western hegemony and by disclosing a more complicated relationship between colonised women and imperialism as they interacted in the case of the Korean 'New Women' movement in the 1920s, a decade in which Korea was subject to Japanese colonisation. My concern is that a perspective focusing exclusively on Western hegemonic domination could paralyse any affirmative evaluation of cultural, economic, structural or gendered changes for both the colonised and post-colonised. A careful look at Korean 'New Women' of the 1920s makes us ask this question: must colonised or post-colonised people always be subjected to a shaming suspicion that everything they have done, thought or felt (even desire and addiction) has been externally (and thus inauthentically) manipulated and distorted?

This investigation also pushes us to weigh more carefully the consequences for women in any colonised society of an analytical stance that – wittingly or unwittingly – fuels such a suspicion. Must women struggling to carve out spaces for their autonomy as women do so only in ways that explicitly deny the vitality of everything which belongs to colonised or post-colonised (except anti-imperial) traditions? If so, does this entrench the presumption that there exist essentially 'pure cultures' or 'better cultures'? Who exactly benefits from the entrenchment of this assertion? While feminist researchers using this anti-imperialist perspective do not intend to do so, they could be subverting the utility of a broader set of criteria for assessing the legitimacy and authenticity of colonised women's efforts at agency. The outcome could then be a shrinking of the already limited ideological and acting space available to many colonised and post-colonised women. Simultaneously, adopting such critical criteria could serve to intensify an already potent masculinised nationalist discourse.

This problem is especially apparent when we try to understand colonised women's movements which were not, or are not, closely affiliated with any nationalist movement. In the colonial and post-colonial context, being stigmatised by an association with 'Western feminism', or any other supposed imperial tendency, does not leave any open space in which indigenous women can construct and articulate their own specific interests and perspectives. I want to illustrate how those analyses which overlook the possibility of such space are inadequate for accurately evaluating the New Women's movement in Korea and the international circulation of feminism.

'New Women in Korea'[4] has been a category used broadly to distinguish early twentieth-century educated intellectual women in Korea from more traditional Korean women.[5] However, more precisely, the 'New Women' activists were a group of women who challenged the moral system of Confucian patriarchy, using a new self-identity that they crafted through modern education in Korea or studies and journeys to Japan and Europe. The New Women's movement in Korea became socially visible in the 1920s, ten years after Japan occupied Korea, in 1910. Women who identified with this movement advocated free love (love between men and women regardless of marriage),[6] free marriage (marriage without the intervention of parents)[7] and the destruction of the dominant feminine chastity ideology. Korean women who openly accepted the label 'New Women' acknowledged being influenced by Western feminism. Denying directly the validity of doctrines of Korean Confucian patriarchy for the first time, the New Women not only comprised the first feminist generation in Korea, they also became the strongest challengers to Confucian patriarchy, a socio-political system which remains a source of cultural oppression of Korean women into the 1990s. Ultimately, the most visible of these New Women became outcasts and died in miserable conditions.

Now, at the end of the twentieth century, reactions to the New Women amongst Koreans vary. Most Korean scholars focus on explaining the reasons for those women's alleged limitations or failures. For instance, Jongwon Lee explains that the failure of the New Women was caused by their being inevitably squeezed in the 1920s transitional conflict, a conflict that erupted when Western culture met traditional culture.[8] Haejung Cho, in much the same vein, argues that their demise was inevitable because of the enormity of the gap between the New Women's Western practices and the traditions of Korean society at the time. Other scholars go further. They assert that Korea's New Women activists were crushed in the conflict of the 1920s because they lacked a nationalist consciousness and thus a sense of societal obligation as colonised women. As articulators of this historical thesis, Jinsong Kim, Sukpoon Park, and Eunpong Park each expresses anger towards New Women for what they claim was those women's indiscreet acceptance of Western feminism and Western culture.[9] The Korean Women's Research Group for Korean Women's History, as recently as 1992, argued that the New Women's lack of nationalist class consciousness was one of their major faults.[10]

These critical evaluations of the 1920s New Women, many of them by Korean feminist historians, shed light on the problem faced by most colon-ised or post-colonised people: what criteria are best used to evaluate the impact of Western culture, especially on women? One way to approach this dilemma is to analyse colonised women's desires and subjectivities, through an examination of the dynamics of how and why the New Women chose certain types of Western feminism. In my examination I shall explore the intersection of and competition of Confucian patriarchy, Christianity, colonialism and nationalism as hegemonic powers shaping the lives of early 1900s Korean women. In particular, I will describe in some detail the impact, mostly positive, of Christianity on Korean women. Consideration of these issues helps establish criteria which can inclusively represent diverse women's interests in colonial or post-colonial contexts.

Haesuk La, Wonju Kim and Myungsoon Kim were prominent leaders of the first generation of New Women. Wonju Kim, an ideologue of the New Women's group, pronounced her ideas in the *Sin Yo Ja* (New Women) magazine she published in 1920:

> Why did we declare ourselves New Women in front of society despite our ignorance and immaturity? ... Because we were going to awaken women to develop themselves through overcoming several cultural shackles that had

oppressed women throughout several centuries. Men would call it destruction or resistance or betrayal. However, look out! You have not treated women as human beings; rather you have despised and raped women like animals … So we are going to liberate ourselves from the whole traditional, conservative, cultural and outdated ideology, as New Women in a new era. This is really our responsibility and obligation and that is the reason why we have to exist.[11] (translated from Korean by the author)

The birth of Korean New Women was not just a natural reaction caused by centuries of Confucian patriarchal oppression. The movement was a product of the complicated meeting of Confucian patriarchy, the expansion of women's modern education, the spread of the ideas of Christianity and Western feminism and the imposition of several foreign governments' imperial power.

Here, an important point must be made. The colonial experience of Korea was significantly different from that of other countries colonised directly by Western imperialists who brought concepts of modernity with their intrusion. Korea, from the end of the nineteenth century to the early twentieth century, experienced imperialism in two forms: the collapse of traditional feudal ideology in the face of Western imperial modernity, and the loss of land and independence through Japanese imperialism. In fact, the history of the relationship between Japan and Korea was not primarily one of domination and subordination, but rather of competition between two countries with similar cultural backgrounds. Japan opened its doors to the West earlier than Korea, so, at the time, some Koreans believed that Japan's early acceptance of Western modernisation made possible both its power and its occupation of Korea. Therefore, regarding the imperialists' cultural and ideological dominance in terms of modernity over Korea, Japan may be best seen not as the dominant force, but as a vehicle or a subsidiary force for Western dominance. Still, the tendency to distinguish the Japanese cultural and ideological impact from Westernisation continues. Furthermore, Japan was not the only vehicle for importing Western discourse: between 1879 and 1910 several imperialist countries, including the US, France, and especially Japan, Russia and China,[12] directly competed with each other to colonise or 'open' the Korean market. Japan won this competition.

It is the resultant separation of, on the one hand, cultural intrusion by Western imperialists into Korea's feudal social order from, on the other, direct colonisation by Japan that distinguishes the Korean case from that of most other colonised countries. It is a separation that has had an important effect on the birth of the Korean New Women's movement. The largely favourable view of Western religion in Korea is one product of this separation. Haesuk Lee explains this tendency: 'In the case of Korea, Christianity is commonly viewed as being separate from imperialism, as Korea was occupied by Japan which was a non-Christian country. Therefore, Koreans could not make sense of the symbiotic relationship between Korean

Christianity and Western imperialism: rather, they evaluated Christianity as contributing to the build up of Korean nationalism.'[13] It was possible, consequently, for Christianity to influence Korean women and the women's movement without provoking a resistance derived from their nationalist consciousness.

At the end of the nineteenth century, when Western imperialism penetrated Korean society in the name of modernisation, it shook the cultural foundations of Confucian patriarchy and its caste system, which were the two central pillars of the Korean feudal system. The subsequent conflict between modernity and tradition was unavoidable. In this conflict, women's status was picked out by many Koreans as the divisive feature that distinguished an oppressive traditional culture from an emancipatory modern culture. In 1888, Younghyo Park, the modernising protagonist of a failed coup against the Korean dynastic regime, insisted on the prohibition of early marriage and polygamy, and the abolition of the law prohibiting women to remarry.[14] Early marriage, concubinage, and the prohibition of women's remarriage in particular became targets of modernising intellectuals' criticism of Confucian patriarchy.[15] One reform bill signed by the king of the Chosun dynasty in 1884 included the prohibition of early marriage and permission for women's remarriage. From this period, women's education was also emphasised. Younghyo Park demanded education for children over the age of six by building up modern elementary and middle schools. Jaepil Suh, an editor of *Doklib Sinmoon* (Independence Newspaper),[16] claimed the necessity of women's education for the improvement of their roles as good wives and wise mothers.[17]

In the middle of this nineteenth-century and early twentieth-century reform movement, many women challenged the traditional women's consent to male dominance and set up new counter-hegemonic discourses. Christianity especially influenced Korean women. Even though Christianity was a patriarchal religion in its Western context, some Korean women found a liberating discourse within it: men and women were equal under God. Korean women reformers found they could use this discourse to attack Confucianism's naturalisation of an unequal relationship between men and women. There is a hint of the degree of Korean women's early involvement in Christianity in one particular statistic. In the mid nineteenth century, the king's father, Daewyungoon, forbade Catholicism and prevented it from spreading by executing Catholic converters. From 1839 to 1848, women accounted for forty-nine out of the seventy-nine people executed.[18] After the first Protestant missionary came to Korea in 1885, the number of Korean Christians reached 200,000 by 1909. Women comprised the majority of Korean Protestants. Hyojae Lee reveals that this was due in large part to the activities of Korean housewives serving as evangelists[19] for the amazing growth of Christianity.[20]

Another way in which Christianity planted the early seeds in the 1920s New Women's movement was by playing a leading role in the expansion of women's education. While the first state-sponsored public school for girls was not opened by 1908 and only three private schools for girls existed in Seoul at the time, Protestants had already built 732 elementary schools, nineteen middle and high schools and one university around Korea. Before 1905, 174 schools for girls were founded by Protestants, and women students comprised 30 per cent of the total 18,000 students attending Protestant schools in 1905.[21] This notable increase in women's schools and women students signified not only the success of a Protestant strategy to spread Christianity through education, but also the growth of the strong desire of Korean women to liberate themselves through the education provided by these non-Confucian religious institutions.

In 1920, the Association of Women's Education sponsored a lecture on the need for women's education in Korea, and over 300 married and unmarried women gathered in the rain to hear the speaker proclaim: 'You need education to achieve human status beyond your current slave status'.[22] In June of the same year, the site of another lecture sponsored by the Association of Women's Education became the scene of utter confusion because so many women had gathered and sought to enter the already packed hall, despite a warning that it was full.[23]

All three of the women who became the most prominent of Korea's New Women grew up enjoying these educational opportunities mainly offered by Protestants. Haesuk La was born in 1896 to wealthy parents. She attended 3.1 Women's School founded by Methodists in 1903[24] and Jinmyong Women's School (a non-Christian private school founded in 1906). Wonju Kim was born in 1896; her father was a Protestant minister and her mother raised Kim like a boy. Wonju Kim respected her mother, later recalling that 'My mother didn't teach any women's morality or women's role and she didn't worry about her style at all. Mother wanted me to be a great man, a hero, not a woman, and did not make me follow any feminine role or any standard'.[25] Wonju Kim's mother's attitude suggests the sort of impact that Christianity in its Korean form had on Korean women at the time. Wonju Kim attended Ewha Hakdang, the first Protestant women's school, founded in 1886. The third of the New Women, Myungsoon Kim, was born in 1896. Her mother was the concubine of a wealthy man of the gentry class. She attended Jinmyong elementary school, Jinmyong Women's School and Ewha Hakdang. The sudden increase of educational opportunities after 1886, while still limited mostly to women from Korea's Westernised upper class,[26] served to create a pool of women from which developed those activist New Women who chose to react to Confucian patriarchy in explicitly untraditional ways.

But beyond these new local opportunities there were the expanded radicalising opportunities to travel to Japan and to Europe. In 1909, Haesuk La went to Japan to study painting at the Tokyo Women's Art College. She was the first Korean female student to formally study Western painting. Her first lover, Sungoo Chai, became ill and died when they were both living in

Tokyo. After returning to Korea in 1913, she taught at Youngsang Junior high school. In 1919, Haesuk La became involved in the '3 1' movement,[27] the biggest national uprising against Japanese occupation, and was prosecuted by the Japanese, though released. In 1920, she married Wooyoung Kim, a graduate of Tokyo University and a lawyer. They were to have four children together. In the 1920s, her activities as a writer, painter and representative of New Women were at their height. From 1927 to 1929, she took a trip to Europe and America with her husband and stayed alone for a few months in Paris. There she fell in love with Lin Chai, a famous Korean religious leader. In 1932, Wooyoung Kim divorced her because of this affair. She tried to go back to Paris, the city of her dreams, but failed. In the years following the divorce, Haesuk La was the target of severe social criticism. She also lost all financial security. She died in 1948.[28]

Wonju Kim lost her free-thinking mother when she was a teenager. At the age of eighteen, to avoid conflicts with her new stepmother, she moved to Seoul. She entered Ewha Hakdang. During this period, she lost her faith in God. She also decided to go to Japan for one year, though her brief time there is not well documented.[29] Like Haesuk La, Wonju Kim, upon her return from Japan, took part in the 1919 anti-occupation 3.1 movement. Serving as an editor of its flagship magazine, *Sin Yo Ja* (New Women), she became actively engaged in the Korean New Women's movement in the 1920s. Twice married and twice divorced, she later became a Buddhist priest. She died in 1971.[30]

Myungsoon Kim likewise studied in Tokyo, attending Tokyo Women's College from about 1910. By 1917, she had become Korea's first modern woman novelist, publishing her first novel, *Whisimwhi Soyo* (Suspecting Girl), in the Korean magazine *Chung Chun* (The Heyday of Youth) in 1917.[31] She went on to publish a collection of poems in 1925, the first such collection by a Korean woman. Myungsoon Kim also worked as a reporter and movie actress. However, from the time she spent in Tokyo, it was her quite liberal relationships with men that were turned into a main target for public criticism against all Korean women who were identified as New Women. Kim disappeared from public view in the late 1920s,[32] though she lived until around 1951.[33]

One crucial commonality of Korean New Women, especially these three prominent New Women, Haesuk La, Wonju Kim and Myungsoon Kim, was their studies in Japan. All three studied in Japan around the same time (La, 1909–13; W. Kim, 191?; M. Kim, 191?). This was a time when Japan was establishing its colonial rule in Korea; but it was also a time when many Japanese feminists were engaged in the debate over their own construction of 'the New Women'. By 1910, the Japanese were instituting a centralised, mobilising, nationalist, oligarchic state which pursued rapid industrialisation at the same time as it was modernising its military. In a Japanese context, the ideas of the New Women seemed to have two major aspects. On the one hand, the term denoted a group of women who asserted their own new self-identity and sexuality. Hiratsuka Raicho, in 1910 the first Japanese woman to identify herself as a New Woman, made no secret of her self-conscious absorption of ideas from Western liberal feminism.[34] On the other hand, Japanese feminist advocates for the New Women saw them as offering a new ideal type of women in Japanese society. Thus, the New Women did not represent only one ideological tendency for the movement's Japanese supporters. L. R. Rodd sums up the debate on New Women among women reformers in Japan:

> Yosano Akiko (1878–1942) advocated a feminism grounded in equal legal, educational, and social rights and responsibilities for women. Hiratsuka Raicho (1886–1971) propounded a doctrine of motherhood that called for state protection of and special privileges for mothers. Yamakawa Kikue (1890–1980) embraced a socialist view of history that traced women's subordination to the system of private property and so set the destruction of that system as her goal. Finally, Yamada Waka (1879–1957) held a more traditional view of women as 'good wives and wise mother' … A major forum for the debate over the 'new woman' was the literary magazine *Seito* (Bluestockings), founded by Hiratsuka Raicho in September 1911 to encourage and advertise the creative talents of women.[35]

However, it seems that the image of the Japanese New Women whom Raicho represented soon became the image most Japanese associated with this actually quite complex movement. In this simplistic form, New Women took on a somewhat negative public image, according to Sharon L. Sievers.[36] In the minds of many non-feminist Japanese, New Women came to represent indulgent and irresponsible young Japanese women who defamed the family and others by satisfying their overdeveloped sexuality.

The Japanese magazine *Seito* in 1913 published translated versions of Henrik Ibsen's *Hedda Gabler* and *A Doll's House*, the latter introducing to Japanese readers the famous character Nora, who declared her own independence and freedom by leaving the house and her husband. While *Seito* also carried socialist and Marxist feminist articles, its editor, Raicho, reported on *Love and Marriage* by a Swedish feminist, Ellen Key (1849–1926). Key emphasised women's new self-identity and the restoration of morality through revaluing motherhood, fostering marriage with love, and permitting free divorce in a real Christian spirit.[37] Raicho herself called on her Japanese readers to esteem motherhood, while challenging Japan's patriarchal system by demanding the recognition of women's and children's rights.[38] Raicho sought not only to introduce liberal feminist ideas but to adapt those ideas to Japanese practice by organising in 1920 the New Women's Association – Japan's first nationwide organisation of female citizens.

Jongwon Lee contends that the appearance of Japanese New Women around 1910–20 directly influenced the three Korean New Women, La and the two Kims, because they were in Japan during the time of the debate.[39]

There is much evidence to support Lee's argument. Wonju Kim was not only the first woman to use the term *Sin Yo Song* (New Women) in Korea; she also changed her name to 'Ilyoup', taking the same Chinese name character as one of the Japanese feminists of the period. Of the two strands of Japan's New Women movement, the Raicho version of feminism seems to have been the more influential among their Korean counterparts. One can see, for example, the same emphasis on Ibsen and Ellen Key. In 1921, La wrote a poem, 'A Doll's House', which adapted to the Korean women's situation the spirit of Nora, who left the stifling atmosphere of the conjugal house for freedom.[40] Korean feminist magazines such as *Sin Yo Song* (New Women) and *Gaebyock* (Opening), carried translated articles by Ellen Key.[41]

On the other hand, it is not obvious that the Korean New Women adopted the Japanese debates, or Raicho's concept of the New Women, in a simple, unadulterated form into their ideology and activism. In the Korean New Women's movement, for instance, there was no emphasis on motherhood or morality. While, like Ellen Key, they insisted that there should be love in marriage, like Ellen Key, most Korean New Women were determined to create the possibility for women to express free love regardless of marriage. Above all, the important distinction between Korean New Women and Raicho's Japanese New Women was the Korean New Women's emphasis on radical personal practices which directly challenged the entrenched Korean principle of feminine chastity. In practice, Raicho rejected the popular emphasis on women's virginity,[42] visited the Yoshiwara, Tokyo's old licensed pleasure quarter,[43] and created a scandal by having relationships with a young boy and with a woman.[44] But, in her political theorising, Raicho did not see criticising the principle of feminine virginity as her main concern, and her personal practices were not deliberately designed to challenge social morality. For the Korean New Women, by contrast, feminine chastity was a main target, and their practices were in quite deliberate defiance of this principle. For the first time in Korean modern history, New Women began to directly challenge the ideology of chastity. Wonju Kim elaborated on the reasoning behind opposition to chastity:

> Through being free from the old system and tradition and ideology, today women are going to revalue the meaning of life; above all, women have to enthusiastically resist the existing morality of sexuality ... there is no chastity without love. However, in the perspective of the existing morality, which has valued chastity, the loves of non-virgin women have been called dirty love. We have to discard this wrong opinion. Chastity never can be a moral concept; it [morality] is a fluid concept that is always changing. Therefore, if a woman who has sexual experience with men thinks that she is sullied because she loses her virginity, it seems to me that that woman disrespects her self-esteem and passion.[45] (translated by the author)

Haesuk La, as a New Woman, also frontally attacked Korea's prevailing feminised chastity ideology and the marriage system. While living in Paris, she, as a married woman, deliberately allowed herself to fall in love with a famous married Korean man. She thought that loving other men as a married woman was taking steps down a path toward becoming a more progressive woman. She wrote, 'Whatever the result, I have to accept this love affair for progress. There are several kinds of ways to become progressive'.[46] Her conviction about freedom of sex was very firm. She declared, 'Women's liberation has to begin with the freedom from chastity ... you can deal with chastity as a kind of hobby or taste'.[47]

However, despite these differences, ideologically the Korean New Women's movement was closely related to Japanese and Western liberal feminism.[48] The ideas of free love and equal rights, for instance, were closely connected to Korean New Women's criticisms of the chastity ideology. Their critique of chastity was based on the denial of gender-specific constraints. Also, their practice of free love was calculated to defy the code of chastity, which victimised only women. In addition, from 1927 to 1929, through study in Paris and travel in England, Haesuk La confirmed her conviction about women's liberation and expanded her perspectives on feminism. In France and England, she was introduced to the issues of abortion, temporary (or tentative) marriage and the suffrage movement.[49] She met Emmeline Pankhurst, a leader of the suffrage movement in England. Once back home, Haesuk La used her writing to introduce to Korean readers Pankhurst's opinion that the suffrage movement was related not only to the issue of women's voting rights, but also to issues of work, chastity and divorce. At bottom, though, Korean New Women were not simple adapters of foreign ideas. Instead, I believe, there is convincing evidence that these women's outspoken and direct denial of chastity and their radical behaviour originated from their analyses of the characteristics of Korean Confucian patriarchy, a system that they came to believe had been built on the ideology of women's chastity for centuries.

Joan Wallach Scott asserts, 'But theories of patriarchy do not show what gender inequality has to do with other inequalities'.[50] The evolution of Korean Confucian patriarchy provides a case, the Korean New Women concluded, which demonstrates that gender inequalities indeed have interconnections with other inequalities. The Chosun dynasty[51] (1392–1910) was a gentry's bureaucratic society. It perpetuated the long-lasting social order in two ways: adherence to the genealogy of a bloodline designed to sustain the caste system and division between the private blood-relation sphere and the public non-blood-relations sphere.[52] By controlling the private sphere very strictly through the creation and maintenance of a patriarchal order, the ruling class sustained the rigid caste system. Haejung Cho, a Korean feminist scholar of the present era, confirms what the earlier New Women suspected: that Chosun dynasty Korea was a family-centred society in which the blood-relations sphere overwhelmed the non-blood-relations sphere. She says, 'the Confucian patriarchy of the Chosun dynasty has to be understood as a subtle coalition between the caste system and blood relations. We have to analyse this patriarchy by centring on the analysis of the dogmatic theory and practice of Confucianism, the clan system and the extended family system by the paternal line'.[53]

The latter period of the Chosun dynasty marked the peak era of the long-developing Confucian patriarchy. Its predecessor, the Koryo dynasty used Buddhism as a ruling ideology, which served to somewhat temper Korean patriarchy.[54] Gender culture was more liberal and women's status was higher than it was to be during the Chosun dynasty. Furthermore, during the early period of the Chosun dynasty (from the end of the fourteenth century to the mid seventeenth century), women's status was higher than it was during its last two centuries, by which time the dynasty's efforts to thoroughly entrench Confucianism had succeeded. For instance, the early laws of the Chosun dynasty guaranteed women's equal inheritance of property and ritual rights for ancestors. However, after the late seventeenth century, when the caste system and absolutism were shaken by the wars with both Japan and, later, Ching China and Japan, and the changes in economic relations and the corruption of the bureaucracy, Korea's ruling class tried to rebuild, extend and strengthen Confucianism in order to reaffirm the existing regime. Hyojae Lee, a feminist sociologist, believes that, at this time, the ruling class consciously adopted a political strategy whereby they would end social instability by victimising women.[55] Through the control of women, legitimised, in the name of Confucian morality, the ruling class wanted to rebuild Confucianism as a ruling ideology and to affirm social stability, and thereby, they hoped, the political survival of the Chosun dynasty as well.[56]

The Chosun ruling class legislated for women's etiquette and manners in striking detail.[57] For example, the mid-dynastic period etiquette laws legitimated two chief ideas of Confucianism concerning women: 'treatment of women as inferior to men', and 'woman's three ways of obedience to men, which meant that, she must follow the way of her father before marriage, acquiesce to her husband's opinions in her marriage and then, after his death, obey her son'.[58] They also used state power to make it impossible for Korean women to inherit property or wealth. Furthermore, the Chosun dynasty law prohibited women's remarriage. Haejung Cho argues that the law prohibiting women's remarriage was one of the by-products of the conflict between men of the ruling gentry class. In order to preserve the honour and the purity of the blood lineage of each clan of privileged gentry, the prohibition against women's remarriage was strengthened. The state's prohibition of remarriage and its institutionalisation of the concept of pure blood lineage together resulted in an almost obsessive state and social anxiety over women's chastity. In the last period of the Chosun dynasty, the virtuous woman who desperately clung to her chastity became the hallmark of a family's honour, not only among Koreans of the gentry class, but among Koreans of all classes.[59] With virtuous women in a family, it was imagined, for instance, that a declining genteel clan had a chance to rebuild the honour and fame of the clan. With such honour, a male farmer, too, could be exempted from state taxation and a slave family could be liberated. To maintain their virtue, many Korean women committed suicide after the death of their husbands, or just because a man had grasped their hand.[60]

The socially supported and state-enforced prohibition of women's remarriage resulted for Korean women in their being coerced into celibate life; for a widow, it meant economic disaster. Because the gendered division into separate spheres was very firm, the widow who could not remarry had no financial power.[61] In short, the rule of 'respecting men and discriminating against women' was an ironbound one imposed on women regardless of the difference of social status, and it translated into women of the Chosun dynasty having to live solely through their restricted roles as reproductive workers and supporters of paternal families or husbands' clans.[62]

While the prohibition of women's remarriage was highly criticised and easily discarded soon after the arrival of Western culture via imperialism, the chastity ideology remained virtually unchallenged. In reality, the chastity ideology still remains potent in South Korean social life in the 1990s and persists today as an important cause of double-standard morality: unlimited sexual freedom for men and no sex outside marriage for women. For all the changes that have shaken and transformed Korean society since 1900, this double standard of morality has survived, serving as the power base of Confucian patriarchal culture. To this day, it restricts women's bodies, space and spirit in the name of preserving and protecting chastity. The New Women were quite aware that their ideological and practical attack on the chastity ideology would be seen by many Koreans as a real challenge to the basic rules of Confucian patriarchy, and thus, in turn, to a social system reliant on the maintenance of the pure paternal blood lineage and the division into separate spheres.

When the New Women asserted women's rights to free love regardless of marriage, and when they denied the legitimacy of the traditional marriage system itself, they were conscious that the themes they were taking up were not by any means trivial in a family-centred society like that of Korea. In the early decades of the twentieth century, marriage was seen by most Koreans to be one of the most crucial ceremonies, and, consequently, one in which fathers and grandfathers had absolute authority to choose brides or grooms for their offspring. Marriage was not an affair between men and women, but between clan and clan, or between family and family. In other words, it was an affair for fathers to manage according to fathers' priorities and strategies. To women, marriage thus meant being a member of the husband's family or clan, while to men, it meant having a wife who would be a supporter of his family and a reproducer to perpetuate his blood lineage. Therefore, the New Women's emphasis on love between men and women, and free marriage without paternal intervention, or their disregard of marriage, were not simply exhibitionists' efforts to shock; they were designed to be direct attacks against the existing marriage system and patriarchal power.

The behaviour of Wonju Kim, Myungsoon Kim and Haesuk La, as well as that of other Korean women who associated with the 1920s New Women's movement, did, however, shock. It was treated as scandalous. Perhaps it was this popular reaction that misled later critics to write off the New Women as trivial. Wonju Kim was divorced twice and lived with men two or three times while not being married.[63] Myungsoon Kim was famous (notorious) for her frequent changes of partner. Haesuk La was divorced after she had a relationship with another married man. Yet, apart from their unusual personal behaviour, they were already famous enough to attract social attention. Haesuk La was the first Western-style woman painter in Korea and was a famous writer. Myungsoon Kim was Korea's first woman novelist and Wonju Kim was a publisher – unusual positions for women at the time. But, taken together with their artistic talents and unique jobs, these women's bold practices that overstepped traditional rules evoked deep controversies. As such, they represented conflicts other than simply those arising from tensions in early twentieth-century Korea between Western modernism and tradition.

Haejung Cho defines the era from 1900 to 1920 as a time when Korean liberal idealism strengthened progressivism, while she sees the era after the mid 1920s as a conservative era, when traditionalists re-emerged to oppose the products of the preceding progressive era.[64] This change in the 1920s was related to a change in the thinking of Korea's colonised intellectuals. After colonisation, Japanese imperialists practised a modernisation policy in its Korean colony. This served to rob many Korean male intellectuals of their will for modernisation, which they had believed to be the only way to empower Koreans. These male intellectuals searched for an alternative way of bringing about their intellectual nationalist restoration.[65] Thus, it was in the 1920s that many once progressive intellectuals came to believe that through deconstructing tradition as a national cultural root and symbol, the New Women's challenge to Confucian patriarchy could weaken the Korean nation's power to stand against Japan

The cultural impact of the New Women's ideology and practice in the 1920s was profound enough to bring about a backlash. Looking back in 1988, Youngsook Shin argued that the negative impact of the New Women was as follows:

> Western liberalism and socialism became dominant ideologies in colonised Korea. Women's insistence on love and marriage began to challenge traditional practices and the family system. However, the concentration on destroying traditional customs was accompanied by severe negative byproducts and disclosed more and more chaos during the transitional period. With the traditional forced marriage, divorce as well as free love and free marriage made women fall into further contradictions, which victimised women: love affairs and adulteries continued to happen. New Women became concubines in the name of second wife and spinster because they could not find spouses, or they committed suicide after homosexual relationships. In 1920,

suicide, divorce, or homicide of women occurred around ten times a day, and women became victims.[66] (translated from Korean by the author)

In *Donga Ilbo* (Donga Newspaper), we can find several contemporary articles that dealt with the danger of the New Women's ideology. 'Recently, all authority has been destroyed. Existing morality and tradition are challenged as to the necessity of their existence ... there is so much freedom and indulgence inside family life that the existing value system is destroyed. Old authority and esteemed persons and institutions are now losing their public value'.[67] The broad anxiety about the contemporary changes in Korean life was converted by many critics into a narrower concern about the New Women's ideology and practices. In this newspaper, one can see how reporters addressed the changes New Women initiated. According to one journalist, 'Now, every woman is in danger ... it is the transition period between traditional rule and modernity. Therefore the rules for women are totally destroyed. Women could easily be victims of this transitional period ... Now women need to choose a balanced way between the two streams thoughtfully'.[68] By comparison with Chosun dynasty society, women's behaviour was severely criticised: 'If women's sexual freedom had happened in Chosun society, would that society have tolerated it? Society calls you prostitutes and moral violators who shatter the chastity concept or criminals who disrupt the social order of the state'.[69]

Yet, many women who would have never taken on the label 'New Woman' for themselves seemed to be embracing some of the New Women's ideas. For instance, in the 1920s, Korea witnessed an increase in divorce litigation in favour of women.[70] Before 1918, there was no concept of divorce in Korea. Wives were simply expelled; it was the husbands' right. In 1918, Japanese colonisers legalised divorce. The first divorce suit brought by a woman was in 1921. While male adultery could not be a reason for divorce, the divorce suits raised by women radically increased. In 1925, the Seoul local court had five to six divorce cases a day. In 1932, the number increased to eighteen divorce cases a day, comprising 5 per cent of marriage cases.[71] When we reflect that women's divorces today still carry a kind of stigma in South Korea, this 1920s increase in divorce shows not only the progress of women's subjective consciousness but also the start of the destruction of the traditional framework.[72] The New Women may have experienced failure in their own lives, but it would be an error, I believe, to equate those private disappointments with a failure of their movement to stimulate new public thinking and action in Korea.

In addition to leading their challenges to love and marriage, the New Women became the pioneers in the redesign of women's costumes. Wonju Kim and Haesuk La analysed the health problems that traditional feminine dress could incur. Conventions in women's formal attire required tightening the breasts severely with bands, so as not to show an allegedly indecent, sexualised body part. As an alternative, New Women recommended wearing a reformed version of the Korean traditional dress, one that was less restrictive.[73] Also, New Women introduced Western-style dresses and short hair cuts. For the New Women, hair and dress styles became symbols used to expose the problems that tradition caused Korean women. They also wielded hair and dress styles as vindicators of their adaptation of Western ideology. These changes of outward appearance, however, played a contradictory role. To many Korean observers, these distinct visual changes merely symbolised the depravity of these women and gave licence to those who heaped severe social disapproval on them. Simultaneously, nevertheless, the New Women became the models of up-to-date fashion in the eyes of many Korean women. Jongwon Lee argues that, despite the publicly voiced disapproval of the New Women's fashions, style change rocketed, and the rapid spread of the New Women's fashions can be seen as evidence of other women's desires to become more liberated and privileged.[74]

From the mid 1920s, many nationalists who had previously advocated women's education as integral to Korea's modernity began to oppose the ideology and practices of New Women. Only a decade earlier they had welcomed challenges to Korean patriarchy as a modern nation-revitalising discourse, especially with regard to women's matters.[75] By contrast, in the mid 1920s, in their revised nationalist discourse aimed now against Japanese colonialism, tradition was reformulated and revalued. For instance, Gwangsu Lee, a famous male novelist[76] and an influential enlightenment activist during the early years of the Japanese colonial era, after 1910, asserted that Koreans could have self-control only through self-enlightenment and called for the destruction of traditional morality. In his first novel, *Mu Jong* (Without Love), published serially in *Macil Sinbo* (Maeil Newspaper) during 1917, Gwangsu Lee criticised the absurdity of the existing marriage system and its perspective on love. He claimed that 'the relation between wife and husband in Korea was a permanent illicit union' and the old perspective of chastity was 'a kind of religious superstition'.[77] However, by the 1920s he had changed his opinion. He began now to celebrate motherhood and to criticise married women who had paid occupations.[78] In his later novel, *Huk* (The Soil), published in 1932, he described a man's conflict in choosing between the traditional woman and the New Woman. Ultimately, his hero chose the traditional woman, because he admired naive women who maintained traditional virtue.[79] Gwangsu Lee's reaction reflected the redirection of Korean nationalists' discourse. Under colonialism, male nationalists thought that the New Women's direct denial of existing patriarchy and sexual morality might cause the collapse of Korean tradition and solidarity.

Japanese colonisers also underwent a change of thinking. They began to move to an ideological and strategic position surprisingly similar to that of the Korean male nationalists. After the popular anti-imperialist 3.1 movement of 1919, the Japanese colonial regime adopted a less oppressive political approach, labelled 'Cultural Politics'. This policy permitted Koreans some freedom of speech, publishing and organisation. It was a policy articulated via indirection and tact. Thus, in order to quash the progressive nationalism of young people who pursued modernity and Korean independence, Japanese officials began to support those Korean conservative legal organisations which advocated deference to Confucianism. Dongjin Kang, looking back, believes that the Japanese wanted to repress the radical ideology of young people by reminding them of the old moral conceptions.[80] At the same time, as part of their cultural political strategies, the colonisers tried to divide the Korean nation by inciting a conflict between the older and younger generations, between intellectuals and ordinary people.[81] For example, during the 1920s, the colonisers awarded large sums of money to sons who were dutiful to their parents and to wives who devoted themselves to their husbands.[82] Furthermore, the Japanese colonial government prohibited the publication of Sin Yo Ja (New Women) after volume number four.[83] The main goal of the Japanese colonial regime throughout the colonial era was the assimilation of Koreans into Japanese culture, not into the modernist strand of Japanese early twentieth-century culture, however.[84] Rather, the colonisers applied to colonised Korea those Japanese concepts of family and state that derived from Japan's one mode of Confucianism. While the Taisho era (1912–1926) was a relatively liberal era in Japan, the state and family concepts constructed in the Meiji era (1868–1912) seemed to continue in both Japan and Korea. The Meiji state defined the state as a family and the emperor as the head of that family. Other family members, while maintaining order and hierarchy among themselves, should be subservient to the head of the family.[85] The Japanese wanted to extend the family state concept into the Korean nation by making Korea a marginalised family member who nevertheless accepted the emperor as the head of the family.[86] For instance, the Japanese policy 'Good wife and wise mother' successfully infiltrated Korea in the 1930s with the growth of nuclear families through industrialisation. According to Haejung Cho, the ideology of 'good wife and wise mother' replaced the rebellious self-identity of the first New Women generation among New Women in the 1930s.[87]

Consequently, by the mid 1920s, both Japan's colonialists and Korea's nationalists had reached the conclusion that they each needed to celebrate and emphasise patriarchy, though in the names of opposing goals. During this period, when colonisation was becoming entrenched and nationalism was seeking popular acceptance, traditional patriarchy was reshaped and restrengthened to serve both sides as a potent weapon in the contest between colonialism and nationalism.

One can deduce the degree of hostility mounted on all sides towards the New Women from their miserable endings. With the flourishing of conservative morality from the late 1920s, Haesuk La could not pursue her dream of building up the New Women's organisations to lead a cultural movement.[88] Furthermore, after her divorce, her 'notorious' reputation weighed heavily on her. She lived in seclusion and died lonely in a clinic in 1948. On 14 March 1949, her name was printed in the obituary section of a local Korean newspaper as a person who fell sick on the road.[89] Wonju Kim also could not overcome the escalating criticism directed towards her. She was tonsured, which was the most important ritual in becoming an ordained Buddhist priest, and cut off every connection with worldly life.[90] Myungsoon Kim's talent and contribution to Korean literature as the first woman novelist and as a poet have been overshadowed by the bad reputation marking her private life. Perhaps more than any other single New Woman, she was made the target of harsh ridicule by contemporary male intellectuals and the media. They seemed to take special pleasure in exposing her humble origins – specifically, her mother's life as a *kisaeng*[91] and concubine of a wealthy official. Even Dongin Kim, a contemporary respected male novelist, wrote a biographical novel[92] about Myungsoon Kim, which deliberately ridiculed and slandered her humble birth and her sex life and that of her parents. The extraordinary pain Myungsoon Kim suffered indicates the persistent power of Korea's caste system. When Myungsoon Kim published her collection of poems, *Sangmyugwhi Gwasil* (The Fruit of Life), she confessed her pain, 'I contribute this book in the name of the suffering, anguish and curse of a young life which has been misunderstood'.[93] Her suffering and conflicts allegedly drove her crazy. She died in a lunatic asylum in Tokyo around 1951.[94]

In trying to understand why the New Women's movement failed, one can take several approaches. Jongwon Lee contends that the appearance and the failure of the New Women's group resulted from the fact that strong forces of the transitional period – marked by the coexistence, from around 1910 through the 1920s, of both a traditional lifestyle and ideology and a modern Western ideology – were at work at the same time as the sudden social changes caused by Japanese colonialism.[95] She describes the first generation of New Women as serving as scapegoats of the conflicts between the new and old cultures.[96] Hyungsil Suh, however, offers quite a different theory.[97] Suh asserts that every period is in some sense 'transitional', and so the reaction against the New Women in the 1920s came from their radical position in the Korean context of the time. Radicalism can be analysed in two ways. One view is related to the strength of Korean patriarchy. The more rigid patriarchy became, the more radicalised women became in order to liberate themselves from its grip. In other words, the New Women's radicalism was necessitated by their desperate situation. A second interpretation of their radicalism is related to a nationalist insistence that the New Women's indiscreet imitation of Western discourse made them too radical. Some late twentieth-century Korean nationalists (and I assume many nationalists thought like this in their time) describe the three leading New Women as victims of false consciousness: their supposedly shallow imitation of the West and its modernisation discourse.[98]

These two positions on the radicalism of the New Women, however, are not mutually exclusive. The desperate necessity for women's liberation that these Korean women felt compelled them to be concerned with women's lives. That is, it was the very imprisoning effects of Korea's own patriarchal system that pushed the New Women to look for alternatives in Japanese, British and Swedish feminist discourses. And before 1910 they were not alone, for, from the end of the nineteenth century to the early twentieth century, many Korean enlightenment thinkers – both women and men – claimed that Westernisation and modernisation offered the only way for Korea to insure its genuine sovereignty. Of course, Korea's male thinkers mainly focused on the development of Western-style technology and the denial of feudalism and the caste system. When they turned their attention to women's education, it was not for the sake of women's equality with men, but for the achievement of an educated motherhood, which they considered necessary for the pursuit of Korean modernisation and the regaining of Korean national power. In other words, these masculinist nationalists did not want the abolition of most women's traditional roles. Partha Chatterjee elaborates the tendency of Indian nationalists to separate the domain of the colonised culture into two spheres, the material and the spiritual, which has some similarities with the case of Korea. He summarises this tendency thus: 'What was necessary was to cultivate the material techniques of modern Western civilisation while retaining and strengthening the distinctive spiritual essence of the national culture'.[99]

However, instead of focusing on technology like Korean men, what colonised Korean women discovered in the West was a different relationship between men and women than that in Korea. Here we can view the dilemma that colonised women experienced. While the national task demanded that the colonised deny colonial hegemonic power, colonised women, on the other hand, wanted to deny the existing traditional patriarchal shackles by using Western feminists' discourse despite its supposed collusion with colonial hegemonic power. What was colonised women's proper position?

Haesuk La went to Europe and America for two years (1927–9) to study painting and to sightsee. She expressed her concern about the cultural gap between the West and Korea. After coming back to Korea, she felt a great yearning for Western modernity. She wrote about this troubling yearning in an essay: 'after experiencing the West, I could not endure my life in this rural Korea which is 2 or 3 centuries behind in the speed of modernisation compared to Europe. Everything in Korea does not fit for me and I feel like an alien in my own country'.[100] This inferiority that New Women felt compared to the West is the most criticised element of the New Women's movement and the main cause of the devaluing of New Women's whole ideology and practice by scholars until now.[101]

To refute the dominant analysis of the inferiority felt by New Women, and to explore another aspect of it, I want to apply Chandra Mohanty's argument to this case. Mohanty denies the difference between Third World women and First World women because Third World women's difference is constructed from the self-centred perspective of Western feminists.

Mohanty argues that this is the otherisation of Third World women whose identities are represented by Western feminists.[102] She says:

> An analysis of 'sexual difference' in the form of a cross-culturally singular, monolithic notion of patriarchy or male dominance leads to the construction of a similarly reductive and homogeneous notion of what I call the 'third world difference' – that stable, ahistorical something that apparently oppresses most if not all the women in these countries. And it is in the production of this 'third world difference' that Western feminisms appropriate and 'colonise' the constitutive complexities which characterise the lives of women in these countries.[103]

On Mohanty's insistence, I want to explore another aspect of colonised women's inferiority to the West. If Western feminists understand Third World women or colonised women's inferiority with a sense of Western superiority, misrepresentations can occur. In other words, I do not think colonised women's inferiority is an opposite concept to Western women's superiority. Colonised women's own sense of inferiority has complicated meanings. From their perspective, this inferiority is not the inferiority of women themselves, because women were not the main agents of male-dominant society. Their colonised inferiority is the result of a society that their men initiated. Feeling the inferiority of the colonised is an important experience that enables women to doubt the hegemonic patriarchal discourse of their own society. If given the chance, this may be related to the discovery of a new paradigm for women because a sense of inferiority can lead to a desire to develop new possibilities. In the case of Korean women, some looked to the West to provide new ideas for their own use. In this model, inferiority could work to reframe colonised women's agency in overcoming their traditional oppression.

Returning to the reasons for the failure of the New Women's movement, Sookhee Oho and the Korean Women's Research Group indicate that the absence of middle-class women, at the time, who could accept and develop New Women's liberal feminism, made the New Women's movement end up simply as radical practices.[104] However, this explanation elicits another set of questions: How possible was it to form a middle class in colonial society? If it was possible, could middle-class women deliver liberal ideology in the colonial context? Were middle-class women free from the influence of nationalism within colonial settings? In other words, I think the backlash against the New Women was not just a simple reaction of existing patriarchal power to radical practices which some liberal middle-class women could accept and follow; rather it can be understood correctly as the meeting of existing patriarchal power and nationalism under colonialism. In the 1920s, Korean nationalism became reified after the 3.1 movement as a prominent ideology. The Korean independence movement was initiated by two groups, socialists and nationalists. The leading nationalists were from the former gentry class who opposed modernisation in favour of keeping the feudal system and morality, and who fought against Western imperialism and Japanese imperialism for almost thirty years. Through their articulation of nationalism, the nationalists revalued tradition in ways connected to the new direction the former progressive intellectuals took at the end of the 1920s. In a similar way to what Chatterjee describes in India's case, Korean nationalism opted for a new patriarchal power to build up national identity and resist Japanese imperialism. In this context, Sookhee Oho doubts the possibility of the success of the New Women movement under colonialism. She says, 'Under the nation's emergency situation, the women's resistance against gendered inequalities had no proper site. Quite apart from men, women themselves thought that new women's insistence was unrealistically indiscreet and could dissipate Korea's power as a nation'[105] (translated by the author).

Overall, I do not think the New Women's movement failed. It is not easy to measure success or failure of such a culturally challenging movement. However, one cannot conclude that, because of their wretched endings, their loss of popularity and the strength of the backlash, the New Women's movement was a failure. Although the three representative women suffered ordeals, they succeeded in changing or at least shaking up some social concepts regarding chastity, love and marriage. Above all, their movement can be counted a success if one asks the question: was their challenge necessary in that society?

The New Women's movement emerged from the conflict between the cultural domination of Western imperialism and Confucian patriarchy. However, the New Women's movement disappeared under the attack of Korean nationalists and Japanese imperialists, and because of the patriarchal cultural reaction. In sum, on the one hand, Western cultural imperialism enabled some Korean women to discover one outlet for refusing indigenous traditional patriarchy. On the other hand, it functioned to reframe the constraints on Korean women by strengthening indigenous patriarchy within nationalist paradigms. The New Women's complicated relation to imperialism reminds us of Third World feminists' present problems: first, the conflict between the appeal of Western feminist discourse and the fear of imperialism underneath Western feminism; second, and the conflict between Third World feminists' denial of tradition as an oppressive system, on the one hand, and Third World nationalists' attempts to revive tradition as an ideological root, on the other hand.

In conclusion, I think we need to try to answer three remaining questions. First, if the New Women's movement had been less radical, would it have succeeded without causing its leaders to end up so sadly? Second, under colonialism, could an authentic form of indigenous nationalism have been created, which managed to embrace the women's rejection of traditionalist values and spirit even though their rejection was in part articulated through the notion of Western feminism? Third, is it possible to build within a nationalist discourse a genuinely feminist politics which can speak effectively to non-nationalistic women's issues? Revisiting specific historical junctures in specific societies, fully acknowledging the multiple currents flowing through those contextualised junctures, offers us, I think, one way to tackle each of these three puzzles and so, hopefully, to establish criteria which can inclusively represent diverse women's interests in colonial and post-colonial contexts.

Notes

1. Chandra Talpade Mohanty, 'Under Western Eyes', in *Third World Women and The Politics of Feminism*, ed. Chandra Talpade Mohanty, Ann Russo, and Lourdes Torres (Indiana University Press, Bloomington, 1991), p. 53.

2. Anne McClintock, *Imperial Leather: Race, Gender and Sexuality in The Colonial Contest* (Routledge, New York, 1995).

3. Mervat Hatem, 'Through Each Other's Eyes: The Impact on the Colonial Encounter of the Images of Egyptian, Levantine-Egyptian, and European Women, 1862–1920', in *Western Women and Imperialism: Complicity and Resistance*, ed. Nupur Chaudhuri and Margaret Strobel (Indiana University Press, Bloomington, 1992), pp. 35–58, and see Barbara N. Ramusack, 'Cultural Missionaries, Maternal Imperialists, Feminist Allies', in *Western Women and Imperialism*, pp. 119–36.

4. The time the New Women emerged (1920–1930) was before Korea was divided into North and South (1945–).

5. S. Chai, B. Lee, Y. Shin and Y. Ahn use the New Women in a broader way in their article, 'Research on Classifying Women for Developing Korean Women's History', *The Collection of Women's Studies Theses*, 10, Korean Women Research Institute of Ewha University (1993), pp. 26–7. They define New Women as follows: 'If we divide New Women up, there were leading New Women who had studied abroad, middle-class New Women who had graduated from high school and had jobs, middle-class homemaker New Women who had been highly educated but lived like traditional women, and working-class New Women who were literate' (translated by the author).

6. According to Korean tradition, men and women could not have sexual relations with each other before marriage or outside marriage.

7. According to Korean tradition, the parents of the bride and groom had absolute authority with regard to decisions about marriage.

8. Jongwon Lee, 'Role Conflict for Korean New Women Under Japanese Colonialism', MA thesis, Spiritual and Cultural Research Institute (Seoul, 1983), p. 60.

9. Jinsong Kim, 'The First Female Western Painter, the Failure of Liberalism', *History and Critic*, Summer (1992), p. 235, and see Sukpoon Park and Eunpong Park, 'La Haesuk: The Distorted Women's Consciousness of New Women', in *Individual Women's History* (Saenal, Seoul, 1992), p. 184.

10. The Korean Women's Research Group for Korean Women's History, *Korean Women's History: Modern Era* (Pulbit Press, Seoul, 1992), p. 125.

11. Wonju Kim, 'Our Demands as Women', *Sin Yo Ja* (New Women), 2 (1920), quoted in Jongwon Lee, 'Conflict for New Women', p. 26.

12. In the Korean colonial context, China seemed less a country colonised by the West than an imperial power which sought to occupy and control Korea.

13. Lee analyses the important roles missionaries played as pioneers in opening the Korean market to imperial interests in contrast to the way they are usually seen. He emphasises the American missionaries' nationalism by discussing a US marine who was also a teacher and who hoisted the Stars and Stripes along with Korean flags in a missionary school. He criticises the educational work of missionaries because it made Koreans worship Western imperialists and Westernisation. See Haesuk Lee, 'What Did American Missionaries in the Early Days Do?', in *Correcting 37 Events of Our History*, ed. the Institute of Historical Problems (Yoksa Bipyong Press, Seoul, 1993), pp. 23–5.

14. Haejung Cho, *Korean Women and Men* (Moonhak Wha Jisong Press, Seoul, 1986), p. 94.

15. Cho, *Korean Women and Men*, pp. 94–5.

16. *Doklib Sinmoon* is the first newspaper written only in Korean.

17. Cho, *Korean Women and Men*, p. 94.

18. Jongwon Lee, 'Role Conflict for New Women', p. 13.

19. According to Lee, one housewife evangelist converted 3,000 housewives in eight months. See Hyojae Lee, 'A Hundred Years of History of Korean Church Women', in *Women, Wake up! Stand Up! Sing!* (Daehan Kidugkyo Press, Seoul, 1985), p. 23.

20. Hyojae Lee, 'A Hundred Years of History of Korean Church Women', p. 31.

21. Haewon Yoon, 'Protestant Schools and Women's Education', in *Women, Wake up!,* pp.113–19.

22. *Donga Ilbo* (Donga Newspaper), 4 April 1920.

23. *Donga Ilbo*, 7 June 1920.

24. Yoon, 'Protestant Schools', p. 113.

25. Wonju Kim, 'I Do Not Know Truth', in *Kim Wonju – Burying Love under a Gray Dress*, ed. Sang-Bae Kim (Solmae Press, Seoul, 1982), p. 38.

26. One interesting feature of women's education during the colonial era was that widows were very eager for their daughters to be educated, especially if the widows only had daughters. Jungsook Kang points out that of 190 graduates of Ewha Women's College in one year, the number of widow' daughters was 52 (the year is not mentioned but it was in the 1920s). See Jungsook Kang, 'Interdisciplinary Studies of the Experiences of Korean Women', in *The Experiences of Korean Women*, ed. Korean Women's Theology Association (Dahan Kidugko Suhwae, Seoul, 1994), p. 95.

27. From 1 March 1919, huge demonstrations were staged in Korea against the Japanese colonial regime for nearly a year. Two million Korean people participated and 7,500 were killed, 16,000 injured and 46,000 arrested. See Mansoo Kang, *Korean Modern History* (Changjak Wha Bibyong Press, Seoul, 1984), p. 46.

28. Kyungsung Lee, 'Women Who Bore the Cross of Beauty', in *A Complete Collection of La Haesuk – Flown Blue Bird*, ed. Jongwook Kim (Sinhung Press, Seoul, 1981).

29. Jongwon Lee, 'Role Conflict for New Women', pp. 38–9.

30. Sookhee Oho, 'The Korean Women's Movement: Focusing on the 1920s', MA thesis, Ewha Women's University (Seoul, 1987), pp. 132–3.

31. Jongwon Lee, 'Role Conflict for New Women', pp. 34–6.

32. Oho, 'The Korean Women's Movement', p. 133

33. Jongwon Lee, 'Role Conflict for New Women', p. 82.

34. Sharon L. Sievers, *Flowers in Salt: The Beginnings of Feminist Consciousness in Modern Japan* (Stanford University Press, Stanford, 1983), p. 175.

35. Laurel Rasplica Rodd, 'Yosan Akiko and the Taisho Debate over the "New Woman"', in *Recreating Japanese Women, 1600–1945*, ed. Gail Lee Bernstein (University of California Press, Berkeley, 1991), p. 176.

36. Sievers, *Flowers in Salt*, p. 175.

37. Ellen Key, *Love and Marriage* (G. P. Putnam's Sons, New York and London, 1911).

38. Sachiko Kaneko, 'The Struggle for Legal Rights and Reforms: A Historical View', in *Japanese Women: New Feminist Perspectives on the Past, Present, and Future*, ed. Kumiko Fujimura-Fanselow and Atsuko Kameda (The Feminist Press, New York, 1995), p. 5.

39. Jongwon Lee, 'Role Conflict for New Women', p. 29.

40. La Haesuk, 'A Doll's House', in *A Complete Collection of La Haesuk*, ed. Kim, p. 331.

41. 'A List of Articles and Theses Regarding Women Under Japanese Occupation', in *Yo Song* (Women), 1 (Changjak Wha Bipyung Press, Seoul, 1985), p. 357.

42. Mikiso Hane, *Reflections on the Way to the Gallows* (University of California Press, Berkeley, 1988), p. 21.

43. Sievers, *Flowers in Salt*, pp.173–4.

44. Sievers, *Flowers in Salt*, p. 225.

45. Wonju Kim, 'Our Ideal, in the Light of Married Women' (July 1924), quoted in *Kim Wonju*, ed. Sang-Bae Kim, p. 233.

46. La, 'The Journey to Europe', in *A Complete Collection of La Haesuk*, ed. Kim, p. 239.

47. La, 'Beginning a New Life', in *A Complete Collection of La Haesuk*, ed. Kim, p. 143.

48. Sievers writes, 'Raicho had made it clear that her visit to the Yoshiwara was made out of curiosity, not social conscience'. See *Flowers in Salt*, p. 174.

49. La, 'An Interview with the Suffrage Movement Women Activists in Britain and America', in *A Complete Collection of La Haesuk*, ed. Kim, p. 309.

50. Joan Wallach Scott, 'Gender: A Useful Category of Historical Analysis', in *Gender and the Politics of History* (Columbia University Press, New York, 1988), p. 34.

51. The Chosun dynasty was founded on and sustained by Confucian feudalism. The king had absolute power over the people, who were divided into gentry, plebeians and slaves.

52. Cho, *Korean Women and Men*, p. 69.

53. Cho, *Korean Women and Men*, p. 69.

54. The influence of Confucianism in Korea appeared six or seven hundred years before the Koryo dynasty was built. With the spread of Confucianism, women's chastity began to be emphasised. During the Koryo dynasty era, Confucianism existed but was not as strong an ideology as Buddhism. See Dujin Kim, 'The Status of Ancient Korean Women' in *Civil Lectures in Korean History*, 15, ed. Giback Lee (Ilchogak Press, Seoul, 1994), p. 34, and HoongSik Her, 'The Status and Role of Women of the *Koryo* Dynasty', in *Civil Lectures in Korean History*, p. 81.

55. Hyojae Lee, *The Korean Women's Movement – The Past and Today* (Jungwoo Press, Seoul, 1989), p. 30.

56. Korean Women's Research Group, *Korean Women's History*, p. 16.

57. Hyojae Lee, *The Korean Women's Movement – The Past and Today*, p. 20.

58. Youngsook Kim, 'The Characteristics of Korean Women's Literature', in *Women of the Yi Dynasty*, ed. Young-Hae Park (Cheong Poong Press, Seoul, 1986), p. 55.

59. Having virtuous women was also an honour to the community or village to which the women belonged. Sometimes, the king bestowed a prize on virtuous women. The prize was a kind of arch, and villagers built the arch in the front of the entrance to the village.

60. Cho, *Korean Women and Men* , p. 76.

61. Youngsook Kim, *Women of the Yi Dynasty*, p. 55.

62. Cho, *Korean Women and Men*, p. 77.

63. Hyungsil Suh, 'Free Love and New Women Under Japanese Colonialism', *History and Critic*, Summer (1994), p. 117.

64. Cho, *Korean Women and Men*, p. 96.

65. Jongwon Lee, 'Role Conflict for New Women', p. 74.

66. Youngsook Shin, 'Research on the Social History of Korean Women Under Japanese Imperialism', PhD dissertation, Ewha Women's University (1988), p. vi.

67. Translated by the author, *Donga Ilbo*, 17 June 1925.

68. *Donga Ilbo*, 10 November 1924.

69. Quoted in Oho, 'Korean Women's Movement', p. 143.

70. *Donga Ilbo* (30 September 1921) dealt with the increase in divorce as a result of fashion.

71. Shin, 'Korean Women's Social History', p. 64.

72. Oho, 'Korean Women's Movement', p. 141.

73. *Donga Ilbo*, 10 September 1921.

74. Jongwon Lee, 'Role Conflict for New Women', p. 45.

75. Oho, 'Korean Women's Movement', p. 146.

76. He was a leading thinker and a novelist who published the first long novel in Korea.

77. Jungwha Byon, 'Short Review of Lee Gwangsu', *Chongae Moonhak*, 13 (1980), p. 225.

78. Cho, *Korean Women and Men*, p. 99.

79. Gwangsu Lee, *Huk* (The Soil), (Bakyoung Press, Seoul, 1966).

80. Dongjin Kang, *The Occupation History of Japanese Imperialism* (Hangil Press, Seoul, 1980), pp. 26–7.

81. Kang, *The Occupation History*, p. 27.

82. *Donga Ilbo*, 30 December 1922.

83. Oho, 'Korean Women's Movement', p. 151.

84. Kang, *The Occupation History*, p. 46.

85. Bernstein, Introduction to *Recreating Japanese Women*.

86. According to Jinsung Jung, the family state concept which focused on representing the Japanese emperor as a god, and the leader of the military, while the Union of Japan, was strengthened by World War II. See Jinsung Jung, 'The Emperor System, Militarism and Women', in *Collection of Materials on Comfort Women II*, ed. The Korean Council for the Women Drafted for Sexual Slavery by Japan (Seoul, 1992), p. 41.

87. Cho, *Korean Women and Men*, p. 99.

88. Oho, 'The Korean Women's Movement', p. 142.

89. Jongwon Lee, 'Role Conflict for New Women', p. 81.

90. Jongwon Lee, 'Role Conflict for New Women', p. 79.

91. *Kisaeng* meant entertainment girls who could play instruments, write poetry and sing classical songs.

92. The name of the novel is *Kim Yonsil Jun* (The story of Kim Yonsil), which is very similar to Myungsoon Kim's original name, Tansil Kim.

93. Quoted in Hosook Song, 'The First Female Novelist, Myungsoon Kim: The Tragedy of Free Love', *History and Critics*, Summer (1992), p. 227.

94. Song, 'The First Female Novelist', p. 228.

95. Jongwon Lee, 'Role Conflict for New Women', p. 73.

96. Jongwon Lee, 'Role Conflict for New Women', p. 77.

97. Suh, 'Free Love of New Women', p. 122.

98. Jinsong Kim, 'The First Female Western Painter' p. 235.

99. Partha Chatterjee, 'Colonialism, Nationalism, and Colonialised Women. The Contest in India', *American Ethnologist*, 16 (1989), p. 24.

100. La, 'I Am Missing the Freedom of Paris', in *A Complete Collection of Haesuk*, ed. Kim, p. 133.

101. Jinsong Kim, ' The First Female Painter', p. 235, and see S. Park and E.Park, 'La Haesuk'.

102. Mohanty, 'Under Western Eyes', p. 53.

103. Mohanty, 'Under Western Eyes', pp. 53–4.

104. Oho, 'The Korean Women's Movement', p. 145, and the Korean Women's Research Group, *Korean Women's History*, p. 125.

105. Oho, 'The Korean Women's Movement', p. 150.

Madrinas and Missionaries: Uruguay and the Pan-American Women's Movement

CHRISTINE EHRICK

International feminism from a Uruguayan perspective: Paulina Luisi's 'map of women's political rights'. Originally published as an insert to Alianza Uruguaya y Consejo de Mujeres, *La mujer uruguaya reclama sus derechos políticos* (Montevideo: Editorial Apolo, 1929). Map owned and photographed by the author, with permission from the Consejo Nacional de Mujeres del Uruguay.

Women's political organising during the first third of this century was, as in our own era, an international affair. More than our own, perhaps, it was an 'internationalist' movement, whose leaders aggressively sought to help form associations and build alliances across national, cultural, and linguistic borders. Like Socialists, Communists, and affiliates of other 'internationals', liberal feminists took advantage of improved and cheaper communications and transportation technology to build a network of contacts across the globe and to forge an international liberal feminist network. The Pan-American women's movement was one sector of this network.

The story of feminism and Pan-Americanism is often told with the United States at the centre of analysis. This article will instead take as its vantage point the small South American country of Uruguay, a nation which stood out among its neighbours during this era as a model of progressive social reform, political democracy and, as we shall see below, successful liberal feminist mobilisation. For the purposes of this article, I define liberal feminism as that ideological branch of the women's movement oriented toward the acquisition of equal political and civic rights for women within a generally capitalist and secular framework, including but not limited to demands for equal access to education and the professions, equal property and citizenship rights and, of course, the vote. This was one of several 'feminisms' that coexisted and competed with each other in Uruguay and beyond during this era. Anarchists and communists involved with the labour movement and the so-called 'Christian feminists' of the conservative Catholic Ladies' League, for example, were also politically active in Uruguay and were connected to their own international and Pan-American networks during these years.[1]

The first 'welfare state' in Latin America, Uruguay was distinguished in the first decades of this century by economic prosperity, a relatively large middle class and advanced social legislation. The latter was largely associated with the figure of José Batlle y Ordóñez, president of Uruguay from 1903 to 1907 and 1911 to 1915 and a leader of the ruling Colorado Party until his death in 1929. During Batlle's second presidential term, Uruguay became the first Latin American nation to legislate the eight-hour day, the first to have a Ministry of Labour and of Industry, and the home of a social security system that became a model for the rest of the continent. Uruguay's reputation as a 'model country' carried over into liberal feminist politics as well. Batlle and his followers saw an elevation in women's status (within certain circumscribed limits, to be sure) as requisite for national advancement, and the result was a political climate favourable to women's political mobilisation in general and to liberal feminist campaigns in particular. This image of Uruguayan liberal feminism was, at least in part, backed up and acknowledged by observers in neighbouring countries. In December 1918, for example, the popular Argentine magazine *Caras y Caretas* published an article on Uruguayan feminism in which the author states that 'within South America, the most defined feminist current is to be found in Uruguay'.[2] Uruguayan liberal feminists even claimed to have been the first to launch a women's suffrage campaign on the continent. Whether true or not, all of this contributed to a strong consciousness among Uruguayan liberal feminists, some of whom saw themselves as the vanguard and as natural leaders of the movement within Latin America. The following was published in 1919 in *Acción Femenina*, the official publication of the

Uruguayan National Women's Council, on the occasion of the group's third anniversary:

> In these three short years of existence, the name of Uruguay has quickly become known in the feminist circles of the entire world ... That is because Uruguay was the first country in South America to initiate a women's suffrage movement; its women have dared to raise their voice for the recognition of their political rights; the first among South American women, they have addressed the established Powers of their country to demand their citizenship rights.[3]

The author of this passage was Paulina Luisi, the most important liberal feminist leader in Uruguay at the time. The first female physician in Uruguay, Luisi was the founder and leader of both the Uruguayan National Women's Council and the Uruguayan Women's Suffrage Alliance, the largest and most influential women's rights organisations in the country and those most associated with the campaign for women's suffrage. In large part due to her efforts – and to frequent trips to Europe – Uruguayan liberal feminism maintained a very high international profile throughout the years in question. Luisi was the only Latin American in the leadership rosters of the IWSA (the International Women's Suffrage Alliance, later the International Alliance of Women, or IAW) during these years, and even spent a few years as acting second vice president from 1923 to 1926.

Luisi's high international profile is immediately evident from an examination of her personal archives, which reveal that she maintained long and in some cases extensive correspondence with many of the leaders of Latin American liberal feminism during these years. In general, these letters report on the state of affairs in the letter writers' political context, they ask for advice, and they lament their own difficult organising circumstances in contrast to the 'greener grasses' of the Oriental Republic:[4] where religion was not stifling the drive for a change in women's roles, where class politics were not so polarised as to make impossible the formation of a broad and diverse women's suffrage campaign, and where progressive government policies provided a nurturing (or at least not hindering) environment for the growth of a healthy and robust liberal feminist movement.

These documents are significant in that they contain the more private discourse of these feminists, and as such provide a very different perspective on the state of the movement and organising strategies from that found in the more diplomatic language of public discourse. At the same time, it is important to emphasise that these letters contain only a small sample of what was surely a wide variety of opinions on the subject of feminism and Pan-Americanism among politically active women in the Americas during these years. There is a process of a priori selection going on here, in that the women Luisi maintained a correspondence with were likely to be those with whom she shared some political or ideological affinity (Luisi herself was sympathetic with the Socialist Party, although she was apparently never a member during these years). Nevertheless, much can be learned from looking at liberal feminist movements throughout Latin America refracted through the Uruguayan experience. Among other things, it helps us to better understand the kinds of circumstances or conditions that either helped or hindered the emergence of strong and healthy liberal feminist movements in various parts of Latin America, and shifts our frame of reference away from the United States which, after all, only vaguely resembles the Latin American reality. These letters also reveal a great deal about the attitude of many Latin American liberal feminists towards their US counterparts. By the 1920s, women's attainment of the vote in the US – coupled with increased North American intervention in Latin American affairs – became a source of tension and disillusionment among some Latin American feminists with this and other international organisations, and would do much to tarnish the (apparent) 'sisterhood' of earlier years. Following a brief overview of the international context, my initial focus will be the importance of the Argentine movement in the foundation of the Uruguayan, and the influence in turn that Uruguayans exercised on the Chilean, Mexican, and (to some extent) Cuban movements during the first third of this century. The second part will focus on relations with European and North American liberal feminists, and the corresponding reaction to that influence/intervention by their Latin American counterparts during an era of growing nationalism and especially anti-US sentiment in the 1920s and 1930s.

The independent nation of Uruguay was created in part as a 'buffer state' between Brazil and Argentina, and Uruguayan national identity still bears that imprint, particularly in terms of the simultaneous threat and attraction of Argentina. Contact and movement between Montevideo and Buenos Aires has always been fluid and frequent, and women's organisations, the labour movement, and other groups in Uruguay were strongly influenced by what were generally earlier developments in Argentina. That Argentine feminists very early on became integrated with the international network of female leaders is reflective of the relatively powerful economic position of Argentina during this time. International conferences were the primary medium through which these liberal feminist networks were forged during the so-called first wave, but participation in these conferences was very expensive, requiring either substantial personal wealth or official government sponsorship (and hence a sympathetic political climate). Thus it is no coincidence that the earliest Latin American representation in these international conferences would come from the wealthiest nation in the region at that time. Ironically, however, the Argentine movement may have suffered from congealing too early, out of step with the 'class blueprint' which would be utilised (unofficially but consciously) by women in other Latin American nations, an issue which will be discussed below. In simplistic terms, the Argentine movement suffered from too strong a presence of aristocratic *damas* (ladies) of the old charitable school. These women, with their more conservative and charity-based ideology, overwhelmed the middle class, reformist and activist-minded professional women, rendering the Argentine Women's Council relatively ineffective as a catalysing force for feminist mobilisation in that country.

The Argentine branch of the National Women's Council, affiliated with the ICW (International Council of Women), was founded in 1900 by Cecilia Grierson.[5] Grierson formed the Argentine Council after attending an ICW meeting in London in 1899, where she was made an honorary vice president of that group. The Argentines, it appears, were entrusted with a proselytising mission to diffuse the project of international liberal feminism among their neighbours. They appear to have faithfully executed this task, at least in the case of Uruguay, where the first Argentine liberal feminists offered tremendous advice and encouragement to potential leaders such as a young female medical student named Paulina Luisi. In South America especially, the first women to receive medical degrees were all but inducted as the 'natural leaders' of the liberal feminist movement in their respective countries, so Luisi would have been the obvious target of Argentine recruitment efforts.

While Luisi was still a student, Argentine liberal feminist Petrona Eyle wrote to her in her capacity as president of the *Universitarias Argentinas* (Argentine Association of University Women, affiliated with the American Association of University Women, or AAUW), recruiting her to join their organisation. Founded in 1902, the *Universitarias* was an important organisation around which the ideology of the female professional as natural feminist leader coalesced in these years. In a letter dated 1 May 1907, Eyle encouraged Luisi and her female colleagues in the university to form an Uruguayan branch of the *Universitarias*, stating that 'although there aren't many of you now, you will always be the nucleus around which others will come together'.[6] It appears that Luisi and others accepted this invitation and joined with their Argentine counterparts in 1907.[7] Important also to Luisi's insertion into Pan-American liberal feminist networks and in her propulsion to the leadership of still germinating Uruguayan liberal feminism was her participation in the Women's Congress (*Congreso Femenino*) held in Buenos Aires in 1910. Organised by the *Universitarias*, the conference brought together more than 200 women, representing Argentina, Uruguay, Peru, Paraguay, and Chile. It seems likely that it was at this conference that Luisi first came into contact with many of the leaders (or soon-to-be leaders) of liberal feminism in South America, and where she would establish her contacts and friendships that would endure for decades afterwards.

Liberal feminism in Uruguay thus owed a great deal to the encouragement and experience of the much older movement on the other side of the Rio de la Plata. But while Uruguayan liberal feminism may have been inspired and backed by the Argentine example, the Uruguayan movement quickly outgrew its mentor in many ways. Following in the footsteps of the Argentine branch, Luisi had the advantage of looking across the river to learn from others' errors. Leaders of the Argentine movement, disenchanted with the outcome of liberal feminist organising (especially that of the Council), offered Luisi advice both before and after the foundation of the Uruguayan National Women's Council. Years earlier, in October 1913, Luisi had received a letter of warning from Council founder Cecilia Grierson. In this letter, which included the statutes of the Argentine Council (apparently requested by Luisi), a disenchanted Grierson advised Luisi not to repeat her mistakes:

> I have had nothing to do with the Council since 1910. We had that Congress [the Women's Congress] and the group ceased to be a Council and has become a literary-musical society (very lovely) but without the direction it should have. It does not represent the intellectuals or the feminine cooperation of the country. I advise you when you form the centre not to be so modest as I because it can happen to you. I will give you some advice, that you reserve for yourself and your *true friends* the executive posts and the councillors ... you need to avoid the formation of cliques as has happened here ... I hope you have more luck than I in the task ...[8]

When Luisi finally founded the Uruguayan National Women's Council in late 1916, her old friend Petrona Eyle sent her this letter, which seconded many of Grierson's earlier admonitions:

> You cannot imagine how much pleasure it gives me and with what interest I have read everything you have sent me about the creation of the National Women's Council of Uruguay ... I think that you will have more luck than Cecilia [Grierson] with her foundation here, because in my opinion (and in that of others also), she erred in giving the Presidency and the leadership to people who could not support her or give the council the direction it should have had. Cecilia thought she was right in attracting all the most distinguished from the point of view of social life, but not from the point of view of education, and most of all they are seignorial, they don't dare to leave a certain small circle of interests that they call *feminismo bien entendido* (feminism as it should be).[9]

As it turned out, Luisi would not be entirely successful in avoiding the pitfalls Eyle and Grierson warned her of, barely surviving an attempt at ousting her by more conservative elements within the movement.[10] But over the long term she was able to maintain her position as the undisputed leader of Uruguayan liberal feminism. Certainly this had much to do with the very different political context in Uruguay, as well as Luisi's obvious leadership skills, but we cannot discount entirely the advantage gleaned from learning from earlier mistakes, particularly that of placing too much authority in the hands of aristocrats, a key element in the 'class blueprint' that was taking shape during these years.

Constructing a strong and influential liberal feminist movement in Latin America during these years was not merely a question of organisational skills and forging strategic alliances. The broader social and political context also exerted an important and potentially defining influence on when and how these groups took shape. Thus while Chilean women were, for example, a visible presence at the 1910 Women's Congress in Buenos Aires, there was a bit of a delay in getting liberal feminist organisations off the ground there, difficulties that had as much to do with the particularities of Chilean society as they did with organisational questions. Letters to Luisi from Chilean liberal feminists imply that, in some cases, hesitation to push directly and aggressively for women's suffrage did not stem from conservatism and a penchant for charity-oriented 'social feminism' within liberal feminist associations, but from concerns about the political impact of women's political participation on national politics. It was a common assumption among Latin American reformers that women remained under the heel of the parish priest and, however much they may have supported women's voting in principle, many feared that in practice women's suffrage would benefit their conservative and Catholic opponents.

Pioneering Chilean feminist Amanda Labarca, for example, expressed deep consternation over the appropriateness of campaigning for women's suffrage in the context of what she saw as a continued stranglehold of clericalism over Chilean women. In a letter to Luisi in 1922, Labarca wondered if 'women's suffrage in Chile would favor the liberal evolution of the country, or would it set it back by strengthening the size and power of the clerical-conservative party?'[11] Earlier that same year, secretary of the International Women's Suffrage Association Mary Sheepshanks wrote to Luisi, stating that Labarca had expressed her fear that if women were given the vote 'they would reverse recently instituted secular education' because of their continued subjugation to clerical control.[12] Two years later, in 1924, Labarca still had reservations, writing that: 'historically, premature social reforms have been a greater source of harm than of good. Could my friends and I be fomenting a premature reform?'[13] Labarca was not the only Chilean liberal feminist voicing these concerns. Journalist and Chilean Council founder Celinda Arregui de Rodicio revealed not only her hesitations but her literary flair in a letter addressed to Luisi about the state of liberal feminism in Chile within the larger international and/or Pan-American context:

> We [Chileans] march very much in the rear guard with respect to women's suffrage, because in Chile everything smells of incense, and until the education of the people clears the air a little we should not hope for too much … here the clergy dominate politics, so that *for now* if they gave women the vote it would sink the country.[14]

Labarca and Arregui de Rodicio's letters also indirectly tell us something about the perception of the Uruguayan movement. Discussion of the fact that 'in Chile' the Church is too strong, and has too much power over women, implies that the author felt that it might not be the case in

Uruguay, and that the relative weakness of the Catholic Church and the secularism of Uruguayan society was an advantage. It is also clear that both Arregui and Labarca were seeking women's suffrage not simply for its own sake, but as part of a larger political project and vision for their country. Otherwise, they would not have been so concerned about the Catholic Church in Chile or its control over women. These documents reveal their authors to be savvy politicians, strongly conscious of their historical role (as they saw it) and proceeding with great care and caution so as not to make any mistakes. They wanted women's suffrage to accomplish certain political goals, for which women's votes served both as a way to change society and as a means to rectify women's civic and political inequality.

These women, therefore, had a clear vision of the ways in which they foresaw the entry of women into politics and were trying to consciously manage both the timing and the terms of that entry. Part of this management had to do with the class composition of their organisations. The challenge was to create an organisation which appeared to cross class boundaries and be universally inclusive of all women, but in which a certain sector of middle-class professional women maintained a firm control. One last document regarding Chile underlines the importance given to the issue of class composition within liberal feminist associations and in society as a whole. Mary Sheepshanks was an important figure in North American and international feminism, for years the secretary of the International Women's Suffrage Alliance (IWSA) and a leader of the Women's International League for Peace and Freedom (WILPF). Sheepshanks had a brother living in Uruguay, and in 1921 she spent several months on his ranch in the interior. It was here that Sheepshanks met Luisi, whom she later described as 'a woman of outstanding ability and genius ... whose vitality and dominating personality would make her a leader in any country in the world'.[15]

Perhaps because of this respect she had for Luisi, or the friendship they may have developed, Sheepshanks maintained a correspondence with Luisi during her South American travels. After leaving Uruguay, Sheepshanks travelled to Buenos Aires and then across the Andes, where she reported back to Luisi on her impressions of the state of liberal feminism in Chile. In a letter dated 15 April 1922 and written in French (their common language) from the capital city of Santiago, Sheepshanks wrote:

> One thing makes me doubt whether it might not be premature to affiliate the *Partido Femenino*[16] here with the International Alliance. I have not located one member during my 18 days here. I have met no one other than Vice President Villaire de Castro, who is enthusiastic, but that is not enough. Another thing: it appears to me that this group contains only working-class women (*ouvrières*) and it should combine all the classes, all the parties ... Might it be possible to wait for a group which unifies working class and bourgeois women? Educated women are not attracted by a purely working class association.[17]

So as not to misinterpret Sheepshanks's words, it is important to cite part of a letter she wrote to Luisi only a month before from Buenos Aires, reporting her critique of the movement in that country:

I saw Mrs Hume, Dr Eyle, Dr Dellepiane, Dr Lanteri-Renshaw, and Dr Moreau.[18] All of them said that the feminist movement is less advanced here than in Uruguay ... Orientalism and luxury seem the worst enemies of the movement ... It is too bad they don't let the Russians enter; a little bolshevism might liven them up a little.[19]

Juxtaposing these two reports tells us a great deal about the ideal 'model' liberal feminists seemed to be following while constructing their movements, and highlights the fact that within the South American context, Uruguay was seen as the best application of that model. What becomes clear from these letters is that there was some sort of ideal blueprint for the formation of these groups in terms of social class: initial formation with a group of upper-class/aristocratic women of the old charitable 'social feminist' school (who lend legitimacy) and bourgeois professional women, but balanced in such a way that the latter are dominant. The second phase – coming later and clearly of secondary importance – is the integration of working-class women. What this means, of course, is that even if working-class women are successfully recruited and integrated into the organisation, it is irrevocably on the terms of the bourgeois liberal feminists, who have long since positioned themselves so as to control the agenda and direction of the group. Uruguayan liberal feminists, to varying degrees, did just that.

The model described above is much easier to sustain in the Southern Cone nations, however, which bear the greatest resemblance to European and North American societies. The social and class structure of most Latin American countries, then and now, does not lend itself easily to the direct application of such models. It comes as no surprise, perhaps, that Luisi's contacts in nations like Mexico and Cuba were radicals within the liberal feminist movement, facing challenges posed in a society where class has assumed a primacy that rendered traditional prescriptions untenable.

In Mexico, deep cleavages along lines of race and class and a historically powerful Catholic Church made the creation of a multi-class, secular liberal feminist organisation extremely difficult, and the political violence and upheavals of the Mexican revolution made for a distinctly different political climate. But despite all of this – and the lack of an explicitly feminist analysis within the ideology of the revolution – this era saw the emergence of unprecedented political space for women and for liberal feminist demands. The most significant of these spaces was in the Mexican state of Yucatan, where the local Socialist government organised two Women's Congresses (*Congresos Femeninos*) in 1916. These conferences attracted hundreds of women – mostly schoolteachers – and were the setting for passionate debates as to what women's role in revolutionary Mexican society should be, revealing the differences and divisions among competing 'feminisms' in a clear and dramatic way.[20]

One of the more prominent participants in these Congresses was Mexican feminist and so-called 'sex radical' Hermila Galindo, who created tremendous controversy with her claims of male and female sexual equality.[21] Both the Uruguayan Women's Council and Luisi were important contacts of Galindo, as she attempted to establish a branch of the ICW in her own country in the years following the 1916 conferences. In 1919, Galindo wrote several letters to Luisi asking the Uruguayan Council to 'amadrinar' (literally, to be the godmother of) a Mexican branch which she hoped to form. It appears that the Uruguayan Council was either unable or unwilling to be that 'godmother', for in December of that year Galindo wrote to Luisi informing her that the Argentine Council had agreed to 'amadrinar' the Mexican Council.[22] In these letters, Galindo laid out her schema in terms of social class for the formation of a Mexican Council. She already had the women of high society; now she intended to get middle-class university women involved (schoolteachers and women professionals), the woman who 'represents the most valuable intellectual element and who gives a positive strength to these organisations'. Finally, she would seek to recruit working-class women, illustrating her desire to loyally follow the 'class blueprint' for liberal feminism.[23]

Galindo, however, was not organising in Western Europe or even in the Southern Cone. She was, instead, trying to organise an ostensibly non-partisan, multi-class association in revolutionary Mexico. In the same December 1919 letter, Galindo told Luisi that she had decided to delay her plans to found such a council because of the unfavourable conditions existing in her country (especially the upcoming presidential elections). She complained about the primacy of class and politics over gender interests in her war-torn country, writing that 'the women of my country are still quite backwards and do not think that before their sympathies for this or that candidate they should look out for the good of their sex'.[24] What is perhaps most interesting about this statement is Galindo's conception of 'modern' and 'backward'. Indeed, it seems almost contradictory that an activist campaigning for women's civic and political equality would lament women having strong opinions about politics. This statement also assumes that there was one set of universal female interests, an assumption which is consistent with the view of middle-class values as universal, a perspective that would classify as 'backward' anyone rejecting those views.

If some liberal feminist leaders resisted the pull of revolutionary politics and sought to maintain a focus on issues of gender, other leaders took another ideological route. Such was the case with Ofelia Domínguez Navarro, a Cuban feminist leader and another of Luisi's 'pen pals' during these years.[25] While very different countries, Cuba and Uruguay share important historical characteristics. Both nations had relatively large middle classes, high degrees of literacy and education for both men and women, a relatively weak Catholic Church, and received a large number of European immigrants during the late nineteenth and early twentieth centuries. But in Cuba, unlike Uruguay (and like Mexico) there was tremendous social unrest and revolutionary convulsion in the early part of this century, as well as a heavily neo-colonial relationship with the United States (foreign capital in Uruguay at this time was predominantly British). Much of the radicalisation of the working class and certain sectors of the middle and professional classes took place during the Cuban people's struggle against the Machado dictatorship in the 1920s and 1930s. Machado responded to this opposition movement, led by university students, labour unions, and some sectors of the armed forces, with stepped-up repression. In this increasingly violent political situation, 'politically active Cuban women threw their support behind the opposition',[26] and many Cuban liberal feminists moved decisively to the left. Among those was Ofelia Domínguez Navarro, a lawyer of lower-middle-class origins who in 1928 led the faction that split off from the Cuban Feminist National Alliance to form the *Unión Laborista de Mujeres* (Women's Labor Union), which had ties to the newly formed Cuban Communist Party.

In her biography of Domínguez Navarro, K. Lynn Stoner states that it was during this second prison term that an ideological transformation from 'socialist feminist' to 'revolutionary' took place.[27] The letters Luisi received support this assertion. In April 1931, during her second prison term, Domínguez Navarro wrote to Luisi from her jail cell. In this letter (written in pencil because, she explained, of the lack of any other writing implement in jail), she emphasised the struggle for women's rights, not in a traditional liberal feminist sense, but by women like herself in the struggle against Machado. 'The women are providing a beautiful example of practical feminism', she wrote. 'Our women are responding and are showing themselves worthy of the rights we are demanding. Many have been imprisoned; without tears, without complaints, without pleading.'[28] About two months later, Domínguez Navarro sent Luisi another letter. Here, her political and ideological transformation is made quite clear. She writes that 'feminism with its political and civic aspirations now seems to me too narrow a mould within which to struggle ... the spirit of the era demands something more just and equitable. I confess that I am living in a moment in which the vision of Russia attracts me'.[29]

In this second letter, one sees nearly the opposite position to that expressed by Mexican feminist Hermila Galindo a decade earlier. While Galindo's view was that concerning oneself with issues outside 'women's interests' was 'backward', now we see a Cuban feminist coming to the conclusion that it is being solely concerned with women's issues which is confining and backward, and that the incorporation of class issues was what the historical moment required. In this case, it is hard to know whether to attribute these differences to location, to the historical era, or to differences in individual political ideologies, but it does suggest some of the crises that were erupting in the Pan-American women's movement, and the issues that were pulling it apart. It is also interesting to note that this is one of the few letters attempting to influence Luisi: Domínguez Navarro was not asking for advice or guidance, but instead was trying to convince Luisi that it was in Cuba that the 'correct' road had been found. Here was a country, unlike the others we have seen, where at least some of the feminist leadership felt no need for 'godmothers' and instead saw themselves as the new vanguard among Latin American women.

This rising sense of autonomy within some sectors of Latin American liberal feminism coincided with the growth of nationalist and anti-imperialist sentiments in Latin America in the 1920s and 1930s. Increased US economic and military presence in the region during and after World War I, coupled with the Mexican and Russian revolutions, combined to create heightened tensions between many Latin Americans and their neighbours to the North. Separate but not unrelated to this was the growing strength of populism in Latin American politics, and the growth of nationalism both on the right and the left. Within the women's movement specifically, the granting of suffrage to US women in 1920 widened the gulf between North American and South American feminists for two reasons. First, in that it fuelled the superiority complex of many North American feminists, who now clearly saw themselves and their culture as superior to that of the South; and secondly, in that, as the years went by, it became obvious to many Latin American feminists that women's participation in North American elections did nothing to bring greater peace to the region or to halt US intervention in Latin American affairs.

Within Luisi's archives, the first real evidence one finds of these growing tensions is in her report on the 1920 Geneva Congress of the International Women's Suffrage Association. This was the first international congress of the IWSA since the end of the First World War (for obvious reasons, the conflict had prevented any such gatherings since 1913). During these interim years women in many nations – including Great Britain and the United States – won full suffrage rights. Consequently, by the time of the 1920 congress women could vote in some capacity in many of the countries of Northern Europe, whereas in much of Latin Europe and the so-called under-developed or colonised world, women were still disenfranchised.

This gap created tensions within the congress itself. Luisi was infuriated with those delegates who, seeing that in their own countries and many others women had gained their political rights, proposed the dissolution of an organisation whose aims had been met. For Luisi, this shortsightedness and lack of an international vision 'demonstrated with this proposition the low opinion that the international feminist world has of the Latin countries'.[30] In a written statement made after the congress, Luisi did little to disguise her contempt for the proceedings, reporting that 'the lively and passionate discussions threatened to divide the Alliance in two sections: the emancipated countries declaring that they had nothing now to do and abandoning the more BACKWARDS (Latin) countries to their fate'.[31] At the end, the conflict was resolved in favour of maintaining the integrity of the IWSA and voting that the International should branch out and take on other issues beyond suffrage. But this division and tension would continue to echo throughout the international feminist movement for years to come and, it appears, made a lasting imprint on Luisi's perspective on feminists of 'the North'.

One of the founders and the first president of the IWSA was North American Carrie Chapman Catt. She and many of her colleagues in the leadership of international liberal feminism suffered from deeply ingrained ethnocentrism that hampered efforts at unity and, at times, provoked the outrage of Latin American feminists, including Luisi. In late 1922, Chapman Catt embarked on a tour of South America in her capacity as head of a new Pan-American Women's Association, founded at the first Pan-American conference of Women held in Baltimore earlier that year. Her tour lasted through early 1923, and took her to Brazil, Argentina, Uruguay, Chile, and Peru. On this and other trips, Chapman Catt kept detailed diaries and wrote letters containing her experiences and impressions of the women's movement in South America and of Latin American society and culture generally. These writings reveal a broader agenda for the Pan-American Women's Association, that of creating an important bridge between North and South as a means to promote greater inter-American relations and cooperation and to strengthen the position and image of the United States in Latin America. In a letter to a friend, for example, Chapman Catt wrote: 'I am convinced nothing on God's earth will prevent a war between the Spanish Republics and the US except careful foreign policy by our government and Pan-Americanism of the right sort'.[32]

What we need to ask, of course, is how Chapman Catt would have defined 'Pan-Americanism of the right sort', inasmuch as it is indicative of the way she defined her position vis à vis her Latin American counterparts. Some insight into this is provided when, in another of these letters, Chapman Catt repeatedly refers to herself and others in her shoes as 'missionaries'. It is interesting to think back to the language used by Mexican feminist Hermila Galindo and ponder the significance of the difference between 'missionary' and '*madrina*' (godmother). While both contain religious overtones and imply unequal power relations, the concept of *madrina* implies a quasi-familial relationship based on mutual obligation. 'Missionary', on the other hand, has embedded firmly within it the notion of Other; that the actor you are trying to convert/assist/ teach is someone very different from you, and from your perspective probably socially, culturally, and/or ethnically inferior. In this same letter, for example, while describing Uruguayan and Argentine society, Chapman Catt writes:

> The climate and the inherited racial inadequacies make the people languorous and willing to put things off until tomorrow. They eat too much ... The waste of food is shocking. In after dinner coffee cups people drink from 3 to 5 lumps of sugar ... Sweets are plentiful and desserts are very sweet. The women are therefore fat and probably less easy to move.[33]

It is also worth noting the way that power relations are gendered in each of these cases. Whereas *'madrina'* signifies female and maternal relations between Latin American feminists, by identifying herself as a 'missionary' Chapman Catt is assuming a more traditionally masculinised role: that of the dominant civiliser in partnership with a subordinate in need of guidance. One can conclude from Chapman Catt's discourse that she in no way considered a Pan-American women's movement as a union among equals, but as a means to 'civilise' this part of the world and improve the image of the United States at the same time. These attitudes on the part of many North American feminists and the increasingly nationalistic and anti-US rhetoric emanating from many Latin American sectors during these years worked to create a wide gulf between many Latin American feminists and their counterparts in the United States.

In response to the continued domination of Western European and North American feminists, some Latin American liberal feminists joined instead with Iberian counterparts in an attempt to form their own international organisation. Paulina Luisi became a leader of the *Liga Internacional de Mujeres Ibéricas e Hispanoamericanas* (International League of Iberian and Hispanic-American Women), an organisation in which she held the post of second vice president for many years. There is some question as to when this organisation was founded, but its official publication, *Feminismo Internacional* began publishing in 1922.[34] The circumstances of its formation and the history of its early years notwithstanding, in later years the Iberian and Hispanic-American Women's League existed in part as an alternative to the Inter-American Commission of Women (IACW), an organisation founded in 1930 and which remained firmly in the control of North American women during the years in question.

Beyond its opposition to the United States, and by extension to the IACW, the politics of the Iberian and Hispanic League are somewhat difficult to classify. The rhetoric is highly nationalistic, and expresses a strong Pan-Hispanic ideology, but vacillates between a right-wing nationalism praising social elites and defending the status quo against 'Yankee imperialism', and a more left-leaning nationalism which decries foreign intervention and calls for more substantive changes in social and property relations. The president of the League during this time was Carmen de Burgos, a Spanish writer from Madrid, and the vice president was Elena Arizmendi, a Mexican citizen living in New York City. Arizmendi's letters also provide insight into the ideological position of the League and its leadership. That one of the main goals of the organisation was to create an organisational structure separate from North Americans, buttressed by a diffuse pan-Hispanicism, is clearly stated in a letter from Arizmendi to Luisi in September 1930:

> I, in the United States, see and know what you don't know and don't see ... The North American women have won all their rights and are now allies of the domineering politics of their men. They have not purified politics ... One thing are the *yanquis* and we are another.[35]

It is a problem common to almost all of these documents that it is nearly impossible to know Luisi's reaction to most of these letters. This was one of the few cases where a copy of Luisi's response (or perhaps a letter she never mailed) is contained in the archive. In this same letter cited above, Arizmendi complains about and expresses her mistrust of the Inter-American Commission of Women and its North American president, Doris Stevens. Luisi's reply to the above letter, dated two months later, states, 'with respect to Miss Stevens, I have known for a long time what to expect from her and her group. It is not news to me'. She goes on to state that, even though she is not living in the United States like Arizmendi, she 'sees and knows' exactly what North American feminists are all about.[36] Perhaps as a result of this changing attitude toward North American feminists, the IACW was one Pan-American women's organisation in which Paulina Luisi appears to have played no part. In fact, Uruguay was notably absent at the IACW foundation and 1930 conference, one of only a handful of Latin American nations not represented at the conference.[37]

For Uruguayans, however, the United States was not the only – nor in most cases the most immediate – threat. Since before Independence, Uruguayan identity had been intimately linked with, and in many ways defined in opposition to, that of Argentina. As stated above, Luisi viewed the Argentine Council as an example of what not to do in the establishment of a feminist movement. It would be to miss an important element of Argentine/Uruguayan relations – and how they translated into the arena of liberal feminism – to overlook the influence of nationalism and concerns about Argentine domination that influenced and permeated Luisi's thinking about her Argentine counterparts (or at least some of them). For whereas for Mexicans and Cubans the major threat to national sovereignty was, by the period after the First World War, indisputably the United States, for Uruguayans that sense of insecurity and threat to the nation was split between fear of the US, the British, and an older and much closer threat based in Buenos Aires.

This fear of Argentine encroachment went so far as to cause problems with the international leadership. Another of the leaders of international feminism to visit Uruguay during this time was Louise Van Eeghen, secretary of the International Council of Women, who spent a few days in Montevideo in December of 1925. She wrote a report on the visit, which appeared in the *Bulletin* of the ICW in May 1926. Van Eeghen was much more laudatory in her report than Chapman Catt, praising the 'intense' feminist activity in Montevideo and the healthy state of the movement,[38] but it is important to keep in mind that this was public discourse and not the private correspondence of Chapman Catt. The letter Van Eeghen sent to Luisi following her visit, however, was very different in tone than the commendation and praise which characterised her public report on her trip:

> I am sorry that I did not have the chance to speak with you, but it seemed to me that you did not want to, fearing that I would meddle in 'internal affairs' [of the Council]. – Let me assure you, my dear Miss Luisi, that the Office of the ICW never intervenes in internal affairs ... I have also learned that you thought that I came with a special mission of the Argentine Council to reorganize the Uruguayan Council. Let me assure you again that a member of the ICW Office does not receive missions from a National Council ... Each Council has its own difficulties and must respond to them themselves, if they choose with the help of the International.[39]

This letter can be interpreted in many ways, and it is impossible to know whether to attribute Luisi's attitude to paranoia or to a legitimate threat to the autonomy of the Uruguayan branch. But it does seem to indicate that, rightly or wrongly, Luisi had developed an equal resentment against both the North American and Western European international liberal feminist leadership, to such an extent that she refused to meet with the ICW's secretary upon her visit to Montevideo.

Further evidence of this concern on Luisi's part can be seen in a letter she wrote to Elena Arizmendi in New York. Here, Luisi writes about what must have been the Third International Women's Congress held in Buenos Aires in 1928, where she was one of the keynote speakers. Arizmendi's concerns, as seen above, were overwhelmingly about US imperialism and domination. Luisi too felt her biggest threat close to home:

> I begin by telling you a few words about the Congress in Buenos Aires: it was good but extraordinarily nationalistic, I would almost say, Argentine. This is no surprise; Argentina is a great nation, it feels strong and independent, not just politically but economically; they will be the *yanquis* of the South.[40]

It is worth noting that the same mistrust of Brazilian feminists on the part of Uruguayans was largely absent, reflecting what continues to be the very different images many Uruguayans have of their northern neighbours. Thus, Luisi was in many ways a product of her national context just as Chapman Catt represented hers. Uruguayans, seeing themselves as caught between the '*yanquis* of the North' and the '*yanquis* of the South', sought to steer an independent course autonomous of either behemoth. One of the concrete results of this vision was an aggressive attempt to cement links between Uruguayan liberal feminists and their counterparts in neighbouring (but less threatening) countries like Chile, Cuba, and Mexico. It seems clear, in sum, that all of these women were seeking to forge a 'Pan-Americanism of the right sort', but the way that was defined was dependent on one's particular class, political, and national vantage point.

Through this material one sees a history of Pan-American liberal feminism directed by Latin American feminists and driven by their own particular national and continental agendas. This research also shows that solid links and networks between Latin American liberal feminist leaders predated Pan-American projects, and provided a crucial base which North American feminist leaders such as Mary Sheepshanks and Carrie Chapman Catt were able to build upon. It also demonstrates the impact of US intervention in Latin America and the growth of nationalism in these countries and within Pan-American women's networks. In 1932, Uruguayan women were among the first in Latin America to be granted the right to vote; more research is needed to determine what impact this may have had on Uruguay's position within Pan-American networks. Finally, these documents help to clarify the complex interactions of feminism and internationalism within the Pan-American arena, one in which multiple and shifting 'feminisms' were refracted through varied and shifting nationalisms and pan-nationalisms, which in turn gave rise to an international movement which was the outcome of, in Leila Rupp's words, a complex interaction between 'conflict and community'.[41]

Notes

1. All translations are the author's. A more detailed discussion of feminist politics within Uruguay at this time can be found in Christine Ehrick, 'Obrera, Dama, Feminista: Women's Associations and the Welfare State in Uruguay, 1900–1932' (PhD dissertation, University of California, Los Angeles, 1997).

2. 'El feminismo en marcha', *Caras y Caretas* (Buenos Aires), December 1918, p. 12.

3. Paulina Luisi, 'Alianza Uruguaya para el sufragio femenino', *Acción Femenina* (Montevideo), August 1919, p. 120.

4. Uruguay's official name is the *República Oriental del Uruguay*, or the Eastern Republic of Uruguay, a designation which refers to the territory's location on the 'Eastern Bank' of the Uruguay River, which separates Uruguay from Argentina.

5. Asunción Lavrin, *Women, Feminism, and Social Change in Argentina, Chile, and Uruguay, 1890–1940* (University of Nebraska Press, Lincoln, 1995), p. 259.

6. Petrona Eyle to Paulina Luisi, 1 May 1907, Archivo Paulina Luisi, Biblioteca Nacional, Montevideo (hereafter PL-BN), Carpeta E.

7. Universitarias Argentinas to Petrona Eyle, March 1907, PL-BN, Carpeta U.

8. Cecilia Grierson to Paulina Luisi, 24 October 1913, PL-BN, Carpeta G.

9. Petrona Eyle to Paulina Luisi, 20 May 1917, PL-BN, Carpeta E.

10. See chapter 4 of Ehrick, 'Obrera, Dama, Feminista'.

11. Amanda Labarca to Paulina Luisi, 19 November 1922, PL-BN, Carpeta L.

12. Mary Sheepshanks to Paulina Luisi, 11 April 1922, PL-BN, Carpeta S.

13. Amanda Labarca to Paulina Luisi, 18 April 1924, PL-BN, Carpeta L.

14. Celinda Arregui de Rodicio to Paulina Luisi, no date, PL-BN, Carpeta A.

15. Sybil Oldfield, *Spinsters of the Parish: The Life and Times of F. M. Mayor and Mary Sheepshanks* (Virago Press, London, 1984), p. 220.

16. I assume that Sheepshanks is referring to the *Partido Femenino Progresista Nacional* (National Progressive Women's Party) which, according to Asunción Lavrin, was founded in February 1920 by Sofia de Ferrari Rojas. It is also possible, however, that Sheepshanks is referring to the *Partido Demócrata Femenino* (Democratic Women's Party), but Lavrin states this group was founded later, in the mid 1920s.

17. Mary Sheepshanks to Paulina Luisi, 15 April 1922, PL-BN, Carpeta S.

18. This list includes many of the most important leaders of Argentine liberal feminism at the time.

19. Mary Sheepshanks to Paulina Luisi, 21 March 1922, PL-BN, Carpeta S.

20. For more information on the 1916 Mérida conferences, see Shirlene Soto, *Emergence of the Modern Mexican Woman: Her Participation in Revolution and Struggle for Equality, 1910–1940* (Arden Press, Denver, CO, 1990).

21. Francesca Miller, *Latin American Women and the Search for Social Justice* (University Press of New England, Hanover, NH, 1991) p. 76

22. Hermila Galindo to Paulina Luisi, 23 December 1919, PL-BN, Carpeta G.

23. Hermila Galindo to Paulina Luisi, 15 January 1919, PL-BN, Carpeta G.

24. Hermila Galindo to Paulina Luisi, 23 December 1919, PL-BN, Carpeta G.

25. Domínguez Navarro knew of Luisi from at least 1926, when she delivered a paper written by Luisi on 'investigación of paternity' to the 1926 Interamerican Women's Congress held in Panama in 1926. In Ofelia Domínguez, *50 años de una vida* (Instituto del Libro, Havana, Cuba, 1971) p. 89.

26. Francesca Miller, *Latin American Women and the Search for Social Justice* (University Press of New England, Hanover, NH, 1991) p. 99.

27. Ofelia Domínguez Navarro to Paulina Luisi, 6 April 1931, PL-BN, Carpeta D.

28. K. Lynn Stoner, 'Ofelia Domínguez Navarro', in *The Human Tradition in Latin America: The Twentieth Century*, ed. William H. Beezley and Judith Ewell (Scholarly Resources, Wilmington, Delaware, 1987), pp. 133–4.

29. Ofelia Domínguez Navarro to Paulina Luisi, 10 June 1931, PL-BN, Carpeta U.

30. 'Congreso de la Alianza Internacional', *La Patria* (Asunción), 1 October 1921.

31. *La Patria*, 2 October 1921.

32. Letters of Carrie Chapman Catt (New York Public Library), Reel 2, Container 2, page 11.

33. Letters of Carrie Chapman Catt, Reel 2, Container 2, pages 12–13.

34. This organisation, unfortunately, has been little studied, and it is difficult to determine its size, influence, or even the details about its formation. Asunción Lavrin states that the first meeting of the Liga took place in Buenos Aires in 1926, but the group was clearly formed earlier than that, as its official publication attests.

35. Elena Arizmendi to Paulina Luisi, 23 September 1930, PL-BN, Carpeta A.

36. Paulina Luisi to Elena Arizmendi, 26 November 1930, PL-BN, Carpeta A.

37. It should be noted that there was no Argentine representative either.

38. Louise Van Eeghen, 'Montevideo et le Conseil National des Femmes', *Bulletin du Conseil International des Femmes*, May 1926, Archivo Paulina Luisi, Archivo General de la Nación, Montevideo, 259/3/62.

39. Louise Van Eeghen to Paulina Luisi, 10 December 1925, PL-BN, Carpeta E.

40. Paulina Luisi to Elena Arizmendi, 26 February 1929, PL-BN, Carpeta A.

41. Leila J. Rupp, *Worlds of Women: The Making of an International Women's Movement* (Princeton University Press, Princeton, NJ, 1997), p. 6.

Inventing Commonwealth and Pan-Pacific Feminisms: Australian Women's Internationalist Activism in the 1920s–30s

ANGELA WOOLLACOTT

If historicising feminist internationalism is an important way for end-of-the-twentieth-century feminists to grapple with its status, problems and possibilities, seeing both historical patterns and variations from them might be an obvious step. Leila Rupp, in her valuable work on the large European- and American-dominated women's international organisations of the early twentieth century, has posited one pattern for that period. Having 'lurched slowly into motion in the years before 1914, gathered steam at the end of World War I, and nearly screeched to a halt in 1939', according to Rupp, these organisations regrouped after World War II and have continued through the rest of the century.[1] This pattern of historical emergence suggests that, while the years just prior to World War I were a foundational moment, the end of the war and then the interwar period were a time of crucial growth and consolidation for feminist internationalism. In this essay, I propose to interrogate one national cohort of internationalist feminists and their interwar activism, Australian feminists' engagement with two smaller and more specifically defined organisations, the British Commonwealth League and the Pan-Pacific Women's Association, in order to explore dynamics within feminist internationalism in this period.

Basing an essay on one national grouping of feminists may seem a paradoxical, perhaps even wrong-headed, approach to internationalism. However, my purpose is to examine the multivalent and even contradictory currents circulating within Australian feminists' internationalism in this period, and thus to raise questions about the global political views informing their activism. Framing such a study around one national grouping allows me to capture these coexisting, diverse currents. On the one hand, the British Commonwealth League (hereafter the BCL), headquartered in London but in which Australian feminists played leading roles, presents distinct evidence of continuity with the nineteenth- and early twentieth-century British imperial feminism which Antoinette Burton has so astutely analysed.[2] On the other hand, the BCL was very much a product of post-World War I internationalist zeal linked to the League of Nations, and also of changing dynamics within the British Empire and the shifting balance of power both between Britain and the white-settler dominions, and between Britain and India. At the same time, Australian women's involvement with the Pan-Pacific Women's Association (hereafter PPWA) signalled a new field of vision, one in which Australian feminists saw themselves as aligned within a Pacific-area international context, a context that at least some associated with the future, perhaps thus implicitly seeing British Commonwealth connections as tied to the past. My aims in this essay include outlining the feminist internationalist activism of Australian women in the context of both of these organisations in the interwar period, assessing the global politics involved, considering their stances as white British dominion women in international contexts and in terms of Australia's colonisation of Aboriginal people, and historicising their activism in the broader picture of feminist internationalism.

The BCL and the PPWA share some of the features of the large international organisations which Rupp has studied, the International Council of Women, the International Alliance of Women for Suffrage and Equal Citizenship (formerly International Woman Suffrage Alliance) and the Women's International League for Peace and Freedom. Like them, the BCL and the PPWA relied upon the active membership of privileged women who could afford to pay their own travel expenses to regular meetings in (for Australian women, often very) distant cities, and who had the leisure to undertake the necessary weeks or months away from home. Moreover, the BCL and the PPWA were both, albeit to different extents, dominated by white English-speaking women. But the BCL and the PPWA each presented a significant challenge to the European and American hegemony of the three larger organisations. The BCL, while its conferences were always held in London and in that way it was congruent with the others, was constitutionally designed to spread organisational leadership between the dominions of the British Commonwealth and Britain itself, and also centrally included India.[3] The PPWA represented the global decentralisation of feminist international organisation even further. Consciously established as a regional focus for feminists distant from Europe, other than the mainland USA and Canada its national constituent committees were all outside the boundaries of Europe and North America, and its conferences moved around the Pacific. Rupp argues that, although in the interwar period they sought with measurable success to become 'truly international', and that 'challenges to feminist orientalism mounted', the large international women's organisations remained, at least until World War II, 'heavily Euro-American in composition and leadership'.[4] Looking at the BCL and the PPWA in this same period allows us to consider the ways in which global power relations operated within feminist international organisations that promised to challenge the entrenched Euro-American hegemony of the larger groups.

Rupp's pattern of historical emergence in fact fits the BCL well. During the British suffrage movement's intensive and militant phase, some Australian women, consciously proud of their own already-enfranchised (since 1902) status, participated in feminist activism in London. In 1911, when prominent Australian feminist Vida Goldstein was invited to help the cause through a lecture tour of England, one of the results of her visit was the formation in London of the Australian and New Zealand Women Voters' Committee, which aimed to draw attention to the fact that Australian and New Zealand women, voting citizens at home, suffered disenfranchisement while residing in the imperial metropole.[5] In 1913, the committee proclaimed that one of its objects was to 'help forward the Woman's Movement in every part of the British Empire'.[6] By 1914, as a result of the visits of Harriet Newcomb, from Australia but residing in London and honorary secretary of the committee, to New Zealand, Australia and South Africa, the British Dominions Woman Suffrage Union (BDWSU) was formed in order that those three countries and Canada should join forces as the self-governing dominions of the empire, and that enfranchised Australian and New Zealand women might help Canadian and South African women also attain the vote.[7] During the war, the BDWSU subordinated its suffrage work in favour of organising clothing for poor London children and war refugees, participating in feminist opposition to special wartime police powers over prostitutes, generally promoting communication among activist women in the dominions and Britain, and in particular organising three biennial conferences.[8] Having changed its name to the British Dominion Women Citizens' Union in late 1918 in honour of both British and Canadian women's enfranchisement, for a few years following the war the union organised regular meetings in London to discuss women's and empire issues.

Perhaps partly because of the retirement from BDWCU leadership of Harriet Newcomb and her (also from Australia) partner Margaret Hodge, between 1922 and 1924 the BDWCU was transformed into the British Overseas Committee of the International Woman Suffrage Alliance. In the summer of 1924, when the British Empire Exhibition staged at Wembley attracted women and men from the dominions and colonies to London to participate in this spectacle and largest-ever imperial exhibition, London-based feminists took advantage of the presence of feminists from around the empire to convene various meetings.[9] The British Overseas Committee erected a stand at the exhibition, especially to attract the attention of dominion women to international feminist issues.[10] It was in this context of renewed imperial feminist activism that in early February 1925 the British Overseas Committee convened a half-day conference on the 'whole question of the organisation of women living in the British Empire, whether enfranchised or still without their citizen rights'.[11] Many years later, M. Chave Collisson, originally from Sydney, recalled how she and Bessie Rischbieth, of Perth, Western Australia, plotted together to arrange the meeting because 'We were impressed by the need to rouse fresh interest in the work and needs of women's action overseas, then somewhat overlooked while British women sought to consolidate their position as full citizens'.[12] To an audience including women from South Africa, Australia, New Zealand and Canada, Collisson urged that there ought to be a central organisation in London to represent the interests of 'Empire women', who would benefit from the dissemination of knowledge about conditions throughout the empire, as well as from an organisation that would work for equal franchise and citizenship, and would provide hospitality to 'empire feminists' while in London. Bessie Rischbieth addressed the need for women to know about legislative changes occurring throughout the empire, and to participate in the changing relationship between Britain and the dominions.[13] If rousing British feminists out of their preoccupation with insular issues and their own partial enfranchisement was one motivation, a platform from which to boost the visibility and importance of dominion feminists, and thus overcome their subordinate status as colonials within the imperial metropolis, was very likely another. And both coexisted with strongly held feminist convictions about women's issues across the empire.

From the February conference, in May the British Commonwealth Women's Equality League was inaugurated, with the motto 'To secure equality of liberties, status and opportunities between men and women in the British Commonwealth of Nations'.[14] By July when it convened its first longer conference, the British Commonwealth League had shortened its name and Chave Collisson was its official organising secretary. The two-day conference was held in a venue very familiar to feminists, Caxton Hall in Westminster, with the announced theme of 'The Citizen Rights of Women Within the British Empire'. Significantly for an organisation which in its earlier incarnations had united white women of the self-governing dominions of the empire, the programmed speakers at this first annual BCL conference included two representatives from Bermuda, one from the British West Indies, and one from Kenya, Charlotte Despard who spoke on behalf of Irish women, and six Indians. The sessions were arranged thematically so that, for example, the afternoon on 'Economic Equality' included a speaker each from Britain, Australia, India and the British West Indies.[15] Speaking in the session on 'Political Equality', Atiya Begum Fyzee Rahamin of India began by proclaiming, 'Here we are the sisters of the vast Empire collected in this hall to-day, irrespective of caste and colour, united by a growing force, fired for the one enthusiasm to demand what is our birthright, Freedom and Equality'. At another point in her speech, Rahamin asserted that she thought 'the Conference a real God-send', and 'begged the co-operation of the Western women in convincing the politician that he must facilitate the establishment, socially and nationally, of the position of women'.[16] In the same session, Mrs MacGregor Ross of Kenya 'begged women when getting political liberty, not to forget the other races. Liberty must go beyond the boundaries of sex and race.'[17] This first full conference, then, seemed to signal that the BCL stood for racial and transnational equality among women of the British Commonwealth and Empire.

While white dominion and British women were still very much in control of the BCL, the process in which the League came to be geographically, colonially and racially more inclusive compels scrutiny, particularly for any exploration of early twentieth-century feminist internationalism. In fact, even prior to World War I, the BDWSU had shown interest in India. Antoinette Burton has demonstrated that debate about Indian women featured in the leading British feminist periodical *Common Cause* in the years immediately prior to the war,[18] which suggests that the BDWSU was very much a part of its British suffrage movement context. At its first conference, in July 1914, Carrie Chapman Catt, president of the International Woman Suffrage Alliance, had spoken on the 'Women's Movement among the Races of the East', and a reception at the International Women's Franchise Club was the venue for an address by Sarojini Naidu on 'Ideals of Indian Womanhood'. Yet, in the same year, a request from the Mussoorie Suffrage Society of North India for inclusion in the BDWSU was apparently rejected, suggesting the possibility that, while the union wanted to hear from and about Indian women, they were not then ready to include them fully as equal participants.[19] By 1918, at least partially through the work of Margaret Hodge, the BDWSU had 'draw[n] the women of India into fellowship, and awaken[ed] an interest in Indian affairs', with events such as a series of Indian teas and an address by Dr Rao on 'India's Position in the British Commonwealth'.[20] The BDWSU's biennial conference that year included a speech on women's suffrage in India, and a 'gala evening devoted to India'. *Jus Suffragii*, the organ of the International Woman Suffrage Alliance, editorialised that the 'bringing together of India and the self-governing British Dominions was perhaps one of the most notable achievements of the Conference'.[21] By 1919, the BDWCU boasted 'an Indian section'.[22] In the wake of the April 1919 Amritsar massacre, when hundreds of unarmed Indian people were shot by British troops, in July 1920 the Women's Freedom League convened a protest meeting of both Indian and British people in Central Hall, London, at which Margaret Hodge of the BDWCU presided.[23]

In September 1919 the BDWCU extended its attention in another direction, hosting an address by Solomon T. Plaatje of the South African Native Deputation, on recent land laws in South Africa and their effects on the native population.[24] According to Vida Goldstein, back in London again after attending the 1919 international women's peace conference in Geneva, and very interested in the work of the BDWCU of which she was a member, Plaatje's talk was symptomatic of a changing postwar global mood. Related to the Paris peace talks, in Goldstein's view, 'The condition of subject races in every country is coming to the front as never before; the slogan of "Self-Determination" has given them such hope & inspiration that they have come out of the seclusion of of [sic] their own countries to London, to Paris, & compelled the attention of the working classes to their own particular grievances against Society & Governments, & to the injust-ices they share in common with white workers. This awakening of coloured & other subject races has been one of the wonders of the war period.'[25]

Goldstein's contention that the war and the global political discussions attendant upon the Paris peace talks had altered race relations world-wide is valuable contemporary commentary, at least as context for an exploration of the shifting imperial and racial politics within which the BCL established its Commonwealth feminist programme in 1925. Particularly given the fact that, at the February 1925 half-day conference where the BCL was first projected, no mention was made of including women of colour – or indeed of any issues other than those pertaining to white dominion women – the racial and colonial politics embodied by the BCL and represented at its annual conferences for the rest of the interwar period, and what those politics can tell us about feminist internationalism in this era, become complex and telling issues which I shall explore below.

Three years after the formation of the BCL in London, sixteen Australian feminists, representing five Australian states and several national women's organisations, and including some women actively engaged with the BCL, attended the first Pan-Pacific Women's Conference in Honolulu in 1928. This first Pacific-rim women's conference included women from New Zealand, the US, Japan, Canada, China, Hawaii, the Dutch East Indies, the Philippines, Samoa, and Fiji. In an expanded definition of the Pacific region, India was represented too: 'India, though not "Pacific," is Asiatic, and no conference which would include other women of Asiatic countries would omit Indian women'.[26] The conference was held under the aegis of the Pan-Pacific Union, a body which sought to promote Pacific-region com-munication through topical conferences often in fields of science or social science. In this connection to a pre-existing organisation, the Pan-Pacific Women's Conference was not unlike the BCL's efforts to hold women's conferences in tandem with Imperial Conferences of heads of state in London, such as the 1926 conference which debated the new status of the dominions. Bessie Rischbieth, 'Chairman' of the Australian delegation to the Honolulu conference and who delivered a plenary address on 'The Influence of Women in Government', later commented that Australian women's participation in the Pan-Pacific conferences was important because 'Australia's opportunity, and we hope her destiny, in the Pacific, is to help liberate the awakening East to a free partnership of nations by freedom of growth', a formulation which posited Australian women as at once leaders and partners in relation to Asian and Pacific Islands women.[27] Perhaps it was both the near simultaneity of the foundation of the two organisations, and her perception that Australian women played leading roles in them, that led Bessie Rischbieth in her 1964 memoir of Australian women's political activism to join the history of the BCL and the history of the Pan-Pacific Women's Association together in a chapter titled 'Brief Histories of Two Kindred Societies'.[28]

Figure 1: Delegates to the first Pan-Pacific Women's Conference in Honolulu, 1928. Above, at the Japanese Consulate; below, Jane Addams addressing a luncheon at the Pan-Pacific Club. *The Mid-Pacific Magazine*, vol. 36, no. 4 (October 1928), p. 302.

Subsequent Pan-Pacific women's conferences were held regularly every few years, until, as Rupp's pattern indicates, World War II caused a major hiatus, from which women recovered their organising slowly and with difficulty. At the second conference in 1930, held again in Hawaii, the organisation called the Pan-Pacific Women's Association was formed; in 1955 at the Manila conference, the name was extended to the Pan-Pacific and South-East Asia Women's Association. The 1930 constitution spelled out the association's aims as being 'To strengthen the bonds of peace among Pacific peoples by promoting a better understanding and friendship among the women of all Pacific countries', and 'to initiate and promote co-operation among the women of the Pacific region for the study and betterment of existing conditions'.[29] While there were national committees within constituent countries, in fact the association's *raison d'être* was largely to stage its international women's conferences every few years, with papers focusing on women's political and legal status, women in industry, social welfare and education, and international relations. Delegates to the 1937 conference in Vancouver believed that that conference marked a significant move away from papers consisting of 'purely factual and statistical information' and towards 'broad international questions'. Ironically enough, it was decided in Vancouver that the 1940 conference, which was never held because of World War II, was to be on 'The Study of Practical Ways and Means of Promoting International Understanding'.[30]

An obvious similarity between the BCL and the Pan-Pacific Women's Association (PPWA) is the fact that they both existed largely in order to convene their regular conferences, despite the BCL's annual conferences being held more often. Yet London's unwavering status as metropolitan venue for the BCL conferences suggests an imperial central grasp on power, which is at odds with the careful geographic mobility of the Pan-Pacific conferences, the first three of which were held in Honolulu, but which then moved in turn to Vancouver, back to Hawaii, then New Zealand, Manila, Japan, Australia and so on. One of the PPWA conference principles was to house the delegates together in one place purposely to build international friendships and understanding,[31] a specific goal that was never enunciated by the BCL and was perhaps less likely to be achieved at conferences in London. A slight factor of difference between the BCL and the PPWA is that while both Australian and New Zealand women were active in both organisations, Australian women held a more dominant role in the BCL (indeed, Australian women were founders and leaders of the BCL, substantially outnumbered any national representation within it other than British, and sometimes even outnumbered that[32]), while New Zealand women seem to have been somewhat more to the fore in the PPWA.[33] Yet Australian women formed their own Pan-Pacific Conference Women's Committee soon after the first conference in 1928, and by 1934 an Australian, Dr Georgina Sweet, had become the PPWA's international president.[34]

Rischbieth, in an article written for the *International Women's News* in 1941 while she was living in London, described the PPWA conferences in stridently romantic terms captured in her subtitle 'Where East and West Meet'. As a result of the conferences held since 1928, Rischbieth claimed (regardless of the forced cancellation of the 1940 meeting) that: 'As an outcome of contact, women now realise that Eastern and Western cultures, deeply different as they are, can be made to blend and harmonise. They know that through the impact of Western Science, coupled with the deeper knowledge of the spiritual laws of the East, a fuller humanity will arise and develop in the process. They realise that we are living in but half the world's culture, and therefore the next step towards world federation is to bring about an adjustment in the relationship between East and West.' Rischbieth's belief in the 'deeper knowledge of the spiritual laws of the East' was based on her commitment to theosophy. Kumari Jayawardena has recently argued that theosophist feminists interested in South Asia came 'nearer the concept of sisterhood' than did Christians during the colonial period, because they 'stood firm against the colonial policies of their own governments'.[35] Yet even in this 1941 peroration to feminist internationalism and its possibilities, Rischbieth's conception of that internationalism was one in which Western women continued as leaders and other women as the objects of their attention. In her concluding exhortation to her readers, she urged: 'I am persuaded that the Pacific is destined to become the new orientation ground for the splendid work already accomplished by the indefatigable effort of women in the international field in Europe. The call goes forth then to the organised women of the Western world to turn their attention to the Pacific as a new stepping-off ground for a wider and richer internationalism.'[36]

Eleanor Hinder, an Australian who served as the programme secretary for the first Pan-Pacific conference in 1928, was a member of the delegation to that conference from China, one of three non-Chinese delegates of a five-member delegation. The constitution of this delegation reflects Western nations' intervention in China, particularly in the treaty ports, and the dominant roles of white women resident there in at least some supposedly Chinese women's organisations, such as Hinder's work for the YWCA of China.[37] (See Figure 2. In contrast to this Western colonisation of the Chinese delegation, it is worth noting that the fifty-one-member delegation from Hawaii – quite separate from the US mainland delegation – included women of Filipina, Japanese, Chinese, Korean and Hawaiian ethnicity.[38]) Yet Hinder's hopes for the first Pan-Pacific women's conference, expressed in an article written on its eve, were founded on more critical distance from the European- and American-dominated international feminist organisations than Rischbieth expressed. While underscoring the historical significance of the large international women's organisations such as the International Council of Women, the IAW, the Women's International League for Peace and Freedom, and the World's YWCA, Hinder pointed out that three of

Figure 2: Delegates to the first Pan-Pacific Women's Conference, Honolulu, 1928: Dr Me Iung Ting, Medical Director, Peiyang Women's Hospital, Tientsin, China; Dr Ellen Leong of Hawaii; and Bae-tsung Kyong of Shanghai. Dr Me Iung Ting reportedly 'electrified the Conference by her dramatic declaration that the time had now come when the women of China demanded the right to speak for themselves, without interpretation of the foreign middlewoman' and Bae-tsung Kyong 'spoke for the Chinese women of the world who endorse the stand taken by Dr Ting'. *The Mid-Pacific Magazine*, vol. 36, no. 6 (December 1928), p. 402.

these were based in London and one in Geneva, which made them remote to women of the Pacific. A Pacific regional international women's organisation, she suggested, could well act as a clearing house for material from these European-based organisations. But, at least as importantly, it would work to inform those organisations about the realities of Pacific women's lives, their concern with basic issues such as education, and the fact that Western-style organisation might not be the only path Pacific-area women envisaged.[39]

Despite Rischbieth's easy assumption of Western women's leadership role, it is important to acknowledge that Australian and New Zealand feminists' serious interest in the Pacific region was unusual in the 1920s and 1930s, and ought at least in part to be read as politically progressive. Although there was overlap between the women who participated in the BCL and PPWA conferences, such as Rischbieth's active role in both, some women chose one international orientation over the other. At a time when Australia's official stance on immigration, the White Australia policy, was explicitly framed to exclude Asians, women who sought to learn more about Asian women's lives and to cooperate with them on women's issues were consciously at odds with their cultural context. Moreover, in developing Australia's connections to Asian and Pacific countries, feminists were engaged in a process of redefining Australia as an Asian and Pacific nation. In the late twentieth century it has become a widely accepted yet profoundly transformative view that Australia is indeed an Asian-Pacific nation; as it is sometimes drily put, Australians have discovered that what they habitually called the Far East is in fact the near north. In the 1920s–30s, such a perspective was transgressive of most Australians' world views, and certainly of Australia's diplomatic and political alignments. In an obituary note on Rischbieth in the *International Women's News* of May 1967, her longtime IAW and BCL British colleague Margery Corbett Ashby wrote: 'To Europeans Australia was a far off member of the British Commonwealth, Bessie Rischbieth showed us Australia as a leading member of the Pan Pacific and later of South East Asia with its deep concern for the women in that vast area. She was ahead of many politicians.'[40] Interwar Australian feminists, including those who were active internationally, represented a spectrum of political views from the left to the conservative, and Bessie Rischbieth fell towards the conservative end.[41] Yet she was a feminist leader on Aboriginal issues within Australia, and regarded as progressive in her advocacy of Australian participation in the Pacific. Further, continuous feminist activism in the Pacific region in this period signalled an internationalist field of vision that broke with the British Empire and Commonwealth mould. Australians involved in the PPWA were developing feminist connections, based not on shared historical ties, but on an assumption that regional commonality could be a basis for overcoming linguistic and cultural obstacles to communication and joint endeavour to improve women's lives.

As Leila Rupp has argued, the interwar period was a crucial time for feminist internationalism. The war had compelled feminists to consider issues of international relations more urgently than before; feminist pacifism (inherently internationalist) had been both challenged and strengthened by it; and in countries where women were enfranchised, internationalist zeal spawned during the war by US President Woodrow Wilson's Fourteen Point Plan, and later by the League of Nations, contributed to women's new definitions of themselves as voting citizens, political actors who could make a difference.

For Australian feminists, postwar internationalism thrived in a significantly altered and evolving national and imperial context. The 'Commonwealth' in the British Commonwealth League's name held doubly resonant significance for Australian women. When the Australian colonies federated into one nation in 1901 they became the Commonwealth of Australia. By 1907 the term 'dominion', which had been applied to Canada since it achieved self-government in 1867, came into use as the official referent for the white-settler components of the British Empire.[42] Yet Australia's particular name continued in such currency that at the 1924 British Empire Exhibition, where the Canadian and Australian pavilions dominated all but the British Palaces of Engineering and Industry, the Canadian pavilion was located on Dominion Way and the Australian on Commonwealth Way.[43] At the same time, the realignments between Britain and its dominions in the immediate postwar years were reflected in the emergence of the term British Commonwealth, to denote the self-governing white-settler dominions in contradistinction to the dependent colonies, whose subordinate status was reflected in their continuing to be called the 'Empire'.[44] These realignments were obvious not only to the dominions and Britain, but to the rest of the world, through such developments as the dominions enjoying separate representation at both the 1919 Paris peace conference, and (as well as India) in the League of Nations; the 1926 Imperial Conference and the resultant Balfour Declaration which laid out the new relationships; and the 1931 Statute of Westminster which elaborated their legalities. To at least some Australian, Canadian, New Zealand and South African feminists, it was of great constitutional significance that, as spelled out in the Balfour Declaration, the United Kingdom and the dominions were now 'autonomous communities within the British Empire, equal in status, in no way subordinate one to another in any aspect of their domestic or external affairs, though united by a common allegiance to the Crown, and freely associated as members of the British Commonwealth of Nations'.[45] Moreover, as relations between the dominions and Britain changed, and new arrangements were devised for intergovernmental consultation, it was important to dominion feminists to support their governments' enhanced voices in Commonwealth and imperial affairs, to ensure their own access to government channels in London and in dominion capitals, and to promote reciprocal arrangements on women's issues such as married women's nationality and maintenance payments to deserted wives.

Bessie Rischbieth recorded in her political memoir that the formation of the BCL as a newly structured organisation for empire women was inevitable in the post-World War I period, because beside the dominions' changing relationship to Britain, the League of Nations had altered international relations and with them the citizenship status of women subjects of the empire.

> Formerly, all matters of International concern, including those affecting women, had to go through the British Government. Under 'Dominion Status' such matters became the responsibility of the National Governments of the respective Dominions. Therefore, with the emergence of the League of Nations, women had to approach their particular National Government in order to place their views before that body. For this reason it became necessary to reorganise the former Dominion Woman Citizen's Union.

Yet, Rischbieth continued, some women (British rather than dominion) were reluctant to acknowledge the changes in intra-imperial relationships:

> Many women in the United Kingdom held what might be described as the old-fashioned Empire viewpoint, and they were considerably concerned over any suggested Empire change. On the other hand, there were members with a sense of the real value and equality of every part of an evolving British Commonwealth. Their attitude was that the Dominions were really self-governing Nations tied with a very close spiritual tie to the Mother Country.[46]

One way in which the BCL reflected changing intra-imperial relations through Australia's new global recognition as a nation in its own right was Bessie Rischbieth's inclusion in the official Australian delegation to the 16th Assembly of the League of Nations in Geneva in 1935, and the report she made to the BCL in London immediately after the Assembly's conclusion.[47] But there is other evidence, to be found in the reports of the BCL annual conferences, of the ways in which the BCL sought to shape feminist activism in the evolving Empire and Commonwealth.

Just as the history of the BCL's precursors reveals both white dominion women's assertion of their leadership roles, and their desires to embrace Indians and other colonised peoples of the empire, the reports of the BCL's annual conferences from 1925 to the outbreak of World War II suggest that both dynamics continued, at times perhaps despite tensions between them. The 1927 conference had as its primary theme the 'Social and industrial position of Women other than British Race, governed under the British Flag'. The preamble of the conference report claimed that 'More than 200 millions of women of other than British race are governed under the British Flag. Enfranchised women can no longer argue that they have no responsibility.'[48] Thus delineating the special responsibilities of British women who could vote, and Australians, Canadians and New Zealanders as the enfranchised women of the 'autonomous communities' in the newly realigned British Commonwealth of Nations, the conference made clear that these women's responsibilities particularly included the 'native peoples' about whom they passed four resolutions. These resolutions ranged from an assertion that 'natives' should be treated equally before the law, to urging the 'Imperial Government' to arrange for the training of 'native' women in maternity work, to urging that all commissions of enquiry into 'native problems' should include 'suitable women' and that women should be appointed 'as protectors of native women and girls'.[49] Commonwealth feminism (as opposed to imperial feminism), then, suggested that the enfranchised (white) women citizens of the dominions, not just British women, were responsible for their less fortunate imperial sisters. Particularly because Australian and New Zealand women had been among the first enfranchised in the world, they readily positioned themselves as modern, educated women, in control of their own lives and bodies, and thus definitionally opposite to 'native women', in a fashion similar to the more recent construction of the 'Western woman', in implicit opposition to the 'average third world woman', which Chandra Talpade Mohanty has described.[50] Despite the fact that the conference paper on 'Chinese Women in Hong-Kong' was delivered by Miss Ho-Tung, and a paper on 'Indian Women and Industrialism' by Munshi Iswar Saran, in other papers, such as that by Mrs Rheinallt Jones on 'The Native Woman in S. Africa', white women spoke about and thus ostensibly on behalf of women of colour. Yet some cross-racial commentary proved controversial. Mrs Neville Rolfe's account of her 'Recent Impressions of India' drew immediate criticism from the floor from Dorothy Jinarajadasa of the Women's Indian Association, who asked for and received time on the second day's programme to express her criticism, and from Mrs S. C. Sen, who used some of her own programmed time for her paper on 'Education in India' also to criticise Rolfe's remarks. Rolfe, secretary general of the British Social Hygiene Council, in her comments on prostitution and venereal disease in India, had suggested that Indian religions, ignorance of science and absence of social responsibility for the poor were largely to blame. In response, Sen denied that Indian religions approved of prostitution, and pointed out that in fact it had flourished under British colonial rule. Jinarajadasa contended that Indians had their own traditions of social responsibility, and described Indian women's current activism on the issue of prostitution. Sen and Jinarajadasa obviously swayed the conference: when Rolfe tried to move two resolutions, the conference refused to accept them for discussion.[51] Clearly, for Sen and Jinarajadasa the issue was not just that of a white British woman representing Indian women, but the specific and critical claims she made.

Notwithstanding the hegemonic preponderance of white women on BCL conference programmes, on top of the racial and class skewing inherent to the perennial London venue, the fact that Jinarajadasa and Sen not only voiced their criticism of Rolfe's representations of Indian women, but prevailed, is significant. This incident at the 1927 conference accorded with, and was probably linked to, the BCL's positioning in the *Mother India* debate. Amid the international controversy which broke over Katherine

Mayo's book *Mother India* (a polemic against the possibility of Indian self-rule) after its publication in 1927, the BCL convened an evening 'conference' in London in 'response to a general desire among women to hear the opinion of Indian men and women themselves upon the subjects dealt with in the book'. The three speakers, all Indian, included Mrs. S. C. Sen.[52] Writing over two years later in *Stri Dharma*, the journal of the Women's Indian Association, Hannah Sen discussed the racial, imperial and anti-colonial nationalist ideological clashes still stirred by the *Mother India* debate. Sen reported, particularly for an Indian readership, on a conference in London in October 1929 on 'Women in India', chaired by MP Eleanor Rathbone. The major provocation at the conference, according to Sen, was a proposal 'for a new and highly paid cadre of Women's Medical Service' to include a research department. The Indian women delegates at the conference 'refused to be drawn into the trap and registered a strong protest against this scheme of exploitation'. Moreover, the Indian women claimed the right to speak for themselves and their societies – which they had not been able to do at the conference – and 'very firmly dissociated themselves from any measure that savoured of patronage or threatened to lead to racial cleavage'. While this whole conference had been an 'unhappy' event in Sen's view, it did produce at least the positive result that some 'British women' and their organisations outspokenly criticised the conference 'in loyal support of the Indian delegates'. One of the three she mentioned by name was Chave Collisson and the British Commonwealth League.[53] Immediately after the BCL's conference on the *Mother India* debate, Collisson had in fact visited India in order to 'make connections for the League in India at Bombay, Madras and Calcutta' with Indian women's organisations.[54] Arguably, then, while perpetuating some imperial dynamics of white women's assuming a hegemonic leadership role, the BCL was at least sometimes sufficiently concerned to let colonised women speak for themselves for it to be possible to see the Commonwealth feminism they were intent on forging as relatively more egalitarian and inclusive than various stripes of imperial feminism.

The BCL's overarching aim was to build 'strong Woman's Empire Political power to be used for good'.[55] The notion of 'good' clearly left much room for interpretation. But the League's methods were straightforward. The annual conferences aimed to expose activist women to information on imperial issues, as well as to provide a venue for women from different countries to meet and discuss feminist concerns. Taking an example again from the 1927 conference, when Mrs. J. D. Rheinallt Jones of Johannesburg had the floor to speak on 'The Native Women of South Africa', she took the opportunity to draw her audience's attention to a bill on the 'Colour Bar' currently before the South African Parliament, which she believed demanded world-wide scrutiny, as well as to urge her audience to inform themselves and to ask critical questions about South African rule in the South West Territory (under League of Nations mandate) and British rule in

Basutoland, Swaziland and Bechuanaland.[56] In between annual conferences, the BCL relied firmly on the power of the letter. Chave Collisson as organising secretary would write, for example, to member societies in constituent countries, to inform them of resolutions passed at the conferences, to urge them to lobby their respective governments on specific issues, and to suggest that they in turn write to member societies in other countries to congratulate them on particular achievements or to offer support in current struggles.

One way in which the BCL's interwar Commonwealth feminism differed significantly from older or other versions of imperial feminism was through broadening London feminists' agendas. The slate of issues presented at BCL conferences included topics not previously adopted by metropolitan feminists: while feminist concern with the empire was anything but new, the BCL addressed itself to a range of issues concerning indigenous women. Australian feminists used their foundational and dominant role in the BCL to ensure that conferences repeatedly considered issues concerning Aboriginal women. Papers on Aboriginal women were delivered at the 1927 and 1929 conferences, and every subsequent conference up to and including 1939; speakers included white Australian feminists who were advocates for and had investigated the living conditions of Aboriginal women, Constance Ternent Cooke of South Australia, Mary Montgomery Bennett of Western Australia, and Edith Jones of Victoria. While these speakers gave their audiences broad-ranging information on the numbers, location, employment, health and welfare of both Aboriginal men and women, they drew particular attention to prostitution and sexual abuse of Aboriginal women.[57] At the instigation of Australian feminists, BCL conferences passed resolutions calling for greater Australian federal government intervention on issues of Aboriginal access to land, employment rights, health and welfare, improved cooperation between federal and state governments on Aboriginal issues, and the employment of white women with official responsibility. Fiona Paisley has argued persuasively that, particularly through their papers presented to BCL conferences in the interwar period, Australian feminists presented and publicised a radical critique of Australian government policy on Aborigines, especially Aboriginal women.[58] Bennett, Cooke, and other leading feminists actively concerned with Aboriginal issues, challenged the premise that government policy 'protected' Aborigines. They claimed that it served white rather than indigenous interests, and called instead for national policy which would effectively protect Aboriginal women from the sexual predations of white men, keep Aboriginal families intact and empower women as mothers, and provide Aboriginal people with the benefits of citizenship which were their rights as British subjects but which they were currently denied.[59] In keeping with the imperialist feminist focus on indigenous women's sexual exploitation by indigenous men, Australian feminists did criticise Aboriginal practices such as girls being married to older men, but they were more vocal about sexual exploitation by white men. Among other recommendations, feminists repeatedly urged the Australian government to employ 'suitable' and concerned white women as protectors for Aboriginal women.

In developing and pushing their radical critique of Aboriginal policy, these feminists actively sought to prod the Australian government into responsible action and to effect improvements in the lives of Aboriginal women. At the same time, they were conscious of their own positioning as white women citizens within Australia, and their and Australia's positioning within the Empire and Commonwealth. As is made clear in a July 1929 letter which Collisson, as organising secretary, wrote to the BCL's Australian constituent societies requesting their active support of BCL conference resolutions on these issues, they believed that feminist protest against the sexual exploitation of indigenous women by white men empire-wide would be helped 'if an active and forward policy in regard to the native race under the control of a young white nation, were set afoot'. Moreover, BCL leaders were anxious to push for an Aboriginal policy that was in no way 'contrary to the principles of our feminism', and to do all they could to 'strengthen the hands of the progressive women' [60] If it is clear that white Australian women activists were claiming an important advisory role for themselves on Aboriginal issues, and hoping to entrench white women in the professional capacity of 'protectors' of Aboriginal women, their activism ought to be seen as more than just self-promotion. In a cultural context in which the belief that Aborigines were dying out was gradually being replaced by calls for their biological and cultural absorption into white society, and government policy was largely based on such racist assumptions so that Aboriginal women rather than white men were penalised for women's sexual exploitation, feminists' work to improve Aboriginal women's lives was both urgent and progressive. In a radical literary departure in the 1920s, white novelists Catherine Martin and Katharine Susannah Prichard depicted the plight of Aboriginal women for the reading public.[61] The very important contribution that Australian feminist activists made on international conference platforms was to take Australian race relations from the obscurity of the nation's backblocks, and place them firmly in the international spotlight. Nevertheless, especially given some evidence that they failed to maximise Aboriginal women's own political power,[62] the implications of their speaking for Aboriginal women demand scrutiny. While by contemporary standards it was a relatively circumspect term, their calling indigenous peoples 'less forward races' immediately indicates their conception of themselves as both superior to and responsible for indigenous women. White Australian feminists sought at once to change Australian government policy to improve conditions for Aboriginal people, to enhance their own power as enfranchised citizens within the Australian Commonwealth, to advance a feminist agenda within the British Empire and Commonwealth, and to underscore their own imperial/international[63] role as white dominion women. As Paisley has recently pointed out, the issue of citizenship was central: white feminists protested Aboriginal women's exclusion from citizenship, because they recognised the importance of their own citizenship that they were actively redefining in national, imperial and world terms.[64] The complexity of these dynamics both defies easy categorisation and reveals the difficulties in the path of feminist inter-nationalism, especially when that internationalism involved the double layering of white colonial/dominion women positioning themselves as authoritative imperial and international voices for women in whose colon-isation they were implicated.

For all the internationalist zeal and altered geopolitical international relations of the interwar period, it is clear that Commonwealth and Pan-Pacific feminisms both shared the white English-speaking women's hegemony of the larger international women's organisations, and in some ways reconstituted other or older forms of imperial feminism. We can see, both in the BCL and the PPWA, contradictions similar to those which Antoinette Burton has identified within nineteenth- and early twentieth-century British feminism: the promise and rhetoric of international sister-hood, towards which white Western women assumed they would naturally lead other women.[65] Assumptions of white Western women's leadership roles saturated the Western-dominated women's international organisations throughout the interwar period, not least the assumption that Western women were well placed as current or potential experts on the status of in-digenous women, and that as experts they should then speak on colonised women's behalf. For example, at its board meeting in September 1936 the IAW resolved to work with existing organisations 'for the protection of native peoples' on the position of 'native women', 'that documents should be collected on the position of native women from Colonial Institutes or Museums in Belgium, France, Great Britain and the Netherlands', and 'to suggest to Auxiliaries in countries with colonial possessions that they should endeavour to get women students to take as their theses the question of the Position of Native Women'.[66] The BCL was in this way very much in accord-ance with its larger internationalist feminist context. By 1930, the second avowed object of the British Commonwealth League, listed in its constitution, was 'To secure for women of the less forward races within the British Com-monwealth the fullest possible preparation for freedom, while safeguarding them from the operations of law or custom which degrade them as human beings'.[67] White dominion and British women thus saw themselves as leaders, advocates and guardians of indigenous women.

When Bessie Rischbieth commented retrospectively in the early 1960s that the annual BCL conferences in London 'have provided a meeting ground for Dominion women, and for the many women of all races, creeds and colours living under the British flag', it could be argued, she was inadvertently revealing that within the BCL some women were more equal than others.[68] The hegemonic role ascribed to white dominion women is even clearer in her formulation that: 'Overseas women who had gained [by 1925] this important new [dominion] status were very conscious of their responsibility to work for the emancipation and citizenship status of the millions of women who were still living in the Colonies and Dependencies under the British flag'.[69] In her most revealing reference, in summation of nearly four decades of BCL work, she alludes to 'the work carried out by the women of the United Kingdom and women of the Overseas Dominions, working in close co-operation',[70] thus ultimately erasing women of colour from 'the work' altogether, other than as constituting white women's 'responsibility'.

The BCL reflected changing intra-imperial dynamics of the interwar period in that it insisted on the equal status with British women of women from the self-governing dominions. In its inclusion of Indian women, and support of their right to speak for themselves, it also reflected the changing balance of power between Britain and India, as India gained international recognition through its representation in the League of Nations, and as the Indian National Congress increasingly gained power within the subcontinent itself. At the same time, the BCL's vision of a united British Commonwealth, tied together in good part by joint loyalty to the British Crown, reflected limitations on at least some members' support for anti-colonial nationalism in the non-self-governing colonies or territories of the empire. While inter-war proposals for Indian self-rule were often discussed within the framework of dominion status, and thus Indian women were potentially equal partners with white-settler dominion women, the BCL did not adopt Indian nationalism as a cause. The BCL can be seen, historically, as a product of a stage of the British Empire in which progressive-minded loyalists advocated a loosening of Imperial bonds in order to maintain imperial and Commonwealth unity.

It is possible to see contrasts between the global politics of the BCL and the PPWA, despite the partial overlap in their constituencies. The BCL, while supporting the continuation of imperial connections, was arguably the more effective of the two organisations in terms of direct advocacy work on feminist issues. Perhaps partly because of the organisation's adherence to an effective central leadership (within which white dominion and British women held sway), the BCL, as mentioned above, relied on directives from the organising secretary in London to urge member societies to lobby their own governments and to support the struggles of societies in other countries. The PPWA, whose organisation consisted of committees within participating countries, and whose conferences, while at first tied to Honolulu, soon moved around the Pacific in a conscious attempt at geographic inclusiveness and international diversity, did not effectively go much beyond the exchange of information and fostering of connections facilitated by its triennial conferences. The PPWA's stronger commitment to internationalism (as opposed to imperial connections) was at least in part a factor of the timing of its birth, in 1928, in contrast to the BCL's roots in its prewar precursor organisations. Ien Ang has recently urged that feminists should not aim to resolve all differences among women, but rather work towards 'a more modest feminism ... predicated on the fundamental *limits* to the very idea of sisterhood'.[71] In this kind of frame, the PPWA's format of meeting primarily to listen to each others' papers and discussion comments, rather than to hammer out a unified agenda, can be seen as more internationalist and perhaps in that sense potentially more progressive. In these decades, however, while the BCL's feminism was constrained by its assumption that, for most non-white women, white women's speaking on their behalf was an acceptable modus operandi, it probably had more global feminist impact.

Writing in the *International Women's News* at the turn of 1941, Rischbieth directly connected the international spheres of the BCL and the PPWA by asserting that the future lay in the Pacific. Reassuring a readership whom she clearly assumed to be Western, she predicted: 'My own conviction is that the Pacific area is a place of vital destiny in coming events and a likely new focus point for the world ... [I]t renews my courage to dwell on the possibilities of this British expansion ground "down under". Such expansion, in the new world – possibly a freer world – would be directed by the three British nations set in the Pacific: Canada, Australia and New Zealand ... Accordingly if the centre of gravity shifts to the Commonwealth and its environs, you may feel assured that it is to an almost wholly British people.'[72] Marilyn Lake has argued that early twentieth-century Australian feminists' concern for Aboriginal women and their links with international women's organisations such as the BCL and the PPWA led them to 'an embarrassed recognition of their own and their country's racism', to an 'active engagement with women from Pacific, Asian and African countries' and to an increasing orientation toward the international arena as their political agenda was thwarted at home.[73] While this positive assessment of interwar Australian feminism has much validity, I contend that we need also to recognise critically the complexity of cross-cultural interactions and to identify the multiple and even contradictory valences in Australian feminists' internationalist activism in this period. The work of the BCL and the PPWA surely did promote international feminist connections, exchange of information and solidarity. To some degree, the BCL decentred imperial feminism and fostered direct representation of dominion and colonial women, albeit at metropolitan headquarters. The PPWA, even more decentring, sought to develop women's cooperation on women's issues across developed/developing, political, racial, religious and cultural divides. And the BCL's concern for direct participation and self-representation by Indian women was racially egalitarian.

Yet few other women of colour spoke at BCL conferences in these decades. Not only were white dominion and British women the self-assured leaders of the BCL, Rischbieth's notion of the Pacific – and thus implicitly the PPWA – as a 'British expansion ground "down under"' indicates that she believed whiteness and Britishness qualified dominion women for leadership roles in the Pacific region as well as the British Commonwealth. Clearly Commonwealth feminism had at least partly moved away from the direct appropriation, representation and silencing of women of colour by white women that characterised versions of imperial feminism, and Pan-Pacific feminism had come into being with a more egalitarian international framework. The internationalist zeal of the interwar period impelled feminists towards cross-cultural and international discussions of women's issues, and internationalist feminist agendas. But assumptions that some women were inherently suited to lead others had left powerful legacies.

Notes

I am grateful to Mrinalini Sinha and the two reviewers for their thoughtful comments on the first version of this essay.

1. Leila J. Rupp, 'Constructing Internationalism: The Case of Transnational Women's Organizations, 1888–1945', *The American Historical Review*, 99 (1994), p. 1575.

2. Antoinette Burton, *Burdens of History: British Feminists, Indian Women, and Imperial Culture, 1865–1915* (University of North Carolina Press, Chapel Hill & London, 1994).

3. It is central to my argument here that I disagree with Leila Rupp's lumping the United States, Canada and Australia as the 'neo-Europes' together with Europe itself as a single global formation of women of European origin. Such a collapsing elides white-settler countries, emergent as nations but still in colonial relationships with European imperial powers, with the imperial powers and the US. In doing so, it obscures the colonial status of white women in these countries and their colonising of indigenous inhabitants, as well as their geopolitical locations, all of which were relevant to their positions within feminist internationalism. Leila J. Rupp, 'Challenging Imperialism in International Women's Organizations, 1888–1945', *NWSA Journal*, 8 (1996), p. 8.

4. Rupp, 'Challenging Imperialism', pp. 11 and 9.

5. 'Australian and New Zealand Women Voters' Committee', *The Vote*, 22 July 1911, p. 164.

6. A. J. R. (ed.), *The Suffrage Annual and Women's Who's Who* (Stanley Paul & Co., London, 1913), p. 14.

7. 'Woman Suffrage Union, British Dominions Overseas', *Jus Suffragii*, 8 (1 January 1914), p. 57.

8. *British Dominions Woman Suffrage Union: Report of First Conference and of First Year of Work*, pp. 3–6; 'British Dominions Woman Suffrage Union, Third Biennial Conference, 1918', *The Vote*, 7 June 1918, p. 277.

9. 'Overseas Suffagists: Reception at Minerva Club', *The Vote*, 6 June 1924, p. 181.

10. *Jus Suffragii: The International Woman Suffrage News*, 18 (1924), p. 146; 'British Overseas Committee Pavilion', *The Vote*, 15 August 1924, p. 263.

11. 'Phyllis', 'In the Looking Glass', *The British Australian and New Zealander*, 5 February 1925, p. 14.

12. 'Bessie Rischbieth, O.B.E., an appreciation by M. Chave Collisson', *International Women's News*, 62 (1967) p. 46.

13. 'British Dominions Women', *The Vote* 13 February 1925, p. 50; 'British Overseas Committee Conference', *Jus Suffragii*, 20 (1925), p. 86.

14. 'British Commonwealth Women's Equality League', *Jus Suffragii*, 20 (1925), p. 133.

15. British Commonwealth League, *Report of Conference 'The Citizen Rights of Women within The British Empire' Caxton Hall July 9th & 10th, 1925.* The Fawcett Library at London Guildhall University holds a collection of all the British Commonwealth League conference reports.

16. British Commonwealth League, *Report of Conference*, pp. 32–3.

17. British Commonwealth League, *Report of Conference*, pp. 35–6.

18. Antoinette Burton, 'The Feminist Quest for Identity: British Imperial Suffragism and "Global Sisterhood"', *Journal of Women's History*, 3 (1991), pp. 59–61.

19. British Dominions Woman Suffrage Union, *Report of First Conference and of First Year of Work*, pp. 2–3.

20. 'British Dominions Woman Suffrage Union', *The Vote*, 24 May 1918, pp. 257–8.

21. 'British Dominions Woman Suffrage Union Conference', *Jus Suffragii*, 12 (1918), p. 156.

22. *The Vote*, 6 June 1919, p. 214.

23. 'Our Indian Meeting', *The Vote*, 16 July 1920, p. 123.

24. 'The League of Nations and Women Overseas', *The Vote*, 26 September 1919, p. 342.

25. Fawcett Library, Vida Goldstein Papers, Box 67, 7/VDG 7, Manifold book – London, July–November 1919, pp. 59–60.

26. 'Pan-Pacific Women's Conference Approaches', *Pan-Pacific Union Bulletin*, n.s. no. 102 (July 1928), p. 9.

27. Bessie M. Rischbieth, *March of Australian Women: A Record of Fifty Years' Struggle for Equal Citizenship* (Paterson Brokensha Pty Ltd, Perth, Australia, 1964), p. 123.

28. Rischbieth, *March of Australian Women*, p. 120.

29. *Women of the Pacific and Southeast Asia: A Record of the Proceedings of the Ninth Conference of the Pan-Pacific and Southeast Asia Women's Association* (The Australian Committee of the Pan-Pacific and Southeast Asia Women's Association, 1961), pp. 19–20.

30. *Women of the Pacific and Southeast Asia*, pp. 20–21.

31. *Women of the Pacific and Southeast Asia*, pp. 21–3.

32. For example, the 1929 BCL conference was supported by thirteen Australian societies, twelve British societies, two New Zealand societies, and one each from South Africa, India, Bermuda, Ceylon and Canada. British Commonwealth League, *Report of Conference Held June 5th and 6th, 1929*, pp. 6–7.

33. Raewyn Dalziel, 'Pan-Pacific and South-East Asia Women's Association 1931–', in *Women Together: A History of Women's Organisations in New Zealand*, ed. Anne Else (Daphne Brasell Associates Press, Wellington, 1993), pp. 88–90.

34. Doris M. Mitchell, *Sixty Years On: The Story of the Pan-Pacific South East Asia Women's Association 1928–1988: Australia's Part* (Pan-Pacific South East Asia Women's Association, Australia, 1977?), p. 4.

35. Kumari Jayawardena, *The White Woman's Other Burden: Western Women and South Asia During British Rule* (Routledge, New York & London, 1995), p. 265.

36. Bessie M. Rischbieth, 'Women's Influence in the Pacific: Where East and West Meet', *International Women's News*, 35 (1941), p. 65.

37. 'List of Delegates According to Countries', *Pan-Pacific Union Bulletin*, n.s. no. 105 (October 1928), p. 13; *Australian Dictionary of Biography*, 9 (1983), p. 304.

38. 'List of Delegates According to Countries', *Pan-Pacific Union Bulletin*, n.s. no. 105 (October 1928), pp. 13–14; and 'List of Delegates to the Pan-Pacific Women's Conference, Honolulu', *Pan-Pacific Union Bulletin*, n.s. no. 104 (September 1928), pp. 9–10.

39. Eleanor M. Hinder, 'Pan-Pacific Women's Conferences in Relation to World Conferences', *Pan-Pacific Union Bulletin*, n.s. no. 102 (July 1928), pp. 11–14.

40. *International Women's News*, 62 (1967), p. 46.

41. See, for example, Kate White, 'Bessie Rischbieth, Jessie Street and the end of first-wave feminism in Australia', in *Worth Her Salt: Women at work in Australia*, ed. Margaret Bevege, Margaret James and Carmel Shute (Hale & Iremonger, Sydney, 1982), pp. 319–29.

42. Karen M. Koral, 'Reflection of a Changing Empire: The British Empire Exhibition of 1924', unpublished MA thesis, Case Western Reserve University, 1994, p. 20.

43. Koral, 'Reflection of a Changing Empire', fig. 1, p. vi.

44. T. O. Lloyd, *The British Empire 1558–1983* (Oxford University Press, Oxford, 1984), p. 279.

45. Lloyd, *The British Empire*, p. 299.

46. Rischbieth, *March of Australian Women*, p. 121.

47. National Library of Australia, Bessie Rischbieth Papers, MS 2004/1/49.

48. British Commonwealth League, *Report of Conference Held June 30th and July 1st, 1927*, p. 7.

49. British Commonwealth League, *Report of Conference Held June 30th and July 1st, 1927*, pp. 9–10.

50. Chandra Talpade Mohanty, 'Under Western Eyes: Feminist Scholarship and Colonial Discourses', in *Third World Women and the Politics of Feminism*, ed. Mohanty, Ann Russo and Lourdes Torres (Indiana University Press, Bloomington and Indianapolis, 1991), p. 56.

51. British Commonwealth League, *Report of Conference Held June 30th and July 1st, 1927*, pp. 25–6, 42–3, 47.

52. 'British Commonwealth League', *The Vote*, 4 November 1927, p. 350.

53. *Stri Dharma*, 13, (1930), pp. 83–5. I am grateful to Mrinalini Sinha for sharing this article with me. For a fuller analysis of the *Mother India* debate, see Mrinalini Sinha, 'Reading *Mother India*: Empire, Nation and the Female Voice', *Journal of Women's History*, 6 (1994), pp. 6–44, and her Introduction to *Katherine Mayo's Mother India*, ed. Mrinalini Sinha (forthcoming, Kali Press, New Delhi, 1998).

54. National Library of Australia, Bessie Rischbieth Papers, MS 2004/7/82, letter from Collisson to Rischbieth, 28 October 1927.

55. British Commonwealth League, *Report of Conference Held June 30th and July 1st, 1927*, p. 5.

56. British Commonwealth League, *Report of Conference Held June 30th and July 1st, 1927*, p. 19.

57. See for example British Commonwealth League, *Report of Conference Held June 30th and July 1st, 1927*, pp. 28–34; British Commonwealth League, *Report of Conference Held June 5th and 6th, 1929*, pp. 28–9; British Commonwealth League, *Report of Conference Held June 18th & 19th, 1930*, pp. 34–40; National Library of Australia, Bessie Rischbieth Papers, MS 2004/7/300 British Commonwealth League Annual Report, June 1931 to May 1932.

58. Fiona Paisley, 'White Women in the Field: Feminism, Cultural Relativism and Aboriginal Rights, 1920–1937', *Journal of Australian Studies*, 52 (1997), p. 114. See also Fiona Paisley, 'Citizens of their World: Australian Feminism and Indigenous Rights in the International Context, 1920s and 1930s', *Feminist Review*, 58 (1998), pp. 66–84.

59. Fiona Paisley, 'No Back Streets in the Bush: 1920s and 1930s Pro-Aboriginal White Women's Activism and the Trans-Australia Railway', *Australian Feminist Studies*, 12 (1997), esp. pp. 121–2. See also Fiona Paisley, 'Feminist Challenges to White Australia, 1900–1939', in *Sex, Power and Justice*, ed. D. Kirkby (Oxford University Press, Oxford, 1996), pp. 252–69.

60. National Library of Australia, Bessie Rischbieth Papers, MS 2004/7/98. Form letter from Chave Collisson written on BCL letterhead, 23 July 1929.

61. Catherine Martin's *The Incredible Journey* (Jonathan Cape, London, 1923) addressed the issue of Aboriginal children being taken from their mothers by telling the story of one such mother's heartbroken determination to get her child back. Katharine Susannah Prichard's *Coonardoo* (1929) represented both Aboriginal women's sexual exploitation by white men and, perhaps more controversially, the possibility of love between a white man and an Aboriginal woman.

62. Paisley, 'Feminist Challenges to White Australia', p. 268.

63. Constance Ternent Cooke spoke on Aboriginal women not only in the Commonwealth/imperial forum of the BCL, but also at the international forum of the Pan-Pacific Women's Conference in Honolulu in 1930; Mitchell, *Sixty Years On*, p. 4.

64. Paisley, 'Citizens of their World', esp. pp. 68–9.

65. Burton, 'The Feminist Quest for Identity', p. 49.

66. Minutes of the board meeting of the International Alliance of Women for Suffrage and Equal Citizenship in Brussels, 9–10 September 1936; Fawcett Library Archives, International Alliance of Women Papers, 2/IAW/10.2

67. British Commonwealth League, *Report of Conference Held June 18th & 19th, 1930*.

68. Rischbieth, *March of Australian Women*, p. 121.

69. Rischbieth, *March of Australian Women*, p. 122.

70. Rischbieth, *March of Australian Women*, p. 122.

71. Ien Ang, 'I'm a Feminist But … "Other" Women and Postnational Feminism', in *Transitions: New Australian Feminisms*, ed. Barbara Caine and Rosemary Pringle (Allen & Unwin, St Leonards, NSW, 1995), pp. 60–61.

72. Bessie M. Rischbieth, 'The Geneva of the Future: An Australian Woman Looks Ahead', *The International Women's News*, 35 (1940–41), p. 42.

73. Marilyn Lake, 'Between Old Worlds and New: Feminist Citizenship, Nation and Race, the Destabilisation of Identity', in *Suffrage and Beyond: International Feminist Perspectives*, ed. Caroline Daley and Melanie Nolan (New York University Press, New York, 1994), pp. 290–91.

The Politics of Pan-American Cooperation: Maternalist Feminism and the Child Rights Movement, 1913–1960

DONNA J. GUY

Feminist cooperation is often difficult to arrange and even more frustrating to implement. According to Leila Rupp, the imposition of European and US approaches has been a critical obstacle to world feminist unity:

> We can see the ways in which the limits to universalism that were embedded in the functioning of the international women's movement helped shape collective identity. Euro-American assumptions, based upon a specific history of gender differentiation in industrialised societies, underlay both the conceptualisation of difference between women and men and the tradition of separatist organising. The notion of transcending nationalism assumed an independent, secure, and perhaps even powerful national existence.[1]

The problems of both nationalism and cultural imperialism were indeed difficult to overcome, but they were not the only dynamics that led to conflict and confrontation among feminists, or among groups of feminists working with non-feminists. One key issue was whether feminism included mother-focused activities. Another factor was the competition for authority among the specialists. Egos could thwart international cooperation as quickly as cultural misunderstandings. These could be exacerbated by the class and racial differences of feminists. People and their special personalities and identities, not nations, made international groups function smoothly. To deal with these problems feminists often had to devise curious strategies to achieve key goals, and the compromises and alliances made on an international level could be quite different from the policies they practised within their own nations.

This is a study of how maternalist feminists, those interested in promoting mother–child issues as part of their efforts to expand the rights of women, influenced the Pan-American child welfare movement. It consisted of two phases. The first phase began in 1913 with a national child welfare congress in Buenos Aires, Argentina, organised by Julieta Lantieri Renshaw and other Argentine maternalist feminists. With the first Pan-American Child Congress following in 1916, this era was characterised by women's demand for state support for institutions that would help children and working-class mothers so that poor children did not end up in orphanages or in foster care. Latin American feminists tried to contact US women, but none attended these early meetings, and efforts from 1916 to 1927 by the non-feminist US Women's Auxiliary Committee to the Second Pan-American Scientific Congress (WAC) created more antagonisms than it promoted Pan-American feminist cooperation.

Furthermore, the women physicians who founded the Pan-American Child Congresses also encountered professional conflict from male physicians more interested in intervening in the family than in helping mothers. This first phase ended in 1927 when the *Instituto Interamericano de Protección a la Infancia* (International Inter-American Institute for Child Protection, IIAPI), founded and controlled by male physicians, took over the Pan-American Child Congresses and excluded female child welfare specialists from active participation in this organisation.

The second phase of the child welfare movement took place from 1927 until 1960. During this era, Latin American IIAPI physicians initially refused to cooperate with feminists, but then they began to understand the important role of female social workers in child welfare work after meeting feminist representatives of the US Children's Bureau in the 1920s. Katherine Lenroot, a key US delegate, chief of the Children's Bureau from 1934 to 1951, and a committed feminist social worker, served as a catalyst to promote broader mother and child welfare programmes in the Americas by focusing on child rights rather than state intervention. As the head of the US delegation in 1930, she provided a role model that led to the re-entry of Latin American feminist child welfare specialists into the Pan-American Child Congresses and shifted feminist strategy from demanding state subsidised and state-controlled child welfare to a more flexible child rights focus. This new model forged both consensus and complementarity, spurred the professional development of female child welfare professionals in Latin America and the admission of the IIAPI into the Organization of American States. And, perhaps most importantly, it brought Latin American women into leadership positions at the Pan-American Child Congresses.

The history of women's efforts to promote child welfare issues in the Americas reveals the complexity of international feminisms. One early example was the effort by non-feminist elite US women to contact Latin American child welfare specialists. On 28 January 1916, Eleanor Lansing, founder (WAC) and wife of the US Secretary of State, invited Dr Julieta Lantieri Renshaw of Argentina to join its international committee and promote the solidarity of Pan-Americanism among women. Lantieri Renshaw, an Italian immigrant to Argentina was a noted physician, feminist, and ardent supporter of female suffrage.

Several months later Lantieri Renshaw angrily declined the invitation in no uncertain terms. US women had not responded to her invitations to attend three feminist congresses she had organised in Buenos Aires in 1910, 1913, and 1916. Particularly galling was the WAC's elite composition and the fact that not a single member of Lansing's committee attended her 1916 Pan-American Child Congress. After all, the meeting dealt with *children*, a fact she chose to underline.[2] Like many Latin American feminists, Lantieri Renshaw believed that child rights were associated with feminist goals and was offended at the lack of interest expressed by US invitees. Rather than work with these elite US women who claimed to support the women of the Americas but didn't turn their desires into action, she decided to berate them and ignore the opportunities to collaborate and educate. Lantieri Renshaw had a difficult personality and had little patience for the wives of diplomats who feigned interest in child welfare. Lansing had more enthusiasm for making strategic friends than for promoting child welfare. The combination of these personalities, as well as the class and professional differences, was too much to overcome.

Protecting the hemisphere's children did become a principal goal of both women, but they shaped their goals and strategies in very different ways. Lantieri Renshaw in 1911 had already formed the *Liga para los Derechos de la Mujer y del Niño* (The League for Women and Children's Rights) as part of her efforts to insert a maternalist feminist perspective in Argentine social policies. After feminists lost control of the Pan-American Child Congresses, her interest in child welfare as a strategy for female empowerment waned and she pursued a career fighting for suffrage until she died shortly thereafter in an accident.

In contrast, Lansing had originally organised the Women's Auxiliary Committee as a social gesture to give foreign wives of visiting scientific delegates something to do, rather than to empower mothers of the Americas. Before the US women decided what to focus on, they contacted Latin American women to secure their support.[3] Yet Lansing's search for a greater goal for the WAC was not directed by those highly qualified Latin American specialists who agreed to join. In fact, they were often snubbed. When the WAC had to choose between inviting the wife of a politician and an activist feminist, they chose the former.[4] They were as unwilling as Lantieri Renshaw to form a truly cooperative venture with women from other parts of the Americas.

The goals of the committee became clear only after 1918, when the WAC identified child welfare as its key interest.[5] This theme legitimated desires for another international meeting, and the WAC published information on Latin American child welfare in their own publications. As they put it:

> Special merit is attached to ... child welfare ... It will be carried on by [this committee] ... until such time when through its convocation ... a Second Conference on Women, even more truly Pan-American in character, will

interpret more broadly its functions and create the means whereby it may
participate in larger measure in all economic and social movements of vital
concern to women and children in the Western Hemisphere.[6]

Despite the good intentions outlined in the confident proclamation of
the WAC, the prospects of women of the Americas constructing a powerful
lobby to promote feminist causes through child welfare issues were fraught
with difficulties. First of all, the leaders of the WAC had no special training
in child welfare. Secondly, they often had a hard time recruiting support
in the US because maternalist strategies were not universally accepted
by US feminists. In fact, many of the women they contacted were busily
organising pro-suffrage rallies.

In contrast, South American women had begun to organise international
meetings on child-focused issues just as male specialists throughout
the Americas, particularly paediatricians and lawyers, were arguing their
cases for improved public health measures and juvenile courts. These men
championed child welfare through family reform, not necessarily through
the empowerment of women, and their professional training and authority
often challenged the view that child rights was a women's issue.

Eventually feminists and non-feminists had to accept each other's
authority in *different professional* specialities in order to accomplish their
hemispheric goals. New possibilities of Pan-American cooperation in child
welfare activities did not come about until the late 1920s when US social
workers began to defend feminist principles of child welfare elsewhere in
the Americas. The professionally trained social workers of the Children's
Bureau opened up a new area of authority, one that did not challenge Latin
American male child welfare specialists. In fact, they supported it because
it offered not only curative, but also preventive strategies. The career of
social work soon opened to Latin American women through the creation of
new schools. This, in turn, helped promote hemispheric solidarity and advanced the development of both national and international efforts related
to child welfare. As part of this process, the efforts of Katherine Lenroot
were central.

The campaign to defend mothers and children was part of a world-wide
phenomenon. The international child rights movement had its origins in
bourgeois legal reform movements in nineteenth-century industrialising
nations of Europe and the US. Its aim was to protect children against ex-
ploitative labour practices, provide an alternative to orphanages through
legal family adoption, and find a way to rehabilitate, rather than punish,
children who broke the law. There was also an emphasis on lowering the
infant mortality rates on the grounds that deaths limited the expansion of
the labour force and thus of capitalism itself.

In 1927, the United States led in the hemispheric battle against infant
mortality. Mexico, for example, had a rate of 193 deaths per thousand,
compared with 68 in the US. Yet Canada, Ecuador, Chile, Paraguay and

Uruguay all had lower rates of stillbirths than the United States. The United States and Canada had the lowest rates of illegitimate births, but ranked high among the American nations for women dying of puerperal fever.[7] These statistics, monitored through national censuses and international publications, provided a strong motivation for the American republics to promote reform. The quest for ways to measure such progress inevitably authorised new professional groups to offer their expertise to their governments, particularly physicians, educators, criminologists, sociologists and social workers. Child reform movements were also linked to religious and medical affiliations.

In recent years scholars have begun to evaluate the role and efficacy of maternalist feminist reformers who participated in the formation of child rescue efforts and the rise of the modern welfare state. Theda Skocpol argued optimistically that the US welfare state made a transition from a male-focused to a female-focused system that provided a range of programmes for women and children. She studied the history of military pensions, working men's compensation, and social programmes for widows, mothers and children. From her perspective, the shift from privileging male patriotism and work in the nineteenth century to the enactment of widow's pensions and school nursing programmes in the Sheppard-Towner Act of 1922 marked a real shift in the history of the welfare state from a system of privilege to one of rights. Feminist historians have not been quick to agree with Skocpol and note that the US system discriminated against many women. Some have observed that the best-organised feminist child welfare reformers in some states were the least effective. They have questioned why feminists helped build programmes that discriminated against non-white women and children in the United States and often set the stage for coercive state intervention there and in Europe, and they have generally seen the phenomenon of feminism as most successful as a springboard for middle-class female reformers.[8]

As the literature on Latin American feminism grows, it appears to have a more positive view of maternalist feminist politics, particularly since the prospects of engaging in successful campaigns for female suffrage were far more difficult there.[9] Furthermore, the existence of legal codes, usually national, explicitly defining family relationships (civil codes) – including limited custody rights of married women over their children – the lack of complete adoption procedures in many countries, and the absence of clear language regarding the rights and responsibilities of mothers, gave feminists a specific reform agenda linked to children and family.

Given these circumstances, it is not surprising that two of the three major meetings organised by Juliet Lantieri Renshaw dealt with maternalist issues. The 1913 meeting was the first National Child Congress. Organised by the League for Women and Children's Rights, the Congress offered papers by specialists in five areas: law, hygiene, infant psychology, assistance and protection for mothers. The League argued that legal reforms were necessary

to help mothers take better care of their children. Thus the last two categories, assistance and protection of motherhood, revealed strong gender
disagreements among participants as well as tensions between secular and
religious institutions (schools, orphanages, hospitals). These sections defined
the basic conflicts between maternalist feminists and others involved in the
child rights movement at the time.

The first signs of strain emerged when Dr Eliseo Cantón made a series of
disparaging statements indicating that the lack of moral qualities in some
mothers necessitated state intervention. His views were countered by
feminist Dr Elvira Rawson de Dellepiane who insisted that economics and
women's individual situations had more to do with whether mothers cared
for or abandoned their children. For that reason she believed that the state
needed to provide homes for mothers so that they could both work and
care for their infants. This exchange of views demonstrated how gender
affected the ways that the child rights and maternalist feminist advocates
justified intervention in families for very different purposes.[10]

There was also strong disagreement about the role of private elitist
charities in the Argentine child rights movement. The largest children's
homes in the capital city of Buenos Aires were operated by a group of
powerful elite women. Their class vision and control over such a large
number of infants and children was challenged by the bourgeois feminist
professional women. As noted by Rawson de Dellepiane, they preferred to
help poor women keep, rather than abandon, their children. Male professionals disagreed with the feminists. They preferred to work with charity
groups.

Since Argentina was the host of the First Pan-American Child Congress
held there three years later in 1916, it was logical that gendered differences
would again emerge. As before, Lantieri Renshaw served as president of
the Congress, although Dr Francisco Súnico was named vice president. The
Mother and Assistance group was headed by Ernestina López de Nelson, a
noted educator, and the members of the national committee were as well
represented by key feminists as by famous male specialists.[11]

The meeting was characterised by strong disagreements between male
and female participants because both groups used the same professional
expertise to claim authority within their own nation state, as well as within
the region. This encouraged competition rather than cooperation. The men
continued to differ with the women about the extent of state welfare. Súnico,
for example, only gave his conditional support to the recommendation that
American nations aid weak children (*niños débiles*). He believed that most
child welfare activities should be handled by charities, not state agencies.[12]
Other areas of dispute included feminist desires to include sex education
in the public schools as well as plans to close down large orphanages and
place children in family-type settings.

It was just at this time that Lantieri Renshaw turned down the offer to join
the WAC. From her perspective these women offered her little support in

her battles with the male physicians. Neither did they present any new ways to tackle the child rights issue.

By the time maternalist feminists organised the Second Pan-American Child Congress in Montevideo, Uruguay, in 1919, they had already lost control of the child welfare movement in South America. Although Dr Paulina Luisi presided over the meeting, male physicians, legal specialists and educators, mostly Latin Americans, had already begun to entrench themselves in the leadership of the congresses and they presented the most papers. This process was facilitated by the increased international participation in the conference, because male professionals were most often sent by their nations to give papers. Rather than work with these men, Southern Cone feminists soon separated themselves from the Child Congresses to pursue other feminist activities. Lantieri Renshaw ran for national deputy in Argentina in 1919. Dr Paulina Luisi was a key Latin American delegate for the League of Nation's investigations of white slavery. Others became involved in national politics, education and welfare activities and left Pan-American child welfare reform to men. The next two meetings of Pan-American Child Congresses held in Rio de Janeiro, Brazil, in 1922 and Santiago, Chile, in 1924 offered fewer and fewer papers by Latin American feminists.

The absence of feminist specialists became all the more significant because reforms of child welfare laws usually followed the hosting of the congresses. Legislators often cited statistics gathered for the congresses to demand the creation of juvenile courts, change criminal and civil codes, devise programmes to help mothers care for their children, and implement child labour laws and adoption procedures. Equally important, in some countries significant sums of money were set aside in national and local budgets for child welfare. If women did not participate, then they could not shape maternalist policies.[13]

Eleanor Lansing's WAC helped maintain a female presence in hemispheric child welfare discussions. In 1924 they held a second meeting in Lima, Peru. Most likely in response to the paper sent by Julia Lathrop, they urged 'childless married women of the continent' to 'interest themselves specially [sic] in founding organizations for the protection of destitute children', and that 'the protection of childhood should be the special charge of women'.[14]

The WAC were doomed to failure because they could only disseminate information rather than instigate new ideas or programmes of their own. Furthermore, by 1927 it became clear that the lives of diplomatic wives and Latin American feminists were too different and too dependent on other variables to continue this collaboration. From that time onward, only by male and female specialists of the Americas combining their efforts, rather than working in gender segregated groups, could they advance the cause of both child welfare and maternalist politics in the Pan-American arena.

As Latin American feminists pursued goals outside of the international child rights movement, plans for a Pan-American children's institute began to take shape in 1919. Male physicians took credit for its creation, and in 1927 the *Instituto Internacional Americano de Protección a la Infancia* (the International American Institute for the Protection of Children) opened its doors in Montevideo, Uruguay, under the stewardship of Dr Luis Morquio, Dr Roberto Berro, and Dr Víctor Escardó y Anaya. Eventually renamed the *Instituto Interamericano del Niño* (Interamerican Child Institute), the group disseminated the latest research and thinking about children in the Americas, and helped organise the Child Congresses. In its early years, the Instituto studiously ignored Latin American feminist child specialists. They published no feminist research, and invited only one Chilean feminist, who had supported the creation of the Instituto, to publish her work there.[15]

Initially, male approaches to Pan-American child welfare did not coincide with those of feminists. One key issue that separated them was whether the IIAPI wanted to target children specifically, or the children and their mothers. In the first case, so-called pure biomedical procedures designed to prevent disease would apply. In the second, a more sociobiological approach was necessary to reach mothers as well as their offspring. While all agreed in theory that mothers played an essential role, male professionals had more difficulty acknowledging this and were reluctant to let feminists speak for these mothers, and, in turn, shape regional policies.

Instead, male professionals viewed the family as a terrain that offered themselves and the state new worlds to shape and influence. They ignored the specific roles for mothers and treated the family as a unit based upon a sanitised poor child monitored by middle-class physicians. They considered private charities, and municipal and national governments as a source of money and power that would enable them to create the modern working-class family that would supply the future generation of citizens. If the state intervened early enough, they reasoned, levels of infant mortality would decline and, equally important, the family would serve as the socialising base of the Americas. Such a mission was so important that only men could undertake it.

An example of the male vision of children and national destiny was expressed at the long delayed 1927 inauguration of the IIAPI when Dr Luis Morquio linked child rights to the construction of the modern state:

> The problem of children has sparked especial interest in all countries in this hemisphere. The concept is rooted in the principles of justice and solidarity. It has nothing to do with charity, no matter how noble ... but rather is an obligation to help abandoned children and those in physical and material misery ... in order to ensure that tomorrow this child can fulfill its mission in dignity, not only for itself, but also for the community and the nation.[16]

From this perspective, both boys and girls had their future missions, so the obligations of adults of the Americas needed to be directed at both. At the same time, mothers and their roles were not discussed.

These physicians supported an authoritarian physician model. In 1923 a section of the *Boletín* of the Pan-American Union was devoted to instructing mothers on the care of their newborn infants. The author, Peruvian physician Dr Rafael Larco Herrera, then requested that the Pan-American Union republish the recommendations in a Spanish-language pamphlet. The instructions dealt with child rearing from pregnancy through infancy until the child begins to walk.

When it came to addressing the mothers, the pamphlet advised that 'Every pregnant mother should immediately put herself under the care of a good doctor or a maternity clinic, and submit to a professional examination'. By submitting themselves to male professionals, women would be bypassing traditional forms of information regarding pregnancy, and depending directly on the doctor. All over Latin America, midwives and female family members or friends delivered far more babies than trained male physicians, so the issue of creating bonds of dependency between Latin American women and their doctors was important to the men.[17] Larco Herrera offered detailed scientific counselling regarding the exact layette expectant mothers should prepare, how to breast-feed and wean the child, and the same advice applied to all mothers.

In December 1927, the First Pan-American Conference on Eugenics and Homiculture met in Havana. Comprised of male physicians from all over the Americas, the group passed twenty-seven resolutions. The thirteenth insisted that 'pregnant women should be compelled to follow the medical prescriptions tending to the care and prophylaxis of the product of conception [i.e. the child]'. The participants also claimed in their eighteenth resolution that the 'child has a natural right to his mother's bosom during the first eight month [sic] of his life, and would only be retired from it by medical prescription'.[18]

These views posed a sharp contrast to the women's approach to mother–child welfare as seen in a 1916 Cuban advice pamphlet published by a female physician entitled *¡Salve su niño!* (Save your Child!). Designed to promote a child-rearing contest sponsored by public health officials, it began forcefully with the statement: 'Every healthy mother should raise her own child ... and the Cuban mothers who hope to win the child-rearing prize by breast-feeding their own children ... will also be contributing at the same time to national prosperity'.[19] It is clear that she had a totally different approach from Larco Herrera and the male doctors attending the Pan-American Eugenics Conference. Her emphasis empowered the mother, not the physician. Although this pamphlet was geared completely toward postnatal rather than prenatal care, Dr Mestre y Havia believed mothers had to educate themselves. In fact, she never referred to doctors in the pamphlet, and made a strong effort to distinguish the various categories of lactating mothers so that there was advice for all.

Construction of gendered reformist roles continued to express itself in Pan-American meetings. After the 1922 Third Child Congress in Rio de

Janeiro, it was decided that there would henceforth be no section on mother and infant welfare. These topics were subsumed within the sociology and paediatrics sections of the meetings – sections dominated by men. The erasure of the mother–child connection from the official organisation of the congresses signalled the end of significant participation by maternalist feminists.

The friendship and mutual respect between Uruguayan physician Dr Luis Morquio and Katherine Lenroot of the US Children's Bureau helped bridge the gender divide within the child reform movement. They met at the 1924 meeting in Santiago, and again in 1927 when both attended the Fifth Pan-American Child Congress in Havana, Cuba. At that time, Lenroot headed the US delegation, and this was also the first time the US participated in a significant way. Equally important, Cuba was close to the United States, which had prominent influence in Cuban politics.

A number of US feminist educators and social workers attended the Havana meeting in December 1927. They participated from a position of strength since female social workers and specialists in mother–child issues had achieved significant visibility in the US. Since 1912 the US Children's Bureau and its all-female directors and staff had expanded its mandate to support campaigns of research in infant mortality, and other programmes affecting mothers and children. For the leaders, Julia Lathrop (1912–21) and Grace Abbott (1921–4), mothers were an essential ingredient of child reform movements. Katherine Lenroot, then sub-director of the Bureau, was well aware of the feminist political agenda of the Bureau.[20]

Lenroot's paper on the prevention of juvenile delinquency, presented in Havana in 1927, focused directly on the need to incorporate parents – both fathers and mothers – into programmes for children at risk. Prevention was far more valuable than subsequent treatment of social and medical ills. If nation-states wanted to decrease the incidence of juvenile delinquency, then they had to help instruct parents on how to monitor their children, not merely turn them over to state care as male juvenile delinquency specialists had been proposing. She also recommended classes in child care for mothers of newborns, as well as more specialised activities for visiting nurses, and scientific studies of juvenile delinquency.[21]

In early 1928 Lenroot published a summary and critique of the Fifth Pan-American Child Congress. She listed as one of several important accomplishments the 'recognition of mothers as the most important collaborators in any efforts developed to support children'.[22] She also argued that it was time to limit the number of themes, and to dwell less insistently on the issue of juvenile courts. Instead she urged members to report only on the actual accomplishments of such tribunals. She recommended combining sessions on sociology and legislation into one called Social Work. Although this designation may have been a matter of simple convenience, it afforded female social workers a clear entry into the discourses of the Pan-American Child Congresses while limiting the participation of male lawyers.

The male physicians who dominated the IIAPI and the Pan-American Child Congresses were willing to be persuaded by Lenroot because her ideas and professional training posed no threat to the authority of physicians. Also, she had a way of promoting collaboration and friendship by arguing in a seductive way that international friendship was at the heart of these congresses and such ideals would lead to an American region united 'in justice, love, in progress, and in civilization'.[23]

Lenroot's influence on Luis Morquio was profound. He was particularly impressed with her social work principles. The year after the Havana meetings, he attended an international child welfare congress in Paris and spoke of the critical importance of social work:

> A new element has been incorporated into welfare services and social defence, one that today plays a preponderant role: *Social Work*, that is a new kind of independent, autonomous service whose goal is to analyse each case individually … in order to prevent damage or to cure it.
>
> This great institution which began in North America, today satisfies the modern tendency which seeks more and more to substitute prevention for assistance.[24]

The lure of social work, personified by the feminist maternalist representatives of the US Children's Bureau, persuaded him and the other members of the IIAPI that the participation of these professional women was central to their grand plans for Pan-American child reform. The need to prevent child abandonment, juvenile delinquency, and other problems that threatened the future citizenry, compelled them to adopt new strategies of cooperation.

In 1930 Katherine Lenroot headed the US delegation to the Sixth Pan-American Child Congress in Lima, Peru. The decision was noteworthy since all the Latin American delegations were headed by males. In her official speech, Lenroot openly equated the participation of women in international endeavours with those of men. Furthermore, she subversively paid homage to the founding mothers and fathers of the hemisphere. As she put it,

> Let us from now on intensify our efforts and our cooperation. The civilizations of Bolívar, Sucre, San Martín and O'Higgins [independence leaders in Latin America] and of Jane Addams [founder of Hull House], Julia Lathrop [founder of the Children's Bureau] and Luis Morquio [founder of the IIAPI], will never be content while children pay unnecessary tribute of life; remain homeless in the streets; suffer from hunger or from lack of housing; are without paternal love and care [carefully including fathers here], or remain out of school. Let us all be conquerors of our own spirits, and of the social environment in all of its aspects … Only thus shall we be able to assure to the American child the glorious patrimony to establish which our forefathers lived and died.[25]

In this way Lenroot had identified women social workers as central to the project of regional nation-state formation, and as important as any hero of independence or any male leader in the Latin American child reform movement. Yet at the same time she emphasised paternal love and patrimony as essential elements. This compromise allowed her to position female social workers *and the founders of the IIAPI* in a more visible position of prestige to influence the future than the founding fathers of Latin American nations.

The US delegation was diligent in its efforts to put mothering on the agenda of Child Congress goals. The group advocated that governments recognise the rights of motherhood, provide prenatal and postnatal care and education for needy mothers, supply adequate aid to needy families in addition to social security, and construct good housing for poor families.[26] There were also resolutions insisting that men assume the legal and social responsibilities of parenting. In general, these recommendations aspired to a common goal – promoting healthy citizens while empowering women – and not all of them could be achieved simply by state intervention.

Lenroot not only criticised, she facilitated. When the IIAPI was having financial difficulties, she tried to get nations to increase their voluntary contributions. She had Spanish translations made of a series of Children's Bureau pamphlets. And she did this without ever criticising or challenging the authority of the IIAPI. She could afford to do so without damaging her feminist credentials, because she recognised a key element of gender relations in the transnational arena: regardless of gender, each colleague has authority within his or her own sphere of influence. The key to international cooperation was to create bonds of non-competitive cooperative desire. Lenroot's lure consisted of skills and theories associated with social work, and the promise to seek funding for the financially strapped IIAPI.

On the other hand, however, Katherine Lenroot quickly learned about the status of the child rights movement in Latin America. Although it is unclear whether she spoke Spanish or had her letters translated, she soon became quite well informed and committed to Latin American issues. In a 10 June 1929 note to Leo S. Rowe, director general of the Pan-American Union, Lenroot urged him to fight for increased US financial support of the IIAPI. She noted that by an Act of Congress the US had joined the organisation in 1928 and paid the voluntary dues, but other Latin American countries had not yet paid, and the organisation was in dire financial straits. Two Uruguayan physicians associated with the Instituto had travelled to the US in January 1928 and stated:

> It would be desirable to have a person from the United States as chief of the social service section if someone well qualified for this work and with a good knowledge of Spanish can be found … It seems very necessary to have a well-qualified social worker on the staff inasmuch as Dr. Morquio, the director, is a pediatrician and Mr. Fournié, the secretary, is an educator.[27]

The memorandum included a clear assessment of which Latin American countries had done the most impressive work on aspects of child rights. Lenroot's interest in Latin America ensured that the job was designed for herself, and subsequently she was nominated by the United States to be a member of the IIAPI International Council.[28] Lenroot eventually persuaded the US to commit $10,000 annually as a firm promise, not a voluntary contribution.

In addition, Lenroot and Grace Abbott helped pull together the US Committee on Cooperation in Pan-American Countries in 1931. Its goal was to promote the IIAPI, encourage the exchange of specialists in child welfare work, fund fellowships for Latin Americans to study social welfare, and promote Pan-American Child Congresses. Its executive committee consisted of distinguished US researchers and child welfare experts, male and female, headed by Dr Neva R. Deardorff, Director of the Research Bureau of the Welfare Council of New York City, and Katherine Lenroot as Secretary. At the first meeting, however, several key Latin Americans were invited, including Dr Gregorio Aráoz Alfaro, President of the IIAPI and head of the National Department of Health of Argentina. These men were invited to give their opinions on all aspects of the plans of the US Committee. Once the US Committee approved its statutes, it contacted foundations seeking funding for fellowships and social work exchange programmes for Latin America, but the Depression intervened and most, though not all, their efforts were thwarted.[29]

Under Lenroot's influence, the impact of female social workers began to be seen in the composition of Latin American delegations attending the 1935 Seventh Pan-American Child Congress, held in Mexico City. Although the Mexican Committee was chaired by male officers, all physicians, a woman was listed as one of the official members of the Education Committee. Furthermore, the selection of Mexican specialists included many women who spoke about the efforts of the Cárdenas government to improve the health and welfare of the Mexican family. They included feminists such as Esther Chapa and Ofelia Domínguez Navarro. Women from other Pan-American countries also participated.[30]

Latin American women still did not hold positions of power within the structure of the congresses, but they once again had the opportunity to demonstrate their expertise and their commitment to mothers and children. They argued for single mothers' rights to pursue paternity investigations. Equally important, congress participants, both male and female, presented a variety of reports about the state of training for social workers in their respective countries. This profession provided Latin American females with new authority to speak about nation and region, and their impact on family dynamics.

In 1939 Lenroot published a lengthy article in the *Bulletin* of the Pan American Union on child welfare in Latin America. She began by quoting the hero of Latin American independence, Simón Bolívar: 'Our society must be a society of sister nations', and then reminded the readers of President Franklin D. Roosevelt's belief in Pan-Americanism.[31] Then she went on to observe that Julia Lathrop had defined child welfare as 'a test of democracy', and noted that efforts in Latin America had led to child welfare advances there as well as in the United States, and the Pan-American Child Congresses had been instrumental in disseminating the latest information. In this way Lenroot once again wove an inclusionary web that linked IIAPI efforts to the efforts of both male and female leaders of the Americas.[32] She concluded by identifying child welfare activities as part of the effort for world peace: 'World peace and prosperity depend, ultimately, upon the health, intelligence, character, and social outlook of the world's citizens. These in turn depend upon the care, protection, and training which the children of the world receive. Thus child welfare is a matter of international as well as national concern'.[33] Once again she reaffirmed the alliance between the men and mothers of the Americas who supported the child rights movement.

At Lenroot's urging, the United States became a more active participant in the Pan-American child rights movement. The US gradually became a leader, rather than an observer, in this aspect of Pan-Americanism. In 1940, the IIAPI voted to invite the United States to host the Eighth Pan-American Child Congress and this became a reality in May 1942.[34] Lenroot was appointed chair of the US organising committee, and her fellow members were all males, including the Surgeon General of the United States – the arch rival of the Children's Bureau – and Dr Henry F. Helmholz, Professor of Pediatrics and a member of the Mayo Clinic. This time Lenroot was not alone as the only female head of a national delegation. The chair of the Mexican delegation was Dr Mathilde Rodríguez Cabo, director of children's assistance in the Secretariat of Public Assistance. In addition, almost every national committee had several women as official delegates, and mostly women as individual delegates.[35]

One way to measure the impact of Lenroot's efforts is to analyse how her Latin American male counterparts valued her efforts. In 1944 Dr Roberto Berro, head of IIAPI after Luis Morquio's death in 1935, argued that at the turn of the century child rights specialists concerned themselves solely with the child. Then the idea of the mother–child unit (*binomio madre e hijo*) emerged and was supported by early male public health specialists. Now the basic unit of study focused on the family.

The emphasis on the family as the basic unit of study, according to Berro, had dominated the Pan-American Child Congresses. He noted that the only exception was the 1916 meeting 'which excluded from its program the theme of pediatrics', a veiled reference to the early disputes between Latin American feminists and male paediatricians. As for recent trends, he noted that 'the last meeting in 1942 in Washington, took a more marked social perspective, without intending for a moment to exclude other approaches, but only to understand … that social problems demand that such studies be undertaken, like all the rest, because they are unquestioned pillars of a complete edifice'. When making these statements, he went out of his way to thank both Grace Abbott and Katherine Lenroot for helping the Uruguayan Children's Council in a number of political matters. Clearly Berro no longer disdained the participation of women in this project.[36]

In 1951, after thirty-six years of government service devoted to the cause of children's rights, Katherine Lenroot retired. At her retirement dinner she was lauded not only for her contributions to US children's policy, she was also characterised as 'one of the great builders of the social work profession both in this country and in Latin America'. Eleanor Roosevelt gave a speech praising her international activities, and Frances Perkins presided over the ceremonies. Although no one from the IIAPI attended, a copy of a letter, dated 17 October 1951, probably penned by Victor Escardó y Anaya or Roberto Berro to Katherine Lenroot, expressed the emotions felt by many at the IIAPI:

> If I had said a few words [at Lenroot's retirement dinner], I would have manifested that the children of your country owe you for all the benefits they have received from the Children's Bureau relating to their welfare, health and well being … I would have expressed … the memory of all the happy hours they experienced because of your caring and opportune intervention … And leaving national limits behind, I would have said that the same is true for the youth of the world, particularly those of the Americas, and that for this reason true Americanism has contracted a debt that can never be repaid and should never be forgotten.[37]

When the men of the Instituto found out that Lenroot had retired from the Children's Bureau, and was therefore no longer an official US delegate, the executive council voted to make her an honorary board member to acknowledge her service to the Americas.[38] Subsequently they invited her to be the IIAPI's representative to the United Nations. They then published an article praising Lenroot. Accompanying the tribute was a photograph of Lenroot gazing directly at the reader.[39] The glamorous photo, published as part of her retirement celebration, made her look more like a movie star than a tireless social worker. For the men who worked with her at the Instituto, she had become a friend, a financial consultant, a social worker, and a magician. The feminists they had once opposed had become an essential element in their Pan-Americanism.

Katherine Lenroot's retirement did not result in the demise of her programme to influence the direction of the IIAPI or the Child Congresses. Dr Elisabeth Enochs, another member of the US Children's Bureau, was asked to replace her. She had been working with the Instituto since 1940 when she began organising a meeting on 'Safeguarding Children in a Democracy'.

In 1960 Enochs, by then president of the executive council of the IIAPI, gave a talk about the Pan-American Child Congresses to the Inter-American

Katherine Lenroot, Retirement Photo. Archivo Histórico del Instituto Interamericano del Niño, Montevideo, Uruguay, a specialised institute belonging to the Organization of American States. Photographed by Gary Hearn and printed with the Permission of the Instituto Interamericano del Niño.

Commission of Women, the official OAS task force on women. She recounted an interview she had conducted with Elvira Rawson de Dellepiane, one of the Argentine feminists who participated in the first Child Congress in 1916, about the history of the Child Congresses. According to Rawson:

> For years there had been talk of the serious problems affecting children in the Americas. We finally decided that the time had come to quit talking and do something about it. The Government of Argentina was involved in a centennial celebration and could not sponsor the Congress officially, but our organizing committee appealed to the Director of the Pan-American Union, Dr. Barrett, through whose good offices all the American Republics made arrangements for their countries to be represented. And so, when the Governments saw how important the Congress proved to be, the men promptly took it out of the hands of the women! [40]

Enochs then elaborated on the great advances of women in Pan-Americanism, identifying great intellectual, social, and political figures, as well as the progress of female suffrage. She chose not to expand upon Rawson de Dellepiane's anti-male comments. Her conclusions linked hemispheric solidarity with child welfare as the joint concern of both men and women. Rhetorically she asked whether women's organisations should be as interested in child welfare as other aspects of Pan-Americanism. In answer, she paid homage to Dr Roberto Berro, and said that his definition of child welfare was one worthy 'of the dedicated support of all America's women'. Berro had observed:

> Very ancient is the feeling of protection for the child as the embryo of society, the nucleus of the family, the receptacle of all that is new, the clay which the human sculptor can mold for good and for brotherhood, which the sociologist should lead toward democracy and which the politician should guide toward peace and freedom.
>
> For centuries the child has been protected, in different ways, at different times, but more recently, in the last half century, concern for child welfare, for the fullness of opportunity and rights for children, have achieved universality and the status of a social science.

Berro had predicted that the next century would become 'the century of the family', not only 'the true depository of the cradle of hope and the future', but also of continental unity.[41] Enoch's homage to Roberto Berro finally laid to rest the conflictive gender divisions that marked the Pan-American child rights movement's early years. It also pointed to the ability of men and women of the Americas to incorporate each other's views for the sake of a common cause.

This tale of international feminism comprised a significant part of the Pan-American campaign to promote child welfare on a hemispheric level. The repercussions of these efforts led to an ambitious body of Child Congress resolutions and the passage of laws in countries that hosted the meetings.[42] The success of these efforts between 1927 and 1960 would have been far more difficult to obtain had men of the IIAPI chosen to work alone, or if the women of the US Children's Bureau, particularly Katherine Lenroot, had chosen to pursue the same tactics on the international level that had brought them success and influence in US politics. Similarly, had Julieta Lantieri Renshaw chosen to work with the WAC, and through that group linked up with Julia Lathrop, the impact of social work on women's careers in Latin America might have taken place much sooner. Clearly individuals, as well as different cultural perceptions of feminism, affected the timing and impact of child welfare movements in the Americas. And without maternalist feminists arguing their views on child welfare issues, more authoritarian models might have emerged. Future considerations of the merits of maternalist feminism should analyse the ideology's impact from this perspective.

Notes

Part of the research for this paper was sponsored by the National Endowment for the Humanities and the University of Arizona College of Social and Behavioral Sciences SB SRI Research Professorship. I would like to thank Gary Hearn, Doris Sommer, Ricardo Salvatore, Osvaldo Barreneche, Julia Clancy Smith, Drew Sherman, Sallie Deutsch, Angela Woollacott, Minnie Sinha, and anonymous *Gender & History* reviewers for their comments on earlier versions of this paper. I would also like to thank Francisco Pilotti, director of the Instituto Interamericano del Niño, as well as archivists Silvana Bruno and Silvia Gagliardi, for their support and cooperation.

1. Leila J. Rupp, 'Constructing Internationalism: The Case of Transnational Women's Organizations, 1888–1945', *American Historical Review,* 99 (1994), p. 1599.

2. US Library of Congress, Manuscript Division, Pan-American Congresses, Women's Auxiliary Committee (hereinafter referred to as USLC, Women's Auxiliary Committee), Box 4. Copy of letter from Mrs Robert Lansing, Pan-American Union, 28 June 1916. Response by Dr Julieta Lantieri de Renshaw, Primer Congreso Americano del Niño, Buenos Aires, 23 August 1916.

3. USLC, Women's Auxiliary Committee, Box 5, newspaper clipping 'Pan-American Union of Women Planned', hand-dated 6 January 1916.

4. This was the experience of Dora Mayer of Peru. After being invited to be a member of the committee in 1916, in 1918 she received a letter saying that her research had been received but her membership had since been revoked and they could not use her findings. They did this to place an elite woman on the Peruvian committee. USLC, Women's Auxiliary Committee, 25 February 1918, Executive Secretary to Dora Mayer.

5. The WAC claimed that even though they credited the International Committee for the idea, it had been decided by the US members. USLC, Women's Auxiliary Committee, Box 4, 21 May 1918, copy of letter from Mrs Glenn Levin Swiggett to Julia Lathrop.

6. *Bulletin of the Woman's Auxiliary Committee of the U.S.* (February 1921), p. 4.

7. *Boletín de la Oficina Sanitaria Panamericana* (June 1930), pp. 655–6.

8. Theda Skocpol, *Protecting Soldiers and Mothers: The Politics of Social Provision in the United States, 1870s–1920s* (Harvard University Press, Cambridge, MA, 1992); Valerie Fildes, Lara Marks and Hilary Marland, *Women and Children First: International Maternal and Infant Welfare 1870–1945* (Routledge, London and New York, 1992); Linda Gordon, 'Social Insurance and Public Assistance: The Influence of Gender in Welfare Thought in the United States, 1890–1935', *American Historical Review,* 97 (1992), pp. 19–54; Richard A. Meckel, *Save the Babies: American Public Health Reform and the Prevention of Infant Mortality 1850–1929* (The Johns Hopkins Press, Baltimore and London, 1988); Seth Koven and Sonya Michel (eds), *Mothers of a New World: Matemalist Politics and the Origins of Welfare States* (Routledge, New York and London, 1993).

9. The literature on the state in Latin America emphasises the role of public health physicians, legal experts and charities, and underplays the role of feminists. See UNICRI, ILANUD, *Del revés al derecho: La condición jurídica de la infancia en América Latina: Bases para una reforma legislativa* (Editorial Galerna, Buenos Aires, 1992); María Ines Passanante, *Pobreza y acción social en la historia argentina: De la Beneficencia a la Seguridad Social (*Editorial HVMANITAS, Buenos Aires, 1987); Angela de Castro Gomes, Ana Frega, Mónica Campins, Horacio Gaggero, Alicia Garro, *Estado, corporativismo y accion social ... en Brasil, Argentina y Uruguay* (Fundación Simón Rodríguez, Buenos Aires, 1992). To understand the role of feminists, consult K. Lynn Stoner, *From the House to the Streets: The Cuban Women's Movement for Legal Reform 1898–1940* (Duke University Press, Durham, NC, 1991). Asunción Lavrin, *Women, Feminism, and Social Change in Argentina, Chile and Uruguay, 1890–1940* (University of Nebraska Press, Lincoln and London, 1995); June Hahner, *The Emancipation of the Female Sex, The Struggle for Women's Rights in Brazil, 1850–1940* (Duke University Press, Durham, NC, 1990); Francesca Miller, *Latin American Women and the Struggle for Social Justice* (University Press of New England, Hanover and London, 1991).

10. *La Prensa* (Argentina), 18 October 1913, p. 13.

11. The list of participants can be found in 'Primer Congreso Americano del Niño', *Boletín No. 3* (Imp. Escoffier, Caracciolo y Cía., Buenos Aires, 1915).

12. 'Congreso Americano del Niño', *La Vanguardia,* (Argentina) 14 July 1916, p. 1.

13. The *Boletín del Instituto Internacional Americano de Protección a la Infancia* (hereinafter referred to as *Boletín IIAPI)* recounted the many ways that the congresses influenced individual countries to change their laws and allocate funds.

14. USLC, Women's Auxiliary Committee, Box 8. Mimeo, 'Informal Report to the Women's Auxiliary Committee by Mrs. G. L. Swigett, the Committee's Official Delegate to the Lima Conference, 24 December–6 January 1925', Resolutions, p. 11.

15. IIAPI Archives, 'Acta de Fundación del IIAPI, 9 de junio de 1927' (Founding of IIAPI, 9 June 1927) indicates that only males were present to sign the document. The Chilean feminist, Cora Mayer, never responded to the letter from Emilio Fournié of 9 August 1927. IIAPI Archives, Copybook No. 1, Letter No. 5.

16. *Boletín IIAPI,* 1 (1927), p. 12.

17. Dr Rafael Larco Herrera, *Métodos para defender la vida del niño: A las madres peruanas* (T. Scheuch, Lima, 1924); the quote is on p. 5.

18. *Actas de la Primera Conferencia Panamericana de Eugenesia y Homicultura de las Repúblicas Americanas* (Official Publication, Cuba, 1928), pp. 322–5. For more on this Pan-American conference see Donna J. Guy, 'The Pan American Child Congresses, 1916–1942: Pan Americanism, Child Reform and the Welfare State in Latin America', *Journal of Family History,* 23 (1998), pp. 272–91.

19. Dra Fidelia Mestre y Hevia, *¡Salve su niño!* (Suárez, Casara y Cía., Havana, 1916), p. 1. Found in USLC, Women's Auxiliary Committee, Box 7.

20. Molly Ladd-Taylor, '"Why Does Congress Wish Women and Children to Die?": The Rise and Fall of Public Maternal and Infant Health Care in the United States, 1921–29', in *Women and Children First*, ed. Valerie A. Fildes, Lara Marks, and Hillary Marland (eds), *Women and Children First: International Maternal and Infant Welfare, 1870–1945*, Wellcome Institute Series in the History of Medicine, 4 (Routledge, London and New York, 1992), pp. 121–32; Lela B. Costin, *Two Sisters for Social Justice: A Biography of Grace and Edith Abbott* (University of Illinois Press, Urbana and Chicago, 1983), ch. 7.

21. Katherine F. Lenroot, 'Prevención de la delincuencia juvenil', *Boletín IIAPI*, 1 (1928), pp. 470–78.

22. Katherine F. Lenroot, 'V Congreso Panamericano del Niño', *Boletín IIAPI*, 1 (1928), p. 557.

23. Katherine F. Lenroot, 'V Congreso', p. 558.

24. *Boletín IIAPI*, 1 (1928), pp. 106–7; 26 (1952), pp. 106–7; the quote is from 2 (1929), p. 260.

25. Sixth Pan-American Child Congress Lima, 4–11 July 1930, *Report of the Delegates of the United States of America* (US Government Printing Office, Washington, DC), p. 38.

26. Sixth Pan-American Child Congress Lima, 4–11 July 1930, *Report of the Delegates of the United States of America*, pp. 52–3.

27. USNA, Record Group 102, 0-1-0-7-12, Memorandum regarding increased support for the US for the International American Institute for the Protection of Childhood. Enclosed in letter from Katherine Lenroot, Assistant to the Chief, to Leo S. Rowe, 10 June 1929, pp. 3–4.

28. In fact she had been appointed by the Department of State on 18 April 1929, with the understanding that she would 'not be authorized to commit or speak for the United States', instructions given to all people appointed as US representatives to IIAPI. USNA, Record Group 102, 0-1-7-12, carbon of letter from Katherine Lenroot to Miss Isabel K. Macdermott, managing editor of the Pan-American Bulletin; IIAPI Archives, Carpeta 10, *ca.* 1929, Luis Morquio to K. Lenroot.

29. USNA, Record Group 102, 0-1-0-7-13, letter from Henry Allen Moe, John Simon Guggenheim Memorial Foundation to Dr Neva R. Deardorff, 16 September 1931; letter from Neva Deardorff to Grace Abbott, including mimeo report of US Committee on Cooperation in Pan-American Child Welfare Work, 27 July 1931, p. 5. IIAPI Archives, letter from Katherine Lenroot to Dr Luis Morquio, 22 June 1929; with the letter came Lenroot's notes on the first meeting of the committee.

30. VII Congreso Panamericano del Niño, *Memoria del VII Congreso Panamericano del Niño*, 2 vols (Talleres Gráficos de la Nación, Mexico, 1937).

31. Katherine F. Lenroot, 'Child Welfare in Latin America', *Bulletin of the Pan American Union* (June 1939), p. 336.

32. Katherine F. Lenroot, 'Child Welfare in Latin America', pp. 336–9.

33. Katherine F. Lenroot, 'Child Welfare in Latin America', p. 348.

34. Eighth Pan-American Child Congress, *Eighth Pan-American Child Congress, Washington DC, May 2–9, 1942* (Government Printing Office, 1942), p. 1.

35. *Eighth Pan-American Child Congress*, pp. 3–16.

36. Dr Roberto Berro, 'Una gran trabajadora social, Katherine F. Lenroot', *Boletín IIAPI*, 25 (1951), pp. 312–15.

37. IIAPI Archives, pamphlet 'Dinner Honoring Katherine F. Lenroot: a Life of Service to Children', 3 October 1951, Washington, DC.

38. IIAPI Archives, Copiador 1951, 17 October 1951, expediente 3167.

39. Dr Roberto Berro, 'Una gran trabajadora social', pp. 312–5

40. Elisabeth Shirley Enochs, 'Pan Americanism and the American Woman', *Boletín IIAPI*, 34 (1960), p. 278.

41. Elisabeth Shirley Enochs, 'Pan Americanism and the American Woman', p. 285.

42. Congresos Pan Americanos del Niño, *Ordenación sistemática de sus recomendaciones 1916–1963* (Instituto Interamericano del Niño, Montevideo, 1965).

Jie Gui – Connecting the Tracks: Chinese Women's Activism Surrounding the 1995 World Conference on Women in Beijing

PING-CHUN HSIUNG AND YUK-LIN RENITA WONG

The Fourth World Conference on Women (FWCW) and its accompanying Forum of Non-Governmental Organizations were held in Beijing in the summer of 1995. An estimated 35,000 women from around the world, and including 5,000 Chinese women, attended the Forum. Preparation and other related activities were under way years before 1995. An unprecedented number of Chinese women were drawn into this process which entailed attending regional preparatory conferences abroad, organising international conferences at home, and participating in numerous meetings to hear and talk about the FWCW. These women used the term *Jie Gui* (connecting the tracks) to articulate their enthusiasm and eagerness to engage in dialogue and exchange with the international feminist community.

This paper examines the opportunities and challenges of *Jie Gui* in the context of international gender politics. Our analysis is derived from, and seeks to contribute to, recent feminist debate about the politics of presentation and re-presentation of Chinese women in Sinology, and about the tension between global and local feminist activism. To analyse the political discourse of international feminist activists, we look with a critical eye at the images of Chinese women that Sinologists have presented in the last decades, as well as appraising more recent developments in the field. Likewise, our findings of Chinese women's gender and national identities call for a dialectical approach to their relationship with the Chinese Communist Party (CCP) state. Focusing on debates and activism surrounding the FWCW, we compare and contrast rhetoric launched by the CCP state and by Western feminist/activist groups with Chinese women activists' interpretations of their own experiences. The term 'Western feminist/activist groups' does not suggest a monolithic, homogeneous entity. However, as we examined the rhetoric and discourse surrounding the FWCW, it became possible to identify groups whose activism was explicitly or implicitly based on a set of Euro-American-centric values and conformed to Euro-American practice. Thus, the term 'Western feminist/activist groups' is used to capture the authority and superiority of those groups evoked in the international politics of presentation and re-presentation.

Through women's reflections and narratives, we uncover and acknowledge Chinese women's agency and subjectivity. Instead of staying at the level of rhetoric and using language and terms inflexibly, Chinese women who participated in the FWCW embraced their specific history of liberation, reflected upon the challenge of the international encounter, and seized new opportunities to define and actualise their causes. Their disposition to connect the tracks with the global feminist activism, however, points up the critical, but so far under-acknowledged, challenge in cross-cultural and transnational exchange that differences of language and terminology present.

To set the stage, we first examine how Sinologists have presented Chinese women over the last decades and the implication of the recent changes in the field to global/local feminist activism. We begin our analysis of gender politics surrounding the FWCW by asking what the FWCW and NGO Forum meant to the CCP state, to Western feminist/activist groups, and to Chinese women activists. To understand Chinese women's activism, we study the ways in which Chinese women's gender and national identities were constructed historically and are playing out in current international political discourse. This lays a solid basis for our analysis that seeks to uncover Chinese women's subjectivity and agency in feminist activism.

Our data concerning the rhetoric and politics of the Western feminist/activist groups are primarily drawn from the discussion in two Internet groups (the Beijing95-L and HKnews), and the homepages of other major Internet groups devoted to the Conference.[1] We used official statements and documents to determine the position of the CCP state. Our data on Chinese women's reflection and narratives in relation to the FWCW mainly come from *Nüxing de fanxiang: Yiqun ceng canyu jiuwu funü dahui guoji choubei huiyi de Zhongguo nüxing de xinsheng jieji (Reflections and Resonance: Stories of Chinese Women Involved in International Preparatory Activities for the 1995 NGO Forum on Women)* which was published by the Ford Foundation in 1995.[2] The stories consist of reflections of Chinese women on their participation in the preparatory process,[3] their observations of the world at large, and dialogues of their shared experiences. Sixty-two women aged from twenties to sixties and two Chinese women's groups, East Meets West Translation Group and China–Canada Young Women's Project, contributed to the collection. They were of diverse professions, including teachers, students, journalists, lawyers, social workers, medical practitioners, researchers, and university professors. The majority of them had played a visible and active role in 'women-work'[4] in China prior to their participation in the FWCW. Some were pioneers of recent women's initiatives[5] in China. We consider these women's personal reflections and narratives particularly significant as they comprised the first group of Chinese women who had entered on the stage of the international women's movement at a time when 'feminism' was still a difficult word to translate into Mandarin, and 'NGO' as a concept was barely out of womb in the Chinese context. In addition to *Reflections and Resonance*, our analysis also draws on the two-week seminar on '*Zhongguo funüyu fazhan – Diwei, jiankang, jiuye*' (Chinese Women and Development – Status, Health, Employment) held in Tianjin in 1993;[6] and the statement of Li Xiaojiang, an outspoken and leading figure in establishing women's studies in China, concerning the issues related to the FWCW.[7]

Over the last decades, one of the central themes in Sinology concerning Chinese women is their relationship with the CCP state. In the late 1960s and 1970s, when Western socialist scholars looked up to China for inspiration and resolution, women in China were presented as having been liberated by the socialist state.[8] After China opened up to Western re-searchers in the late 1970s, high expectations soon gave way to disillusion-ment, criticism, and cynicism. The appraisal of the CCP's monumental accomplishment was replaced by the notion of socialist patriarchy that oppresses Chinese women.[9] Most recently, Chinese women are said to have come to reject the CCP state. In her analysis of the Chinese women's subject positions in discourse, Tani Barlow looks at the historical emergence and political context of three Chinese words for 'women': *funü, nüxing,* and *nüren*. According to Barlow, *funü* was used in the 1960s and 1970s when the official notion of womanhood resembled the image of 'women hold up half the sky'. It signified the Maoist woman who fought to be man's equal. *Nüxing* and *nüren*, in contrast, have been forged in the 1980s and 1990s to challenge the Marxist CCP's dogmatic representation of women. *Nüren* (womanhood) puts a specific emphasis on gender difference, while *nüxing* (female sex) indicates that women are reclaiming their sexuality. Together, Barlow argues, *nüren* and *nüxing* stand for a rejection of, and historical departure from, the CCP's monopolised representation of the Chinese woman as *funü*.[10]

Although Sinologists' presentations of Chinese women have gone through several phases, the CCP state has persistently been portrayed as a static entity vis-à-vis Chinese women. The CCP state, by subscribing to the Marxist approach to women's liberation, has been alternatively praised for liberating the Chinese woman or for oppressing her. Until recently, Chinese women have mostly been seen as passive victims. Such a portrayal of Chinese women ignores the fact that Chinese women have actively negotiated their position vis-à-vis the CCP state throughout its history.[11] Barlow's analysis, although relatively sophisticated, is also problematic, because her understanding of the relationship between *funü, nüxing,* and *nüren* assumes a linear, historical progression from one concept to the next. In real lives, as we will show in our analysis, the sense of womanhood of individual Chinese woman embraces *funü, nüxing,* and *nüren* simultaneously. More specifically, in Barlow's analytical framework, *funü* – taken to denote a particular version of womanhood constructed by the CCP state, is opposed to *nüxing*, and *nüren*. This framework does not allow any infusion or articulation among these three protocols, a phenomenon which is evident as we examine the attributes and transformation of Chinese women's gender and national identities.

To understand Chinese women's agency and activism surrounding the FWCW, it is essential to recognise the nationalist component of their gender identity. However, an engendered national identity does not imply a complete surrender to the official agenda and position. Rather, Chinese women have been actively renegotiating their relationship with the CCP state. A gender identity that is intertwined with national identity presents a conceptual paradigm that is different from the oppositional position implied in the NGO model embedded in Western feminist activism. Moreover, the CCP state is not alone in its claim to present and re-present the Chinese woman. In the context of international gender politics, Chinese women's gender and national identities are constructed and contested in both the national and international arenas. Consequently, Chinese women have to simultaneously assert themselves against both the CCP state and their Western counterparts.

In recent years, critical analysis of the politics of presentation and re-presentation has generated heated discussion on paternalism and stereo-types of Third World women in Euro-American feminist writing.[12] Western feminist Sinologists have been urged to rethink their understanding of the Chinese woman as research subject. As a result, scholarly attention is no longer entirely devoted to Chinese women's oppression and subordination. Exploration of women's agency, power, and resistance has led scholars to appreciate the ways in which Chinese women define and interpret their own world and experiences.[13] Moreover, discussion on methodological and epistemological issues has challenged the relationship between Western feminist Sinologists and their Chinese women informants. To rectify the persistent hierarchical relationship between Western feminist Sinologists, the theory producers, and local feminist scholars, the suppliers of raw materials, translations of the work of key Chinese women thinkers and researchers are included in scholarly publication for the first time.[14] Observations and analyses made by Chinese women scholars in diaspora have gradually transformed the indigenous woman from informant to 'analyst and producer of feminist discourse in her own right'.[15] These new developments are significant because they mark the end of an era when Western feminist Sinologists dominated the presentation and re-presentation of the Chinese woman. They also begin to rupture the monolithic, hegemonic notion of the Chinese woman as the Other in Western feminist discourse.

After decades of exclusion, the voices of Chinese women have finally entered the discourse of global feminism. The analytical paradigm proposed by Mohanty to deconstruct the homogeneous, hegemonic construct of the Third World Woman has made its way into the study of Chinese women. With diverse voices entering the field, the 'reconstruction' that was missing in Mohanty's original proposal is transforming the portrayal of

Chinese women.[16] The implication of these new developments for global/ local feminist activism is instructive. In knowledge building, the reconstruction takes the form of involving local women to speak for themselves. In practice, it takes a lot more to 'connect the tracks' between global and local feminist activism. Constructive dialogue requires the parties involved to be able to 'understand struggles and envision dreams woven from different languages and cultural contexts'.[17] Unfortunately, many commonly used terms in Western feminisms do not translate easily or clearly into Chinese, or any other languages, because their implied cultural, political, and/or historical meanings are often lost in translation. How to break through cultural and ideological paradigms which underlie language usage remains a challenge in cross-cultural dialogue. Besides, local activists often employ diverse strategies and approaches in their struggles. Therefore, to recognise local women's subjectivity and agency, Western feminist/activist groups must go beyond any rigid usage of terminology, and, most importantly, become open to a paradigm of feminist activism that may be different from their own.

Before going into Chinese women activists' own view of the FWCW and their strategies, we would first examine the discursive rhetoric of the CCP state and Western feminist/activist groups around the FWCW. Gertrude Mongella, the secretary of the FWCW, once asked the press to focus on women's issues, rather than on China. In her words, 'This is not a conference on China. It is a conference on women'.[18] However, in view of the fact that China was hosting the Conference, it was unrealistic to expect this. The Chinese government had gone out of its way to win the bid to host the Conference with the expectation that it would raise its international profile by showing how the proletarian revolution had liberated Chinese women. In contrast, many outspoken Western feminist/activist groups saw the Conference as an opportunity to bring China in line with international standards of human/women's rights. The Conference was once declared as providing a chance for '36,000 feminists [to] meet 1 billion communists', while attending the Conference in Beijing was equated to going to Hitler's Germany in 1939 for a human rights conference.[19] The Chinese government's decision to move the site of the NGO Forum away from Beijing further fuelled the already heated protests by some prominent Western human rights and women's organisations. Such highly contentious political undertones came to shape and regulate debates surrounding the Conference. The dispute regarding women's status in contemporary China is a typical example.

In order to broadcast its record on women's liberation, the Chinese government put out two documents in 1994: *Country Report on the People's Republic of China's Implementation of the Nairobi Strategy to Enhance Women's Status* and a White Paper on *The Situation of Women in China*. In both documents, the Chinese government argued strongly that the proletarian revolution led by the CCP had liberated Chinese women from a feudal, imperialistic past. According to the CCP state, Chinese women now enjoy an unprecedentedly high status 'which had remained unattainable in Chinese society over millennia'.[20] Although conceding that 'the condition of Chinese women is still not wholly satisfactory', the government attributed this to 'the constraints of social development and the influence of old concepts'.[21] The White Paper claims,

> The Chinese government is making every effort to develop the economy, strengthen the legal system, eradicate all backward ideas of discriminating against and looking down on women and promote equal rights for men and women in all spheres of social life as stipulated in Chinese law. This will speed the realisation of the various development goals of the Nairobi Strategies in China before the end of this century.[22]

Throughout these two documents, the CCP is accredited with all the progress and advancement Chinese women have experienced. They also assert the CCP state's unquestionable commitment toward gender equality.[23]

Feminist/activist groups outside of China dispute claims made by the Chinese government. For example, a report entitled *An Alternative View of the Status of Women in China* dismisses any positive, direct linkage between CCP policy and improvement in women's status. The report argues that '*in fact*, the status of women had improved before the CCP came into power in 1949' and 'what women in China have gained is the fruit of a whole century of struggle' rather than the CCP's accomplishment as pronounced by the Chinese government. Instead, it targets the CCP as the main source of abuse and oppression. For example, regarding women's individual rights, the report states:

> The White Paper [of the Chinese government] says that Chinese women enjoy the right to life and health as men do, and the law safeguards women's reproductive rights. *In actuality*, the one-child policy being sternly carried out at all levels, the suffering of a lot of women and the abuse or even killing of girls are facts of life many people are familiar with.[24] (emphasis ours)

Moreover, some human rights groups that joined in the dispute emphasised China's restrictions on association and expression. Under such an authoritarian state, their rhetoric suggests, Chinese women could only be considered victims. Thus, the introduction of Amnesty International's report on Chinese women's human rights made a strong but general statement:

> Locked up for years for joining the pro-democracy movement. Doing forced labor in punishment for political crimes. Hideously tortured with a range of specially designed implements. Harassed and persecuted for promoting human rights. This is the experience of many women of independent minds at the hands of the Chinese authorities ... Many have been detained, restricted or harassed for exercising fundamental rights such as freedom of expression or association.[25]

Throughout the debate, both the CCP state and those Western feminist/ activist groups which publicised their views on Chinese women's status claimed the authority to speak for Chinese women. They quoted different statistics to construct a hegemonic 'reality'. In their attempt to expose the oppression of Chinese women, these feminist/activist groups outside of China employed terms such as 'in fact', 'actually', 'reality', thereby implying that only they could penetrate the truth that the CCP state was seeking to obscure. In the process, they manage to 'establish *their* authority on the backs of non-Western women, determining for them the meanings and goals of their lives' (original emphasis).[26] In contrast, the CCP state held on to its paternalist position vis-à-vis Chinese women. It attributed existing problems to the static categories such as 'feudalism', 'backwardness', or 'underdevelopment'. However, by positioning itself as the legitimate guardian of Chinese women's welfare, the CCP state was a target only to be discredited by Western feminist/activist groups. The oppositional position implied in the rejection bears its theoretical roots in feminist analysis of the capitalist state in the West. It also projects a Western feminist activist model that is embedded in the NGO framework. Before further examining the implications of this particular conceptual paradigm for global/local feminist activism, it is important to see the Conference through the eyes of Chinese women.

For many Chinese women, participation in regional preparatory conferences for Beijing 95 was their first trip abroad, first attendance at an international conference, first contact with NGO activities, and first meaningful dialogue with foreign activists and feminists. Generally speaking, the encounter proved extremely informative, stimulating, and uplifting. Whenever they talked about their experiences abroad, these Chinese women began their narratives on a positive note. For example, 'my trip to Malaysia leaves me a strong impression', 'my trip to Northern Europe has made me ponder over a number of issues', and ' [over the last years] I have gone abroad for a number of women's functions. The biggest gain is that my life has changed'.[27]

At the personal level, the chance to enter the international arena provided individual women with an opportunity to forge new perceptions about themselves, renegotiate their marital relationships, and/or challenge those societal norms and practices that once governed their everyday lives. Deng Chunli, a lecturer at the Chinese People's University, gives a vivid, elaborate account along these lines:

> My most recent trip [abroad] has made me feel increasingly confident …
> After coming back, I became even more determined to work for women …
> Many people around me look at me in a strange way. One day I went out
> with [one of] my girl friends. My neighbour said, 'Here they come again,
> two feminists going out.' My husband also said, 'You're so annoying. Have
> you got a women's contagious disease or what, talking about the Women's

Conference all the time? What can you women do?' Now, I just do what I like. I pay no attention to his grumbling. Perhaps he can't really understand me now, but I'll try to make him understand gradually. In the meantime, I feel I need to do something to show him that women can in fact accomplish things. Besides, after having contacted so many women, I have come to realise that women have limitless potential, even greater than that of men. We women can bear heavier burdens. We have more merits than flaws. Women are persevering and determined. Our capacity to withstand suffering, and to be empathetic and tolerant certainly surpasses that of men. My husband says that I have changed, that I'm no longer lovely nor gentle. My reply is that I have come to realise that I used to expect too much of myself. Why should I have to be so gentle and virtuous? Besides, who decides what is 'gentle' anyway? I should simply do what I have to do'.[28]

At the professional level, being a host of the FWCW gave women activists in China unprecedented opportunities to engage in exchanges with international women's groups. In an article entitled 'How Do We Face the World? – Some Thoughts on Connecting the Tracks', the author Xie Lihua, editor-in-chief of the journal *Nongjianü baishitong (Farming Women Know It All)*, explained how the political context of *Jie Gui* has changed drastically in less than a decade. In their first encounter with a Spanish women's group in 1985, Xie and her colleagues were completely shocked and dumbfounded when the Spanish leader remarked on how the group had been promoting 'the sexual pleasure movement' and claiming that women should have the same sexual rights as men and that sex should not be only for men's enjoyment. 'At the time,' Xie stated, 'it was like hearing an alien voice from the moon. We could not engage in exchange, nor any meaningful dialogue. All we could do was nod our heads, with blank looks on our faces'.[29]

The political, historical context of that encounter is significant:

> Although the first World Conference on Women had been held in Mexico City in 1975, and the UN had accepted a proposal by the Conference that 1976–1985 be declared the 'UN Decade for Women', my colleagues and I on the staff of the journal *Women of China* did not even have this basic information. We used to think anything related to foreign countries should be the responsibility of the Foreign Affairs Department, and whether or not to connect the tracks [with foreign countries], or how to connect the tracks had nothing to do with us or our work.[30]

Clearly, as late as a decade ago, no one could even imagine 'connecting the tracks of Chinese women's movement with the world'. As Xie put it, 'we didn't understand women in the outside world. Their understanding of us was even poorer.'[31]

Xie's first experience in attending an international conference brought her a new realisation of 'the dialectic relationships between the indigenous/ Chinese and foreigners'.[32] By then, the journal *Farming Women Know It All,* a popular magazine catering to rural women, had been in press for about a year. Although Xie and her journalist colleagues had brought the magazine along to the conference, they were not sure how the international community would receive such a 'rustic magazine'. She and her journalist colleagues, in Xie's words, 'felt like country bumpkins' who, at the beginning, were very reluctant to tell others who they were and what they had been doing.[33] However, she later recalled, when she showed up at the book exhibition with the magazine,

> My anxiety suddenly evaporated. Among numerous magazines focusing on the image of labouring women, *Farming Women Know It All* was the most outstanding one. This unexpectedly positive reception made a colleague of ours decide not to present the popular magazine she had brought, because it had a beautiful blonde on the cover. Its fate was the same as that of the pretty dresses [we had made for and brought to the conference which are now sitting] at the bottom of our suitcases. When she privately showed her magazine around, she was asked 'is your magazine for the poor or the rich?'[34]

This experience allowed Xie to come to an awareness of the commodification problem of women in the mass media. It also made her wonder out loud how many of 'the forty to fifty periodicals and magazines on women published by the All-China Women's Federation, the largest one of which has a circulation of two million copies' were in fact 'presentable' at the Fourth World Conference on Women.[35]

Underlying these reflective narratives is a search for women's identities that has been evolving among Chinese women scholars and activists since the 1980s.[36] Their participation in regional preparatory conferences for the FWCW allowed them to further articulate their gender and national identities in the context of global feminist activism. Born years before the Cultural Revolution (1966–76) and growing up in the era of 'women hold up half the sky', many of these women, although they claim not to have personally experienced discrimination, have come to fight against gender inequalities in contemporary China. To understand their conviction, we need to reconstruct the historical path of their activism.

Chinese women who experienced the Cultural Revolution as the formative experience of their lives faced a paradoxical environment when they began their careers. On the one hand, the overall sociopolitical climate favoured gender equality. The official rhetoric and government policies were based on the Marxist notion of gender liberation. On the other hand, this liberation was built, in turn, upon a denial of gender difference and a presumption that 'what men can do women can do'. Many women of this cohort reported that they strove to become 'men's equal' by consciously or unconsciously keeping themselves from being 'ordinary women'. The following examples are typical.

I was born in 1951 ... I am now the editor-in-chief of *Farming Women Know It All* ... I was a soldier for fourteen years. I was once a leader in the military's propaganda section. I simply went from the world of men to the world of women. I felt no sense of inequality or being discriminated against in that man's world because I was the leader of male soldiers. After I went to the Women's Federation, probably owing to increased contact with incidents of darkness and backwardness, I found that sexual inequality does exist. Then I developed a sense of purpose. I hope that we all will do something about this inequality. I have no special skills, I just worry about the fate of the country and its people.[37]

I have gone abroad for a number of women's functions. The biggest gain is that my life has changed. [Going abroad] inspired me to identify with women (*nüxing*) ... I had been in the army for 24 years. I didn't work for the All China Women's Federation. Therefore, I once joked that I went from a place where there was no women's restroom to one where there is no men's. When I was a soldier, I looked down on women. I felt that they had the collective short-comings of all human beings. I was once proud of the ways in which I was different from other women. Others attributed my success to the fact that men did not treat me like a woman, they treated me either as a colleague or a competitor. I was quite proud of this judgement because [I thought] at least I did not have all the negative attributes of being a woman. At that time, I took pride in not identifying myself with my gender group.[38]

Liu went on to say:

I have heard some women cadres maintain that their success is due to the fact they do not perceive themselves as women. They claim that they are successful women. But deep down in their hearts, they have not identified with other women. Instead, they look down upon women. The assumption behind this type of statement is that women are weak and cannot be suc-cessful in society. It fails to recognise that women have long been denied the opportunities for social participation and so could not fully realise their potential and demonstrate their unique qualities. Success should not be the privilege of a particular sex. Therefore I think it is very important to study women's issues.[39]

These 'iron women' belong to the so called 'Cultural Revolution generation'. Like the previous cohort, which came of age before 1949, they, too, feel a sense of 'liberation' and often talk about 'gender equality'. However, the life experiences of these two cohorts are quite different. Women of the older generation, as clearly demonstrated by Rofel, gained their sense of liberation by comparing their life before and after the 1949 Revolution. A female factory worker, Rofel argues, would be perceived as a 'broken shoe' prior to the 1949 Revolution because she had crossed gender lines. The 1949 Revolution provided women with the political and ideological leverage to become widely praised 'proletarians'.[40] In contrast, women of the Cultural Revolution cohort drew their sense of 'liberation' from being different from the 'traditional', 'ordinary' woman, who came to symbolise weakness, inferiority, and backwardness. They therefore took great pride in feeling and becoming 'men's equals'. Many Western feminists have judged the experiences of these particular two cohorts of women to have been anything but 'liberating'. Not only did they tend to turn the 'iron woman' generation into a cultural and historical 'Other', they also portrayed these women as victims betrayed by a monolithic and patriarchal socialist state.[41] Such a framework leaves no room to recognise, much less articulate, the personal, political meanings of socialism for the iron women generation. Yet the preceding excerpts show that these women, whose commitment and sense of mission to further women's welfare and gender equality derived from their gender and national identities, could think and speak for themselves.

Since the 1980s, rather than completely rejecting 'what men can do, women can do', a pervasive ideological doctrine of their generation, Chinese women activists have struggled to fight against discrimination inflicted on women by market capitalism. The emphasis on women's self-esteem, self-confidence, self-reliance, and self-cultivation is aimed to a great extent at transforming the 'ordinary' woman. In this *Sizi* Campaign (Self-cultivation in four aspects), there is no sign of a rejection of the *funü* and the CCP state, as suggested in Barlow's analytical framework. Instead, the historical path of these iron women's 'liberation' continues to inform their analysis of the roots of the problems. It also influences their proposals for change.

Their spirit also impacted on the younger generation. Ge Youli, who was in her early thirties, reflected on her mother's experience of 'liberation' in the 1950s–60s and her own experience of gender inequality since the 1980s.

> Mum is an optimistic, independent woman with a strong character. School education in the fifties gave her confidence that 'women can hold up half the sky'. The employment, salary and social welfare system under the planned economy also provided her with confidence and structural support. She worked very hard and won many certificates of merit. Mum often says to me confidently, 'As long as you work hard and keep improving yourself, women are not worse than men'. At that time, she genuinely believed that the country had created all possible conditions for the equality of men and women. The rest was up to women themselves. As a mother, she gave me physical and spiritual freedom to escape the inhibitions of my childhood. Mum's spirit accompanied and influenced me throughout my primary and high-school years.[42]

Instilled with her mother's confidence, Ge was unprepared for the experience of gender inequality she was later confronted with in university, at work, and in the society at large since the economic reform of China. After participating in various international activities around the FWCW and observing how women in other countries fought against gender inequalities, Ge came to a new understanding of gender equality and her mission in the country,

> I finally understood: women's issues are global and China is no exception ...
> I also remembered my retired mother whose understanding about the equal-
> ity between men and women now requires new contents. The social injustice
> against women hidden in the planned economy has resurfaced, and even
> strengthened, with the growth of the market economy. The elimination of
> such injustice requires the concern and efforts of the whole society and,
> moreover, the struggle of a future generation of daughters.[43]

Ge's reflection on gender equality differed from her mother's. But together with other women activists of different cohorts in China, she also perceived a close link between her notion of self, her sense of mission to further women's welfare, and her devotion to the nation. Similar to many women's movements in other Third World countries, the women's move-ment in China has a history grounded in the context of anti-imperialism and the formation of a strong nation. During the early twentieth century, the Qing dynasty's slow implosion and the imperialist West's invasion invoked the Chinese intellectuals, primarily male, to emancipate China from the Manchu rule, from Western imperialist occupation, and, more fundamentally, from the Confucian canon. Emancipating women from Confucian familial traditions, raising women's status, and strengthening the nation were considered inseparable projects. Initiated by male intel-lectuals, the anti-footbinding and the mass female literacy movements at the time aimed at advancing women for the construction of a modern nation. Acknowledging this tradition of a male-initiated women's move-ment and its relation to the formulation of national identities, many leading women activists in contemporary China do not consider their engagement with feminism necessarily in opposition to men, nor to the state.

> In China, it was male scholars and thinkers who had first advocated for
> women's liberation. This is a tradition. Today, women come to their self-
> awakening and can speak for themselves. But men's perspective and voice
> should still be taken seriously and listened to, even if it is a different voice.[44]

> I never think that women's interests are in absolute contradiction with that of
> the state's. On the contrary, I have always cherished the tradition in which our
> society has constantly backed women's liberation, and our state has made
> continuous effort to assist women.[45]

> In China, the relationship between women and men is more of cooperation.
> This is related to the path and the process of Chinese women's liberation ...
> Since the beginning of this century, the Chinese women's movement has never
> been an independent movement. It was either linked to the nationalistic

revolution, or to the socialist revolution. Men and women have worked hard together for women's liberation.[46]

The tradition of dedicating themselves to the welfare of the nation and the people is still pronounced among women activists in contemporary China. In the international activities preparing for the FWCW, they took pride in being Chinese women, and vowed to do something for the country.[47] They saw their future as connected with 'hundreds of millions of Chinese women' and felt it was up to them to make the country more prosperous.[48] In other words, Chinese women's sense of self and agency is very much intertwined with their commitment to China as a nation, and people, and particularly to Chinese women. This suggests that, in the context of feminist activism, these Chinese women activists' national identity is very much a part of their gender identity. Nevertheless, their engendered national identity does not imply an acquiescence to the official nationalist discourse. Li Xiaojiang refused to comply with the CCP state's agenda of glorifying its success in elevating Chinese women's status in the NGO Forum in the name of nationalism. She chose not to participate in the NGO Forum. Li stated,

> To have the image of the Chinese government tied so closely with an international conference relating to the fate of all women in the world is really disappointing. It has put the Chinese women in a very awkward position: Even at the NGO Forum, no individual can make a speech out of her own will or relate any of women's problems on behalf of them ... In a situation like this, being a Chinese woman means that I have no alternative but to keep silent when I have to make a choice between the State and Women, for to whatever extent women's right might have been stripped off at the Conference, outside the Conference, China is still marching on her arduous course towards democracy. What I can do is to expect the Chinese government to become more advanced and show more tolerance, so that women will be allowed to do something for themselves while the State continues to try all its efforts to help women, so then women will not only be asked to speak for the country, but also be given the right to speak for themselves; and so that women will not only be required to demonstrate their growth and achievement, but also be permitted to tell of their problems encountered in daily life.[49]

Li's difficult decision to be absent from and keep silent during the FWCW resulted from her negotiation between her agency as a woman and her simultaneous subject position as a Chinese citizen committed to the development of the nation. It marked a complex relationship between Chinese women and the state. Such intertwined and yet conflicting gender and national identities challenge the feminist individualist subject of much of liberal feminist theory. The experiences of these Chinese women activists suggest the necessity of conceptualising collective selves in the theorisation of agency and subjectivity. The collective selves embody a consciousness which grounds in multiple, often opposing, positions. Within the context of collective selves, women activists negotiate various positions and propositions, rather than taking a simple or single counter-stance. It is also a consciousness of acting collectively with moral conviction.[50]

Therefore, Chinese women's relation to the state is quite different from models developed by Western feminists who have fundamentally positioned women in opposition to the state. The Western models emphasise the state's domination over, and suppression of, women, in the capitalist system.[51] For women in socialist China, their relationship with the CCP state and China as a nation is not so straightforward. Rather than taking a confrontational stand, Chinese women's activism simultaneously draws upon the existing system and works on new initiatives. Recognition of this strategic difference and conceptual paradigm of Chinese women's activism is necessary to comprehend Chinese women's agency and subjectivity. The alternative forms of activism chosen by Chinese women also challenge the colonial authority of Western feminist/activist groups in global feminist activism.

Given the diverse historical development underlying women's construction of their subjectivities and agency, their conceptions of language and terms circulated in global feminist activism are also doomed to vary across cultures and nations. In international encounter, therefore, the first step is to bridge the language gap between the parties. This entails more than a straightforward word-to-word translation. Luo Xiaolu's story is very informative in this regard.

My trip to Northern Europe made me think over a number of issues. When I introduced myself in our first workshop, I said, 'I'm not a feminist [*Nüquan zhuyizhe*]'. Following our introduction, the moderator introduced the group as a 'feminist organisation'. So I felt sort of dumb … In the past, I had learned about feminists from some articles and thought they were against men. By the time we left Finland, the woman who coordinated our visit said at the farewell banquet, 'I would like to give you the title of Finnish honorary feminist. Even though you claim that you are not a feminist, I think you're indeed a feminist. Why? Because you have done so much for women'. I felt her definition is rather accurate … After I got this puzzle clarified, I realised that many aspects of women's issues transcend national boundaries and other differences. Women throughout the world face many common problems. However, we have little opportunity to communicate, especially between China and foreign countries. In China we talk about 'women-work' [*funü gongzuo*], while women elsewhere speak of the 'women's movement' or 'feminism'. This difference is caused by a lack of communication. So, I feel the first thing we need to do is communicate, among ourselves and with women abroad. Even though people may have different ways of doing and thinking things, or may even have different starting points, our goal and objectives are the same.[52]

Luo is not the only Chinese woman who is reluctant to call herself a feminist. And, this has to do with the terms feminist and feminism in the Chinese context. When the term 'feminism' was first introduced to China in the early twentieth century, it was used in connection with the suffrage movements in Europe and North America of the time. The Chinese equivalent, *nüquan zhuyi,* literally means the 'ism' of women's rights. The term 'feminist movement' has ever since been understood as a political movement that particularly strives for women's formal, legal rights. In the context of China's proletarian revolution, the terms 'feminism' [*nüquan zhuyi*] and 'feminist movement' (*nüquan zhuyi yundong*) have been associated with bourgeoisie class values and interests.[53] Although the terms 'feminist' and 'feminism' have taken on new meanings since the 1980s, many Chinese women scholars and activists still prefer to refer to themselves as being involved or interested in 'women-work' (*funü gongzuo*).

The Beijing conference drew attention to a critical but so far under-acknowledged and under-investigated issue: the existence of cultural and ideological barriers underlying language differences to cross-cultural communication among feminist activists from different countries. Such barriers are often mediated through different usage of terminology or abstracts. Not recognising these differences and barriers is particularly detrimental to non-Western women whose native language is usually not used in international events. Because they use non-mainstream terminology and languages, non-Western women are often not being heard and understood in international dialogue. Moreover, given the existing hierarchy in international politics, Western feminist/activist groups have much more power to impose their own categories and terminology upon their non-Western sisters. As Du Fangqing noted in the seminar on 'Chinese Women and Development',

> [Cultural and language barriers] are not only differences of terminology and concepts. What is important is also the operational bias guided by certain models. Some Western scholars often apply their presumed model framework in the study of Chinese women, which is often inapplicable or even flawed.[54]

In the process, these Western scholars either come to assume a position of speaking for, and about, their non-Western sisters, or they turn their non-Western sister into an 'Other' who is to be judged by Western norms and standards.

The debate over whether or not there are NGOs in China, and whether the All China Women's Federation (ACWF) can be considered as an NGO, is a typical example. Two positions have dominated the heated discussion of this: a unanimous, accusing 'No' from Western feminist/activist groups on the one side, and a defensive 'Yes' from the Chinese government on the other. Western feminist/activist groups base their conclusion on the

NGO model prevalent in the West, and on their assessment of the powers of the Communist-dominated Chinese state. According to them, the Chinese state possesses enormous power to limit the scope of NGO activities. Through restrictive registration procedures, penetrating controls, and arbitrary crackdowns, the CCP exercises complete control over the NGO sector in China. Therefore, as one statement put it, 'for an NGO to act effectively in safeguarding and promoting women's rights, it must be allowed to function independently of any government agenda', and 'the ACWF is not an NGO and don't let anyone tell you otherwise'.[55]

Many sources suggest that, at the beginning, this accusation caught the Chinese government completely by surprise.[56] The government really had no clues as to what the issue was about, and why there was a problem.[57] Later on, an official position was developed. In an interview, Kang Ling, vice chairwoman of the NGO Forum Committee, laid out the government's position:

> Many friends argue that NGOs should depend mainly on international force to achieve their goals, but I do not think so. What these organisations are fighting for is in the immediate and long-term interests of their country and people and, therefore, they should be close to the government instead of keeping far away, so that they can persuade and lobby for policies, and keep an eye on their implementation.[58]

The Chinese official went on to cite instances where the ACWF or other women's organisations had been successful in working within the state system.

A discussion of whether there are 'real' NGOs in China, and whether the ACWF is a 'real' NGO, is beyond the scope of this paper.[59] However, this debate is relevant to our quest for Chinese women's subjectivity and agency in feminist activism on three grounds. First, Western feminist/activist groups have employed a rather rigid ideological framework on which the concept of NGO is based and a set of Euro-American-centric criteria to evaluate what organisations can be classified as NGOs. Their approach implies that the only way women can promote and safeguard their interests is through NGOs that assume an oppositional position vis-à-vis the state. The CCP state, in contrast, upholds an entirely different model, a model that reflects its self-proclaimed commitment to women's liberation and reiterates its state-sponsored, mass-line politics without considering other alternatives. Rather than talking toward one another, the international community and the CCP state have both taken up positions that force them to talk against and across each other.

Secondly, in the process, the image of a suffocating, totalitarian social state is perpetuated. This is done jointly by the Communist state, Western feminist/activist groups, and the mass media. Adopting an antagonistic position, the CCP's defensive attack on so-called 'negative foreign influences' proves to be hasty and political. It counteracts its concerted effort to clear away the authoritarian image. This image, on the other hand, conveniently prevents Western feminist/activist groups from seriously considering possible flaws in their own position concerning the relationship between the state and NGOs. In effect, any reference to women's initiatives in conjunction with the CCP state is viewed with suspicion.

Thirdly, Chinese women's voices and experiences have been suppressed and marginalised. To illustrate this point, let us once again turn to their narratives.

In her essay, entitled 'How Do We Face the World? – Some Thoughts On Connecting the Tracks', Xie Lihua compares and contrasts the ACWF with NGOs she visited in Senegal. The differences in terms of size, structure, and financial resources are striking:

> In Senegal, and indeed in all of Africa, no country has a top-down women's federation like China's. Though their NGOs are as numerous as mushrooms after a spring rain, they remain very weak because of their loose organisation. FDEA, the organisation that received us, is one of the three largest NGOs in Senegal, yet it has only a dozen members. Therefore, in countries like these, women could not launch vigorous nation-wide activities such as 'Double Learning, Double Competing', 'Women Making Contributions' … Comparatively speaking, the advantages of the Women's Federation in China are obvious. First of all, the majority of our federation cadres need not worry about how to make a living; we have fixed salaries given by the government, and we can wholeheartedly throw ourselves into our work. The staff of NGOs abroad must first solve their own financial problems, before they can help other women. Furthermore, we have organisational networks at every level, but they have only separate project groups, which do not even have fixed places to work.[60]

Although the ACWF has some advantages, Xie turns her critical eye on its long-lasting weaknesses:

> Perhaps because of the difficulties they [the NGOs in Senegal] are facing, they show an indomitable vitality; and maybe because we have a well-organised system and network, we lack the sense of being our own masters, and usually are not active participants. We just wait for orders or arrangements from above.[61]

Such frailty, according to Liu Bohong, has to do with the historical roots of women's liberation in China. Employing a comparative framework, Liu observes:

> In my opinion, the Western women's movement has involved a subjective, self-initiated, and bottom-up process. It has been part of a larger social movement. For example, in the States, there were the civil rights movement, the student movement, and the women's movement in the sixties.

[Individuals] realised that, as subjective agents, they should liberate themselves in the course of social development. In our country, however, we have the Party leadership. It is the liberation of class and nation that has brought changes in, and protection of, women's status. The achievement and realisation of women's rights has actually taken place from the top down.[62]

A by-product of such a top-down approach to women's liberation is that although Chinese women are formally entitled to legal rights, in real life these rights are often compromised. Luo Ping refers to those formal, legal rights as 'principles' and 'unreal', and considers what women actually experience as 'life' and 'reality'. In her words:

On legislation and reality: women in our country have been protected by many legal codes and so enjoy legal equality with men. This is a rather historic achievement. In real life, unfortunately, many of the entitlements are either compromised or absent. In the West, as we witness in Northern Europe, although women don't have that many laws to protect them, they have a lot more rights than us In real life. This is why they do some things that we in China would never see or hear of. On principle and life: equality between men and women, the rights to vote and stand for election, non-discrimination against women in employment and promotion are all principles. Principles are written on paper, with no substance … Life is strange and complicated. It is full of lives with many twists and turns. People often develop their own strategies to fudge on regulations from above. Principles can guide life, but can also be put aside. They can glitter, they can also fade away and become mere fossils. Chinese women enjoy more rights in 'principles' than in their real lives. 'Principles' are unreal, but 'life' is real.[63]

No wonder many Chinese women did not think that the Law on the Protection of Women's Rights and Interests, promulgated in 1992, was necessary.

Many women never expected such a law. Nor have women realised that they need to refer to this legislation. It was like waking up one morning to find there was this Law on the Protection of Women's Rights and Interests. That's how I feel about it. I never felt I needed such a law. Nor did my friends. We never even thought about our 'needs'. As long as there is the Constitution, it's fine.[64]

A number of critical themes pertinent to Chinese women's subjectivity and agency emerge from their discussion on NGOs and the ACWF. First and foremost, Chinese women activists have definitely developed their own positions regarding women's activism in China, which differ from both that of the Western feminist/activist groups and that of the Chinese government. On the one hand, they recognise the advantages for a women's organisation such as the ACWF: extended national networks, sizeable staff, and secure financial resources. On the other hand, they clearly detect the embedded problems and disadvantages of such a national organisation.

Secondly, the comment on not needing more laws to protect Chinese women's rights and interests has multiple meanings. In principle, the statement suggests that these Chinese women activists have not challenged the legitimacy of the CCP's claim that it represents the interests of Chinese women. It accepts the CCP, and the policy of the ACWF which is primarily drawn from Marxist doctrine. In practice, however, these Chinese women argue that, in their everyday lives, legislation is necessary, but not sufficient, to ensure gender equality. The gap between the 'superficial rights' to which women are formally entitled and the unequal treatment women experience in 'reality' urges them to raise strong demands for changes in the way women-work is carried out by the ACWF and the Chinese government.

Thirdly, Chinese women activists' discussion on issues surrounding NGOs goes beyond the rigid framework and abstract categories that have entrapped many Western activist/feminist groups and the CCP state. By adopting a comparative framework, Chinese women activists ground their discussion in the everyday. Their analysis is strengthened by their · observation of women-work abroad and their activist involvement at home. As a result, their proposals for change and action reflect their subjective understanding, and draw upon the energy of a larger number of women's groups to rectify the weakness of China's existing system. The following excerpt is typical:

> The women's movement in China is at the stage of reflection and self-examination. It is time for it to enter a new stage. The international women's movement is developing rapidly, though with some new problems. In China, the women's movement has not made much progress, and women's understanding of their own liberation is rather narrow … In Latin America, there are numerous women's organisations that represent and provide services to women of different classes. They are the result of women's own consciousness and initiatives. The organisations inform and educate. In China, we don't have such organisations. Most people expect the government to solve women's problems. Since I visited Argentina, I not only think women should push the government for solutions. More important, we need to get organised to solve our own problems. We can start by making changes little by little, and family by family. The tiny drops will one day join together to become a flood of revolution that can change the way society thinks about women, and create a living space where men and women are equal and harmonious.[65]

Underlying such incremental, not-so-glamorous, everyday endeavours is these women activists' perception of feminist activism. Again, this perception is articulated in the context of what they witness abroad:

> At the Conference [in Manila], 'confronting the government', and 'fighting against men' can be heard everywhere. These feisty speeches won the

applause of many, but we weren't thrilled or uplifted. Quite the opposite. We felt suppressed and heavy-hearted. We constantly ponder one question: how should an NGO carry out its work and influence the government so that the latter can change from its opposing, un-supportive position to a support-ive position. Ultimately, this is a question of how to carry on the women's movement. As I reflect on the Conference, I think the [Western] women's movement should avoid three traps. First, the task of NGOs should be to influence the government, and to win over their support and protection – not to take an oppositional stand to fight against the government. Fighting against the government is not a good strategy. Otherwise, with the deepening of misunderstanding, NGOS would find they have less and less room for their work.[66]

Another woman commented:

I used to know very little about the international women's movement and foreign women's organisations. My Manila trip has not only made me under-stand better. It also allows me to compare [the situation in the Philippines] to the situation in China. In addition to participating in the formal meetings, Guo Jianmei and I met representatives of many women's legal organisations. We visited their offices and hot lines. The organisation members were all very warm and active. They had stable funding sources, so their work is well organised and of a high quality. However, China has just started this kind of work, so there is a huge difference. Moreover, the women in Manila were very gender conscious. They knew that their work was on behalf of women, and they drew a very sharp distinction between men and women. Some even said that they wanted to step on men. They saw men as their enemies. They said they wanted to struggle against the government for more power. These women wanted to struggle against the government for their rights. This is different from the women's movement in China. In China, the differences between men and women are not so great. I suggest that we unite with men to achieve progress for humanity. I think 'non-government' [*fei zhengfu*] does not mean 'against government' [*fan zhengfu*]. In order to have power, especially legal status, women must win the support of the government and change the government's concept of women, but not fight against it.[67]

These excerpts reveal vivid attributes of Chinese women's activism. They clearly illustrate that women activists in China, at least at this historical juncture, propose to take up a dual approach: they intend to renegotiate their relationship with the state on the one hand and organise their own action-oriented groups on the other. This double focus derives from an assessment of the strengths and weaknesses of the ACWF in China *and* NGOs abroad. In contrast to the Western, single-focus approach that advo-cates and insists upon the NGO's uncompromising opposition to the state, Chinese women activists see values of working with, and winning support from, the state. Although it will require more than good will to build partnerships with men in feminist activism, the presence of a conscious effort to renegotiate Chinese women's relationship with the status quo is unquestionable. In marked contrast to this lively dynamism, both the CCP state and many Western feminist/activist groups continue to hold fast to outdated positions. By stubbornly insisting that they alone speak for the Chinese woman, and by continuing to indulge in political rhetoric, they demonstrate that they have failed to appreciate the strength and character of Chinese women's activism.

Since 1975, the United Nation's World Conferences on Women have generated enormous energy from women's groups around the globe. Although the Conference has come to symbolise the highest form of global feminist activism, it has also been an arena where women's groups from the North and South are confronted by tensions between universalism and localism and between internationalism and nationalism. While women activists in China perceived the Conference of 1995 as a beginning to connect local initiatives with global feminist activism, heated exchanges between the host CCP state and outspoken Western feminist and human rights groups overshadowed their efforts.

Although recent criticism of the hegemonic authority First World feminists have claimed over their Third World sisters has created spaces for Chinese women scholars to articulate and present their own interpretation and experiences in Western gender discourse, in practice, the CCP state and Western feminist/activist groups continue to dominate the presentation and re-presentation of the Chinese woman. In the name of confronting an authoritarian, oppressive socialist state, some prominent Western feminist/ activist groups assume the authority to speak for and about the Chinese woman. The CCP state, in contrast, sanctions a glorified version of women's liberation, and hence perceives any discussion of women's problems in contemporary China as a betrayal of, or threat to, its rule. Chinese women's own voices, however, have been marginalised in the midst of all this talk about them.

In global feminism, genuine partnership between local and international feminist groups requires the involvement of local women to speak for themselves. By examining Chinese women activists' reflections and narratives, we show the historical development of Chinese women's activism. Chinese women's engagement with feminism is grounded in the context of anti-imperialism, nation-building, and a self-awakening of their gender identity. Their intersecting gender and national identities demand a conceptualisation of collective selves in the theorisation of agency and subjectivity. To recognise Chinese women's subjectivity and agency, we argue, one must realise that Chinese women's activism is a departure from the NGO model embedded in Western feminist activism. Instead of confronting the state, Chinese women activists take a dual approach. That is, they simultaneously draw upon the political and financial resources of the state/ ACWF, and work on new, local initiatives. Rather than fighting against men, Chinese women activists build on the tradition of the women's movement in China and talk about winning the support of, and working together with, men to transform the entire society. Although Chinese women activists share with their international counterparts the same dream of achieving gender equality, their approach and strategy are rather different. To judge Chinese women's activism with a single-focus approach would inevitably appropriate Chinese women activists' agency over, and subjective understanding of, their destiny. Thus, an openness to alternative visions and practices is the key to alleviating the conflict and tension between global and local feminist activism.

Feminists and activists in global activism must also begin to address the language barriers that are evident in current international feminist dialogue. It is essential not only to pay attention to spoken words that have different meanings, but, even more important, to recognise the cultural and ideological paradigms which underlie language differences.

Notes

The two authors have put an equal amount of thinking and work into this paper. Their names are arranged in alphabetical order. The authors thank the co-editor of *Gender & History*, Professor Mrinalini Sinha, and the two anonymous reviewers for their careful reading and helpful suggestions on the early version of this paper.

1. Originated in San Jose, US, Beijing95-L was launched on 22 January 1995 as a listserv discussion forum of the FWCW. Available Email: beijing95-l@netcom.com. Topics included pre-conference events, non-governmental organisation information, international formal and informal reports on the current status of women, job, volunteer, and organisational opportunities related to the conference, and post-regional and post-conference follow-ups. In the data that we collected from this list, there are lots of cross-postings distributed by Human Rights Network (HRNet). Available Email: hrichina@igc.org. HKnews, on the other hand, is launched by The Alliance of Hong Kong Chinese in the United States (AHKCUS) and incorporated in the state of Hawaii. Available Email: hknews@ahkcus.org. Its main objective is to promote democratic development and human rights in China and Hong Kong. It sends out Hong Kong and China news reported in published media through the Internet. The other major world wide web homepages on the Conference included those of the NGO Forum Daily available at http://www.womensnet.apc.org/beijing/forum, the National Organisation for Women (NOW) of the United States available at http://now.org/now/home.html, the UN Women's Conference available at http://www.iisd.ca/linkages/women.html, Virtual Sisterhood available at http://www.igc.apc.org/vsister/vsister.html, and WomensWeb Canada available at http://crc.web.apc.org/womensweb.

2. Wong Yuen Ling (ed.), *Nüxing de fanxiang: Yiqun ceng canyu jiuwu funü dahui guoji choubei huiyi de Zhongguo nüxing de xinsheng jieji* (*Reflections and Resonance: Stories of Chinese Women Involved in International Preparatory Activities for the 1995 NGO Forum on Women*) (The Ford Foundation, Beijing, 1995). The Ford Foundation put out both Chinese and translated English versions. All the excerpts we include in this paper are our own translations from the Chinese text. We decided not to use the English version because we find its translation problematic in a number of ways. For example,

the phrase *Nühaizi zhangda weileyao jiaren* is translated as 'When girls grow up, they have to get married' in the English version (Ge Youli, p. 5). This translation does not adequately preserve the original meanings of *weileyao* (for the sake of, for the purpose of) and *jiaren* (being married off). A better translation would be 'Girls grow up for the sake of being married off' (Ge Youli, p. 4). The English version, 'My grandma was forced to bind her feet when she was a girl, and yet my mother was lucky enough to go to university' (Yue Mei, p. 54), has added meanings which were not there in the original writing which simply states, 'My grandma had to bind her feet when she was a girl, and yet my mother was able to go to university' (Yue Mei, p. 41). More serious problems arise when the English translation misleads the reader. For example, reflecting on the character of women's activism in China, Xie states, 'We women haven't organised our-selves into various action-oriented groups. We just depend on the government. Because everything is handed down to us by the government, because government has planned everything for us, our consciousness and spirit of participation in self-liberation remain somewhat weak' (Xie Lihua, p. 219). We find the following English translation very misleading, 'We have no independent women's organisations. We depend totally on the government. Everything is decided and planned by the government. We have a poor spirit of participation in self-liberation' (Xie Lihua, p. 297). In order to allow the reader to check either the Chinese or English version, we include page numbers of both editions. The first number is from the Chinese edition, and is followed by the one in the English edition.

3. With domestic and international support, more than a hundred Chinese women participated in various international preparatory activities for the 1995 NGO Forum on Women. These activities included six regional meetings: Asia Pacific Symposium of NGOs on Women in Development, Latin American and Caribbean NGO Forum on Women, Vienna NGO Forum 1994, African NGO Forum on Women, NGO Regional Preparatory Committee for ESCWA, and the Nordic Forum; three NGO consultations parallel to preparatory meetings of the United Nation's Commission on the Status of Women; and the NGO Fora of the three United Nations World Conferences held during this period where Women's NGOs have honed their skills and priorities for Beijing; The NGO Forum of the Vienna Human Rights Conferences, and the NGO Forum of the Copenhagen Social Summit. Their international donors included the Ford Foundation which initiated the project in 1993, Canadian International Development Agency, Swedish International Development Agency, Danish International Development Agency, Global Fund for Women, International Women's Rights Action Watch, UNIFEM, and UNFPA. See Wong (ed.), *Reflections and Resonance*.

4. 'Women-work' refers to all kinds of service provision and activism in relation to women in China. For further discussion of 'women-work' in China in relation to feminism, see the quote on p. 483 of this paper and our subsequent discussion.

5. Since the early 1990s, a spontaneous wave of establishing women's groups has swept through China. In response to mounting problems women face in contemporary China, women scholars and former/retired Women's Federation cadres establish new organisations to provide services for women. These organisations are non-government-run and many receive funding from sources outside of China. The Jingling Family Center and the Women's Hotline in Beijing are the two most well known among these women's initiatives.

6. Du Fangqin (ed.), *Zhongguo funüyu fazhan – Diwei, jiankang, jiuye (Chinese Women and Development – Status, Health, Employment)* (Henan People's Publishers, Zhengzhou, 1993). Funded by the Ford Foundation, this seminar was jointly organised

by the Chinese Society for Women's Studies (CSWS) in the US and the Center for Women's Studies in Tianjin Normal University in the summer of 1993. Five members from the CSWS presented feminist perspectives on gender issues, and over twenty scholars in China delivered reports on their research projects on domestic women's problems. Over one hundred women nation-wide, from both academia and the Women's Federation, from all over China attended the seminar. The seminar was not particularly directed at the FWCW. But women researchers in China later regarded the Tianjing seminar as the beginning of the 'large-scale landing of Western feminism in China', cited in Wang Zheng, 'Maoism, Feminism, and the UN Conference on Women: Women's Studies Research in Contemporary China', *Journal of Women's History*, 8 (1997), p. 141. The application of Western feminist theories to the analysis of Chinese women's problems and the cultural and language barriers in cross-cultural dialogues were among the heated discussions in the seminar. It paved the way for the FWCW where women activists in China made their efforts to 'connect the tracks' with the international feminist communities in its largest scale.

7. On 11 October 1995, Christina Gilmartin delivered the statement on Li Xiaojiang's behalf, '*Wo weishenmo jujue canjia 95 shijie funü dahui NGO luntan*' (Why I Refused to Participate in the NGO Forum at the 95 Fourth World Conference on Women – Women, State, and Individual), at the J. K. Fairbank Center for East Asian Research, Harvard University.

8. See Elizabeth Croll, *Women in Rural Development: The People's Republic of China* (ILO, Geneva, 1979); Delia Davin, *Woman-Work: Women and the Party in Revolutionary China* (Clarendon Press, Oxford, 1976); Marilyn B. Young, (ed.), *Women in China: Studies in Social Change and Feminism* (University of Michigan, Ann Arbor, 1973).

9. See Phyllis Andors, *The Unfinished Liberation of Chinese Women: 1949–1980* (Indiana University Press, Bloomington, 1983); Kay Ann Johnson, *Women, the Family and Peasant Revolution in China* (The University of Chicago Press, Chicago, 1903), Judith Stacey, *Patriarchy and Socialist Revolution in China* (University of California Press, Berkeley, 1983); Margery Wolf, *Revolution Postponed: Women in Contemporary China* (Stanford University Press, Stanford, 1985).

10. Tani E. Barlow, 'Politics and Protocols of Funü: (Un)Making National Woman', in *Engendering China: Women, Culture, and the State*, ed. Christina. K. Gilmartin et al. (Harvard University Press, Cambridge, 1994), pp. 339–59.

11. Two recent articles on women's involvement, positions, and resistance to China's Birth Planning Policy are exemplary in this regard. See Tyrene White, 'The Origins of China's Birth Planning Policy', in *Engendering China*, ed. Gilmartin et al., pp. 250–78; Yuk-Lin Renita Wong, 'Dispersing the "Public" and the "Private": Gender and the State in the Birth Planning Policy of China', *Gender and Society*, 11 (1997), pp. 509–25.

12. See Chandra Mohanty, 'Under Western Eyes: Feminist Scholarship and Colonial Discourses', in *Third World Women and the Politics of Feminism*, ed. Chandra Mohanty et al. (Indiana University Press, Bloomington, 1991), pp. 51–80; Aihwa Ong, 'Colonialism and Modernity: Feminist Re-presentations of Women in Non-Western Societies', in *Theorizing Feminism: Parallel Trends in the Humanities and Social Sciences*, ed. Anne C. Herrmann et al. (Westview Press, Boulder, 1994), pp. 372–81; Gayatri Chakravorty Spivak, *The Other Worlds: Essays in Cultural Politics* (Methuen, New York, 1987).

13. See Richard W. Guisso and Stanley Johannesen (eds), *Women in China: Current Directions in Historical Scholarship* (Philo Press, Youngstown, NY, 1981); Gail Hershatter, 'Modernizing Sex, Sexing Modernity: Prostitution in Early Twentieth-Century

Shanghai', in *Engendering China*, ed. Gilmartin et al., pp. 147–74; Emily Honig and Gail Hershatter (eds), *Personal Voices: Chinese Women in the 1980s* (Stanford University Press, Stanford, 1988); Susan Mann, 'Learned Women in the Eighteenth Century', in *Engendering China*, ed. Gilmartin et al., pp. 27–46.

14. Gilmartin et al. (eds), *Engendering China*.

15. Lisa Rofel, 'Liberation Nostalgia and a Yearning for Modernity', in *Engendering China*, ed. Gilmartin et al., pp. 240. On Chinese women's activism, three recent publications are especially informative: Wang Zheng, 'A Historic Turning Point for the Women's Movement in China, *Signs*, 22 (1996), pp. 192–9; Wang Zheng, 'Maoism, Feminism, and the UN Conference on Women: Women's Studies Research in Contemporary China', *Journal of Women's History*, 8 (1997), pp. 126–52; Zhang Naihua and Xu Wu, 'Discovering the Positive Within the Negative: The Women's Movement in a Changing China', in *The Challenge of Local Feminisms: Women's Movements in Global Perspective*, ed. Amrita Basu (Westview Press, Boulder, 1995), pp. 25–57.

16. Mohanty identifies two steps in examining the 'intellectual and political construction of third world feminisms'. The first is to deconstruct and dismantle the hegemonic position of Western feminisms in the presentation and re-presentation of the Third World women. This is followed by a construction of 'autonomous, geographically, historically, and culturally grounded feminist concerns and strategies'. See Mohanty, 'Under Western Eyes', p. 52. In the paper, nevertheless, Mohanty only focuses on the first step.

17. Sharon K. Hom and Xin Chunying, *English–Chinese Lexicon of Women and Law* (UNESCO and CTPC, Paris and Beijing, 1995), p. 18.

18. Daniel J. Shepard, 'Mongella Urges Focus on Beijing', *Beijing95-L* (Online), 13 August 1995. The message was distributed by HRNet to Beijing95-L. Shepard was a reporter of the Earth Times News Service.

19. The statement '36,000 feminists meet 1 billion communists' was made by Helen Ross, 'China Survival Kits' (Online), available: http://pages.prodigy.com/NY/gonzo/beijing.html. It was cross-referenced in the world wide web homepage of UN Women's Conference. At a hearing debating whether or not the US should participate in the FWCW, Chris Smith, the US House representative and chairman of the International Relations Committee's Panel on International Operations and Human Rights, stated that 'going to Beijing in 1995 is analogous to going to Hitler's Germany in 1939 for a human rights conference'. (No author), 'Panel Debates China Conference', *HKnews* (Online), 18 July 95.

20. *The White Paper: The Situation of Chinese Women* (Information Office of the State Council of the People's Republic of China, Beijing, 1994), p. i.

21. *The White Paper*, pp. ii–iii.

22. *The White Paper*, p. iii.

23. There is a clear discrepancy between the state's rhetoric and practices. Ample examples illustrate that government officials turn a blind eye when discriminatory practices occur. A report prepared by Human Rights in China (HRC), entitled *Caught between Tradition and the State: Violations of the Human Rights of Chinese Women* (Human Rights in China, New York, 1995), documents the incidents at great length and discusses how they have compromised women's rights.

24. Zhang Kai, 'An Alternative View of the Status of Women in China Today', *Beijing95-L* (Online), 28 August 1995. The article was first published in a magazine titled *October Review*, on 30 July 1995, and re-posted in Beijing95-L.

25. Amnesty International, *Women in China: Imprisoned and Abused for Dissent* (Amnesty International, London, 1995), p. 1.

26. Ong, 'Colonialism and Modernity', p. 372.

27. Guo Jianmei, '*Xiantan shuoshao zhiyi: Zhongwai funü gongzuo luetan*' (Dialogue One: Chatting on Women-Work in China and Abroad), in *Reflections and Resonance*, ed. Wong, p. 216 / p. 293; Lou Xiaolu, 'Dialogue One', p. 222 / p. 301; Liu Bohong, 'Dialogue One', p. 224 / p. 303.

28. Deng Chunli, 'Dialogue One', pp. 217–18 / p. 295–6.

29. Xie Lihua, '*Wuomen ruhe mianxiang shijie? Guanyu "Jie Gui" de duanxiang*' (How Do We Face the World? – Some Thoughts On Connecting the Tracks), in *Reflections and Resonance*, ed. Wong, pp. 50–51 / p. 68.

30. Xie Lihua, 'How Do We Face the World?', p. 51 / p. 68.

31. Xie Lihua, 'How Do We Face the World?', p. 51 / p. 68.

32. Xie Lihua, 'How Do We Face the World?', p. 52 / p. 69.

33. Xie Lihua, 'How Do We Face the World?', p. 52 / p. 69.

34. Xie Lihua, 'How Do We Face the World?', p. 53 / p. 70.

35. Xie Lihua, 'How Do We Face the World?', p. 53 / p. 70.

36. The new development is often referred to as the women's studies movement because it involves setting up women's studies programmes in the universities. For an examination of the movement and its implication, see Wang, 'Maoism, Feminism, and the UN Conference on Women'; Zhang and Xu, 'Discovering the Positive Within the Negative'; Ping-Chun Hsiung, 'The Women's Studies Movement in China in the 1980s and 1990s', paper presented at the Conference on Education and Society in Twentieth Century China, 26–8 September 1997, organised by Ontario Institute for Studies in Education of the University of Toronto and the Joint Centre for Asia Pacific Studies, York University and University of Toronto. Hsiung's analysis pays specific attention to the interplay of personal and institutional aspects of the movement.

37. Xie, 'Dialogue One', p. 214 / pp. 291–2.

38. Liu, 'Dialogue One', p. 224 / p. 303.

39. Liu, 'Dialogue One', p. 224 / pp. 303–4.

40. Lisa Rofel, 'Liberation Nostalgia and a Yearning for Modernity', in *Engendering China*, ed. Gilmartin et al., pp. 226–49.

41. See Johnson, *Women, the Family and Peasant Revolution in China*; Stacey, *Socialist Patriarchy and Revolution in China*; Wolf, *Revolution Postponed*.

42. Ge, 'Girls Grow up for the Sake of Being Married Off', p. 5 / p. 7.

43. Ge, 'Girls Grow up for the Sake of Being Married Off', p. 7 / p. 10.

44. Du Fangqin, '*Zai zhongxifang jiaoliuzhong tuozhan Zhongguo funü yanjiude xinshiye yu xinfangfa*' (The New Perspectives and Methods of Developing Chinese Women's Studies in the East–West Exchange), in *Chinese Women and Development*, ed. Du Fangqin, p. 10.

45. Li, 'Why I Refused to Participate in the NGO Forum at the 95 Fourth World Conference on Women'.

46. Li Xiaojian, *Guanyu nürende dawen* (*Questions and Answers About Women*) (Jiangsu People's Publishers, Nanging, 1997), p. 57. The quote comes from a speech which Li delivered in Germany in early 1995, which was reprinted in *Questions and Answers About Women*.

47. Ge, 'Girls Grow up for the Sake of Being Married Off'; Yue, '*Huidao zizhiren zhongjianlai: Gei huaren funü yanjiu xuehui pengyoumende xin*' (Coming Back to My Own People: A Letter to My Friends in the Chinese Society for Women's Studies), in *Reflections and Resonance*, ed. Wong, pp. 41–5 / pp. 54–60.

48. Yue, 'Coming Back to My Own People', p. 45 / p. 60.

49. Li, 'Why I Refused to Participate in the NGO Forum at the 95 Fourth World Conference on Women'.

50. Chandra Mohanty, 'Cartographies of Struggle: Third World Women and the Politics of Feminism', in *Third World Women and the Politics of Feminism*, ed. Mohanty et al., pp. 1–50.

51. Catherine A. MacKinnon, 'Feminism, Marxism, Method, and the State, An Agenda for Theory', *Signs*, 7 (1982), pp. 515–44.

52. Luo, 'Dialogue One', pp. 222–4 / pp. 301–2.

53. Since the early 1980s, Chinese women scholars have come to learn that feminism entails more than a demand for women's legal rights. The term is now translated as *nüxing zhuyi*, the 'ism' of female sex. This new translation's emphasis on unique female characteristics reflects Chinese women's recent search for gender identity. Thus, the change from *nüquan zhuyi* to *nüxing zhuyi* represents a shift in Chinese women's struggles in the twentieth century. See Sharon K. Hom and Xin Chunying (eds), *English–Chinese Lexicon of Women and Law*, pp. 128–31.

54. Du, 'The New Perspectives and Methods of Developing Chinese Women's Studies in the East–West Exchange', in *Chinese Women and Development*, ed. Du Fangqin, p. 8.

55. Kris Torgeson, 'Speaking for Chinese Women: Freedom of Association and Preparations for the 1995 World Conference on Women', *Human Rights Network – HRNet* (Online), available Email: hrichina@igc.org (3 September 1995). The article was first published in the journal of Human Rights in China (HRC), *China Rights Forum*, Winter (1994).

56. Wang, 'A Historical Turning Point for the Women's Movement in China'; Wang, 'Maoism, Feminism, and the UN Conference on Women'.

57. At the preparatory conference in Manila, 1993, the Chinese delegation was challenged because it included members of the ACWF, which was not considered as an NGO. This incident was said to bring the NGO issue to the Chinese authorities' attention for the first time (personal communication).

58. Jiang Wandi, 'The Special Way of Chinese NGOs' (Online), available: http://www.womensnet.apc.org/beijing/forum (2 September 1995). It is the world wide web homepage of the NGO Forum Daily.

59. As they examine the relationship between the state and society and the possible transformation of the state's hegemonic control, some analysts maintain that the CCP state is not as omnipresent and suffocating as many others have claimed. Although the communist state possesses oppressive, iron-fisted power to strike down any overt challenges, its giant bureaucratic system is fragmented and ineffective in most of its routine operations. Such a system therefore leaves enough room for individual, clandestine negotiation and manipulation. For further discussion, see X. L. Ding, 'Institutional Amphibiousness and the Transition from Communism: The Case of China', *British Journal of Political Science*, 24 (1994), pp. 293–318; Yia-Ling Liu, 'Reform from Below: The Private Economy and Local Politics in the Rural Industrialization of Wenzhou', *China Quarterly*, 130 (1992), pp. 293–322; Vivienne Shue, *The Reach of the State: Sketches of the Chinese Body Politic* (Stanford University Press, Stanford, 1988). Specifically, two recent papers examine the relationship between the ACWF and women's new initiatives in the past years. Hsiung focuses on how the women's studies programme in universities draws upon the ACWF's political resources, while Milwertz's case study shows the linkage between the ACWF and *Dagongmei zhi jia* (Migrant Girls Club), a new organisation established in 1996 to provide services to migrant girls in

Beijing. See Hsiung, 'The Women's Studies Movement in China in the 1980s and 1990s'; and C. Milwertz, 'Organizing Rural Women Migrants in Beijing', paper presented at the Oxford Women's Studies Network Conference, 20 September 1997.

60. Xie, 'How Do We Face the World?', pp. 53–4 / pp. 71–2.

61. Xie, 'How Do We Face the World?', p. 51 / p. 72.

62. Liu, 'Dialogue One', p. 219 / p. 297.

63. Luo Ping, 'Reflections on My Impressions of Northern Europe', in *Reflections and Resonance*, ed. Wong, p. 150 / pp. 205–6.

64. Guo, 'Dialogue One', p. 219 / p. 297.

65. Le Ping, 'Thoughts on the New Era', in *Reflections and Resonance*, ed. Wong, pp. 193–4 / pp. 262–4.

66. Guo Jianmei, '*Nanwangde Manila huiyi*' (An Unforgettable Preparatory Conference in Manila), in *Reflections and Resonance*, ed. Wong, p. 157 / p. 215.

67. Ma Yinan, 'Dialogue One', in *Reflections and Resonance*, ed. Wong, p. 218 / p. 296.

Unifying Women: Feminist Pasts and Presents in Yemen

MARGOT BADRAN

In campaigns to achieve national sovereignty and to implant new state systems women have participated as active agents, promoting gender egalitarian notions of citizenship.[1] States themselves have both mobilised women to serve their own internal political agendas and used women to signal to the outside world an egalitarian and democratic construction of citizenship they do not necessarily deliver.[2] There is a distinct tension between states' needs to articulate the equality that is fundamental to democracy and (masculinist) states' intentions to reproduce gender inequalities. This tension constitutes a potent site for feminist exploitation.

The literature on women's activisms and on gender and the state in Middle Eastern Muslim societies, produced in the 1980s and 1990s, has brought into view complicated politics and projects. In her introduction to *Women, Islam, and the State,* Deniz Kandiyoti writes: 'The ways women are represented in political discourse ... and the social movements through which they are able to articulate their gender interests are intimately linked to state-building processes and are responsive to their transformations'.[3] Marnia Lazreg, Sondra Hale, Parvin Paidar, and I show ways women both came forth as active participants in national liberation and revolutionary movements and were used by states for their own purposes in analyses of gender politics in Algeria, Sudan, Iran, and Egypt.[4] The equality of citizens was promoted when women's active support was needed, such as in campaigns for national independence, or in oppositional movements aimed at radical state transformation. When new state power was sufficiently secured the avowed equality of citizens was replaced by expressions of gender inequality. Shifts to gender inegalitarian discourse occurred in early postcolonial contexts,[5] such as liberal nationalist Egypt and socialist Algeria; at moments of the ascendancy of political Islam to state power, such as Iran and Sudan; and at a time of recuperation of lost state sovereignty as in Kuwait.[6]

Gendered citizen inequalities around the globe exhibit certain basic historical patterns, albeit in highly different contexts. These have included differential access to political rights[7] and discriminatory laws regarding such matters as marriage, divorce, child custody, and property rights – called personal status laws in Muslim societies. Modern states have often been quicker to grant equal political rights to women than to institute gender egalitarian personal status laws.[8] Typically, modern nation-states have accorded high visibility to gender equal political rights as indices of democracy. However, they have been more quiet about the few numbers of women elected to legislative bodies. States have also tended to be silent about their gender discrimination in laws regulating rights in the family. Moreover, personal status rights are often not conceptualised as citizens' rights.

Activist women's discourses and politics of citizenship in the West and the Middle East have varied in significant ways. Typically, in Western countries, women's movements to gain rights to vote and to be elected have been campaigns directed exclusively at obtaining female suffrage. Western suffragists developed discourses of citizenship and equal gender rights around the trope of political rights. In Western countries women have organised separate campaigns to reform laws regulating family relations and property rights. In Middle Eastern countries women's movements, first appearing at moments of national liberation and new state formation, have articulated a discourse of political rights and personal status rights within a unitary framework of citizens' rights. For example, Egyptian feminists in the early 1920s[9] and feminists from countries of the Arab East in the mid 1940s simultaneously demanded equal political rights and more egalitarian personal status rights (they accepted a gender complementarian model rather than a model calling for full equality).[10] In the 1990s Palestinian feminists are participating in the building of a new state, calling for gender egalitarian citizens' rights.[11]

Although Arab feminists in post-colonial societies articulated a comprehensive gender egalitarian construction of modern citizenship, they have faced fundamental difficulties which have yet to be resolved. In most post-colonial countries of the Middle East, secular law (based mainly on the French model) governs the 'public sphere' while religious law is left to regulate matters of personal status construed to belong to the 'private sphere'. In this way 'the citizen' is constituted as a 'public citizen' and member of the secular state and the equality central to democracy is confined to the (public) citizen. Individuals are constituted as members of a religion in the private sphere to be governed by personal status codes constructed out of readings of Islam (or Christianity). Male religious specialists entrusted with the interpretive task have conducted patriarchal readings of Islam which have formed the bases for gender inegalitarian personal status laws. This has created an awkward dichotomy in nationals who are constituted as equal (public) citizens but unequal (private) members of religions. Arab feminists Nawal El Saadawi and Fatima Mernissi have decried the particular oppressiveness of this split for women.[12]

Striking exceptions among Middle Eastern countries where the notion of gender egalitarian citizenship was expressed across public/private divisions were states which opted for fully secular laws. These states, from above, enacted remarkably (if imperfect) gender egalitarian personal status codes through which they intended to signal their political projects of secular modernity. These states included Turkey (1926) and the People's Democratic Republic of South Yemen (1974). Although the specifics of national experience varied, these secular codes had differential consequences across classes and regions within these countries. With the discourse for gender equality in personal status matters located strictly within a secular modernist context there was no space for a religious modernity. In the 1980s and 1990s, Islamists, speaking the language of ordinary people, have attacked secular modernity.[13] During this same period, feminist activists and scholars in the Middle East have assailed the limits of 'state feminism' and exposed its patriarchal dimensions.[14] ('State feminisms' have been discredited elsewhere as well following the collapse of communist and socialist regimes.)[15]

At the end of this century, with movements of political Islam over more than two decades and with the continuous spread of Islamism, new discourses of citizenship and of modernity are being more widely defined within a religious framework. Post-colonial secular states and secular political parties understand the political imperative to rethink Islam; they are aware that Islam is the major political and cultural idiom of the popular classes. The split between a 'secular public sphere' and a 'religious private sphere' (never as sharp as alleged but nevertheless vexing) is collapsing. In the 1990s, women from within Islam and Islamist movements in far-flung places around the globe – from Malaysia, to South Africa, to Iran, to the United States – have begun to articulate a holistic gender egalitarian construction of citizenship within the framework of an Islamic modernity.[16] I have argued elsewhere, along with Ziba Mir-Hosseini, Afsaneh Najmabadi and others, that this 'Islamic feminism' constitutes the new radical feminism within the Muslim world.[17]

The Republic of Yemen (ROY), which is neither a post-colonial secular state nor an Islamic republic, offers a different political and cultural space for feminist expression. In the new unified Yemen, the constitution and all laws – civil, personal status, commercial, and criminal, are based on the *shari`ah* (Islamic law) and consequently all the courts are shari`ah courts. There is no secular/religious dichotomy and no related public/private distinction. This, of necessity changes the nature of the gender debates. Yemeni women in their gender activism are not bogged down in public/private and religious/secular debates (as are women from post-colonial Muslim societies); rather, as Yemenis, they articulate their feminism from the location of 'integrated space'. Yemeni women do not have to justify their feminism as culturally authentic, as most women in post-colonial societies feel compelled to do. Positioned within a (national) religious culture but not from within a (national) Islamic republic, Yemeni women activists, and others, take 'Islamic embeddedness' for granted. Yemeni 'feminists' are not engaged in re/interpretation of Islamic religious texts, as, for example, Iranian 'feminists'. Yemeni women as 'feminists' are pointing to contradictions in men's discourse and practice of citizenship – within a culture of religious modernity – and exposing their patriarchal politics.

In 1990, the Republic of Yemen was forged out of the former Yemen Arab Republic (YAR, or North Yemen) and the People's Democratic Republic of Yemen (PDRY, or South Yemen). The amalgamation of the nationalist republican regime of the north and the socialist regime of the south signals for many the supremacy of the former over the latter. In the project of fashioning unity the trope of equality – of all citizens under the law – permeates the new discourse. Taking a gendered look at the project and process of unification, this paper suggests that women both act as its primary agents and reflect its deepest inequities. While they have multiple identities, affiliations, and allegiances which might divide them, women are united by gender – by experiences of gender – in ways men are not. For women gender is not merely a card in the game of political expediency in which the state and political parties engage.

Women behaving as feminists (without labels) are exposing and contesting re/assertions of patriarchal excesses that threaten national unity and the equality of citizens fundamental to the self-declared democratic project. Equality, seen through the prism of gender, is most striking in the arena of the constitutional affirmation of formal political rights. Gender inequality is most apparent in the Personal Status Code which preserves masculinist hegemony.[18] I argue that Yemeni women in functioning as feminists are at the forefront of the struggle to unify the new republic. I do not suggest, however, that women do not have differences, for they do. Rather I claim that women, through their gendered experiences, share things they identify with, which furnishes them with a unity upon which to build. To demonstrate this I look at two signal events in the recent history of gender and nation: the parliamentary elections of 1997 and the simultaneous attempt to impose a revised personal status law. In the first instance, women mobilised themselves to exercise their political rights and were also mobilised by the state and male-dominated political parties. (However, men were more sanguine about women as voters than as candidates.) In the second, women mobilised themselves while most men took cover. An examination of these two events reveals the split masculinist agenda in the construction of the new state and how the equality declared to be at the core of this project is subverted. At the same time, it illuminates the dynamics of Yemeni women's feminism.

Yemeni women today are heirs to two separate feminist pasts. The Yemen Arab Republic in the north was created in 1962, ending the Zaidi Imamate which had been established in 1918 following the demise of Ottoman rule (initiated in 1872). Influences of Nasirite Egypt which had supported the republicans in the revolution against the Imamate were discernible in the construction of the new nationalist state. In the south, the People's Democratic Republic of Yemen was established in 1967 following an anti-colonial struggle against a long-standing British occupation. The Aden Colony and Protectorate, which had come under the control of the British Colonial Office in 1839, experienced more direct colonial rule from 1937 to 1967.

While the story of women's nationalist activism to drive the British out of the south is still to be written, the pattern of intersecting nationalist and feminist awareness and activism seems to echo that of women in Egypt at the beginning of the century and in Sudan at mid century.[19] With the end of British colonialism and the establishment of the People's Democratic Republic of Yemen in 1967, the new socialist state embarked on the most progressive social programme in the entire Arab world. The PDRY Constitution of 1978 made it a state responsibility to deliver rights to women within a framework of equality. Article 36 read: 'The State shall ensure equal rights for men and women in all fields of life, the political, the economical and social, and shall provide the necessary conditions for the realization of that equality'. The Family Law promulgated in 1974, was legendary in the Arab and Muslim world, rivalling the Turkish Civil Code of 1926 and the Tunisian Personal Status Code of 1956 as an egalitarian instrument.[20]

However, the gender equality that the Family Law confirmed was diminished by a provision in the constitution indicating that the state upheld the conventional ideology of women's work in the home. It was not radical enough to declare that men likewise have responsibilities for work in the home. The constitution read: 'The State shall also work for the creation of the circumstances that will enable the woman to combine participation in the productive and social work and her role within the family sphere'. This resembled the Egyptian Constitution promulgated in 1971 at the beginning of the Sadat era (in the turn from Arab socialism to open-door capitalism), specifying that the woman's public roles and responsibilities had to be co-ordinated with her family roles. This, as Egyptian feminists had been quick to protest, constituted a shift away from the more gender egalitarian Nasirite Constitution of 1963.[21]

In socialist Yemen there was no room for competing ideologies or for independent political parties. The General Union of Yemeni Women, which was formed in 1968 under the aegis of the state, became an instrument of 'state feminism'.[22] The Union organised literacy classes and provided instruction in practical skills including health and child care, sewing, and typing. Meanwhile, through its government agencies, the socialist state provided new educational and work opportunities for women. They were offered jobs in the government bureaucracy, mainly clustering in the lower levels, where they were employed in clerical positions. However, a small cadre of professional women was also formed. The most notable departure from convention occurred when women were able to occupy the post of judge, something still beyond the reach of women in most Arab countries.[23]

Religion in the PDRY was not abolished. Article 47 declared Islam the state religion. However, religion was made a private matter. During the period of Arab socialism in Egypt, Islam was likewise declared the state religion. There is a distinct difference between religion furnishing a dominant political idiom and religion operating as a matter of individual belief and moral guidance. There is no necessary connection between socialism and aetheism, as anti-progressives would later allege when the political framework of the state shifted with the establishment of the unified state in 1990.[24]

In the north, the building of a new state and society immediately following the establishment of the YAR in 1962 was impeded by the fighting that persisted for most of the decade between republicans (backed by Nasir's Egypt) and the royalists (backed by neighbouring Saudi Arabia). In 1970 the new constitution of the YAR declared the equality of rights and duties of all citizens. The state exhibited certain Nasirist influences, especially during the presidency of Ibrahim al-Hamdi (from 1974 to 1977, when he was assassinated). Centrifugal forces, especially the power of the tribes, impeded the creation of a strong and progressive state.[25] The Family Law issued in 1978, which preserved patriarchal privileges,[26] bore resemblance to the conservative Egyptian Personal Status Code – an artefact inherited and preserved by Nasir's socialist state – that Egyptian feminists had been trying to reform for half a century.[27]

Although the principle of equality was enshrined in the constitution, the state never made gender equality part of a vocal discourse. Women, however, staked out new lives for themselves with quiet assistance from the state, which in certain ways smoothed their entry into public life. In the 1960s (before the promulgation of the constitution) and, especially, the 1970s, they began to pioneer in obtaining primary and secondary school education. Some continued their higher education at Sana`a University (established in 1970) or abroad, especially in Egypt. They also broke ground taking up jobs teaching and radio broadcasting (children's and family programmes) and later in television announcing.[28] In 1965 women established the Yemeni Women's Association (YWA) with branches in different parts of the country. The YWA had a social programme similar to that of the Women's Union in the south, providing instruction in literacy, health, child care, and practical skills. The YWA branches offered sites for women to gather outside the house and also helped in the building of a national women's network.

Yemeni women's separate feminist pasts have left a dual legacy. Northern women acquired a set of lessons about masculinist culture and power. They had to enact a piecemeal feminism, pioneering incrementally to stake out new roles and a claim on public space. Women from the north received limited help from a state, which was unable and unwilling to play a prominent role in their support. The state, at the same time, accorded women as feminist activists (in function but not in name) room to manoeuvre. Northern activist women, taking nothing for granted, acquired political acumen that has stood them in good stead. They had few illusions about the power or endurance of patriarchal relations and beliefs. These northern women operated largely with their own vision of how they wished to constitute their lives in a new society they were helping to shape.

Women of the south, as beneficiaries of gender gains within the project of the socialist state, were stranded with its decline. The 'state feminism' of the PDRY did not penetrate very deep into the patriarchal bedrock, nor very far from Aden into the hinterland. In the mid 1980s, at the time of the factional strife in the PDRY, signs of incipient conservatism began to appear in Aden as women's dress grew more modest.[29] The 1980s was also a time when university enrolments of women increased dramatically.[30] Women in the south who had benefited from the opportunities and protections of the socialist state seemed to believe their gains would never be rescinded. They behaved as feminists, if by that is meant shaping lives of their choice by accessing the new options offered them. But, they did not embrace a feminist ideology or identity as this was pre-empted by the state. When the socialist regime collapsed, the fragile gains of 'state feminism' went with it.[31] Women in the south, who had not honed feminist skills, nor refined a feminist sensibility and politics to draw upon, were bereft when the umbrella of state protection closed. Some women survived, but many of the older generation fell by the wayside. It would be the task of the younger generation, those most recently equipped with the educational opportunities the state had offered, to forge a feminist future.

Northern women had acquired an acute gender consciousness and developed practical feminist skills, through their experience in piecemeal pioneering, but they had no legitimate political space. Southern women had been able to exploit the educational and professional benefits conferred under 'state feminism', but they did not have the independent ideological space in which to develop a feminism of their own.[32]

The two Yemens were united in 1990 to form the Republic of Yemen, which constituted the realisation of long-held vision and was the result of a fraught political process.[33] The constitution of the new republic, approved by referendum in 1991, provided for a parliamentary democracy. It explicitly stipulated that all citizens had 'equal political, economic, social, and cultural opportunities'.[34] The Electoral Law of 1992 declared both men and women eligible to vote from the age of eighteen and to run for parliament at thirty-five.

Islam was declared the religion of the state, as it had been in both the YAR and the PDRY. Now, however, the shari`ah was affirmed as 'the main source of legislation'.[35] (Islah tried without success to boycott the 1991 constitutional referendum, insisting that the shari`ah be 'the only' source of legislation.)[36] The constitution also made explicit that the equality of women and men must be understood within the context of the shari`ah.[37] It has already been noted that in Yemen all laws – civil law, personal status law, commercial law, and criminal law are cast within the framework of the shari`ah and that all courts are shari`ah courts. This is unlike other constitutional states (excepting the Islamic republics of Iran and Sudan) which declare Islam to be an important or sole source of legislation. Egypt, for example, where the constitution affirms Islam to be 'the' source of legislation, retains a complicated secular and legal system. Shari`ah courts handle only personal status cases; national (or secular courts) handle all other cases. I would like to stress again that in the Republic of Yemen there is no debate about secular versus religious law, and therefore no dichotomisation of a 'secular public sphere' and a 'religious private sphere'. Gender issues are debated within a holistic Islamic framework.

During the year of the unification a plethora of political parties surfaced.[38] The major parties included the General People's Congress (GPC, founded by President Ali Abdullah Salih in the 1980s); the Yemen Socialist Party (YSP) a carry-over from the former PDRY; and the Yemen Islah (Reform) Party (YIP), an Islamist grouping.[39] Each of these parties formed women's divisions, but the highest decision-making levels were retained by the male hierarchy. The Yemeni Women's Organization (YWO) was formed out of the old Yemeni Women's Association in the north (which had a feminist leadership in Sana`a in the 1970s but was taken over by Islamist women in the 1980s) and the Women's Union of the former PDRY. The new Women's Union has continued to function in the north at the local level where the branches have sustained their social projects.[40] In the south, the leadership of the old PDRY Women's Union in Aden, which has been in disarray, exacerbated by the Civil War of 1994, is trying to regroup.[41] The YWO, however, has been all but moribund at the national level. Lack of state support of this quasi-governmental organisation and an old-guard leadership with split residual loyalties have contributed to this.[42] The National Women's Committee (NWC), formed in 1996 under a decree from the prime minister, now constitutes the paramount quasi-governmental women's organisation at the national level.[43]

Parliamentary committees were created to formulate laws for the unified state. The notion of equality of citizens, enshrined in the constitution and upheld by the political parties, was to be the guiding principle. Islah, for example, in its 'Political Action Programme' issued in 1997, states: 'The essence of equality is the equality under the law between members of society', and goes on to pledge, 'The YIP shall work effortlessly [sic] to strengthen the principle of equality among all members of society'.[44] The drafting of the new personal status law (as the family law would be called in the unified Yemen) became the official responsibility of the men of the Constitutional Committee and the Shari`ah Committee of the unified Parliament. In shaping the new personal status law there was a contest between northern liberals and conservatives while southerners did little to defend the previous PDRY law.[45]

Absent from the official parliamentary committees, women tried through other means to influence the construction of a new personal status law. Raufa Hassan accepted the request of a GPC/Islah coalition to chair a conference to discuss a new law. After making a surprise appearance at the conference, the president of the country asked her to form a committee of women and men from north and south, including representatives from the Women's Union, Ministry of Justice, Ministry of Legal Affairs, and independent lawyers to study the question further. The committee tried to find a middle way between the previous family laws of the north and south. As Raufa Hassan put it, they wanted 'a law society would accept without having women lose the ground they had gained in the Family Law of the south'. They submitted their report in timely fashion, but 'debate lasted forever'.[46]

In Ramadan of 1992, at a moment when popular attention would be elsewhere, a personal status law was 'suddenly' enacted.[47] The new law was devoid of any suggestions made by the men and women of the committee Raufa Hassan chaired. Later, she and Radiyya Shamshir, a lawyer from the south,[48] discovered that a deal had been struck between the GPC and the Socialist Party. The Socialists would get a free hand in designing the education law but would give way on the personal status code (this was a move by the GPC to court the Islah Party).[49]

When the new law was announced, women in the south mounted strong public protest. Under the banner of the recently formed Organization for the Defense of Democratic Rights and Freedoms, hundreds went out in protest demonstrations.[50] Women in the north, despite their strong disappointment, made little overt public outcry. Instead, activist leaders continued to forge ahead from their professional bases, settling in for a long haul.

The gender-egalitarian model of the PDRY Family Law of 1974, that was by-passed, had included such provisions as: minimum marriage ages for females and males of sixteen and eighteen, respectively; free choice in marriage for both women and men; the abolition of polygamy, except under extreme conditions; divorce to be initiated by either spouse in front of a judge; and court-determined child custody.[51] Instead, the 1992 Personal Status Law of the united Republic of Yemen, a slightly improved version of the 1978 Family Law of the YAR, affirmed an ideology of gender inequality within the family, stamping a conventional patriarchal model of the family upon the new statutory law. The law set the minimum marriage age at fifteen for females. The law did not enunciate the principle of free choice of spouses but simply declared that marriage by force was invalid. Polygamy was allowed, but the existing wife was to be informed of her husband's intention to marry another woman. A man's ability to end a marriage by repudiation was still possible, but a woman could obtain financial redress only if a judge considered the repudiation to be unfair. A woman could also petition a court to end her marriage.

The new Personal Status Law regulating gender relations and controlling women within a restrictive legal framework reflected the dominant post-unification political culture. In this law, equality was subverted in principle and practice. This was done unobtrusively and under the justification of a narrowly interpreted shari`ah. It was an adumbration of what was to come.

If the ability of Yemeni women to vote and be elected to parliament is an indicator of equality and democracy, as the highly vocal attention paid to women's political rights in Yemen would have it, a closer look is required. In the parliamentary elections of 1993 and 1997 the state and the political parties made highly visible efforts to mobilise women to vote for the success of male-dominated political parties.[52] Women's votes were crucial in the coming to power of the GPC/Islah coalition in 1993 and in the victory of the GPC as the paramount party in 1997.[53] Islamists candidly acknowledge the critical support women's votes had offered to Islah.[54]

Women mounted their own campaigns to support the exercise of their rights as voters and candidates in the elections in 1993. With the benefit of experience and a heightened sense of urgency, they continued even more vigorously in 1997.[55] Raufa Hassan, a parliamentary candidate in 1993, organised a nation-wide project for the Support and Increase of Women's Participation in Elections.[56] The project conducted political awareness campaigns among women throughout the country. The effort extended into the remote mountain villages where tribal leaders were often enlisted to help the female coordinators in mobilising local women.[57] Their strategy was to build a permanent structure by training a large network of women as governorate and constituency coordinators, first to help women register and later to encourage them to cast their votes on election day.[58] Activist women employed Islamic discourse in promoting women's exercise of their political rights. Raufa Hassan taped an interview with Muhammad Tantawi, the Shaikh al-Azhar (rector of al-Azhar University), in which he confirmed women's right to vote and to be elected to parliament. It was later distributed in cassettes in the parliamentary elections of 1993 and 1997 in Yemen.[59] The project also conducted seminars on women's right to vote and to be elected in Islamic law.

If the male mainstream was mobilising women and eagerly courting their support at the ballot box, men were more resistant to supporting women as candidates for parliament. Rashida al-Qiyali, an outspoken Islahi, pointed to false promises of political support made by the male-dominated parties, saying: 'They told us they would take our hands. They took our hands, not to parliament, but to the voting booths'.[60] If the GPC was not explicit about this, Islah made no pretence in opposing women's candidacy for parliament. It is worth noting that Islah did not advance Islamic justifications for women's exclusion from parliament. On the contrary, they acknowledged women's membership in parliament was permitted within the shari`ah. They claimed rather an instrumental reason, saying they did not want women to be exposed to the rough and tumble of campaigning. At the same time they insisted they did not wish to support women as candidates unless they could win.[61] Meanwhile, despite the GPC's liberal rhetoric, its real stance was manifest in its lack of serious backing for women candidates.

Women activists worked hard to support women candidates. The project for the Support and Increase of Women's Participation in Elections ran workshops for women candidates, offering practical training on how to conduct a campaign. The project also created the Women Candidates' Fund to offer material support to the contestants. The composition of the Fund's executive committee, which included heads of women's divisions in the GPC, Islah, the National Women's Committee, and independents, testified to an element of women's unified activism on one level and to women's complicated political manoeuvres on another, simultaneously expressing loyalty to gender and party.[62]

In the first national elections in 1993, women came out to vote in large numbers. But in 1997 only twenty-one ran as candidates, less than half the number of the previous election.[63] Without serious support from men in the political parties, women stood very little chance of success. In both elections it was women from the south who were elected, and each time there were only two. In 1993 the new women parliamentarians were from the Socialist Party: Hawla Sharaf and Muna Basharahi.[64] In 1997 (after a bitter and bloody civil war between the North and South in 1994), Socialist men and women abstained from the elections. In the 1997 election the two successful candidates were from the GPC: Oras Sultan Naji and Uluf Bakhubaira.

The high visibility the state and political parties accorded gender equality citizens' political rights (if only actively backing women's ability to vote) renders more striking the invisibility surrounding the 1997 revised draft for a modified personal status law, encoding still less egalitarian relations between women and men than provided for in the 1992 law.[65] The supporters of this new draft kept it highly secret. They apparently hoped that with the distractions of Ramadan and preoccupation with the coming elections less than three months away, the Personal Status Law draft revision would pass in parliament without notice. However, word of the proposed revision leaked out.

When women learned of the regressive draft for a modified personal status law they swung into action. Since unification nothing had unified women like the spectre of this draft law. Women from the north and south, from the General Congress Party to the Islah Party to the independents, and across generations, joined forces. It was only after extreme difficulty that women were able to obtain a copy of the proposed draft in order to examine its content for themselves. The proposed changes included among others: elimination of a minimum marriage age; removal of the requirement that a man inform his wife of his intent to marry another woman; ending women's ability to act as legal witness; and the validation of a marriage by force if partners subsequently agree.

There was limited time to halt the process. Women organised themselves from their professional bases and from within their political organisations, using all the resources available to them to mount a swift campaign. There were several focal points of activity. The Empirical Research and Women's Studies Center at Sana`a University, under the direction of Raufa Hassan, formed a Law Committee to examine the new draft. Composed of female and male graduate students, among whom were a judge and lawyers, it was headed by Ahmad Sharaf al-Din, a professor in the Faculty of Shari`ah and Statutory Law, who also teaches in the Women's Studies Center.[66] The committee, which addressed the most repressive articles, marshalled Islamic arguments in formulating their refutations.

The women lawyers' office, called *al-Ra'idat* (the Pioneers), the first and only one of its kind (established in March 1996), adopted a similar strategy of singling out the most offensive articles and preparing Islamic arguments against them. Al-Ra'idat founders Nabila al-Mufti (from Ibb in the north) and Shada Muhammad Nasir (from Aden in the south) held *nadwas* (seminar-like discussion groups) of women during Ramadan to spread the word and discuss the issues. They also used the press to widen the scope of action, contacting such papers as *al-Ayyam* and *al-Shura*.

Women's homes likewise became sites of activism. Suad al-Amri (whose father is ambassador to London) held meetings in her house, gathering friends, acquaintances, and colleagues among the young generation, rising professionals (many of whom are engaged in development work).[67] Lawyers Nabila al-Mufti and Shada Muhammad Nasir attended these meetings, offering detailed explanations of the proposed changes contained in the draft. The women also invited the prominent religious scholar and specialist in Islamic jurisprudence, Murtada al-Mahadhwari, to one of their gatherings. Shada Nasir, who took her law degree from Aden University in the eighties (continuing advanced studies in Prague), stressed the importance for women to be well grounded in Islamic law in order to help shape the personal status law.[68] (Her colleague Nabila al-Mufti predicts that women will become specialists in Islamic jurisprudence and in the future will help formulate codes responsive to women's needs.)[69]

Members of the Women's Section of the Islah Party, like the other women who had been kept in the dark (although it was widely believed that Islah was behind the regressive modifications), expressed concern and they too conducted their own investigation.[70] During Ramadan the Islah women invited women of various political and ideological persuasions to an *iftar* (the breaking fast meal at the end of the day) which became another venue for women to collectively air their complaints about the prospective law. The Women's Section also quietly pressed the Islah leadership not to support the proposed draft.[71]

When supporters succeeded in getting the draft passed through parliament, the only recourse for the women was to persuade the president not to sign the bill. The Women's Studies Center contacted Abd al-Karim al-Aryani, the Minister of Foreign Affairs.[72] Al-Raidat worked through a counsellor to the president (the Minister of Legal Affairs in the current government).[73] It was suggested to the president that there were efforts under way to alienate women from the GPC. The women's interventions worked. The president did not sign the bill. If the GPC had been willing to back the proposed personal status law for political gain – either to curry favour with Islah or to be seen more widely as supporting a 'religious' project – following the public exposure of the draft and outcry by women, it was no longer expedient to do so. Islah publicly feigned ignorance of the draft. However, tucked away in the party's 'Political Action Programme' was an item calling for 'Overcoming obstacles in the way of early marriage', a euphemistic call to eliminate the legal minimum marriage age and a hint that Islah had a hand in the regressive draft.[74]

Women not only saved the day but were put on the alert. The Women's Studies Center, which had already targeted law as one of the its four major areas of study, will intensify its research on women and law. This is yet another expression of a wider move under way among women activists in different Muslim countries to re-examine the Qur'an and other religious sources upon which the shari`ah is formulated in order to help achieve more gender egalitarian laws.[75] It will also continue to closely monitor future draft laws. Center director Raufa Hassan affirms: 'The next task will be to help create a [personal status] law that will come out of the society itself. This must be done through a process of intellectual and cultural development'.[76] Meanwhile, the women lawyers believe they have an important role to play in implementing the present law and promoting legal literacy.[77] Female activists agree with Nabila al-Mufti that women cannot play a role in formulating laws that promote the equality the Yemeni constitution and democratic project proclaims until they are sufficiently represented in parliament.[78]

There is a dissonance between people's perceptions and the purveyors of a conservative personal status discourse, certainly within the urban population. Research conducted among women and men in diverse socio-economic quarters of Sana`a in 1997 disclosed widespread ignorance of the personal status law; both the 1992 law and the 1997 revised draft. Strikingly, the research also revealed that people assumed that the proposed changes would constitute a liberalisation of the law, and so they did not view them negatively.[79]

When government officials, members of parliament and politicians promote conservative (or reactionary) policies and legislation, such as the Personal Status draft, a typical justification they give is that the people would not accept a liberal law. They blame the 'culture' and conservative habits – of ordinary people. Political power brokers attempt to construct and control the discursive representation of the people, and especially women, for their own political ends. Their loud proclamations of the principle of equality and their muted impositions of inequality announce their awareness that they are manipulating, and not merely responding to, the wishes of the people in general and of women in particular.

There is a consistency in Yemeni women's embrace of the ideals of democracy and in their resolve to put these into practice. It is significant that women in Yemen have the right to vote and to be elected to parliament;

and the country can justly take credit for being the first in the Arabian Peninsula to grant women the full rights all citizens in a democracy are due. Yet, there is a gender difference in the attempts to apply these rights. Yemeni women encouraged other women to exercise their right to vote. Yemeni men attempted to mobilise women to vote, largely as a function of partisan politics. Women also encouraged women to run as candidates; however, here there was less consensus. Most Islahi women did not support the idea of women running for parliament. In general, men did not encourage women to run for parliament; some, notably Islahis, actively opposed the idea of women running. Women running for parliament would not serve men's interests.

It was not ideology or constituency politics that brought women across a wide spectrum together in militant activism. It was transgressing the bottom line of what was acceptable in women's everyday lives. Moreover, it was the crossing of the bottom line in exactly what women had always been told was *their* sphere: family relations and personal life. The conservative personal status law that had been intended to control women produced the opposite effect of politicising them. Their unleashed fury empowered them and dissolved barriers among them. This is not to say that women retracted other loyalties, especially party loyalties, but that they coalesced around a gender issue.

When they collectively mobilised to oppose the regressive personal status draft, women had acted on an issue that directly affected their everyday lives. Women established a linkage between democracy and the principle of equality inherent in it, in both public life and private life. They insisted on the principle and practice of equality of citizens in both political rights and personal status. Linking what male politicians wanted to keep distinct and separate was made more dramatic as the national elections and efforts to enact a new regressive personal status law occurred simultaneously. Yemeni activist women insist that equality is indivisible as a democratic principle. Selective equality is illogical and anti-democratic – and threatening to Yemen's unification process.

At this moment in Yemeni history when women have attained equal rights to vote and to be elected, it is a blatant form of masculinist expediency to promote women's ability to vote only to harness it to male political purposes. It is also a masculinist expediency to stall women's ability to become members of parliament. A significant number of women in parliament might create a force that would change the politics of gender. At the moment when women legally enjoy their political rights, one way to contain women is through a conservative personal status law that re-enforces male control over them in the context of the family. Activist women understand this.

In Yemen, women practise feminism. They do not label it. They grasp the sly masculinist manipulations of discourse and practice. Women are exposing the fraudulent contradictions between rights given in principle and withheld in practice, between equality declared and equality subverted.

Yemeni women are not allowing themselves to be merely a pawn in the game of masculinist politics. It is a pragmatic moment, not an ideological moment. They are engaging in practical politics that does not call attention to itself. Yemeni feminist activists are refusing to get caught up in a binary secular/religious framework. Activist women across the spectrum speak an Islamic language as they practise their feminism and a feminist language as they practise Islam. Women have consolidated around personal status legislation based on the shari`ah. In broad outline they agree on a more advanced interpretation than men, across the political and ideological spectrum, advance. Is this feminism? Is this progressive Islamism? Is this Islamic feminism? These are not questions these feminist activists ask. They do not, as noted, call themselves feminist activists. Rather, the term describes their actions.

Through their activism Yemeni women are making a distinctive contribution to the discourse of feminism in Middle Eastern and Islamic societies. Unlike most women elsewhere in the region, they have been able to consolidate as women around critical gender issues while retaining their loyalty to a political party or remaining committed to non-partisan independence. They have narrowed a gap common elsewhere between Islamist women and non-Islamist women. Yemeni women are insisting on the unitary nature of citizenship, inclusive of the 'public' and the 'private', and the necessity of equality in the construction of citizenship: equality of north and south, of women and men. Yemeni women activists acted swiftly to expose and confront the contradictory projects of the highly touted national elections (with the prestige that women's ability to vote brought the country) and the regressive draft for a revised personal status code, the secrecy surrounding which belied its problematic nature. Full equality expressed in a progressive personal status code will be achieved as part of a longer process, rather than all at once (as with the implementation of women's right to be elected to parliament). Yemen cannot unify without women playing integral roles, nor can Yemen become a functioning democracy without women fully taking part. Women and men, alike, understand this. But, it will be the women who will have to make this happen – which, as we see, they are doing. Yemeni women's activism is a vibrant illustration of the local feminisms Amrita Basu reminds us are constitutive of the story of 'women's movements in global perspective'.[80]

Notes

1. Research for this paper was conducted in January and February, and from August to mid November in Yemen (mainly Sana`a but also in Aden) under a grant from the American Institute for Yemeni Studies. During this time I had interviews and extended conversations with many women in Yemen to whom I wish to express my gratitude for information and insights which have contributed to the shaping of this paper. From

23 August to 18 September, as part of my grant, I co-conducted a Workshop in Gender Research Skills with Raufa Hassan, director of the Center for Empirical Research and Women's Studies, Sana`a University. This study has benefited from research done during the workshop by the student participants: Evelyn Anoya, Narges Erami, Abd al-Hakim al Hamdani, Majda al-Qarmuti, Sabah al-Huthi, Samira Muhsin, Miryam Rashid, Nabil al-Shamsani, and Farah Usmai.

2. Many states, for example, have signed international conventions such as the United Nations Human Rights Convention or CEDAW, signalling acceptance of human rights and women's rights while silently failing to honour them in practice.

3. Deniz Kandiyoti (ed.), Introduction, *Women, Islam and the State* (Temple University Press, Philadelphia, 1991), p. 2.

4. See Marnia Lazreg, *The Eloquence of Silence* (Routledge, London, 1994); Sondra Hale, *Gender Politics in the Sudan: Islamism, Socialism, and the State* (Westview Press, Boulder, CO, 1997); Parvin Paidar, *Women and the Political Process in Twentieth-Century Iran* (Cambridge University Press, Cambridge, UK, 1995); and Margot Badran, *Feminists, Islam, and the Nation: Gender and the Making of Modern Egypt* (Princeton University Press, Princeton, 1994).

5. Amrita Basu (ed.), *Women's Movements in Global Perspective* (Westview Press, Boulder, CO, 1995), p. 14, makes an important observation when she writes: 'women's activism seems to have borne greater dividends in contemporary nationalist struggles than in earlier anticolonial movements'.

6. On experiences in Algeria, Egypt, Iran, and Sudan see note 4; and in Kuwait see Margot Badran, 'Gender, Islam, and the State: Kuwaiti Women in Struggle, Pre-Invasion to Postliberation', in *Islam, Gender, and Social Change*, ed. Yvonne Haddad and John Esposito (Oxford University Press, New York, 1998), pp. 190–208.

7. They also include rights to retain citizenship after marriage, to assume citizenship in the country of one's spouse, and the ability to pass one's citizenship to one's children.

8. It is important to note that it should not be assumed that modern states in the Middle East (or elsewhere) necessarily promote more or necessarily promote less gender egalitarian laws than premodern societies. Historical experience is complicated. For example, on law and gender in various places under Ottoman rule see Amira El Azhary Sonbol, *Women, the Family, and Divorce Laws in Islamic History* (Syracuse University Press, Syracuse,1996). Modern states in the West have adjusted some of their laws repressive to women before granting women the vote, as, for example, in England where a women's property law was instituted before women were granted suffrage; but despite specific advances women in most countries, after acquiring the vote, have had to continue long struggles to gain better divorce laws, laws relating to reproductive rights, and the like.

9. While Egyptian feminists articulated a unitary discourse on citizens' rights, out of expediency, they prioritised their activist struggle, giving immediate attention to achieving personal status rights and postponing the fight for equal political rights. See Badran, *Feminists, Islam, and Nation*.

10. Badran, *Feminists, Islam, and Nation*, ch. 12, pp. 223–50.

11. See, for example, *Women in Contemporary Palestine: Between Old Conflicts and New Realities*, edited and published by the Palestinian Academic Society for the Study of International Affairs (Jerusalem, 1996).

12. Nawal El Saadawi, 'The Political Challenges Facing Arab Women at the End of the Twentieth Century', and Fatima Mernissi, 'Democracy as Moral Disintegration:

The Contradiction between Religious Belief and Citizenship as a Manifestation of the Ahistoricity of the Arab Identity', in *Women of the Arab World*, ed. Nahid Toubia (Zed Press, London, 1988), pp. 8–26 and 36–43 respectively.

13. For example, on the Turkish experience see Nülifer Göle, *The Forbidden Modern: Civilization and Veiling* (University of Michigan Press, Ann Arbor, Michigan, 1996).

14. In Turkey, for example, male legal headship of the family was inscribed in the Civil Code of 1926, as second wave Turkish feminists disdainfully pointed out. See Yesim Arat, 'Kemalism and Turkish Women', *Women and Politics*, 14 (1994); Yesim Arat 'On Gender and Citizenship in Turkey', *Middle East Report* (1996); and Yesim Arat, 'Women's Movement of the 1980s in Turkey: Radical Outcome of Liberal Kemalism?', in *Reconstructing Gender in the Middle East*, ed. Fatma Müge Göcek and Shiva Balaghi (Columbia University Press, New York, 1994); Nükhet Sirman, 'Feminism in Turkey: A Short History', *New Perspectives on Turkey*, 3 (1989), pp. 1–34; and Tekeli, Sirin, 'The Emergence of the Feminist Movement in Turkey', in *The New Women's Movements: Feminism and Political Power in Europe and the USA*, ed. Drude Dahlerup (Sage Publications, London and Beverly Hills, 1986).

15. For example, in the case of China see Mayfair Yang, 'From Gender Erasure to Gender Difference: State Feminism, Consumer Sexuality, and Women's Public Sphere in China', in *Spaces of Their Own: Women's Public Sphere in Transnational*, ed. Mayfair Yang (University of Minnesota Press, Minneapolis, 1998).

16. For example, in Kuala Lumpur, Malaysia, Sisters in Islam have issued several booklets on feminist rereadings of the Qur`an; on South Africa, Farid Esack, *Qur'an, Liberation and Pluralism: An Islamic Perspective of Interreligious Solidarity Against Oppression* (Oneworld Press, Oxford, 1997); on Iran, Ziba Mir-Hosseini, 'Stretching the Limits: A Feminist Reading of the Shar`ia in Post-Khomeini Iran', in *Feminism and Islam: Legal and Literary Perspectives*, ed., Mai Yamani (New York University Press, New York, 1997), pp. 285–320, and Afsaneh Najmabadi, 'Feminism in an Islamic Republic: "Years of Hardship, Years of Growth"', in *Islam, Gender, and Social Change*, pp. 59–84; and in the United States, Amina Wadud-Muhsin, *Qu'ran and Woman* (Penerbit Fajar Bakti, Kuala Lumpur, 1992).

17. See Mir-Hosseini, 'Stretching the Limits: A Feminist Reading of the Shar`ia in Post-Khomeini Iran'; and Afsaneh Najmabadi, 'Feminism in an Islamic Republic: "Years of Hardship, Years of Growth"'; and Margot Badran, 'Toward Islamic Feminisms: A Look at the Middle East', in *The Hermeneutics of Gendered Discourse and Space*, ed. Asma Asfaruddin (forthcoming, Harvard Monograph series); and Badran, 'Feminisms and Islamisms', in *The Journal of Women's History*, special issue on Women and Fundamentalisms (forthcoming).

18. Seema Kazi notes this common pattern in Muslim countries in 'Muslim Law and Women Living under Muslim Laws', in *Muslim Women and the Politics of Participation: Implementing the Beijing Platform*, ed. Mahnaz Afkhami and Erika Friedl (Syracuse University Press, Syracuse, 1997), pp. 141–6; Nadia Hijab, 'Islam, Social Change, and the Reality of Arab Women's Lives', in *Islam, Gender, and Social Change*, pp. 45–56, speaks of this in the context of Arab society; and Boutheina Cheriet in the case of Algeria in 'Fundamentalism and Women's Rights: Lessons from the City of Women', in *Muslim Women and the Politics of Participation*, pp. 11–17. Feminists in Arab countries have been less successful in obtaining equal rights in the 'private sphere' than in the 'public sphere', as I discuss in the case of Egypt for example in 'Independent Women: More than a Century of Feminism in Egypt, in *Arab Women: Old Boundaries, New Frontiers*, ed. Judith Tucker (Indiana University Press, Bloomington, 1993), pp. 129–48.

19. See Margot Badran, 'Dual Liberation: Feminism and Nationalism in Egypt from the 1870s to 1925', *Feminist Issues* (Spring 1988), pp. 15–24; Badran, *Feminists, Islam and Nation*; and Carolyn Fleur-Lobban, 'Women and Social Liberation: The Sudan Experience', in *Three Studies on National Integration in the Arab World* (Association of Arab-American Graduates, North Dartmouth, MA, 1974).

20. For an analysis of the PDRY Family Law of 1974, see Maxine Molyneux, 'Legal Reform and Social Revolution in Democratic Yemen: Women and the Family', *International Journal of the Sociology of Law,* 13 (1985), pp. 142–72 and republished in an abbreviated form as 'The Law, the State and Socialist Policies with Regard to Women: The Case of the People's Democratic Republic of Yemen 1967–1900', in *Women, Islam, and the State.*

21. There is no necessary link between ideology expressed in a constitution and in personal status laws. It was also under Sadat that the 1929 Egyptian Personal Status Code was modified in a way more responsive to women's needs.

22. The Yemeni Women's Society, established in Aden in 1946 under the leadership of Ruqaiya Luqman, appears to be the first of its kind and private precursor to the GUYW.

23. See Helen Lackner, *The People's Democratic Republic of Yemen: Outposts of Socialist Development in Arabia* (Ithaca Press, London, 1985), pp. 114–18. In Egypt, for example, where women are not allowed to function as judges, there was a recent demonstration in the press of women's ability to fill positions as judges in Islam citing religious texts, including the Qur'an and Hadith. See the two-part article in *Al-Ahram Weekly* by Zeinab Radwan, 'Sitting in Judgement', 16–22 April, p. 14, 1998 and 'Robbing Wise Men of Their Reason', 12–29 April 1998, p. 15.

24. In Egypt at mid century, Inji Aflatun argued that there was no contradiction between Islam and leftist ideologies. See her books: *Thmanun Maliyun Imra'a Ma`na* (Eighty Million Women with Us) (Cairo, 1948) and *Nahnu al-Nis'a al-Misriyyat* (We Egyptian Women) (Cairo, 1949).

25. See Paul Dresch, *Tribes, Government, and History in Yemen* (Clarendon Press, Oxford, 1989).

26. The situation before the Family Law of 1978 was complex. See for example: Hassan al-Hubaishi, *Legal System and Basic Law in Yemen* (Billing and Sons, Worcester, UK, 1988). Martha Mundy, in 'Women's Inheritance of Land in Highland Yemen', *Arabian Studies*, 5 (1979), pp. 161–87, shows legal advantages women gained – on paper – regarding inheritance rights with the creation of the 78 statutory law and how this was subverted in rural areas.

27. See Badran, *Feminists, Islam, and Nation*, ch. 7, 'Recasting the Family', pp. 124–42.

28. See Amatalrauf al-Sharki, 'An Unveiled Voice', in *Opening the Gates: A Century of Arab Feminist Writing*, ed. Margot Badran and Miriam Cooke (Indiana University Press, Bloomington, 1990), pp. 375–85. .

29. Conversation with Valentina Alwan, 2 November 1997, and with other women from Aden.

30. These two phenomena, increase of conservative dress and increase of women at university, should not be taken as contradictions. The more daring entry of women into university would have come with the first path-breakers of the seventies. Also, neo-religious conservatives typically encourage the education of women.

31. Interview with Mona al-Attas, 31 October 1997, who said: 'Before the state in the South protected women but the new state does not'. Molyneux, 'Women's Rights and Political Contingency', p. 422, notes (in a different context) that the PDRY

Constitution contained 'many commitments to state intervention on behalf of women'. She provides an analysis of the general political and economic decline of the PDRY and its gender consequences; see esp. pp. 427–9.

32. For a comparative perspective on 'state feminism' see Mayfair Yang, 'From Gender Erasure to Gender Difference: State Feminism, Consumer Sexuality, and Women's Public Sphere in China', who writes in reference to Maoist China: 'state feminism also made it difficult to sustain a critical gender perspective and an independent feminist discourse mounted by women themselves, issuing from their own experiences'. For a brief account of women from the previous two Yemens a year and a half into the new unified state, see Sheila Carapico, 'Women and Public Participation in Yemen', *Middle East Report* (November–December 1991), p. 15 .

33. On this process, see Charles Dunbar, 'The Unification of Yemen: Process, Politics, and Prospects', *Middle East Journal*, 46 (1992), pp. 456–76; Siobhan Hall, *Yemen: The Politics of Unity* (Gulf Centre for Stategic Studies, London, October 1991); and Fred Halliday, 'The Enigma of Yemeni "Unity"', ch. 4 in *Revolution and Foreign Policy: The Case of South Yemen, 1967–1987* (Cambridge University Press, Cambridge, 1990); and Sheila Carapico, 'The Economic Dimension of Yemeni Unity', *Middle East Report* (September–October 1993), pp. 9–14.

34. Art. 18 of the 1991 Constitution.

35. Art. 2 of the 1991 Constitution.

36. See Sheila Carapico, 'Elections and Mass Politics in Yemen', *Middle East Report* (November–December 1993), pp. 2–6.

37. Art. 27 of the 1991 Constitution.

38. See Sheila Carapico, 'Elections and Mass Politics in Yemen'.

39. Muhammad Qahtan, the head of Islah's political division, in an interview with Rochdi Younsi, 9 September 1997, explained the long build-up of Islah and his own involvement in what was previously an underground network from 1974. The Islah Party constitutes an expedient amalgam of tribal forces headed by Shaikh Abdullah al-Ahmar, head of the Hashid confederation and the Muslim Brothers with a strong urban base. It has three strands: extremely conservative, moderate, and 'liberal'.

40. In an interview on 2 November 1997 in Sana`a, Samira Muhsen described the programmes of the Taiz branch.

41. Ihsan Ubaid (the president), Ruqaiyya Sayyid Muhammad Ali, Ilhsan Salam, and Howla Sharaf from the YWU, in an interview in Aden, 18 January 1997, gave a version of this tortuous process.

42. D. Dorman, A. N. al-Madhaji, M. Aidarus, S. Beatty, Z. Ismael, and M. de Regt, *Yemeni NGOs and Quasi-NGOs: Analysis and Directory: Part II, Directory* (Sana`a, 1996), pp. 81–3. Sheila Carapico stresses the divergent agendas of the Northern and Southern women within the new Union as a primary reason for its disarray. See 'Yemen between Civility and Civil War', ch. 9 in *Civil Society in the Middle East*, ed. A. R. Norton (Brill, Leiden, 1996), pp. 287–316.

43. Headed by Amat al-Alim al-Suswa, this body was created in the aftermath of Beijing. A fuller discussion of its complicated mandate to serve women and the state is beyond the task of this paper.

44. Yemen Republic Islah Party, 'Political Action Programme' (1997), official English translation, a 38-page document.

45. See Molyneux, 'Women's Rights and Political Contingency', p. 427, who writes that the Socialist Party 'made no significant effort to defend their own law. Instead, they abandoned the 1974 code on the family much as they had other distinctive, secular,

and socialist laws regulating social practices'. Carapico, 'Yemen between Civility and Civil War', p. 310, says the Yemeni Organization for the Defense of Democratic Rights and Liberties, a human rights organisation created in Aden in February 1992, 'prepared to challenge the Personal Status Law'.

46. Interview with Raufa Hassan by Sabah al-Huthi and Rochdi Younsi, Sana`a, 2 September 1997.

47. Molyneux, 'Women's Rights and Political Contingency', p. 243, citing a Yemeni legal expert, writes that the 1990 Personal Status Law contained elements from the League of Arab States' Unified Model Arab Personal Status Law, which is an indication of their wanting state of enlightened legal paradigms. See the discussion of personal status and family laws in the YAR, PDRY, and ROY, in Republic of Yemen Women National Committee, 'Status of Woman in Yemen' (Sana`a, May 1996), pp. 16–18; and also Anna Würth, 'The Legal Status of Women in Yemen', unpublished report (March 1994), CID/WID Project, Bureau of Applied Research in Anthropology, Dept of Anthropology, University of Arizona; and Anna Würth, 'A Sana`a Court: The Family and the Ability to Negotiate', *Islamic Law and Society* 2 (Leiden, 1995), pp. 320–40. I would like to thank Anna Würth for sharing her knowledge of law and the courts in Yemen, and especially for discussing the (then) impending draft revision of the personal status law.

48. Raufa Hassan and Radiyyaa Shamshir were both to run unsuccessfully for parliament in the 1993 elections, running respectively as an independent and Socialist.

49. Interview with Raufa Hassan by Sabah al-Huthi and Rochdi Younsi, Sana`a, 2 September 1997.

50. See Molyneux, 'Women's Rights and Political Contingency', pp. 428–9 and 'Masira Istinkar wa Ihtijaj Nisawiyya' (Display of Feminist/Women's Condemnation and Denunciation), `Adan, 28 April 1992.

51. Raufa Hassan in an interview with Rochdi Younsi, Sana`a, 2 September 1997.

52. For a general account of the 1993 elections, see Renaud Detalle, 'The Yemeni Elections Close Up', *Middle East Report* (November–December 1993), pp. 8 12.

53. In 1993, out of the 301 seats in parliament, the GPC won 123 and Islah 62 (*The Economist*, March 1997), p. 46. In 1997, the GPC won about two-thirds of the seats and Islah about 54 ('GPC Rides High', *Yemen Times*, 5–11 May 1997). See Carapico, 'Yemen between Civility and Civil War', p. 300, who says that women played a major role in Islah's successful voter registration campaign in which they mobilised large numbers of women voters.

54. See Janine Clark, 'Women and Islamic Activism in Yemen', *Yemen Update: Bulletin of the American Institute for Yemeni Studies*, 39 (1997), pp. 13–15.

55. In 1993, 15 per cent of the eligible women voted as opposed to 77 per cent of the men. Fifty women were among the 3,600 parliamentary candidates who remained in the running until the end. See Sheila Carapico, 'Elections and Mass Politics in Yemen'. In 1993, women were 19 per cent of the registered voters and, in 1997, 30 per cent. 'Yemen's Elections are Given High Marks by Observers', *Yemen Times* (5–11 May 1997).

56. On her campaign, see David Warburton, 'A Campaign Rally in San`a', *Middle East Report* (November–December 1993), p. 12.

57. They concentrated on the constituencies with the lowest voter participation rate in the 1993 elections.

58. In January 1997 the author attended one of these two-day workshops which conducted training seminars for women to act as constituency coordinators from all over the country. At the closing ceremony women from different political parties, especially the GPC and Islah, as well as independents were in evidence.

59. The author was present at the interview with Muhammad Tantawi at his office in al-Azhar in Cairo in February 1997.

60. Interview with Rashida al-Qiyali by Miryam Rashid, Sana`a, September 1997. She observed that all the political parties marginalise women.

61. Interview with Muhammad Qahtan by Margot Badran, Sana`a, January 1997. Rashida al-Qiyali told Miryam Rashid: 'The good thing about Islah is that they are honest about the [woman's] issue'.

62. The women on the executive committee of the Fund include: Amat al-Razzaq Jahlaf (GPC), Amat al-Sallam Ali Raja (Islah), Amat al-Alim al-Suswa (National Women's Committee), and Raufa Hassan (independent).

63. Women constituted an important presence in the voter monitoring procedures on election day.

64. Hawla Sharaf is from Aden and Muha Basharhi from Hadhramaut.

65. Molyneux, 'Women's Rights and Political Contingency', p. 419, note 4, makes this point.

66. Members of the committee from the Center included: Muhammad al-Qabatri, a judge; Hanan Bahmaid, Abd al-Hakim al-Hamdani and Najat al-Shami, lawyers; and Fathiyya al-Haythami and Sa`id al-Mikhlafi. There were also human rights activists, and journalists.

67. The author attended one of these meetings at the end of January 1997. In discussions with women there, and also in an interview with Suhair al-Amri and Bushra al-Mutawakkil, Sana`a, 15 January 1997, I learned about the concerns of the rising generation of professional women, whose gender consciousness, advocacy, and activism grows out of their own personal and work lives.

68. Shada Nasir emphasised this in an interview with Majda al-Qurmati and Narges Erami, Sana`a, 2 September 1997.

69. Interview with Nabila al-Mufti by Samira Muhsin and Evelyn Anoya, Sana`a, 3 September 1997.

70. When I interviewed members of the Islah Women's Division in Sana`a in January 1997, they seemed genuinely to be unaware of the draft.

71. Interview with Muhammad Qahtan by Margot Badran, Sana'a, October 1997.

72. Interview with Raufa Hassan by Rochdi Younsi, Sana`a, 2 September 1997.

73. Interview with Nabila al-Mufti by Samira Muhsin and Evelyn Anoya, Sana`a, 3 September 1997.

74. Yemen Republic Islah Party, 'Political Action Programme'. See full citation in note 44.

75. See note 16; also Barbara Stowasser, *Women in the Qur'an, Traditions, and Interpretation* (Oxford University Press, New York, 1994), and Stowasser, 'Gender Issues and Contemporary Qur'an Interpretation', in *Gender, Islam, and Social Change,* pp. 30–45.

76. Interview with Raufa Hassan by Rochdi Younsi, Sana`a, 2 September 1997.

77. Shada Nasir emphasised this in an interview with Majda Abd al-Qurmati and Narges Erami, Sana`a, 2 September 1997.

78. Interview with Nabila al-Mufti by Samira Muhsin and Evelyn Anoya, Sana`a, 3 September 1997.

79. This research was conducted by students from Sana`a University and the University of Chicago during the Workshop in Gender Research Skills held at the Center for Empirical Research and Women's Studies, Sana`a University in August and September 1997.

80. This is taken from the subtitle of Basu's book, *The Challenge of Local Feminisms: Women's Movements in Global Perspective.*

FORUM

International Feminisms: Latin American Alternatives

ASUNCIÓN LAVRIN

Feminism was born wrapped in one great hope: that it would be good for all womankind, and able to embrace all women, to dispel all national, racial and cultural barriers. Because it was developed concurrently in many parts of the world – sometimes as a groping desire not well articulated, sometimes as a clear elaboration of much meditation – it had an apparent promise of universality that led many women and men to believe that some day it would be a global canon for all humankind. Time has proven that the femaleness of all women is not enough to achieve a unity of purpose that must overcome the many cultural factors that make gender a reality different in each society. Further, feminism, like any other ideological and cultural construct, is not held within a strict mould that remains impervious to chronological change. The aspirations of the first feminists – those who evolved roughly between 1900 and 1940 – took new courses as new generations sought different routes to solve their problems, or some of the original goals were achieved. The meaning of women's or feminists' needs vis-à-vis their own social environment therefore takes myriad subtle forms that demand careful attention to unravel. By now the pluralism of feminism is well established, and we are dealing with feminisms as an experience that is not necessarily shared in the same degree or within the same conceptual frames even at the national level, let alone in the international arena.

In the international forum, some academic cultural centres, endowed with the power of their prestige and long history of research and engagement on the topic, have become predisposed to see a 'universal' pattern of feminism, acceptable and applicable to all situations and all women. The definitions of feminism elaborated in European countries and in the United States from the mid 1850s onwards have been assumed to represent all feminist interests. We confront today many objections to a universal discourse, coming from areas that were until recently regarded as the periphery of intellectual debates, but where the needs and the cultural heritage of most women do not fit the parameters devised elsewhere. Thus, we face international feminisms with two problematic issues. One is whether West European and North American interpretations of feminism can serve the needs of the rest of the world; the other is the possible breakdown of an ideology that has served well so many women's causes into a number of compartmentalised expressions, which serve local issues, but have lost the binding ties that permit the recognition of a common experience in womanhood.

Assuming that feminism is a cultural construct that does not accept unquestioned transference of thoughts and answers from one period to another or from one nation or one area of the world to another, is it possible to save its 'international' character without losing the wealth generated by its internal diversity? This question has elicited many answers, and here I will simply outline some thoughts that may facilitate further discussion without attempting to cover all the facets of this complex issue.[1] As an academic historian I conceive international feminisms to be a comparative and interdisciplinary subject, which implies the exchange of theories, as well as openness to a dialogue in which the 'popular' understandings of its meanings, and 'pragmatic' approaches to reaching women at the level of their daily needs become valid objectives. The marketplace of feminisms should not take the approach of multinationals but maintain the spirit of the national and local 'economies' of womankind.

Taking the latter line of inquiry, Latin America offers an interesting case-study in the dialogue of national and international feminisms. Locked in one vast continent, these nations form within themselves an international scenario. They share some common historical, cultural, and political experiences, but have developed idiosyncratically, forcing us to focus on national and international issues whenever we attempt to tie the nations together under the banner of common gender concerns. Continental Latin America comprises a variety of ethnicities and races, social classes, economic problems, and cultural traditions, and is a macrocosm in which we find reflections of the experience of women world-wide.

Historically, Latin American feminisms have also had ties with other cultures that served as inspirational beacons. Latin American feminists developed a strong vocation for internationalism, not only as an intellectual orientation, but as a validation of their aspirations for a political and juridical personality. Francesca Miller has argued that since the beginning of the twentieth century Latin American women's participation in international conferences helped to counterbalance their alienation from politics by the local androcracy, and their ostracism from male-controlled international diplomacy conferences.[2] The First International Feminine Congress in Buenos Aires in 1910 was a forum for the discussion of a broad spectrum of topics, and was attended by representatives from all over Latin America as well as from Europe. Significantly, most of the discussions revolved around social issues, not suffrage or political rights, which were beyond them at the time. What seemed to bind all women together were universal themes of family and labour, as well as a desire to come to grips with the meaning of feminism itself.[3]

Participation in international conferences gave personal and political strength to those returning home as well as to those who had stayed behind. For example, Sofía Alvarez de Demicheli made a news splash in her native Uruguay after her lucid participation in the 1933 Inter-American Conference, where women pressed for the recognition of women's civil rights. A committed feminist, she proceeded to help support the cause of women's suffrage in her country, where women first participated in a national election in 1938.

The history of women's presence and activities in the Pan American Union Conferences is indicative of the nature, goals, and obstacles faced by early twentieth-century feminists. They succeeded in making statements against United States imperialism in the area, but did not pursue what today we may call a North South confrontation. Rather, they collaborated with the United States in seeking the ratification of international women's rights, such as the right to a single nationality, in The Hague International Court. The 'imperialism' of the male sex at home was never described in so many words by the participants in such conferences, but was more explicitly addressed by feminist activists in their relentless pursuit of the elimination of male supremacy in the laws defining gender relations in the family. Before 1940, feminists targeted warfare as another expression of patriarchal values enforced upon humanity in general, founding organisations to promote world peace. Unfortunately, pacifism became a 'feminine' activity, suffused with emotionalism and bound to become a lost cause in an increasingly militarised decade. The return to war in 1940, and of peace in 1945, were unique experiences that turned feminists' interests from international pacifism to issues of political 'empowerment' through suffrage, international political domination, and economic dependency. Although some countries had already adopted women's suffrage by 1945, female enfranchisement was largely a post-World War II achievement. Suffrage was a universal political concept rather than a tool for reshaping politics, insofar as many countries wavered between democratic and dictatorial regimes, and few offered a consistent channel for active female political participation in the national arena. Whether practised or not, the right to vote was an intellectually enabling tool that by the 1970s permitted the politicisation of women's activism – a consciousness of their own capabilities – and an incisive analysis of their roles in the economies and in the formulation of politics.

Before the 1960s, internationalism helped women's feminist groups to examine their own situation in the light of the values and practices of women of other cultures who, nonetheless, shared common problems owing to their gender. An analysis of the circumstances confronted by other women led feminists to adopt for themselves whatever was adaptable to their own nations. They were also led to the consciousness of the idiosyncracy of their respective national circumstances. Further, international meetings help self-examination at a personal level, bonding at a group level, and the softening of rough edges born of hard-core cultural assumptions. Seven international meetings known as *encuentros* have been renewed in Latin America beginning in 1981 in Bogotá, with other important ones taking place in Peru (1983), Mexico (1986), Argentina (1990), and Chile (1996). For the participants, they validate gender as a bonding element, and help identify the premises of universal female oppression. While today international conferences may not give the same feeling of 'empowerment' to women they did at the beginning of the century, they still help to define national agendas, and to redefine techniques of organisation and persuasion, after the flurry of state and private activities focused on women that followed the Decade of the Woman that began in 1975. Internationalism has not been, however, the only route open to women for political participation in the national arena. Nationalism and internationalism have coexisted with differing degrees of strength born out of circumstances over which women had no control. While a small group of middle-class educated women was projecting itself in the international arena, other women (or sometimes the same women) were founding female organisations and even women's parties, from which they launched a variety of national, social and political campaigns.

This historical framework helps us to understand certain 'traditional' continuities in Latin American feminisms, while underlining the departures experienced as a response to new historical circumstances. Beginning in the 1960s, Latin American nations devoted enormous energy to development, and struggled to find a way between the ideological and economic commitment to capitalism and the social inequalities that led many people to assume that Marxism was a panacea for all problems. The tension created by such antagonistic forces led many important countries to a return to authoritarian and repressive regimes. Neither Marxism nor military regimes proved to be fertile ground for the consideration of gender issues. The military encouraged a return to traditional gender roles, while engaging in new forms of violence that included activities against women. Nonmilitary regimes and revolutionary regimes relegated gender issues to a secondary place in their agendas or failed to carry institutional changes into meaningful personal changes. The reliance on centralised states to provide answers for gender legal issues and for the welfare of women and children has maintained men in control of the most important mechanisms of social change. Latin America has the dubious distinction of being the source of the concept of overbearing masculinity or *machismo* as the signifier of male-dominated gender relations.

Yet, the same forces that led to authoritarian regimes were at the bottom of a budding redefinition of women's social and economic role, as well as a new mode of thinking the rights of women within the universal rights of peoples. Gross economic inequalities began to affect the material structure of the family, forcing more women to assume active roles to salvage households from increasing poverty. Migrating to other countries was one alternative taken by some; becoming part of multinational industries was another; going into the streets as members of the 'informal' economy was a third option. The feminisation of poverty and the increasing number of female heads of households have raised deep concerns among segments of the economic and intellectual leadership, and have reactivated the role of 'action' feminism. After 1975 the revitalisation of international feminisms world-wide had a profound influence on Latin America. In a world of mass communications, educated middle-class as well as working women became aware of the ground swell of contemporary feminisms and began to formulate their own responses to the lingering problems of national economic decline and the solutions adopted to stall it: neoliberalism and political conservatism. In this critical period the seizure by the military of a large portion of South America activated the hidden political resources of women in the name of human rights.

There are many voices in an environment characterised by its diversity, and the attempt to coordinate them has taken time and effort. Beyond and above the different topics discussed in national and international encounters, the main agenda of these meetings has been the search for unity in diversity, the creation of personal bondings, and a better understanding of the many meanings of feminism. Nationalism and all the centrifugal forces that may cause a cacophony of noises rather than a chorus of stated purposes are serious obstacles if not threats to creating an intercontinental feminist spirit, and confrontations have been inevitable. However, the debate over finer points of ideological standing and political strategies has been aptly identified as essential for keeping channels of communication open among national groups and a venue for an ultimate mutual understanding. Internal democracy within feminist groups has been regarded as essential to maintain the vitality of feminism at the national and intercontinental levels. Also identified as an important need is learning about the social and economic conditions of the nations and the continent to give women the tools to criticise economic and political schemes and meet the most pressing challenges to themselves and society. The encounters have also reiterated a number of themes: the need to establish broader networks; the right of reproductive freedom and legal abortions; the need to secure access to the mass media; the search for stronger support to low-income women; the duty to extend the meaning of democracy (as equal participation of all and respect for the individual) to the home, the work place, and the school.[4] These may be considered the distinguishing features of Latin American feminism in the 1990s.

The agenda of recent national and intercontinental encounters is politically very different from those congresses of nearly a century ago.

Participants have no doubts about their duty and right as women to self-determine the future of womanhood, renouncing all accommodation to traditional patriarchal values. They also realise that continental encounters cannot replace the collective reflection of problems at a regional or national level to achieve a balance of national and international interests, essential for the survival of feminism as an expression of diversity. The intense self-analysis resulting from these meetings has yielded a formula of conciliation: the respect of individuality within a feminism that is aware of the 'pluralism of difference'.

Women in Latin America were ready to assume a new role in the 1980s, and the surge of their activities is the result of a feminist thought with roots stretching back to at least the beginning of this century if not earlier, and a foundation of legislated reforms adopted between the 1920s and the mid 1970s. National and international factors pushed women towards even greater activism and a better understanding of gender roles in the 1980s, but the role of protagonist for women's causes emerged slowly and against difficult odds for women of all social sectors. Anywhere in Latin America, feminist politics are difficult to separate from national politics, given the centrality of the state and the nature of the political systems. Unlike countries with stable electoral systems, Latin America presents an assortment of political regimes which include democracies, nations subject to violent internecine political wars, local or national *caudillismo* (bossism), and nations with revolutionary regimes. This variety of political circumstances demands feminist expressions and activities suited to meet these peculiarities.

The integration of women into political parties remains problematic, but a necessary step for feminism to achieve national validity and effective means to change local and national gender issues. The need to exercise power within the established parameters of the national state creates for each national feminist movement a problem that cannot be replicated elsewhere and that also creates serious internal divisions. How can international feminisms reconcile the disparity of political circumstances under which women live and which they must address to achieve their gender-based claims? The viability of feminist organisations depends on the degree of internal political freedom as well as the admission of women to the national dialogue as equal partners with men, who still dominate the politics of all nations world-wide. Politics may serve as the yeast that accelerates the development of feminism as a yearning for democracy within democratic regimes, as was the case with several countries in South America in the 1970s. In more stable regimes such as that of Costa Rica, or in countries where democracy seems to be thriving after many crises, such as Venezuela, the issue of how to address legal and social rights and create new mental attitudes about gender relations has become one of the key strategies to overcome ideological divisions among women and create a unified gender 'front'. The limited numerical representation of women in the congresses of certain nations has led to the formation of women's caucuses regardless of political orientation. Argentines and Brazilians, among others, have pushed for the adoption of legislation that guarantees the election of a fixed number of women to congress, a formula that may gain in strength and popularity among other nations, although it will be a highly debated and opposed solution. At a global level these strategies may not be feasible given the disparity of political systems under which women live, but feminists and women in general must realise that looking for an insertion in the political system under which they live is essential to their success. Addressing the many slippery problems involved in the nature of the political regimes that feminists must confront is one of the greatest challenges to international feminisms, because political regimes are embedded in national or regional cultures, and are a ground with which women are not well acquainted and within which their power is limited.

Given the harrowing experience of nations under military regimes in the 1970s, the close association of Latin American feminists with the issue of human rights is not surprising. The now world-known Argentine Madres de la Plaza de Mayo and their less well known counterparts in Chile, Uruguay, Nicaragua, and Honduras, became icons of mobilisation in the name of motherhood, activating political power from the ubiquitous domestic space. They gave motherhood and family the political strength that was the dream of early twentieth-century Latin American feminists. The denunciation of torture and murder by plain women theretofore 'apolitical' had a deep ethical content and gained respect precisely because the archetype of selfless motherhood was above political commitments and had deep cultural roots. Ironically, in Latin America the model created by the Madres has received much criticism in the 1990s, especially from feminists for whom the Madres perpetuated the polarity between women–femininity–mother and men–masculinity–state. The specificity of their demands – always presented within the framework of the individual experience and the temporality of a precise situation – has been deemed insufficient to alter the power relationship between men and women. Others disagree, seeing in the Madres a potential venue for the discussion of large national problems at a pragmatic level, meaningful for those who participate in it and enhancing the power of the alliance of motherhood and human dignity in an effective way, an example worth studying by feminists elsewhere. After all, the Madres obtained global visibility and respect, and helped to weaken the military's arrogant disregard for human rights. Other Latin American Madres movements have had less visibility and less immediate success, and there is no indication that their example has been copied elsewhere. The Madres may be an idiosyncratically Latin American phenomenon. For international feminism the issue of motherhood as a political tool remains an issue of whether the value ascribed to motherhood is an asset transferable from the socialisation to the politicisation of the genders.

While the Madres did not use a feminist approach, they shared with feminist groups a thirst for human rights that has become one of the latter's

most innovative contributions to universality. In the 1980s, feminists succeeded in calling attention to the international nature of the subjection of
women as well as to the fact that the violence exercised by military and
authoritarian regimes affects women as much as it affects men. Up to then,
the call for human rights was enunciated in terms that represented men
rather than men *and* women. Feminisms world-wide may profit from the
adoption of human rights as part of its agenda. Costa Rican Alda Facio,
a dedicated supporter of this ideological marriage, posits that, because
feminism is concerned with issues that affect all women regardless of
nationality or ethnicity, it is capable of embracing and contesting all forms
of discrimination. All other political ideologies have been born out of
concern with male issues and have been tainted by the exercise of gender
discrimination in their formulation and developing stages. In her view, a
redefinition of human rights from a female viewpoint includes the rights of
females and males, of rebels and conformists, of the right and the left, and
is far more inclusive than other ideologies. Facio's endeavour to make
feminism a universal ideology through the lens of human rights deserves
attention now and in the future. She represents the direction in which some
Spanish American theorists are moving today. Argentine Elizabeth Jelin,
acknowledging the difficulties implied in drawing up a 'list of basic human
rights, from which to locate and denounce violations against women',
still concedes that the sensitivity to the violation of human rights may be
converted into a strategy to deter violence and different forms of subordination and marginalisation. Feminists should try to resolve the tensions
between women's rights and human rights by combining the struggle for
the 'recognition of women's rights as human rights', while challenging the
definition of human rights as male and Western.[5]

In the early 1980s, the late Chilean Julieta Kirkwood also travelled the
political road of feminism to tie human rights, the desire for democracy,
and the revindication of women, in a manner that may also serve to inspire
international feminisms. In her case, Kirkwood addressed the special case
of a nation with a respectable history of constitutionality that fell under
the grip of a military regime in 1974. Looking at the ideology of the right
and the left Kirkwood saw a world in which non-feminist ideologies
incorporated women into schemes directed by men whose ideas of social
redemption relegated women and gender issues to secondary and expend-
able places.[6] Women remained in silence because they did not perceive
themselves as the subjects of their own revindication. To counter that
silence, she proposed *protagonismo*, living one's own role as a woman, a
position that consciously avoided any ideology or movement in which
gender was not recognised as a category of oppression.

Kirkwood understood that male authoritarianism was more than a
political or a military experience. It was also a familiar situation experienced by women at home, at school, and at work. Its ubiquity, she thought,
gave women the opportunity to analyse the politics of gender relations and

understand the essence of the exercise of power within patriarchal societies. The struggle against political authority could and should be taken into the realms of the family, sexuality, and the sexual division of work. She also supported a feminism without class barriers. The goal of feminism was to learn how to recognise oppression, its reasons and effects, and to assume the praxis of doing what was necessary to eliminate it. Her formula to activate women in a political sense was to make them conscious of what was denying them their sociopolitical participation, and, by 'saying no to don't', to deny the man-created alterity of women. Her formula may be fruitfully put to the test and used in areas which are either suffering from the same political woes or are emerging from them. The situation of Eastern European countries where, after decades of Marxist authoritarianism, women are returning to self-analysis without ideological shackles, is comparable to the post-dictatorship period that Kirkwood anticipated for Latin American feminists. While democracy may be a desirable political system, it is not a global reality, and international feminisms must seek formulations, like those evolved in Latin America, to provide alternatives suited to the specific social and political realities of women. For women under authoritarian regimes, engendering human rights is a feasible goal that will find a sympathetic hearing in a world increasingly sensitised to discuss the polyvalent meaning of 'human'. Kirkwood's challenge demands that women take a decision born out of personal reflection that can be nurtured in 'popular' movements of poor and working-class people, as well as those self-identified as feminist. In both instances the personal awareness must relate to the political situation in a realistic manner, cogent to the culture where it develops, and must be defined by the actors themselves. The key to both is the creation of an atmosphere of social respect for women as human beings, out of which may evolve self-respect and introspection by women, the source of strength envisioned by Kirkwood and other Latin American feminists. One cannot forget, however, that while the struggle against authoritarian (and traditionally patriarchal and paternalistic) regimes may call for female solidarity, the latter does not guarantee an immediate or amicable resolution of all problems affecting women .

Class and race remain among the most divisive factors in national and international feminisms. The issue of race has not always been present or discussed in Latin American feminisms. Poverty, as a significant feature in many women's lives, has been regarded as powerful enough to become the central theme for numberless organisations dealing with poor women. Yet, race as an underlying factor has recently become an issue in some areas such as the Andean countries, where a *majority* of the women are indigenous, or in areas with a strong component of peoples of African descent, such as Brazil. The terrain of race is ambiguous, because race itself is ambiguous in a continent with 500 years of racial mixing, and in which political violence and instability, and economic struggle are powerful enough to obscure the meaning of race.[7] If, in the past, race has been 'subverted' or neglected at the national level as part of ideological, political, or even economic programmes, it is apparent that it is beginning to emerge as an element of consciousness among black and indigenous women's groups. Race is a potentially divisive factor because it is associated with strong cultural elements that separate world-views and create different interpretations of women's roles and gender relations. For example, Andean indigenous groups have traditionally mobilised around unions and labour issues in which women have collaborated with men against a well defined economic and social exploiter. The class solidarity created by the struggle plus the historically traditional social concept of gender complementarity leads them to believe that a feminism based exclusively on the assertion of women's rights is alien, especially if it is spelled by an urban and mostly white middle class. Although development and labour studies focusing on women identify poor women in terms of class and not race, the latter may act as a wedge within the elaboration of national or international feminisms.

Some representatives of indigenous nationalism separate themselves from any form of feminism, which they feel is white and 'foreign' to their cultural heritage. Recently, Vivian Arteaga Montenero, a veteran Bolivian feminist, and María Eugenia Choque Quispe, an Aymara of the work-group on Andean Oral History, came into conflict over the issue of the validity of feminism for all women. Choque Quispe assumed an antagonistic position against 'Western' feminism with clear racial connotations. She denounced non-indigenous women as exercising a form of domination seeking to change the nature of indigenous society, to which feminism was an alien and unnecessary ideology. 'The contradictions implicit in feminism do not reach the Indian woman of the ayllu because ayllu and feminism are antagonistic systems.' Hers could be the voice of many non-Western or non-white women elsewhere. Arteaga Montenero argued the relevance of gender over any other factor and denounced the nationalism of indigenous ideologies as hiding the existence of gender domination among Aymara and Quechua men.[8] This split illustrates the divisiveness that may debilitate feminisms, nationally and internationally. However, we cannot establish that all indigenous women feel like Choque Quispe. Numerous successful consciousness-raising workshops have been carried out among indigenous women, and it is also possible to detect significant changes in their attitude on gender and oppression.

The process of acquiring racial or ethnic consciousness within Latin American feminism is very recent, and most groups have been formed in the late 1980s or early 1990s. The first international encounter of black women took place in the Dominican Republic in 1992, in an attempt to build a politically oriented body that would give voice and exposure to the problems specific to black women.[9] Such meetings are feminist in nature but address specificities that other women must recognise, as well as a desire to establish paradigms of self-identity. Is this a possible model to give a voice to groups marginalised within international feminism? It is perhaps too soon to tell, but not too soon to assume that we must find a place to discuss how racial and class differences affect the perception of feminism and may lead to further fragmentation and less unity. One key concern is how to maintain a balance between the issues of race and the imperative of gender that must remain a constant to preserve the political objectives of feminism. On the other hand, the lack of resolution to concerns expressed by indigenous women and women of African ancestry may produce painful rifts. This may happen if racial or ethnic nuances are not addressed upfront with the intention of accommodating them. In Latin America race and class are very intertwined. Dark-skinned women are often at the lower rungs of the educational and economic ladder, but dark skin per se is not a precondition for poverty or social marginalisation. Feminism has to avoid conflating poverty and colour under gender, and assume that gender will be strong enough to iron out differences that, while not ignored, have not been adequately addressed. By itself, gender self-consciousness does not enable women to overcome negative individual circumstances of race or ethnic affiliation and which demand a social awareness that feminists must espouse. Since the late 1980s, Latin American feminist groups have proclaimed the need to broaden their social base to ensure that class and race are taken into consideration in the construction of an inclusive movement, overcoming lingering fears that too much specificity may weaken the view of feminism as based on gender solidarity aiming at global transformation. Choque Quispe notwithstanding, non-white and non-affluent women's nuclei have not rejected feminist venues for self-expression, while the *encuentros* have reiterated the need to nurture the concept that each economic group, each nationality, and each race, brings its own share of wealth into the definition and practice of feminism.[10]

The realisation that feminisms everywhere confront serious class and ethnic challenges should lead us to consider the need to understand how non-academic women understand feminism, what guides them to join those 'women movements' that sporadically agitate our nations, and how we could establish bridges of understanding between the diverse elements that form our societies, to assume positions vis-à-vis national and international feminisms. Women from the lowest levels of the educational rungs are today conscious of the oppression exercised by men in the name of *machismo* and traditional rights. However, their solutions to this problem are as varied as their educational, economic and ethnic backgrounds. In 1991, Colombian Eulalia Yagarí González, an indigenous Chami woman running for a place in a regional parliament, expressed nationalist sentiments when she stated that 'we need a policy for liberating women, but I don't mean a policy like the ones introduced here from Europe and North America'.[11] In her own direct way she expressed the same distrust of 'foreignness' stated by other women elsewhere in Latin America. Does this mean a rejection of internationalism per se and an endorsement of a

narrow nationalism? Not necessarily. The liberation of women is acknowledged as a universal principle, but Yagarí González underlined the need
to search for solutions to problems specifically Colombian. In 1984, a
leading Nicaraguan intellectual Milú Vargas Escobar defined her hopes for
a 'society in which we may see with our own eyes; touch the world with
our own hands; translate experiences in our own minds ... remove the
mask of exploitation, illiteracy, discrimination, hunger and poverty that has
been imposed upon us and became encrusted in our skin throughout
centuries of being exploited by imperialism'.[12] Within the framework of an
ongoing *national* revolutionary regime, Vargas Escobar was reiterating the
subjective nature of women's liberation. Vargas's words describe a political
and a personal imperialism, both signified and enforced by men, foreign
and national. These women represent the ambivalent attitudes of many
Latin American women who desire a liberation designed by themselves for
the universal problem of male domination as they experience it in their
countries and their homes.

It has been argued that theory is necessary to feminisms for opening
channels of understanding across national boundaries because theory has
the universal quality that makes feminism international. This may be true
among women of similar levels of education. Yet, the dilemma of how to
make theories accessible to women without formal education becomes
more puzzling the more sophisticated the theories become. When one turns
the pages of such media publications as *Feminaria,* produced in Buenos
Aires, or *Género y Sociedad,* produced in the Dominican Republic, the
erudite academic discussions of the latest theoretical North American and
European feminists certainly exude the aroma of exotic hothouse flowers.
Doubtless, some of the principles discussed in academic circles have found
their ways downward in a remarkable process of simplification and adjustment to daily life, as well as social service to the community of women.
Women participating in *encuentros,* meeting in spaces beyond their homes
or their countries, searched for a personal understanding of feminism and
the diversity and unity among women, and for practical solutions to make
feminism work with all women. One may say that theoretical constructs
have been less discussed than the practical purposes of self-discovery, the
understanding of the daily life problems of other women, and the understanding of how national politics impinge upon women's lives. Perhaps the
most important task of international feminism is to find that ample theoretical framework capable of embracing the largest number of female
experiences.

The articulation of the personal, the regional, and the national into a
universal formula understood by the largest number of women remains the
most elusive objective of the feminist search for an international consensus.
Yet, there is hope. While in the past the difficulty of global communication
hindered the search for mutual recognition, today we have much better
tools to engage in the process of understanding the differences among the

multiple manifestations of women's activities and the place that 'feminism' occupies in their agenda. As some Chilean feminists put it: think globally and act locally. For some leading feminists, the issue is how to avoid being 'named' or defined from centres of intellectual power outside their own experience before they learn all they need about themselves. As writer and academician Lucía Guerra Cunningham states, 'approaching the problems of Latin American women from the parameters already extensively elaborated in Europe and the United States implies, in our opinion, recycling them in a uterine space of violence and dispossession'.[13] Peruvian Virginia Vargas, an advocate of international feminisms acknowledges that 'the experiences of oppression and subordination, and the resistance to them, are expressed in so many different ways that there cannot be one global explanation which encompasses all conflicts'. The emancipation process must articulate more than one exclusive and privileged axis. It may well be that the flexibility that postmodernist analyses permit will accommodate a diversity of feminist voices, but much depends on the ability of postmodernist analysts to make themselves understood.

I believe that we are closer to the creation of feminist paradigms in close touch with the broader features of Latin American culture than may be assumed. In my understanding, the large feminist and women-oriented literature across the disciplines is an expression of a cultural self-recognition that bears an indisputable Latin American character, despite the many national and political approaches of such writings. The construction of a supra-national category of gender, comprising a body of women-citizens speaking in multiple voices, is a reality that has been taking shape in the last twenty years, but with strong historical roots that go back over one hundred years.

Latin American women's writings and voices tell us that we should not approach contemporary feminisms in that area through a 'post-colonial' lens applicable to other parts of the world. The colonial past of the area is chronologically 'remote', insofar as independence from Spain was achieved by 1825 – with the exception of Cuba and Puerto Rico, which remained as colonial enclaves until the end of that century. Explanations of women's status or gender relations using colonialism as an experience within memory become more difficult than for other areas. The model of 'foreign' elements diametrically opposed to a native culture becomes questionable as we learn that Spaniards, Portuguese, indigenous people and Africans exchanged cultural traits and engaged in a biological and cultural *mestizaje* (blending). However, we may engage the concept of colonialism fruitfully if we recall that social and economic walls, constructed around the ruling colonial European elite, gave priority to its objectives and pre-eminence to its values, and created models of gender behaviour and relations that became a model for several centuries and are still detectable in our societies. Is it possible to speak of North American or Euro-centred feminisms exercising undue influence as a form of cultural imperialism – on

Latin America? I believe that the longstanding influence of leftist ideologies, the nationalist undercurrents of Latin American nations, and the socio-economic problems of our nations help prevent a take-over of theories constructed elsewhere, without previous rewording and adaptation to our own needs. Revolutionary regimes, such as those of Cuba and Nicaragua, resorted to the political power of Marxism, to offer strong resistance to 'bourgeois', i.e. North American and European formulated, feminisms. In Nicaragua some feminists were working on the reformulation of the regime's position vis-à-vis concepts of international feminism when the political revolution 'collapsed' in its first elective trial. In Cuba, the duration of the regime has allowed its leadership to formulate and reformulate positions that have changed from vociferous opposition to feminism to an official 'hospitality' attitude towards it in the mid 1990s. In neither country did the mobilisation of women generate any special sympathy for foreign models, and the adjustments that took place in gender relations had more to do with their internal political needs than with international ideological pressure. In non-revolutionary countries, nationalism is but one element conspiring against the wholesale import of ideas. Traditional conservatism and cultural machismo are strong obstacles to the development of feminism itself that will inevitably – even as they lose ground – exert pressure for a reformulation of feminism more attuned to regional and national cultural features. These are some of the reasons why I argue that Latin American feminisms are responding, as they must, to national and cultural pressures, even as they ponder on the universal values of gender-constructed ideologies.

Under historical analysis, the possibilities of revealing the multifaceted nature of Latin American feminisms will allow us not only to stretch the boundaries of our own understanding, but to welcome the experience of women elsewhere, as well as let them see that the mirror of womanhood reflects an imperfect but challenging view that comprises multi-ethnic and multi-racial components. Latin American feminisms have given some key concepts and experiences to the debate of feminisms in the international arena: the extension of the concept of the struggle for political democracy to the home as the initial step in eroding the patriarchal grip of husbands and fathers; the need to engender the concept of human rights to formulate a global concept of female as human and therefore respectable; the debate over the validity of empowering women by casting maternal images (*marianismo*) in critical national as well as in daily political circumstances; the validation of women's economic role in society by academic analyses, whose ultimate symbolism lies in contesting the intellectual hegemony of national and international male economic planners; the reflection on how behavioural stereotypes remain in the allocation of power to women even in 'revolutionary' regimes. Not all feminists believe in using the image of a sacrificial but powerful mother (as Mary, the mother of Christ and thus *marianismo*) as a satisfactory way of politically empowering women, but the fact that in some instances the maternalist position has yielded significant power in Latin America remains a challenge for feminists everywhere because maternalism may not necessarily have the same significance and ability to empower women in other parts of the world. Since two important revolutionary regimes have attempted to (and in one case succeeded) reshape social and economic structures without undue change in gender relations, international feminisms of the twenty-first century should take note that 'revolutionary' ideology must include gender to be a true venue of change for women's status. It is also crucial to remember that the cultural weight of androcentrism can become a substantial obstacle to strictly political ideological solutions to change in gender relations.

In learning about the possibility of alternative forms of expressing power, and of envisioning gender roles under different cultural circumstances, we can see the value of the study of a region such as Latin America, where feminisms reflect the pluralism of the rest of the world. The amplification and revalidation of international feminisms will not necessarily mean a globalisation of feminism as a hegemonic force, but an understanding of the fact that globalisation means recognition of the national and the supra-national in a fruitful exchange of mutual appreciation.

Notes

1. See, Peter Waterman, 'Hidden from Herstory: Women, Feminism and New Global Solidarity', *Economic and Political Weekly* (Bombay), 30 October 1993, and 'Feminism and Internationalism in Latin America: A suitable case for treatment?', unpublished, 1996. For the history of Latin American feminisms, see June Hahner, *Emancipating the Female Sex: The Struggle for Women's Rights in Brazil, 1850–1940* (Duke University Press, Durham, 1990); K. Lynn Stoner, *From the House to the Streets: The Cuban Woman's Movement for Legal Reform, 1898–1940* (Duke University Press, Durham, 1991); Asunción Lavrin, *Women, Feminism, and Social Change: Argentina, Chile, and Uruguay, 1890–1940* (University of Nebraska Press, Lincoln, 1995), and 'Unfolding Feminism: Spanish American Women's Writing, 1970–1990', in *Feminisms in the Academy*, ed. Domna C. Stanton and Abigail J. Stewart (The University of Michigan Press, Ann Arbor, 1995), pp. 248–73; Virginia Vargas, 'The Feminist Movement in Peru: Inventory and Perspectives', in *Women's Struggles and Strategies*, ed. Saskia Wieringa (Gower, Brookfield, 1988), pp. 136–55. This short bibliography by no means exhausts the topic. A key channel for international communication is *mujer/fempress* a monthly magazine edited in Santiago de Chile as an alterative feminist network.

2. Francesca Miller, 'Latin American Feminism and the Transnational Arena', in *Women, Culture, and Politics in Latin America* (University of California Press, Berkeley, 1990), pp. 10–26.

3. See Lavrin, *Women, Feminism, and Social Change*, ch. 1.

4. See, for example, *Memoria del IV Encuentro Feminista Latinoamericano y del Caribe* (n.e., Taxco, Mexico, 1987); Nancy Saporta Sternbach et al., 'Feminisms in Latin America: From Bogotá to San Bernardo', *Signs*, 17 (1992), pp. 393–434; Diana Bellesi

et al., 'VII Encuentro Feminista Latinoamericano y del Caribe', *Feminaria*, 10 (1997), pp. 28–36.

5. Alda Facio, 'Repensarnos como mujeres para reconceptualizar los derechos humanos', *Género y Sociedad*, 3 (1995), pp. 1–54; Elizabeth Jelin, 'Engendering Human Rights', in *Gender Politics in Latin America*, ed. Elizabeth Dore (Monthly Review Press, New York, 1997), pp. 65–83.

6. Julieta Kirkwood, *Ser política en Chile. Las feministas y los partidos* (Facultad Latinoamericana de Ciencias Sociales, FLACSO, Santiago de Chile, 1986).

7. In a homogeneously black country such as Haiti, poverty subverts gender in the perception of self–appointed feminist women. Olga Benoit, Haitian head of a forum for rural women and market sellers, identifies the institutionalisation of male domination, *machismo*, as the greatest obstacle to the acceptance of feminist premises at even the lowest levels. See interview with Olga Benoit and Marie Frantz Joachim in Gaby Kuppers (ed.), *Compañeras: Voices from the Latin American Women's Movement* (Latin America Bureau, London, 1994), pp. 34–9.

8. Vivian Arteaga Montenero, 'Jornada sobre feminismo y política', in *Feminismo y política*, (Coordinadora de la Mujer, La Paz, 1986), pp. 63–5.

9. See *Especial/Fempress*, 1995, a special edition of the Chilean-based feminist magazine, dedicated to discuss issues raised by black women across Latin America. Also, *mujer/fempress* , no. 131 (September 1992), p. 7.

10. *Memoria del IV Encuentro*, p. 96; 'El feminismo de los 90: Desafíos y propuestas', summary for the *V Encuentro Feminista Latinoamericano y del Caribe*, in *mujer/fempress*, no. 111 (January 1991), pp.4–6.

11. Kuppers, *Compañeras*, p. 143.

12. Ileana Rodríguez, *Registradas en la Historia: 10 años del quehacer feminista en Nicaragua* (CIAM, Managua, 1990), p. 154.

13. Lucía Guerra Cunningham, 'Alternativas ideológicas del feminismo latino-americano', *Feminaria*, 5 (1992), pp. 1–2.

FORUM RESPONDENTS

Feminisms and Internationalism: A View from the Centre

LEILA J. RUPP

As numerous literary works and films, as well as feminist standpoint theory, have reminded us, our understanding of what has happened in the past or what is happening now depends heavily on the angle of vision provided by our particular vantage points. Asunción Lavrin provides us here with a thought-provoking portrait of feminisms – 'born wrapped in one great hope' – from the perspective of Latin American women's history. I picture her standing somewhere between Mexico and Argentina, circling slowly in order to survey what goes on around her. When she turns her gaze to the far north and northeast, feminisms in the United States and in Western Europe look very different from her southern standpoint.

What I would like to do here is to fix my vision on some of the same subjects from a different angle. I am, I guess, on a ship in the Atlantic, a ship that is theoretically able to sail to any continent but in fact inclined to ply the seas between North America, Britain, and northern Europe. I look, that is, from the perspective of the major international women's organisations that formed in the late nineteenth and early twentieth centuries: the cautious and inclusive International Council of Women (1888), the feminist International Alliance of Women (1904), and the progressive Women's International League for Peace and Freedom (1915).[1] Theoretically open to women all across the globe, these groups primarily organised elite, Christian, older women of European origin. Yet in the 1920s and 1930s the three bodies did succeed in adding national sections in such places as Argentina, Egypt, India, and Rhodesia. However limited their internationalism might have been in practice, their commitment to global organising makes the view from their vantage point at the very least supra-national. From this perspective, I would like to consider four issues that Lavrin raises in her essay: the relationship of nationalism and internationalism, the definition of 'feminism' or 'feminisms', the inclusiveness of feminisms, and the question of what, if anything, women might have in common across time and space.

Lavrin suggests that Latin America 'offers an interesting case-study in the dialogue of national and international feminisms' because of course it comprises many countries and cultures yet shares some unifying characteristics. I would suggest further that the perspectives of women from Latin America, as well as Asia, the Middle East, and Africa, have historically challenged the notion that nationalism and internationalism are polar opposites. Lavrin points out that internationalism fuelled the national struggles of Latin American feminists, that a 'balance of national and international interests [is absolutely] essential for the survival of feminism as an expression of diversity'. My own work on the international women's organisations shows that women from colonised or dependent countries often fought for national autonomy as a prerequisite for internationalism, encountering resistance from women who took their own national identity and independence for granted. Where a woman stood in the world system, that is, had a powerful effect on her understanding of the relationship of nationalism and internationalism. Further, the notion that women from Third World nations are too nationalist to be good internationalists – common in the movement I studied as well, I think, as today – ignores the fact that all feminisms are grounded in nationalism. They differ in part depending on when they emerged in relation to the securing of national autonomy. Thus Egyptian feminism in the 1930s looked 'too nationalist' to the British and US women involved in the international women's movement, but that was only because they took their own nationalist interests for granted.

Perhaps the central question with which Lavrin grapples is whether it is possible to define or conceptualise 'feminisms' without either forcing a Euro-American mould onto the rest of the world or allowing the term to shatter into such tiny shards that they cannot be glued back together. I would argue that, in order to conceptualise feminisms globally, we need to think about them organisationally and tactically as well as ideologically. Verta Taylor and I suggest in a forthcoming article in *Signs* that we need to move away from a purely ideological approach to defining feminisms by looking, instead, at how women constructed, sometimes through conflict with one another, different levels of collective identity or 'we-ness'.[2] In the case of the international women's movement in the early twentieth century, we distinguish organisational identity (based on affiliation with a particular group), a broader movement identity that subordinates individual social movement organisations to the cause of feminist internationalism, and an even more inclusive solidary gender identity. We argue that such an approach avoids a static notion of identity and also allows us to see how feminists with conflicting interests and ideas were (and are) able to talk across their differences.

Applying this scheme to the general problem of feminisms and internationalism, we would recognise that women belong to specific national and international bodies to which they feel loyalty, that they also claim labels such as 'feminist' or 'humanist' that bind them across organisational and national boundaries even as they struggle over the meaning of those terms, and in addition that they, at times, embrace a diffuse gender solidarity on the basis of, for example, potential motherhood. I see all of these levels in Lavrin's essay, as women organise on the national level to fight for suffrage, as they come together with women throughout the Americas in the Interamerican Commission of Women conferences, as they mobilise in the name of motherhood in Argentina, Chile, Uruguay, Nicaragua, and Honduras. Rather than debate what represents 'women's rights' and what 'human rights', a multilevel collective-identity approach recognises that in disagreements like that between Vivian Arteaga Montenero, the Bolivian feminist, and María Eugenia Choque Quispe, the Aymara who rejects Western feminism as imperialist, what is important is that they are talking to each other.

The debate between Arteaga Montenero and Choque Quispe gets to the heart of the question of the inclusiveness of feminisms. Here I think we must distinguish between the possibilities for inclusiveness and the realities of exclusion. The history of the international women's movement is instructive. Despite grand proclamations of their global nature, the international organisations – by virtue of their choice of official languages, sites for conferences, election of leadership, and so on – mirrored and perpetuated the dynamics of global power. But one has only to compare, say, the congress of the International Council of Women in London in 1899 with the United Nations Fourth World Conference on Women in Beijing in 1995 to see the possibilities for inclusiveness across class, race, ethnicity, religion, nationality, and sexuality.

In other words, I would argue that feminisms are not *necessarily* exclusive of the groups of women who have historically been marginalised. Rather, structural barriers, often unintended although sometimes consciously erected, have made feminisms inaccessible or irrelevant to such women. Yet it has not been and will not be enough simply to lower the barriers, to invite new groups of women to join the party on the same old terms. Instead feminisms must both become accessible and also change in response to an expanding constituency. I am optimistic that this has begun to happen.

Which brings us to the question of what, if anything, women have in common. Despite all the important progress we have made in breaking down the notion of a universal 'woman', what is striking from an international and historical perspective is how deep the roots of the idea of difference between women and men go. Women in the international women's movement clung to the belief that women, as potential or actual or 'social' mothers, had an interest in preserving life that made them opponents of war. They built solidarity around women's reproductive capabilities, their susceptibility to gendered violence, and their lack of political power. They did not (perhaps because of their elite status) rally around women's economic disadvantage, a theme that has become central in the contemporary move-ment and that speaks to the question of responsiveness to an expanding constituency. Economic disadvantage, like issues of reproduction and bodily integrity, links elite women in corporate America bumping up against the glass ceiling with the poorest peasant woman in the Sudan without pre-tending that their problems are the same.

So where does all of this leave us? I would suggest, in conclusion, two things. First, we need to view feminisms and internationalism from multiple angles, from national, comparative, and international locations. Lavrin sug-gests what Latin American feminism adds to the picture. Margot Badran's portrayal of the centrality of European feminist leaders in the memories of Egyptian feminists shows the lack of reciprocity in international feminist circles, since the records of the European-based feminist circles are quite silent about Egyptian and other Third World participants.[3] Mala Mathrani's work on Indian women's activism in the international women's movement points out the compatibility of nationalism and internationalism.[4] We need to advance on all fronts by continuing to explore national feminisms, by engaging in more comparative work of the kind undertaken by Karen Offen, and by expanding our horizons to feminisms practised at a global level.

Second, I would argue optimistically for the promise of global femi-nisms. If nationalism and internationalism do not have to act as polar opposites; if we can conceptualise feminisms broadly enough to encompass a vast array of local variations displaying multiple identities; if we work to dismantle the barriers to participation in national and international women's movements; if we build on the basic common denominators of women's relationship to production and reproduction, however multifaceted in practice; then we can envisage truly global feminisms that can, in truth, change the world.

Notes

1. See Leila J. Rupp, *Worlds of Women: The Making of an International Women's Movement* (Princeton University Press, Princeton, 1998).

2. Leila J. Rupp and Verta Taylor, 'Forging Feminist Identity in an International Movement: A Collective Identity Approach to Feminism', *Signs*, forthcoming.

3. Margot Badran, *Feminists, Islam, and Nation: Gender and the Making of Modern Egypt* (Princeton University Press, Princeton, 1995).

4. Mala Mathrani, 'Nationalism or Internationalism? All-India Women's Confer-ence, 1927–1947', paper presented at the annual meeting of the American Historical Association, Atlanta, January 1996.

Feminisms and Internationalisms:
A Response from India

MARY E. JOHN

The relations between feminism and internationalism have invariably been entangled ones, with local and global questions increasingly co-implicating one another. If this is true of the Indian context I am familiar with, Asunción Lavrin's welcome essay indicates that the Latin American context is no exception either.

Nonetheless, it has been somewhat disorienting to read about feminist initiatives and problems from the perspective of a continent that lies, culturally speaking, considerably to the West of India, but is at the same time also part of 'the South'. Lavrin's essay not only exposes the extent of my/our ignorance of 'other others', but, even more important, it highlights the elusiveness of 'internationalism' as a concept and a goal. Does such an internationalism imply total blindness to questions of national affiliation? If not, what are the criteria by which it would seek to differentiate nations and national contexts? What sorts of commonality would it look for or hope to cultivate? For it is obvious – today more than ever before – that while an internationalist perspective must, by definition, take one beyond national concerns, dominant transnational (global?) forces preposition us to look in certain directions rather than others.

From the Indian side, I can vouch for the fact that there has been little pressure to think about possible connections to Latin America. This is in spite of the historic misnaming of the 'indios' by the conquistadores five centuries ago, or Latin American influences of more recent decades such as dependency theory, liberation theology, or, at a different level, the charismatic inspiration of Che Guevara. But these have been transient presences in India, insufficient to build on, and with no immediate feminist implications. If truth be told, Indians, even educated ones, are more likely to know of a figure like Eva Peron through the Bombay remake of the US musical *Evita*, rather than her campaign for Argentinian women's suffrage.

I do not know whether (or in what ways) the Latin American situation is different from ours, nor what place – if any – India has in feminist debates there. If my response is, therefore, something of a shot in the dark, I see it also as an important opportunity to try and initiate a dialogue where no parameters or agendas have been laid out in advance. The challenge would be to try and rethink some of the assumptions that undergird Indian feminism and internationalism in the light of what Lavrin has to say. Though her essay raises many pertinent questions, I would like to concentrate on the two which are of special comparative value for feminist debates in India: the prevalence of *pluralism*, and the legacy of *colonialism*. Significantly enough, the question of pluralism figures already on the first page and effectively sets the tone for the essay as a whole. Colonialism, in contrast, is only explicitly addressed at the end, and that too in order to signal its experiential remoteness from most present-day problems.

This, then, is my point of entry for a possible dialogue. India may not be a continent; nevertheless, it too has had a long and complicated history of pluralisms, disparities and divisions. Such formative experiences (which the Indian state attempts to manage through proclamations of 'unity in diversity') bring us in the vicinity of Latin American realities. The question of colonialism, on the other hand, queers the pitch. It is not so much that colonialism still presses itself upon us (independence was won fifty years ago), but that its legacy is far from being settled. The question of the dominance or hegemony of colonial rule; the uneven transformation of modes of existence both economic and cultural; problems concerning ongoing or new dependencies – Third World, neo-colonial, post-colonial; the reconstitution through colonial and Western frames of the very notions of pluralism and difference themselves – all of these are live issues yet to be resolved.

Let me begin with how colonialism has been tackled in Indian feminism. The colonial legacy is nowhere more apparent than in the special 'recasting' of gender, women's rights and feminism, beginning at least from the nineteenth century, but with resonances up to the present day.[1] As the ongoing bearers of 'Indian tradition', middle-class feminists can still be accused of betrayal and inauthenticity since their feminism becomes equated with westernisation.[2]

Preceded as it was by a century of social reform (involving specific relations of inequality among British officials, missionaries from various parts of the Western world, and Indians – both men and women – from different castes and regions of the country), 'feminism' is first mentioned around the turn of the twentieth century.[3] Compared to the wealth of scholarship on nineteenth-century figures, debates and controversies, the twentieth century unfortunately remains somewhat sparsely researched as yet.[4] This also means that the history of international feminist relations (such as those between the nationalist-feminists of the All India Women's Conference and British suffragettes during the 1920s) has yet to be written. There are glimpses, moreover, of alternate internationalisms during this time. The year 1931, for instance, was witness to a series of related feminist interventions: the passing of the resolution on fundamental rights, including women's equality, by the Indian National Congress; the adoption of a similar resolution by the Communist Party of China; and a gathering in the same year of the Congress of Asian Women for Equality in Lahore (now in Pakistan).[5] Though more is known about Western connections, we still lack a nuanced sense of the commonalities and divergences undergirding Western women's agendas in India – ranging from Katherine Mayo's infamous indictment of 'Hindu barbarism' in her widely circulated book *Mother India*, to the more 'sympathetic' views of Annie Besant, Irish anti-imperialist campaigner based in Madras, whose vision of India's 'future' was constructed on a nationalist and Brahmanical Hinduism.[6]

The period leading up to independence in 1947 was to witness the crisscrossing or blocking of numerous feminist concerns. The critical domains of reproduction, contraception and population control, which first gained ground during the 1920s and 1930s, illustrate how a 'women's issue' could be caught in the cross-currents emanating from: the first Indian eugenics societies, the neo-Malthusian League, Gandhian nationalists, and the non-Brahmin movement, not to speak of Margaret Sanger from the United States and Marie Stopes from Britain.[7]

This historical background partly explains why Lavrin's claim that 'Latin American feminists developed a strong vocation for internationalism' (p. 520) is echoed somewhat differently in India. The international relations of Indian feminists were fractured by the inequalities of colonialism, the contested priorities of the nationalist movement, and also by other conflicts.

The decades following independence – the fifties and sixties – have acquired the somewhat misleading label of the 'silent period' in the Indian women's movement. This is mainly because of the enormous hope and legitimacy vested in the Indian nation-state under Jawaharlal Nehru, a state explicitly committed to the ideals of democracy, socialism and non-alignment. Such a political climate seemed to relativise prior feminist initiatives; but the swift repression of left-wing oppositional struggles in which women were active (such as the Telangana struggle) was also a contributing factor. Whatever the real significance of the less-known decades of the fifties and sixties, there can be no doubt that a fresh phase of feminist activism began during the critical conjunctures of the 1970s, which witnessed the emergence of a range of rural and urban movements, often in direct confrontation with an increasingly centralised state.[8]

The Progressive Organisation of Women in the southern city of Hyderabad was one of the first militant women's groups to be formed during the early 1970s, followed by the mushrooming of various groups in different parts of the country.[9] International inspiration came as much from Maoism and the 'speak bitterness' meetings of Chinese women as from Western socialist-feminisms and the early consciousness-raising campaigns. On the more academic side, the Committee on the Status of Women (set up at the initiative of the Department of Social Welfare of the Government of India in anticipation of the UN Women's Year of 1975), produced a remarkable document known as the *Towards Equality* report. Its wide-ranging findings proved that the living conditions of the vast majority of Indian women had actually deteriorated since independence – a revelation that shattered the complacencies of a generation of feminists who had come of age in the post-independence period. Deeply nationalist in its framework and assumptions, this text played a very significant role at the UN conference in Mexico City, and was ultimately more widely circulated abroad than at home.[10]

It is not easy to capture the range of activities undertaken by a newly resurgent movement during the 1970s and 1980s – including diverse campaigns against rape, 'dowry deaths', hazardous contraceptives, bad working conditions, and so on; lobbying for changes in government policy and legislative reform; and the emergence of women's studies as the academic arm of the movement. While local problems and interventions were emphasised, the burden of accountability was seen as resting mostly on the state. Thus, international issues were not commonly invoked as a major focus or rallying point. Feminism was adopted as a self-description more easily by some than by others. Differences and lines of tension between women's groups were constitutive of this phase of the movement from its very inception. Such tensions were often those between organisations affiliated to political parties, especially those on the left, and others who claimed 'autonomy' for themselves.

Nearer the present, the 1990s seem to be something of a watershed decade. On the one hand, the increasing international visibility of the movement and the growth of feminist scholarship from India have brought Indian debates into transnational fora of various kinds – activist, academic, governmental, and NGO. Overshadowing this, however, has been another worrisome development – the annexation and redeployment of feminist initiatives by the state, political parties and resurgent Hindu Right-wing forces in particular, and by international agencies, to mention the most important. Though some Indian feminists were relieved to see that the fourth world women's conference in Beijing and Huairou in 1995 appeared to reaffirm the vitality of women's movements world-wide (in contrast to explicit attempts at Nairobi in 1985 to deflect attention to 'gender sensitisation' techniques at the expense of critiques of patriarchy and development), others were deeply concerned over the more subtle but comprehensive influence of international donor agencies, from the very preparatory process for the conference and the selection of representatives, to ongoing attempts to mould agendas.[11]

The most disorienting aspect of contemporary developments, however, is that the more straightforward meanings attached to terms such as 'local' and 'global' no longer seem adequate. Thus, for instance, we are only beginning to recognise that the processes of globalisation (to which India is a relative latecomer) give birth not only to highly visible *trans*national movements and influences, but to equally significant transformations *within*

Entessar, Nader (1989)

To Kurdish Mosaic η Discord

Third World Quarterly

Vol 11, No 4

pp 83 – 100

national boundaries as well. As for conceptions of the local, doubts have been raised for some time about the problematic nature of the 'Indian' or the 'indigenous'. For if 'Hindu religion' and 'caste' (to mention the two most common markers of a quintessentially Indian identity) are constructs that have been irreversibly transformed by the colonial encounter, then affirmations of Indian authenticity cannot claim immunity from the processes of modernity.

Questions relating to the local, the national and the global have thus become difficult and contentious issues, and a great deal hinges on the context and the particular standpoint from which they are deployed. In other words, these terms have not shed their older meanings, even though these are being renegotiated on many levels. India is now going through yet another period of transition, when very little holds still and the relationship of the past to the future appears particularly uncertain. Moreover, current pressures on the Indian nation-state are multi-dimensional to say the least. The policies of globalisation, liberalisation and the 'opening up' of the economy to international market forces (after four decades of autarkically planned, state-led development) have been accompanied by the political prominence of the Hindu Right, by growing caste cleavages and disparities, and by regional reassertions of various kinds. This also means that the paradigm inhabited by the nationalist feminism of earlier decades, in which urban middle-class feminists with their largely unexamined default identity as upper-caste Hindus assumed the right to speak in the name of the majority and for their welfare, is no longer viable.

One of the more positive outcomes of all these developments is that we are being forced to take a fresh look at 'pluralism' and 'diversity', both within the nation and beyond. If feminism is not singular, neither is internationalism. It has become more important than ever to understand the different stakes involved in laying claim to local, national, and international arenas. Nationalism – with an effectively upper-caste Hindu slant – has played a pre-eminent role vis-à-vis colonialism and Western domination in recent Indian history. It has therefore had the power to shape, further or hinder international links. But 'foreign' influences may look very different when seen 'from below', as the subaltern, predominantly lower-caste locations and careers of Islam and Christianity in India might suggest. To take another more recent example, the increasingly visible gay and lesbian movements in India have drawn sustenance both from their local ties to the Indian women's movement, and from their international connections to the identity politics of sexuality in the West.[12]

Taking pluralism more seriously than we have so far would involve re-examining the feminist concepts (such as patriarchy and gender) that we deploy in our respective contexts. Our notion of pluralism must respond to power-laden global and national realities – it cannot be an abbreviation for the sort of relativism where hermetically sealed cultures and their discrete patriarchal arrangements coexist without friction. At least in recent history, our differently gendered contexts have evolved out of situations of contestation, through processes of mutual, if unequal, implication. The fact that the world today is not only divided, but is, by all accounts, heading towards increasing disparities between regions and peoples, has definite consequences for conceptualising gender relations. I am, therefore, genuinely unclear about Lavrin's 'imperative' that gender 'must remain a constant to preserve the political objectives of feminism' (p. 529). If there is a common condition that feminism must address, it is one of unequal patriarchies and disparate genders. The imperative, then, is to recognise how asymmetries and structures of privilege may have prevented solidarities; and to fight on many fronts to enable the development of more viable feminisms.

The failure of certain international feminisms from the West which had assumed the right to speak for all women everywhere is only too well known. What alternate possibilities and fresh dangers might be in store for us, as Indian feminists address themselves to new international challenges? Let me conclude by briefly alluding to some fledgling efforts currently under way which have the potential – yet to be realised – of sharpening and giving new direction to local/global questions.

My first example is a project (in which I am also involved) of dialogic exchange and translation between a group of French and Indian feminists. Initiated a few years ago, the project aims to collectively produce two edited volumes, one on feminism in India for publication in France, and its twin, a collection on French feminisms for Indian readers. As a venture falling within the ambit of academic 'cultural exchange', it is possibly unique in its feminist origins and especially in its two-way structure. Contemporary inequalities between France and India are sustained as much by the weight of 'high theory' that has come to stand in for feminism in France, as by the otherness of India, still orientalised and seen as a victim-nation of the 'Third World'. While essays have been selected with an eye to how well they might travel and be relevant for their new French/Indian addressee, we do not conceive of translation as an effort to try and 'close the gap'. Rather, translation involves making available to the 'global' reader as much as possible of the 'local' contexts, histories and debates that produced the original essays. Rendering explicit those aspects of context which are usually taken for granted (and thus naturalised), and consciously cultivating a sensitivity to present problems, might not only enlarge our respective worlds, but, no less significantly, encourage us to see ourselves remade in another language and, therefore, in a new light.

A different kind of regional internationalism has been gaining momentum during the last decade. This relates to the growing importance of South Asia as a supra-national region – in government diplomacy and military strategy, as an economic zone for trade and investment, and for feminist engagement and coalition-building. Indeed, feminists have been at the forefront of the recent rediscovery of the Partition of British India in 1947. They have retold the violent births of Pakistan, India and East Pakistan (now Bangladesh), by drawing from the hitherto suppressed perspectives of the millions of people, especially women, whose lives were disrupted under conditions of incredible uncertainty regarding their ultimate destination or homeland.[13]

Compared to my previous example of feminist collaboration across national frontiers, the geopolitics and ethnic conflicts of South Asia present very different challenges and difficulties. For example, the Indian authors of a volume on women's experiences of the Partition begin by acknowledging that their initial plans to work on a three-country oral history of women's experiences had to be changed.[14] In the South Asian context, feminists from India also have to contend with India's dominance in the region, and the disproportionate influence wielded by Indian perspectives across our borders. (I wonder what lessons Latin American feminisms might have to offer on analogous intra-regional, inter-national asymmetries.) This is not to detract, however, from the heightened awareness of the complicated pasts of the subcontinent, which has inspired more concerted attempts to question the claims and policies of the Indian state, whether on the role of the Indian army's 'peace keeping forces' in Sri Lanka, or on the politically volatile claims about mass Bangladeshi 'infiltration' into Indian border states and metropolitan cities.

Apart from the increased attention being paid to the South Asian region, 'India' is also being evoked and mobilised across the globe by a newly emergent diaspora. Suddenly (or so it would seem), people from countries with such disparate historical connections to India as Britain, the United States, Canada, Trinidad, Guyana, Fiji, Mauritius, South Africa and Australia, are affirming the Indian within themselves. Repercussions on gender relations, especially in the form of women's unique roles in maintaining community identity, are also apparent. Though the temptation to view these developments as derivative nationalisms and revivals of 'Indian womanhood' is considerable, especially in view of the coordinated global activities of right-wing organisations such as the Vishwa Hindu Parishad (VHP), this may have to be resisted. The specific political-cultural content of, and motivations behind, invocations of 'India' have to be examined in relation to the particular local circumstances that produced them – in a bi-racial African and East Indian society like Trinidad; after the world-historic defeat of apartheid and under Nelson Mandela's Rainbow Coalition in South Africa; in relation to the new racism epitomised by the rise of the One Nation Party in Australia; or in the emergence of yet another 'model minority' in the United States. In this area too, feminists have once again had to strain against dominant versions of nationalism and Indian patriarchy in order to make room for diasporic negotiations of gender, citizenship and identity.[15]

This brings me to my final theme for the exploration of internationalist agendas: South–South relations and feminism. For all their importance, efforts along these lines have been particularly tenuous and difficult to sustain. The history of the making of the 'Third World' (initially composed of the newly independent states of Africa and Asia, and subsequently joined by Latin America) has clearly left its imprint in feminist circles, as the ongoing use of the phrase 'Third World feminism' would attest. Feminists in India and elsewhere have been particularly active in building solidarity against the negative fallout of structural adjustment programmes initiated by the World Bank and the IMF since the 1980s, given all the evidence that it is poor women who would bear the brunt of the 'social cost' of such programmes.

However, alongside the recent redivision of the globe into North and South, a more subtle remapping of the Third World into zones of 'success' (Southeast Asia), 'failure' (Latin America) and 'collapse' (sub-Saharan Africa) has been taking place. This is an important development that has not received the critical attention it deserves. As I have argued elsewhere, in globalising India, the image of being sandwiched between the two options of sub-Saharan Africa to the West and Southeast Asia to the East, has become quite a potent one, even in development and progressive circles.[16] This is why, in my view, the most effective response to globalisation and current proclamations about the 'end of the Third World' would be the forging of alternative South–South linkages.

Comparative work across the South has the potential of displacing the hegemony of the West as our default frame of reference. Instead of looking for, or expecting to find, homogeneity in Third World places, feminist engagements can help lift the largely subterranean histories of lateral con-nections and influences above the threshold of visibility. A fascinating potential case here would be the complex local mobilisations of – and relationships between – the Argentine Madres de la Plaza de Mayo (and similar mothers' struggles in other parts of Latin America), and the series of Mothers' Fronts which emerged in different regions of Sri Lanka from 1984 onwards to protest the 'disappearance' of Sri Lankan men by the state.[17] Contrary to Lavrin's assumption, therefore, it would seem that the 'Madres' are not an idiosyncratic Latin American phenomenon; and I am sure that there are other relationships yet to be excavated.

My purpose in discussing these examples of newly emergent internationalisms – more egalitarian and dialogic Western collaborations, new perspectives on the South Asian region and the Indian diaspora, and attempts to rethink South–South relations – is to try and provide specific content to the plural forms that feminist internationalisms can take. As we approach the twenty-first century in the global context of a uni-polar world order, struggles by women and by feminists have never been more critical for thinking about and working toward a more democratic and equal world. If there is no single universal method that will take all of us there, the specific paths being forged in particular locations must be our starting point. This forum has provided an invaluable opportunity for demonstrating how entangled yet apart our distinct histories have been, and how much more needs to be built as we struggle for and towards a less unevenly shared – a common – future.

Notcs

1. The classic text to have foregrounded these issues is Kumkum Sangari and Sudesh Vaid (eds), *Recasting Women: Essays in Colonial History* (Kali for Women, New Delhi, 1989).

2. Some of the conceptual problems concerning feminism in India and the West have been addressed in my book *Discrepant Dislocations: Feminism, Theory, and Postcolonial Histories* (University of California Press, Berkeley, and Oxford University Press, Delhi, 1996), and in a subsequent essay, 'Feminism in India and the West', in *Cultural Dynamics* (in press).

3. Some general overviews of the nineteenth and twentieth centuries are to be found in B. R. Nanda (ed.), *Indian Women: From Purdah to Modernity* (1976; Vikas, Delhi, 1996); Radha Kumar, *A History of Doing: An Illustrated Account of the Movements for Women's Rights and Feminism in India* (Kali for Women, New Delhi, 1993); Susie Tharu and K. Lalita (eds), *Women Writing in India: 600 B.C. to the Present*, vols I and II (Feminist Press, New York, and Oxford University Press, Delhi, 1991 and 1993); Geraldine Forbes, *Women in Modern India* (Cambridge University Press, 1996).

Recent studies of the nineteenth century include Mrinalini Sinha, *Colonial Masculinity: The 'Manly' Englishman and the 'Effeminate' Bengali in the Late Nineteenth Century* (Manchester University Press, Manchester, 1995, and Kali for Women, New Delhi, 1997); Sudhir Chandra, *Enslaved Daughters: Colonialism, Law and Women's Rights* (Oxford University Press, Delhi, 1997); Uma Chakravarti, *Rewriting History: The Life and Times of Pandita Ramabai* (Kali for Women, New Delhi, 1998).

4. The important exception here is the figure of Gandhi, who has received considerable feminist and international attention over the years. See also Aparna Basu, *Mridula Sarabhai: Rebel with a Cause* (Oxford University Press, Delhi, 1996).

5. I am indebted to Vina Mazumdar for bringing this to my attention.

6. See Mrinalini Sinha, Editor's Introduction to Katherine Mayo's *Mother India* (Kali for Women, New Delhi, forthcoming). For a discussion of Annie Besant in the context of the non-Brahmin movement, see V. Geetha and S. V. Rajadurai, *From Iyotheedass to Periyar: Towards a Non-Brahmin Millenium* (Samya, Calcutta, in press).

7. Barbara Ramusack, 'Embattled Advocates: The Debate over Birth Control in India, 1920–40', *Journal of Women's History*, 1 (1989); S. Anandhi, 'Reproductive Bodies and Regulated Sexuality: Birth Control Debates in Early Twentieth Century Tamil Nadu', in *A Question of Silence? The Sexual Economies of Modern India*, ed. Mary E. John and Janaki Nair (Kali for Women, New Delhi, in press).

8. Ilina Sen (ed.), *A Space Within the Struggle: Women's Participation in People's Struggles* (Kali for Women, New Delhi, 1990); Nandita Gandhi and Nandita Shah, *The Issues at Stake: Theory and Practice in the Contemporary Women's Movement in India* (Kali for Women, New Delhi, 1992); Indu Agnihotri and Vina Mazumdar, 'Changing Terms of Political Discourse: Women's Movement in India, 1970s–1990s', *Economic and Political Weekly*, 30 (1995).

9. K. Lalita, 'Women in Revolt: A Historical Analysis of the Progressive Organisation of Women in Andhra Pradesh', in *Women's Struggles and Strategies*, ed. Saskia Wieringa (Gower, Aldershot, 1988).

10. For a further analysis of this report and others, see my essay 'Gender and Development in India, 1970s–1990s: Some Reflections on the Constitutive Role of Contexts', *Economic and Political Weekly*, 31 (1996).

11. Indu Agnihotri, 'The Fourth World Conference on Women: A Report from China', *Indian Journal of Gender Studies*, 3 (1996). Agnihotri points out that 'for the first time the Indian government was forced to have a mediated relationship with its own NGOs through an Inter-Agency Facilitating and Coordinating Bureau, which itself is a creation of donor agencies' (p. 122).

12. See for instance, Sherry Joseph, 'Gay and Lesbian Movement in India', *Economic and Political Weekly*, 31 (1996).

13. Urvashi Butalia, 'Community, State and Gender: On Women's Agency During Partition', *Economic and Political Weekly*, 37 (1993); Ritu Menon and Kamla Bhasin, 'Recovery, Rupture, Resistance: Indian State and the Abduction of Women during Partition', *Economic and Political Weekly*, 37 (1993).

14. Ritu Menon and Kamla Bhasin, *Borders and Boundaries: Women in India's Partition* (Kali for Women, New Delhi, 1998), p. vi.

15. For some examples of recent work, see Tejaswini Niranjana, "Left to the Imagination": Indian Nationalisms and Female Sexuality in Trinidad', in *A Question of Silence? The Sexual Economies of Modern India*, ed. Mary E. John and Janaki Nair; Kamala Visweswaran, *Fictions of Feminist Ethnography* (University of Minnesota Press, Minnesota, 1994, and Oxford University Press, Delhi, 1996); Aparna Rayaprol, *Negotiating Identities: Women in the Indian Diaspora* (Oxford University Press, Delhi, 1997). See also Kalpana Ram and J. Kehaulani Kaunavi (eds), *Women's Studies International Forum*, Special Issue on Migrating Feminisms (forthcoming).

16. Mary E. John, 'Globalisation, Regionalisation and the Remapping of the Third World', paper presented at the conference on 'Rethinking the Third World: History/ Development/Politics', University of West Indies, Jamaica, December 1996.

17. Malathi de Alwis, 'Motherhood as a Space of Protest: Women's Political Participation in Contemporary Sri Lanka', in *Appropriating Gender: Women's Activism and the Politicization of Religion in South Asia*, ed. Amrita Basu and Patricia Jeffrey (Routledge, London and New York, 1997).

International influences can also be used to rewrite local history in non-fortuitous ways. De Alwis discusses how the first Mothers' Fronts amongst minority Tamils in northern Sri Lanka were effectively erased from memory by some of the Sinhala organisers of the later Mothers' Fronts in the south of the country, who claimed inspiration from the Argentinian Madres alone.

Feminist Representations:
Interrogating Religious Difference

SHAHNAZ ROUSE

The problematic in Lavrin's piece I address here states: 'is it possible to save its [i.e. feminism's] "international" character without losing the wealth generated by its internal diversity?' (p. 520), the issue at stake being that of identity and difference. Building on Lavrin's insistence on contextualisation and situatedness as imperative to discussions on/of feminism(s), the context I examine is that of 'Muslim' women in the Middle East and South Asia, and its accompanying tensions and questions. I use all three terms reluctantly and cautiously, recognising that space limitations preclude any thorough examination of these regions' complexity and diversity. The term 'Muslim women' is yet more problematic since it begs the question as to its meaning, and to whom it refers. I have chosen this combination to raise a key and vexed issue - of religious difference.

Contentions surrounding feminism in these regions revolve largely around this religious dimension. This applies internally to feminist movements, to their detractors, and to their supposed international 'supporters' (among 'Western' feminists). The terrain of religious difference permits an interrogation of the politics of resistance and agency, debates surrounding power relations, issues of cultural 'authenticity', voice and representation. It also (re)addresses ideas of knowledge construction and related epistemological and ontological concerns. In teasing out these matters, I hope to add both theoretically and strategically to Lavrin's contribution.

Debates around religious difference and feminist struggles are contingent on whether 'Muslims' and therefore 'Muslim' women constitute a majority or a minority. My focus is on the former. Contexts like the Indian one where Muslims – though numerically large – constitute a minority will not be interrogated.

Debates on religion in these parts of the majoritarian 'Muslim' world frequently occur in response to internal and external articulations of identity and difference. The collapse of the Soviet Union and the construction of the 'New World Order' has led many to see themselves targeted as the new 'enemy'. Pervasive negative representations of the 'Islamic' world and 'Muslims' have created a heightened sense of besiegement. The result is a shift towards a defence of Islam (and Muslims) not only among those previously on the right, but also among segments of the left, and within feminist circles.

This sentiment is aided by a sharp critique of liberalism and liberal regimes. Structural adjustment policies leading to an intensification of capitalist regimes of power – and I would like to stress that the present order is an intensification, with fewer barriers than previously, but not 'new' as is being generally portrayed – today combine material and cultural/ symbolic resources, racheting up a sense of estrangement from local 'secular' regimes. The sense of political impotence reflected by/in the state is constructed and read today – unlike previous periods – increasingly in cultural terms.

This shift involves a move away from a materialist focus to a right of centre, culturalist, even a 'civilisational' focus. While feminists in parts of the regions I am addressing here are imbricated in this reconfiguration, the initial impetus has come not from within feminist movements and struggles but from 'without' (in a multiple sense): as a reaction to representations of 'Muslim' women as necessarily oppressed and always subordinated to men – representations which thereby cast them as 'victims' lacking agency (and reinforcing interventionist positions of both some 'Western' feminists and imperialism); as feminists 'outside' their culture, i.e. alienated from it (a position actively taken by Islamist groups and by those left-segments who continue to insist that feminism is a bourgeois product, a secondary issue); and as a reaction to state structures.

These structural and representational dilemmas have led to an emphasis on 'cultural authenticity' among some women activists – both Islamists and non-Islamists. In the latter instance it remains unclear whether this stems from a valid recognition of distance from and relevance of feminist struggles to women of marginalised classes on the part of middle- and upper-middle-class 'secular' women, and is therefore a tactical and inclusive move; or whether it simply reflects a non-reflexive adoption of notions of religious and cultural difference which reify and essentialise such differences, reproducing ultimately a kind of 'orientalism in reverse', i.e. an ontology of difference, and a new 'exclusiveness'.

Regardless of this inherent ambiguity, these dynamics suggest a reactive-ness among women's groups, formulating agendas within existing hegemonies of power structures – at the level of the state and civil society. They serve ultimately to reinforce reactionary structures and ideologies by giving them centrality discursively, reconstituting them as effective regimes of surveil-lance. This effect obtains not only from the practices of those proposing a defence of 'Islam' and culture, but also from those mounting a defence of 'secularism', since the language and categories of secularism are often used without reference to their context and manipulation by dominant groups. Though couched as resistances to these precise groups and struc-tures, they help reinforce the positions and authority of those already in power. Instead of suggesting experience as the starting point of analysis and struggle, experience gets recast through hegemonic discourses and agendas. This is most obvious, albeit not exclusively limited to so-called 'Islamic feminists' and to many living in the metropole who evoke an ontological basis for religious difference in their work, which shuts out any real discussion of what this means, its multiplicity and complexity. It results, on both sides, in a denial or lack of recognition of actual difference, which is substituted for by a polemic of difference read a priori onto 'Muslim' women.

Thus far I have focused on the problematic aspects of recent developments: the erasure of 'real' difference through its actual silencing, ensuing difficulties surrounding activism in those arenas considered as part of one's 'culture' posited in terms of a moral authority (often religiously articulated) – female genital mutilation, dress, sexuality, marriage and divorce being key among them – and a suggestion yet again that some women are more representative than others of the interiority of a given society and culture. What I propose now is a rethinking, a shift in focus.

Debates around religious difference have provided a necessary corrective to previously existing focuses on capitalism and modernisation, and their accompanying ideologies, but it remains imperative that they be accompanied by an interrogation of their own imbrication within existing structures of power and privilege. This holds as much for those from within these societies as those without. Indeed, the very issue of inside/outside needs to be rethought in relation to late capitalism. What is clearly called for is a retreat from a polemics of difference – whether posited in secular or religious terms – to a politics of experience. In other words, two issues need to be overtly addressed: to what extent are feminists framing the debate representative of those for whom they speak? How do the concrete circumstances that construct women's lives create the languages in which they (we) speak? I would argue that, overall, 'secular', Islamist and 'pro-Islamist' voices represent women from different factions of the *same* class reflecting combined and uneven processes of capitalist development. Debates around the authenticity of 'secularist' versus 'Islamist' or pro-Islamist feminists repress awareness of their class similarities, by framing their differences simply in/through discourse. There are signs that a recognition of identicality *is* emerging; for example, recently 'Islamist' and 'secular' feminists came together in Pakistan under the banner of Women Against Rape (WAR) to organise jointly on issues of violence against women. The ability to work together on specific issues, without subsuming each other's voices, represents a significant step forward but leaves considerable space to be traversed vis-à-vis women from the popular and most especially producing classes. Debates and confrontations limiting the definition and articulation of feminism to a select class of privileged (middle-class) women are fraught with inconsistencies and problems. Their respective claims to representation and authenticity continue to deny agency to women who are not actively mobilised in either camp. Above all, they evade consideration of not only the multiple meanings of being 'Muslim' but also the articulation of religious identity with alternative sites of identity construction and ensuing problematics, regimes of policing and constructions of need and desire.

What is called for is a return to 'the everyday as problematic' (as suggested by Dorothy Smith). The starting point here is not discourse but experience, fraught as that notion may be, and implicated as it is, in representation itself (in the dual sense, figurative and literal). Rather than assuming we know what being religious means, we must interrogate its multiple meanings and languages, and its intersections with what Smith terms as 'relations of ruling'. Rather than posing cultural authenticity in reified, de-historicised ways, we need to examine how capitalism creates difference in seemingly totalising ways but which if examined more closely reveal the close link between existing differences and power relations: secular and religious discourses themselves being two of these.

It becomes obvious then that the languages we speak are closely linked to the spaces we occupy in concrete relations of ruling. It should also become clear that while we may seem to have a choice in the matter, these choices are not open-ended. The positions we assume and the languages we speak – secular feminist, Islamic feminist, organised feminist, outside the organised domain – all reflect the zones of possibilities available to us (to borrow from Raymond Williams). Rather than base our positions and alliances on these languages therefore, I am suggesting we recognise a multiplicity of languages and abandon any attempts to prioritise them in a hierarchy of value. Instead, it might be beneficial to examine the processes through which we connect with each other, the actual ability to formulate projects and possibilities in ways that further gender justice. Feminist frameworks must interrogate the relation between hegemonic discourses and institutional structures, through practices that overturn their combined authority. Insistence on recognition of a multiplicity of practices and discourses of localised relevance would constitute such a (new) beginning.

Borderland Feminisms: Towards the Transgression of Unitary Transnational Feminisms

JAYNE O. IFEKWUNIGWE

In her mapping of the multiple genealogies which have given birth to contemporary transnational feminisms, Lavrin acknowledges the yet unresolved tensions between and among first-wave universalist feminist politics of exclusion and third-wave feminist politics of differences which include as they fragment. In retracing the footsteps of first-wave feminism, she points to the biological essentialism which provided the reconstructive basis for third wave feminisms. That is, our 'femaleness … is not enough to achieve a unity of purpose'. Rather, as political theories and social practices, contemporary third-wave transnational feminisms operate on the assumption that global gender categories are historically located and socially and culturally constructed. Moreover, within their specific local domains, women occupy varied and layered positions based on simultaneous lived experiences of 'race', ethnicity, class, religion, sexuality, age and disability among other structures. Yet, these transnational feminist politics of inclusion predicated on the social recognition of multiple lived experiences of women have left feminisms' political project without a singular platform upon which to build coalitions across differences.

Compounding this fragmentation is the fact that even in their multiple formations, (post)modern feminist paradigms still claim legitimacy based on false binarisms; that is, 'black' or 'white', 'First World' or 'Third World', 'southern' or 'northern'. In particular, my response interrogates the oppositional 'racial' categories 'black' and 'white'. The common presumption is that the meanings of 'blackness' and 'whiteness' are both portable and fixed. In fact, though the maintenance of privilege and power may be the universal logic underpinning 'racial' ideology, the local meanings of what it means to be 'black' or 'white' do not always travel. For example, 'black' feminisms in Britain incorporate the experiences of women who in the United States would be excluded from 'black' feminist discourses. On both sides of the Atlantic, no textual space exists within these dual(ing) discourses for borderland feminisms which speak against the generalising tendencies of both mainstream 'white' majority and 'black' minority feminist theorisings. Borderland feminisms transgress contrived 'racialised' differences and transcend bounded 'national' identities. Borrowing from Anzaldua's notion of a _mestiza_ consciousness, borderland feminisms thrive at:

> that juncture ... where phenomena tend to collide. It is where the possibility of uniting all that is separate occurs. This assembly is not one where severed or separated pieces merely come together. Nor is it a balancing of opposing powers. In attempting to work out a synthesis ... its energy comes from continual creative motion that keeps breaking down the unitary aspect of each new paradigm.[1]

In other words, borderland feminisms stage debates which do not resolve but rather elucidate both the discursive and political problematics of oppositional feminisms whether unitary or fragmentary in nature.

Borderland women whose parentage positions them at multi-ethnic, multi-cultural and multi-racial intersections are at the front lines of social and geopolitical change.

'White' (English) mothering, 'black' daughters?

> The relationship between mother and daughter stands at the center of what I fear most in our culture. Heal that wound and we change the world.[2]

> A child is made in its parents' image. But to a world that sees only in 'Black' and 'White', I was made only in the image of my father. Yet, she has moulded me, created the curves and contours of my life, coloured the innermost details of my being. She has fought for me, protected me with every painful crooked bone in her body. She lives inside of me and cannot be separated. I may not be reflected in her image, but my mother is mirrored in my soul. I am my mother's daughter for the rest of my life.[3]

As part of broader international feminist agendas, Lavrin points to the politicising potential of the social institutions of motherhood. Feminist psychoanalytical, anthropological and sociological analyses are also replete with at times ambivalent recognition of the primacy of the mothering role in the social rather than biological reproduction of gendered identities. In my ongoing feminist autoethnographic work on narratives of borderland subjectivities in England, I address the ways in which at different life stages and across age, class, ethnicity, and locality women attempt to position themselves in a racially polarised society which denies them full womanhood.[4] Their testimonies reveal painful psychosocial consequences for individuals whose lived realities defy the false one drop rule wherein one known African ancestor designates a person as 'black'.[5] Within pre-established 'bi-racialised' social contexts, all the narratives speak to a desire for 'racial' reconciliation and an integrated sense of self which can embrace both 'white' maternal and 'black' paternal sociocultural inheritances. In ideal circumstances, all of the borderland women wish to be liberated from political discourses which mandate compulsory 'black' affiliation and silence indigenous and diasporic ethnic/cultural inheritances which are infinitely more complex and dynamic.

However, to appropriate Rich, the 'great unwritten story' is that which critically acknowledges the fact that, at times, young borderland girls first witness the complex world of womanhood through everyday interactions with their 'white' English female caretakers.[6] Through the psychosocial processes of 'white' English mothering, the primary culture the women I spoke with inherit is 'white' English. Societal assumptions based exclusively on their physical appearances frequently deny this reality. Furthermore, society tells them that they must deny this socialising fact and remember that they are 'just black'.

As told to me, their evocative testimonies shed light on paradoxes of identity and affiliation for borderland women whose 'white' English mothers or mother-surrogates have been central socialising influences. 'Racial' regulation, in the form of the one drop rule, collapses ideas about 'race' and culture in general and disallows 'white' English maternal and cultural influences in particular. For example, the four borderland feminists featured in this text all have 'white' English (Yemi, Bisi and Ruby) or 'white' German (Similola) birth mothers and 'black' Nigerian (Yemi, Bisi and Ruby) or 'black' Tanzanian (Similola) birth fathers. Yemi and Bisi were raised by their 'white' English birth mother in Nigeria. Ruby and Similola, were raised by 'white' English women, who were the matrons in the English and Welsh children's homes where they spent their formative years. However, based on locality, family circumstances, social class, and ethnicity, these four women all deploy different strategies to make sense of the contradictory and fluid processes of becoming borderland women.

As Yemi remembers:

> We were at home with our mother and our father. Although my mother worked, she was the primary influence in our house – culturally. We didn't really know very much about Yoruba culture. We just didn't.

Similarly, Similola recounts:

> When I was growing up the main influence was the ['white' English] house mother in the children's home, who totally dominated my life up until I was sixteen years old. Her views were my views.

As Bisi recalls, despite their best intentions, sometimes 'white' mothers do not completely understand the extent to which their own 'white' privilege separates them from the 'everyday racism'[7] which their borderland daughters face:

> A lot of the modern consciousness I have of being African and being 'black', which is not the same thing, is probably in spite of my mother. Being 'black'

in the sense that I feel now, that would be in spite of her. It's not something she agrees with ... She has very little knowledge of how racism operates and how it affects people ...

Furthermore, as Ruby describes it, 'white' grandmothers of borderland granddaughters grapple even further with their own 'white' daughters' 'transracial' transgressions which 'contaminate' allegedly 'pure blood lines':

> That period of time with my Gran brought out very much to the fore what her attitude to me was and why it was like that. It was eighty per cent because of the colour of my skin; the other twenty per cent was the fact that I was an illegitimate child. For my grandmother and her generation that was quite a shameful thing. But had I been a 'white' illegitimate child it would have been very different. So as I say eighty per cent because of the colour – she didn't want to be associated in the blood line with a 'black' granddaughter.

At the same time, one could argue that in spite of their 'white' privilege, 'white' mothers or carers of borderland daughters could themselves be considered borderland feminists. In fact, I have spoken with politicised 'white' mothers of borderland children who describe a shifting 'double consciousness'. This constant negotiation of 'racialised', sexualised and gendered status is associated with the differential ways in which 'the public' responds to them depending on whether or not they have their designated 'black' children in tow. Hence, one could argue that borderland women and their 'white' mothers/carers are both potentially equipped with the social tools for building transnational coalitions across the 'black'/ 'white' feminists' divide. Yet, amid all the feminist academic attention paid to mothering and mother/daughter relationships, very little if any textual space attends to this strategic political possibility. Both 'black' and 'white' feminists have also neglected specific lived realities of racially problematised 'white' mother/borderland daughter dyads.

As borderland daughters and their 'white' mothers illustrate, fostering social, cultural and political allegiances which do not merely pivot around the centre, but instead subvert manufactured and real differences among women, is one way for international feminisms to 'embrace the largest number of female experiences'. Hence, transnational borderland feminisms can be forged from a collective consciousness of both the falsity and fluidity of 'racial' categories as well as from the recognition of the slippery nature of local 'national' identities in light of globalisation and diaspora(s). However, as they are manifest in local milieux, differential lived realities and legacies of (post)colonialisms, sexisms, class oppression, and ethnic discrimination must be acknowledged and interwoven with any transnational borderland feminist praxis.

Notes

I extend boundless gratitude to the women who generously gave their time and retrieved joyful and painful memories in order to make this ongoing organic project possible.

1. G. Anzaldua, *Borderlands, La Frontera: The New Mestiza* (Aunt Lute Press, San Francisco, 1987), p. 78.

2. A. Levins-Morales, '... And Even Fidel Can't Change That', in *This Bridge Called My Back: Writings By Radical Women of Color*, ed. C. Moraga and G. Anzaldua (Kitchen Table Press, New York, 1981), p. 56.

3. N. Onwurah, *The Body Beautiful* (film) (British Film Institute, London, 1990).

4. J. Ifekwunigwe, *Scattered Belongings: Cultural Paradoxes of 'Race', Nation and Gender* (Routledge, London and New York, forthcoming, 1998).

5. N. Zack, *Race and Mixed Race* (Temple University Press, Philadelphia, 1993).

6. A. Rich, *Of Woman Born: Motherhood as Experience and Institution* (Virago, London, 1977).

7. P. Essed, *Understanding Everyday Racism: An Interdisciplinary Theory* (Sage, London, 1991).

REVIEW ESSAYS

Some Trajectories of 'Feminism' and 'Imperialism'

ANTOINETTE BURTON

In the fifteen years since Valerie Amos and Pratibha Parmar first wrote their germinal essay 'Challenging Imperial Feminism' in the Britain-based collective *Feminist Review* (1984), what was considered a controversial argument about the historical relationships of Western feminism to imperial ideologies, institutions, and practices has become a commonplace of feminist scholarship. Their claim that 'the "herstory" which white women use to trace the roots of women's oppression … is an imperial history, rooted in the prejudices of the colonial period' has not only been documented, it has formed the basis for a new critical historiographical practice: one which insists that, like gender, the category of feminism itself emerged from the historical context of modern European colonialism and anti-colonial struggles, and that therefore histories of feminism must engage with its imperial origins as well as its national(ist) legacies.[1] Debates about the racist foundations of women's suffrage arguably took root earlier in American than in British historiography, thanks in large measure to the work of Ellen Dubois and Angela Davis – both of whom were at pains to track the ways in which suffragists and other female reformers were either co-opted into relying on racist rhetoric to achieve their party political ends, or unselfconsciously used the apparent naturalness of whiteness as the platform from which they might reform – read, 'civilise' – ante- and post-bellum African Americans.[2] As identity politics gained ground in the North American academy in the 1980s, and white middle-class feminists were exhorted, if not compelled, to confront the racist presumptions of their political practices, feminism's unbecoming history became the very grounds for demanding new critical practices in women's studies – as the work of Audre Lorde, Adrienne Rich, Cherrie Moraga, and Gloria Anzaldua from the late 1970s and 1980s attests. Indeed, as Amos and Parmar observed, it was the presence of feminists of colour and the influence of black feminist theory and politics which forced the kinds of reconceptualisations – of feminism, of empire, of history, of the nation – from which there is, now, no turning back.[3] Nor should the influence of the Birmingham School (which pioneered materalist cultural studies) be discounted here: though critical race and feminist politics were not and are not institutionalised in Britain in the same way as in the US, their effects on Anglo-American historical production cannot be underestimated. In this sense, Paul Gilroy's *The Black Atlantic* tracks a series of historical criss crossings which are echoed by the transatlantic influences which have put British and American feminists in dialogue for two decades – a trajectory not as well recognised or well documented as the impact of black feminist critique on women's studies, perhaps, but which has nonetheless shaped many women's and feminist historians in the Anglo-American West.[4] The impact of these exchanges has been nothing less than monumental for scholarship on feminism and imperialism. As Catherine Hall has insisted in *White, Male and Middle-Class*, her collection of essays on feminist history in the British context, feminists can no longer afford the kind of historiographical amnesia which has characterised much of women's history if they are to be accountable to the complexities of 'women's' struggles in the past and mindful of the necessities of women's political commitments in the present.[5]

To be sure, the long Western feminist tradition of claiming the moral high ground, of seeking exemption for responsibility from certain forms of 'patriarchal' power – what Jane Marcus, tracing it back to Virginia Woolf, calls the practice of 'registering objections' – has produced some resistance to feminist critiques of feminist history.[6] One might even argue that some of the 'backlash' against postmodern and poststructuralist feminism has been the result of the ways in which attention to race and colonialism have tended to displace, or at the very least interrogate, the apparently coherent category of 'women' via a more fragmented and contingent set of subjectivities, so that 'the' subject of feminism is no longer self-evidently gendered, let alone above critique.[7] Such engagements cast light on feminist theory's historical attachment to Marxism, and more specifically to Marxist grand narratives – suggesting that race and class and gender rarely coexist placidly inside the much-touted 'holy trinity', but often vie in feminist analyses for priority and even dominance as historians attempt to find and to read primary evidence in ways that are equally respectful of historical context and cultural meaning. Because of the explosion of postcolonial studies onto the academic scene, not just since the 1980s but dating from de-colonisation and before (as the work of Frantz Fanon testifies), feminists have by no means been the only audience for or producers of these ideas. Their contributions coincided historically with an increasingly pervasive curricular (though institutionally still relatively marginalised) interest in the relationship between so-called oppositional groups and regimes of power, whether ideological, institutional or both – in part because the traditional equation between agency and resistance has been put to the test in a variety of venues, from subaltern studies to feminist theory to Black British cultural studies to critical race theory to whiteness studies. By now, the notion that Euro-American women, especially in their quest for 'emancipation' and political equality through the formal mechanism of the vote, were often complicit with the racism of colonial regimes at home and abroad is so generally available that Edward Said felt licensed to claim in *Culture and Imperialism* (1993) that Western feminists have historically been 'uncomplaining members of the imperialist consensus' emanating from the European metropole – without, incidentally, citing any of the historical work, feminist or otherwise, which has leant credence to such a contention.[8]

The fact that arguments about the colonial contexts and imperial presumptions of modern Western feminism have been mainstreamed, and relatively quickly, in the last decade should not distract us either from the considerable accomplishments of the scholarship or from the research and criticism that remains to be done. Careful literary and historical work by Moira Ferguson, Clare Midgley, Vron Ware, Billie Melman and Reina Lewis in the British imperial context has made it impossible to refute the claim that white British women's historical experience, in all its complexity and variation, was bound up culturally, economically and politically with imperial concerns and interests. The relationship between anti-slavery and feminism has proven a particularly fruitful site of inquiry, highlighting connections between the slave trade and imperial policy which raise more questions than answers, as Midgley has gone on to show in work since the publication of her first book on the topic, *Women Against Slavery.*[9] Research in this field, including my own on imperial suffrage, has tended to focus on activist women, whether writers or reformers or both, a focus which has prompted some to query its middle-class preoccupations and others, like Inderpal Grewal, to call for more attention to the ways in which empire entered into and shaped the lives of ordinary women across class as well as differentially throughout the British Isles.[10] To these critiques I would add the necessity of interrogating the ways in which the nation – with its often implicit Englishness – has, perhaps unwittingly but nonetheless fairly consistently, been consolidated in this recent work, *Burdens of History* included. Destabilising the nation ought to be part of the political project of feminist scholarship on empire, lest the nation itself be re-naturalised as the logical site of origin, or even made invisible (again) as the grounds upon which women's already complex subjectivities are formed. In this sense, it is not the monographs on 'feminism and imperialism' as historical artefacts (conceived largely in the 1980s), but rather recent work on feminism as a historiographical practice trained on empire as a subject which offers some of the most important and indeed, revolutionary perspectives on the intersections between the 'new imperial studies' and feminist history. Catherine Hall's essays (some of which are collected in *White, Male and Middle-Class*, others of which are to be found in *New Left Review* and various edited collections) make the stakes of this approach indubitably clear by insisting that 'domestic' society, politics and culture were constantly made and remade by empire – a phenomenon which brought systems of gender, class, religion, sexuality, race and ethnicity consistently to bear upon the apparently self-contained institutions and practices of 'the Island Nation' in the nineteenth century.[11] Similarly, Mrinalini Sinha's *Colonial Masculinity* explicitly and deliberately insists on masculinity and the concept of 'imperial social formation' as rightful objects of feminist inquiry, and in the process demonstrates how insufficient the categories of 'nation' and 'empire' are for understanding the systems of patriarchal racism which structured global power relations in the nineteenth century.[12] 'Women' as such are not absent from these studies; nor are men or feminists, for that matter. But they are treated simultaneously as agents and products of local, regional and geopolitical power in ways that attend to the material conditions they faced as well as the cultural capital they both embodied and wielded. Most important, this new work aims to critique the complicity of history-writing in the production and the maintenance of ideologies heretofore understood as imperial – especially with respect to the originary status of the nation, a status made possible by imagining Britain as the 'mother country' and 'her' citizens as benign civilisers concerned only with bringing the 'natural' social order to 'natives'. More work remains to be done to denaturalise the easy association of Britain with 'home' – especially since even some of the most interesting new scholarship can end up glossing the important contention that nation does not historically precede the empire, but is fundamentally constituted by it.[13] Here, Ann Stoler's work on gender relations and sexuality in the Dutch East Indies is enormously helpful, not least because it disproves the often implicit claims of British imperial exceptionality by arguing that metropolitan Dutch culture was (also) made by its imperial investments, rather than the other way around.[14]

That ideas about gender, sexuality and women's place have been crucial to this process, there can be little doubt – though admittedly, whether practitioners of traditional national histories will be willing fully to countenance the implications of such arguments in their research and teaching remains to be seen. In what seems like a replication of the system of geopolitical hierarchies inherited from the nineteenth century, much of the historical work around the categories of 'feminism' and 'imperialism' in the West would seem to have been researched in the British context, with scholars of French and Dutch feminism only recently taking up the subject.[15] There is no reason to expect that the British model could or should be emulated, though it is worth noting that in part because of the relationships between imperial power and colonial archives, Algeria appears to be emerging as the centre-piece of French historiography in the same way that India has come to be reproduced as the 'jewel in the crown' of the new imperial studies. In observing this, it is not my intention to occlude the important work that has been done in national contexts which are neither fully 'European' nor properly 'non-Western', two among these being Australia and Ireland. In fact, these are sites of incredibly innovative scholarship which undermines the stability of the discourses around 'feminism' and 'imperialism' by suggesting that the coherences they appear to embody are actually effects of longstanding imperial traditions with resonances far beyond fortress Europe. Chilla Bulbeck has called Australian feminism a 'hybrid' case; and Northern Ireland may be said to be one of the last colonial outposts of the British Isles.[16] A number of Australian and Irish feminist scholars are struggling with the legacies of British imperialism for their national/colonial cultures in ways that have the capacity to transform, if not unravel, our presumptions of how empire colonised white women – efforts which need further inquiry as to what the best approaches are for historicising and critiquing that kind of ideological work. What these and other literatures point to is, possibly, the beginning of an end to nationally bound historical projects and the emergence of a more transnational approach to writing women's and feminist history in the new century: an approach which is not necessarily sanguine about the end of the nation, but one which conceives of nations as permeable boundaries, subject to a variety of migrations, diasporic contests, and refigurations not just after colonialism but throughout its history as well.[17]

Given the proliferation of work on 'Western' women, feminism, and imperialism in the last decade, it behoves us to remember that the chief purpose of Amos and Parmar's 1984 essay was not to clear the way for a more politically accountable historiography of Euro-American women's movements, but rather to make space for histories of black women, women of colour, and by extension, anti-colonial and nationalist women – historical figures arguably cast in relative academic anonymity because the template for feminist history had privileged certain Western values and in turn had shaped a feminist past which seemed self-evidently white, Western, and middle class. It is not too much to say that as a result, before the 1980s, it was possible for even some of the most accomplished feminist historians in the West to express surprise that there had been women's movements and feminist cultures outside Europe and North America before the 1960s, even as they failed to realise the neocolonialist effect this kind of ignorance was having on the production of postcolonial counter-histories. The publication of Chandra Mohanty's 1988 article, '"Under Western Eyes": Feminist Scholarship and Colonial Discourses' – which, significantly, also appeared in *Feminist Review* – offered an enormously influential analysis of the insufficiency of Western epistemological frameworks for recovering, let alone understanding, the cultural and historical meanings of women's experiences and structural locations outside the West.[18] To be sure, work on feminist movements outside Europe had existed before this: Kumari Jayawardena's broad-ranging book *Feminism and Nationalism in the Third World* (1986) documented struggles for women's emancipation in Turkey, Egypt, Iran, Afghanistan, India, Sri Lanka, Indonesia, the Philippines, China, Vietnam, Korea and Japan in an impressive survey whose breadth has proven one of its distinguishing features, especially in comparison with the more specialised studies of colonial nationalist women's efforts which have been produced since. Although Jayawardena pointed to the contradictions which the quest for 'female emancipation' might generate among women passionate about nationalist struggles but cognizant of the patriarchal bargains which had often been struck between male colonisers and indigenous male elites, she did not reject the designation 'feminist' as an appropriate descriptor of their actions, as Madhu Kishwar did in the South Asian context.[19] And yet this tension – between reading non-Western women's activities and struggles as 'feminist' on the one hand, and recognising the culturally specific, politically charged influences and constraints they encountered as they tried to reconcile a woman-centred agenda with the exigencies of anti-imperial politics, often in the context of military struggle, on the other – has helped to shape historians' accounts of what non-Western women did in the name of liberation[20] from the nineteenth century to the present.

Perhaps not surprisingly, monographic treatment of Third World women's history (feminist and otherwise) written in English has followed if not the flag, then at least the British imperial archive, with India and Egypt dominating the historiographical landscape in the 1990s. In both contexts, recent scholarship has been informed by two decades of research, some of which focused on social issues with political resonance like birth control, some of which was dedicated to making the memoirs of individual women available for teaching and further research.[21] Whether they take an empirical social history approach (see Aparna Basu and Bharati Ray, *Women's Struggle: A History of the All India Women's Conference, 1927–1990*, and Beth Baron, *The Women's Awakening in Egypt*), a more high-political approach (Barbara Southward *The Women's Movement and Colonial Politics in Bengal*), a self-consciously gender-centred approach (Margot Badran, *Feminists, Islam and Nation: Gender and the Making of Modern Egypt*), a comprehensive survey approach (Radha Kumar, *The History of Doing: An Illustrated History of Indian Feminism and Women's Movements*), or an individualist approach (Kumari Jayawardena, *The White Woman's Other Burden*), many of the scholars working in this field have combined the quest for recovery with an attempt to frame women's work and women's words in the complex political and cultural contexts out of which they were produced.[22] What they share, in addition to a commitment to restoring certain heretofore under-appreciated women to history, is a conviction (long characteristic of women's and feminist history) that the stories they excavate do not simply shed new light on national, imperial or 'mainstream' accounts of modernity, but in fact require us to reconsider the inadequacy of those narratives which occlude women's participation, and even of those which acknowledge it but fail to recognise how thoroughly systems of gender, sexuality and 'feminism' shaped national, colonial and anti-colonial cultures. In the South Asian context, Kumkum Sangari and Sudesh Vaid's collection *Recasting Women* has been absolutely consequential in this regard, arguing as it does that *all* responsible historical scholarship recognises 'that each aspect of reality is gendered' and that, in the colonial context no less than in any other, feminisms and patriarchies of all kinds exist in dialectical relation to one another.[23] The significance of this for subaltern studies (which has been, with the somewhat phenomenal exception of Gayatri Spivak, remarkably disengaged from these debates) can be fully appreciated in Kamala Visweswaran's recent essay 'Small Speeches, Subaltern Gender', which admirably rewrites the history of Indian women's agitation and resistance into the Gandhian 1930s as part of a larger theoretical critique about the centrality of feminist analyses to the politics of nationalist narratives.[24] The extent to which elite women's words, however small and elusive, still dominate, is as pervasive a problem in non-Western women's histories as it is in the historiography of feminism and empire in the West – and perhaps more so, given both the ways in which colonial archives were designed to privilege only those 'native' voices which left a (literally) legible trace, and the ways in which indigenous cultures often relied on the oral as much as the written for transmission and preservation of knowledge.[25] Feminist historians will undoubtedly continue to owe a great debt to ethnographers and other researchers interested in the evidence of culture, even as they must be wary of that discipline's long historical associations with the colonial enterprise itself.[26] Whether historians of Third World feminism will pursue a comparative, transnational approach when the stakes of using the nation as investigative framework are, arguably, higher even than for scholars of Western women and feminist movements, promises to be one of the most compelling questions left unanswered by feminist work in the 1990s.[27]

As with the literature on Western feminism and empire, recent research on countries and cultures which have less self-evident (or less well known) relationships to European empires represents some of the most interesting work in the field to date – as scholarship by Janet Afary, Mansour Bonakdarian, and Hammed Shahidian on Iran illustrates. There, especially in the twentieth century, the clash between religious values and secular, modern politics offers a different model than the South Asian or Egyptian cases – raising important questions not just about fundamentalisms and feminisms but about the ways in which what Shahidian calls 'prefabricated frames of analysis' can distort even anti-orientalist intellectual inquiry.[28] Perhaps tellingly, her discussion of the challenges posed by Iranian women's history falls under the rubric of 'International Trends', a recently developed section of the *Journal of Women's History* in which most of the reflection on non-European topics tends to occur. If the categories of 'feminism' and 'imperialism' appear to break down here as elsewhere, it is because they clearly fail to capture the complexities of colonial domination, complicity and resistance in situ – and, perhaps more significantly, because in the end (much like 'internationalism' itself[29]) they betray the orientalist histories from which they have emerged, as well as the lingering purchase of those histories on even some of the most critically engaged work of the present.[29] Historians have much to learn from current debates about citizenship and difference, especially those which take the fact of colonialism as their point of departure without reifying it either as a system of dominance and resistance or as a historical phenomenon readily accommodated by the post- in postcolonialism. Once again, *Feminist Review*, which sponsored so much important debate in the 1980s about the legacy of imperialism to feminist theory, practice, and politics, continues to track these themes – as recent issues on 'Nationalism and National Identities', 'Thinking through Ethnicities', 'Feminist Politics – Colonial/Postcolonial Worlds', 'The Irish Issue: the British Question', and 'Citizenship: Pushing the Boundaries' – have regularly illustrated.[31] As has always been the case, contemporary feminist and anti-imperial scholarship needs historical research which not only 're-orients western feminisms', but interrogates the impact of colonial legacies on feminist genealogies precisely so that it does not lose its capacity to envision complexly democratic futures.[32] A rigorous critique of the traditions of liberal individualism which modern, especially pre-1945, feminisms and imperialisms persistently articulated, alongside sustained critical analyses of the gendered self and the racialised nation which those historically bourgeois formations attempted to cast as the only legitimate conditions of citizenship, would seem to be crucial to furthering a politically engaged debate around these questions.

Notes

1. Valerie Amos and Pratibha Parmar, 'Challenging Imperial Feminism', *Feminist Review*, 17 (1984), pp. 3–19.

2. Ellen Carol Dubois, *Feminism and Suffrage: The Emergence of an Independent Women's Movement in America, 1848–1869* (Cornell University Press, Ithaca, 1978), and Angela Y. Davis, *Women, Race, and Class* (Vintage Books, New York, 1983). For a recent study that uses the frame race, class and gender but seeks to complicate it with the Asian-American experience, see Judy Yung, *Unbound Feet: A Social History of Chinese Women in San Francisco* (University of California Press, Berkeley, 1995).

3. Audre Lorde, *Sister/Outsider: Essays and Speeches* (The Crossing Press, 1984); Adrienne Rich, *Blood, Bread, and Poetry: Selected Prose, 1979–1985* (Norton, New York, 1986); Gloria Anzaldua and Cherrie Moraga (eds), *This Bridge Called My Back: Writings by Radical Women of Color* (Kitchen Table Women of Color Press, New York, 1981); Gloria Anzaldua, *Making Face, Making Soul: Haciendo Caras: Creative and Critical Perspectives by Women of Color* (Aunt Lute Press, San Francisco, 1990).

4. See Paul Gilroy, *The Black Atlantic: Modernity and Double Consciousness* (Harvard University Press, 1993); Padmini Mongia (ed.), *Contemporary Postcolonial Theory: A Reader* (Arnold, London, 1996); Houston A. Baker, Jr, Manthia Diawara and Ruth H. Lindeborg (eds), *Black British Cultural Studies: A Reader* (University of Chicago Press, 1996); and Hazel V. Carby, *Reconstructing Womanhood: The Emergence of the Afro-American Woman Novelist* (Oxford University Press, New York, 1987).

5. Catherine Hall, *White, Male and Middle-Class: Explorations in Feminist History* (Routledge, London, 1992).

6. Jane Marcus, 'Registering Objections: Grounding Feminist Alibis', in *Reconfigured Spheres: Feminist Explorations of Literary Space*, ed. Margaret R. Higgonet and Joan Templeton (University of Massachusetts Press, Amherst, 1994), pp. 171–93. Thanks to Laura Mayhall for this reference.

7. Daphne Patai, *Professing Feminism: Cautionary Tales from the Strange World of Women's Studies* (Basic Books, New York, 1994); Diane Bell and Renate Klein, *Radically Speaking: Feminism Reclaimed* (Spinifex Press, Victoria, Australia , 1996); Teresa L. Ebert, *Ludic Feminism and After: Postmodernism, Desire, and Labor in Late Capitalism* (University of Michigan Press, Ann Arbor, 1996); and, most recently, Chilla Bulbeck's *Re-Orienting Western Feminisms* (Cambridge University Press, 1998).

8. Edward Said, *Culture and Imperialism* (Vintage Books, New York, 1993), p. 53.

9. Moira Ferguson, *Subject to Others: British Women Writers and Colonial Slavery, 1670–1834* (Routledge, London, 1992); Clare Midgley, *Women Against Slavery: The British Campaigns, 1780–1870* (Routledge, London, 1992); Vron Ware, *Beyond the Pale: White Women, Racism and History* (Verso, London, 1994); Billie Melman, *Women's Orients: Englishwomen and the Middle East, 1718–1918* (Macmillan, London, 1992); Reina Lewis, *Gendering Orientalism: Race, Femininity and Representation* (Routledge, London, 1996); see also Midgley, 'Anti-Slavery and the Roots of "Imperial Feminism"', in her edited collection *Gender and Imperialism* (Manchester University Press, 1998), p. 161–79.

10. Antoinette Burton, *Burdens of History: British Feminists, Indian Women, and Imperial Culture, 1865–1915* (University of North Carolina Press, Chapel Hill, 1994); Inderpal Grewal, *Home and Harem: Nation, Gender, Empire and Cultures of Travel* (Duke University Press, Durham, 1996).

11. Hall, *White, Male and Middle Class*; see also 'Histories, Empires and the Postcolonial Moment', in *The Post-Colonial Question: Common Skies, Divided Horizons*, ed. Iain Chambers and Lidia Curti (Routledge, London, 1996), pp. 65–77; 'Imperial Man: Edward Eyre in Australasia and the West Indies, 1833–66', in *The Expansion of England*, ed. Bill Schwarz (Routledge, London, 1996), pp. 130–70; 'Rethinking Imperial Histories: The Reform Act of 1867', *New Left Review*, 208 (1994), pp. 3–29.

12. Mrinalini Sinha, *Colonial Masculinity: The 'Manly Englishman' and the 'Effeminate Bengali' in the Late Nineteenth Century* (Manchester University Press, 1995).

13. See for example Anne McClintock, *Imperial Leather: Race, Gender and Sexuality in the Colonial Contest* (Routledge, London, 1995) and Susan Meyer, *Imperialism at Home: Race and Victorian Women's Fiction* (Cornell University Press, Ithaca, 1996).

14. Ann Stoler, *Race and the Education of Desire* (Duke University Press, Durham, 1995); and, with Frederick Cooper (eds), *Tensions of Empire: Colonial Cultures in a Bourgeois World* (University of California Press, Berkeley, 1996). See also Frances Gouda, *Dutch Culture Overseas: Colonial Practices in the Netherlands Indies, 1900–1942* (Amsterdam University Press, Amsterdam, 1996) and Julia Clancy-Smith and Frances Gouda (eds), *Domesticating Empire: Race, Gender, and Family Life in French and Dutch Colonialism* (University of Virginia Press, Charlottesville, 1998).

15. See Clancy-Smith and Gouda (eds), *Domesticating Empire*; Joan Scott, *'Only Paradoxes to Offer': French Feminists and the Rights of Man* (Harvard University Press, Cambridge, 1996); and Marnia Lazreg, 'Feminism and Difference: The Perils of Writing as a Woman on Women in Algeria', in *Conflicts in Feminism*, ed. Marianne Hirsch and Evelyn Fox Keller (Routledge, London, 1990), pp. 326–48 and Lazreg's book, *The Eloquence of Silence: Algerian Women in Question* (Routledge, New York, 1994).

16. See Chilla Bulbeck, 'Hybrid Feminisms: The Australian Case', *Journal of Women's History*, 6 (1994), pp. 112–25 and her *One World Women's Movement* (Pluto Press, London, 1988); the special double issue on Irish women published by the *Journal of Women's History*, 6, 4/7 (1995); Catherine Candy, 'Relating Feminisms, Nationalisms and Imperialisms: Ireland, India and Margaret Cousin's Sexual Politics', *Women's History Review*, 3 (1994), pp. 581–94); and essays in the *Feminist Review* special edition, 'The Irish Issue: the British Question', v. 50 (1995).

17. See for example my 'Who Needs the Nation: Interrogating "British" History', *Journal of Historical Sociology*, 10 (1997), pp. 227–48; Catherine Candy, 'Relating Feminisms'; Grewal, *Home and Harem*; Fiona Paisley, 'White Women in the Field: Feminism, Cultural Relativism and Aboriginal Rights', *Journal of Australian Studies*, 52 (1997), pp. 113–25; Angela Woollacott, '"All This is the Empire, I Told Myself": Australian Women's Voyages "Home" and the Articulation of Colonial Whiteness', *American Historical Review*, 102 (1997), pp. 1003–29; and Leila J. Rupp, *Worlds of Women: The Making of an International Women's Movement* (Princeton University Press, 1997).

18. Chandra Mohanty, '"Under Western Eyes": Feminist Scholarship and Colonial Discourses', *Feminist Review*, 30 (1988), pp. 61 88; also reprinted in her collection, edited with Ann Russo and Lourdes Torres, *Third World Women and the Politics of Feminism* (Indiana University Press, Bloomington, 1991). For a critique, see Sara Suleri, 'Woman Skin Deep: Feminism and the Postcolonial Condition', *in Colonial Discourse and Post-colonial Theory: A Reader*, ed. R. J. Patrick Williams and Laura Chrisman (Columbia University Press, New York, 1994), pp. 244–56.

19. Kumari Jayawardena, *Feminism and Nationalism in the Third World* (Zed Books, London, 1986); and Madhu Kishwar, 'Why I Do Not Call Myself a Feminist', *Manushi: A Journal About Women and Society*, 61 (1991), pp. 2–7.

20. I use this term advisedly, following Aparna Basu's discussion of the relationship of feminism to women's liberation in her essay, 'Feminism and Nationalism in India, 1917–47', *Journal of Women's History*, 7 (1995), pp. 95–107. See also the special issue of *Women's History Review*, edited by Barbara Ramusack and myself, called 'Feminism, Imperialism and Race: A Dialogue Between India and Britain' (vol. 3, no. 4, 1994).

21. See for example Barbara Ramusack, 'Embattled Advocates: The Debate Over Birth Control in India, 1920–1940', *Journal of Women's History*, 1 (1989), pp. 34–64; Cynthia Nelson, 'The Voices of Doria Shafiq: Feminist Consciousness in Egypt, 1940–1960', *Feminist Issues*, 6 (1986), pp. 15–31; Geraldine Forbes (ed), *Memoirs of an Indian Woman*, by Shudha Mazumdar (M.E. Sharpe, New York, 1989); Roushan Jahan (ed), *Sultana's Dream by Rokeya Sakhawat Hossain* (The Feminist Press, New York, 1988); and Margot Badran (ed.), *Harem Years: Memoirs of an Egyptian Feminist, by Huda Shaarawi* (The Feminist Press, New York, 1986).

22. Aparna Basu and Bharati Ray, *Women's Struggle: A History of the All India Women's Conference, 1927–1990* (Manohar Publications, New Delhi, 1990); Beth Baron, *The Women's Awakening in Egypt: Culture, Society and the Press* (Yale University Press, New Haven, 1994); Barbara Southard, *The Women's Movement and Colonial Politics in Bengal, 1921–1936* (Manohar, New Delhi, 1995); Margot Badran, *Feminists, Islam and Nation: Gender and the Making of Modern Egypt* (Princeton University Press, 1995); Radha Kumar, *The History of Doing: An Illustrated History of Indian Feminism and Women's Movements* (Verso, London, 1994); and Kumari Jayawardena, *The White Woman's Other Burden: Western Women and South Asia During British Rule* (Routledge, New York, 1995).

23. Kumkum Sangari and Sudesh Vaid, Introduction to their edited collection, *Recasting Women: Essays in Colonial History* (Kali for Women, New Dehli, 1989), pp. 3, 5.

24. Kamala Visweswaran, 'Small Speeches, Subaltern Gender: Nationalist Historiography and its Ideology', in *Subaltern Studies IX*, ed. Shahid Amin and Dipesh Chakrabarty (Oxford University Press, Delhi, 1996).

25. A notable exception in the South Asian context is Stree Shakti Sanghatana, Lalita, Ke et al., *We Were Making History: Life Stories of Women in the Telangana People's Struggle* (Zed Books, London, 1989).

26. See Stoler, *Race and the Education of Desire,* and Timothy Burke, *Lifebuoy Men, Lux Women: Commodification, Consumption, and Cleanliness in Modern Zimbabwe* (Duke University Press, Durham, 1996).

27. This is a strategy being pursued by Philippa Levine in her research on prostitution in the British empire (see her forthcoming *The Sexual Politics of Race: Venereal Disease and Prostitution under British Colonialism*) and by Mrinalini Sinha in her research on the circulation of Katherine Mayo's controversial text *Mother India*, in the contexts of Britain, South Asia, and the United States in the 1930s. See Sinha's introduction to the new edition of *Mother India* (Kali for Women, Delhi, forthcoming). This is also the recommendation of M. Jacqui Alexander and Chandra Mohanty in their edited collection *Feminist Genealogies, Colonial Legacies, Democratic Futures* (Routledge, London, 1997).

28. Janet Afary, *The Iranian Constitutional Revolution, 1906–1911: Grassroots Democracy, Social Democracy, and the Origins of Feminism* (Columbia University Press, New York, 1996); Mansour Bonakdarian, '"The Woman Question" and the Iranian Constitutional Revolution [1906–1911] in the British Press', *Nimeye Digar*, 2nd series, 3 (1997), pp. 123–45; and Hammed Shahidian, 'Islam, Politics, and the Problems of Writing Women's History in Iran', *Journal of Women's History*, 7 (1995), pp. 113–44. See also Deniz Kandiyoti (ed.), *Women, Islam and the State* (Temple University Press, Philadelphia, 1991).

29. For an enduringly valuable discussion of internationalism and its imperial implications, see Cynthia Enloe's *Bananas, Beaches, and Bases: Making Feminist Sense of International Politics* (University of California Press, Berkeley, 1989).

30. For an example of the persistence of the complicity/resistance model, see Mala Mathrani, 'East–West Encounters and the Making of Feminists', *Journal of Women's History*, 9 (1997), pp. 215–26

31. See volumes 44, 45, 49, 50, 57 respectively.

32. Here I draw self-consciously on the work of Bulbeck *in Re-Orienting Western Feminisms,* and Alexander and Mohanty (eds) in *Feminist Genealogies, Colonial Legacies, Democratic Futures.*

Feminisms and Transnationalism

FRANCESCA MILLER

Leila J. Rupp states at the opening of her new book *Worlds of Women: The Making of an International Women's Movement*, 'I see my work as part of a transnational history that we are only beginning to write'.[1] Using Rupp's fine history of women's organising in the early twentieth century as a starting point, this essay will consider new work by feminist scholars addressing international relations, the history of women's transnational organising, and the complex of transnational feminist interactions that are at once local and global in the late 1990s. Drawing specific examples from work on women of the Americas, the essay will also explore the ways in which increasingly subtle understandings of gender informs the new literature.

First, etymology: the terms 'feminisms' and 'transnationalism' arose at specific historic moments, and their roots are relevant to the ensuing discussion. In previous work, I used the term 'transnational' to distinguish certain activities from formal intergovernmental activities carried on at the international level, that is, to make it clear that the participants met together not as representatives of their governments but as individuals or representatives of civic organisations, clubs, unions and other local or regional entities.[2] The term 'transnational' came into general use in the 1920s, in reference to trans-Atlantic trade, but the first print use of which I am aware occurs in Randolph Bourne's 1917 essay 'Trans-National America', wherein Bourne advocates a kind of 'multicultural United States', theorising that a citizenry composed of many immigrant groups would be less likely to wage war against the countries from which they came.[3]

'Feminisms' is a politically strategic term that came into play in the late 1980s. It is intended to deny the claiming of feminism by any one group of feminists and to signify the multiplicity of ways in which those who share a feminist critique may come together to address issues. 'Feminisms' acknowledges that specific historical and cultural experiences will differently construct understandings of gender at different times and places. 'Feminisms' is meant to create discursive space in a fraught arena. It is quintessentially historical, resisting homogenisation, generalisation, nostalgia.

In undertaking a literature review of 'feminisms and transnationalism' it is appropriate to recognise the historiography of this effort: early in this

century a number of feminist scholars attempted to write feminist international activism into the historical record. Mary Wilhelmine Williams,
author of the most widely used United States textbook on Latin American
history from 1930 to 1955, included material on feminist activism in the
region in her chapters on inter-American relations. In 1927 Emily Green
Balch edited *Beyond Haiti* with the intention of influencing United States
policy in the Caribbean. Leila Rupp, citing Mary Beard's 1946 book, *Women
as a Force in History*, points out that 'women committed to the international
women's movement understood the importance of keeping records'.[4]

In *Worlds of Women,* Rupp examines three transnational women's organisations: the International Council of Women, founded in Washington, DC,
in 1888; the International Woman Suffrage Alliance, founded in Berlin in
1904; and the Women's International League for Peace and Freedom,
founded at The Hague in 1915. Rooted in the progressive values and
growing trans-oceanic internationalism of the late nineteenth century, the
membership of the organisations 'mirrored the dominance of European or
European-settled, Christian, capitalist nations in the world system'.[5]

Women elsewhere were organising transnationally as well as locally in
this same period, certainly in the Americas,[6] with an eye to bringing pressure on national governments and to creating political space where women
could debate and bring international attention to issues. But what seems to
distinguish the organisations under examination in *Worlds of Women* from
others formed in this period is the women's construction of 'a collective
identity' as feminist internationalists. Rupp states, 'not only did women
share a common belief in some sort of loyalty to an entity beyond their
motherlands', but they believed that, in the interwar years, 'questions of
labor legislation, nationality, and the traffic in women could only be addressed on the international plane'. The often-intense friendships that
developed among women internationalists via correspondence, congresses,
and, in the case of WILPF, at their Geneva headquarters, helped sustain the
women's work over time and across distance. Rupp makes a convincing
argument that the contentious debates that occurred within the women's
organisations – over suffrage, women's right to work versus protectionism,
birth control and social hygiene – were not a sign of weakness but a necessary and valuable part of the organisational process. Assessing the results
of half a century of women's transnational efforts, Rupp concludes: 'It was
through the League of Nations that feminist internationalists succeeded in
putting their issues on the international agenda ... the history of international
governance would not have been the same without the participation of the
transnational women's groups'.[7]

In the final chapter, 'International Matters', Rupp points out the extent
to which the ICW, IWA and WILPF were disrupted by World War II, but
asserts that 'the embers of women's activism, smoldering in the ashes of the
League of Nations, flamed anew as the legacy of internationalism passed
to the new United Nations ... yet when the delegations took their seats at

the founding conference, only a few included women ... the Australian, Brazilian, Canadian, Chinese, Dominican Republic, the United States and Uruguay'.[8] Rupp, her focus firmly on the three major transnational women's organisations of the interwar years, does not point out that five of the seven delegations that included women representatives are from the Western Hemisphere. This was no accident.

Rupp cites Brazilian delegate Bertha Lutz's letter to her close friend Carrie Chapman Catt: 'Your Brazilian daughter and the Latin American women with Australia have been doing great battle to get an article into the Charter giving women representation and participation on equal terms'. [9] By 1945, the history of women's transnational organising in the Western Hemisphere spanned nearly sixty years, beginning with the Pan-American Scientific Congresses of the 1890s.[10] Rupp's new work significantly enlarges our knowledge of the history of women's transnational organising; conversely, the interposition of the history of women activists' organisational efforts in the Americas – Mexican schoolteachers, Cuban club women and independence fighters, Uruguayan socialist suffragists, Argentine labour organisers and journalists, Chilean educators, adds a dimension to the history of feminisms and transnationalism that both enriches and destabilises the 'Euro-American' ('American' understood as the United States and Canada) paradigm of women's international organising.

In *Latin American Women and the Search for Social Justice*, I posited that it was women of the Americas who, with years of transnational experience and success in lobbying the Inter-American Conferences of American States on feminist issues, argued successfully for the inclusion of the phrase 'the equal rights of men and women' in the charter of the UN. In San Francisco in 1945, a delegation from the Inter-American Commission of Women (IACW) that included Bertha Lutz, Minerva Bernardino of the Dominican Republic and Amália Cabellero de Castillo Ledón, chair of the IACW and delegate from Mexico, made a forceful case that precedent had been set in international law by the 'Declaration in Favor of Women's Rights' adopted at the Eighth International Conference of American States at Lima in 1938.[11]

Rereading this assessment in the light of Rupp's research opens up new possibilities of interpretation. Looking at Rupp's description of the disruption the war caused for the 'Euro-American' women's internationalist organisations highlights the fact that the transnational activities of women of the Americas were far less disrupted by the war: the 1938 Lima conference is one example, but, perhaps more importantly, Latin American, Canadian and United States women were deeply involved in the common effort to unite the Americas in the defence of democracy during the war years.[12] In her study of the Chilean women's movement in the 1940s, Corinne Antezana-Pernet states that 'World War II acted as a necessary catalyst in the formation of a broad, ambitious women's movement committed to the defense of democracy and its extension to women'.[13] Latin

American women continually made their presence felt at the inter-
American conferences, despite the wariness felt by some toward aligning
with US women, a concern Christine Ehrick delineates in her contribution
to this journal, 'Madrinas and Missionaries: Uruguay and the Pan-American
Women's Movement', in which she documents Uruguayan internationalist
Paulina Luisi's discomfort with the 'missionary' attitudes of certain visiting
feminist organisers from the United States. Argentine feminist Alicia Moreau
de Justo was similarly cautious but ultimately supported the efforts of the
Franklin Delano Roosevelt administration to unite the hemisphere as the
Second World War threatened.[14] While the embers of the great women's
international organisations smouldered in Europe, women of the Americas
provided an active continuity of exchange, recruiting new allies in the
democratic opening of the period. Moreover, these American women who
had been active on behalf of feminist and women's issues prior to the
war were present in force at the conferences that met to plan postwar
international strategies.[15]

Speaking on the *Jim Lehrer News Hour*, 26 February 1998, historian
Doris Kearns Goodwin observed, 'In a way, the UN is only eight years old'.
Goodwin makes reference to the near-immediate eclipse of the stated goals
of the UN by the perceived urgencies of the Cold War. Among those who
called for staying true to the original intent of the founders of the UN were
the women who gathered at the Primer Congreso Interamericano de Mujeres
in Guatemala City, 21–7 August 1947. Two hundred women, representing
women's organisations from British Columbia to Brazil, from Minnesota to
Argentina, Mexico to Ecuador, called on the foreign ministers gathered in
Rio de Janeiro to 'honor the original intent of the Charter of the UN ... and
not give it a militaristic interpretation', arguing 'that the expansion of communism will be contained not by force of arms but through the improvement of the living conditions of the people'.[16]

Yet in the 1990s, despite the efforts of pioneering feminist scholars such
as Cynthia Enloe, the history of women's transnational activities has not
been incorporated into an understanding of international relations, far less
into the analysis of foreign policy.[17] In her book *Feminist Theory and International Relations in a Postmodern Era*, Canadian political scientist Christine
Sylvester asks, 'How can femin*ism* leave an indelible mark on the field [of
International Relations] when femin*ists* are absented from the literature?'[18]
She writes that 'one of the characteristics of IR is that it presents itself as
gender-blind, as a realm of objective human knowledge'. Sylvester's project involves employing feminism-sensitive research, in which the gender
categories 'men' and 'women' are understood in a multiplicity of ways –
people called men, people called women, 'men' dressed as nation states,
soldiers, decision-makers, 'women' evoked as the ' " 'Chiquita Bananas' of the
international political economy", "the Pocahontas" of diplomatic practice'.[19]

Though sympathetic to the fact that the words and deeds of 'women
worthies' who did not keep to their assigned places 'at home ... have been

lost ... or simply ignored because they are the views of people called women', Sylvester is more concerned with disrupting political theory via feminist theory than with writing women into the historical record: 'We cannot become obsessed with the effort to exhume women worthies at the expense of exploring the possibilities for identity hyphenations, meta-morphoses, and mobilities that can homestead IR in new ways'.[20]

In *Feminism and International Relations*, Sandra Whitworth agrees with her colleague Sylvester that 'the discipline of IR has been dominated by the realist approach to international relations [wherein] analyses of women or of gender issues were [deemed] simply inappropriate to the study of "states, power and anarchy"'. Whitworth undertakes a comparative analysis of the International Planned Parenthood Federation (IPPF) and the International Labour Organisation (ILO) to 'discover the ways in which knowledge about sexual difference is sustained by international institutions and the possible avenues for changing those understandings'.[21] The ILO, founded in 1919 as an international agency of the League of Nations and incorporated into the United Nations in 1945, is charged with assessing and proposing inter-national labour legislation. Whitworth writes, 'From its beginnings, the ILO has developed policies which quite explicitly recognize certain assumptions about the appropriate role of women and men in the family, labor force and society'. She examines the ways in which ILO policies historically reflect 'particular and changing understandings of gender relations', tracing the debates over protectionism in the 1930s through women's entry into the workforce in the post-World War II era and demands for equality, concluding with the shift in ILO policy in the 1980s from seeking equal employment conditions for women to the recognition that men as well as women may have family responsibilities. She credits that shift to the influ-ence of the women's movement and the UN Decade for Women.[22]

Whitworth convincingly links the founding of the International Planned Parenthood Federation to the Cold War: 'The creation in the West of an elaborate network of international organizations aimed at coordinating trade, finance, oil and security [to contain the USSR] ... the association of birth control, global stability and the promotion of peace ... population control policies became part of the American Cold War strategy'.[23]

The IPPF's immediate prototype was the Planned Parenthood Federation of America, formed from the merger of Margaret Sanger's Clinical Research Bureau and the American Birth Control League in 1942. The gender role assumptions of 1950s America were embedded in the IPPF charter; Whitman writes that what began as 'a movement to defend women's reproductive freedom effectively became an organization concerned with the far more "respectable" enterprise of promoting family and social stability'. Through her case studies of the ILO and the IPPF, Whitworth demonstrates the ways in which 'gender is both reflected in international institutions and is in part organized by those institutions', and succeeds in developing 'a feminist account of international relations which takes into account gender relations'.[24]

While recognising the resistance of IR to feminist theory and valuing both the difficulty and the clarity of Sylvester and Whitworth's intellectual work, I am struck by how much these projects would be enriched and nuanced through reading feminist history. For example, Whitworth's assessment that the IPPF was founded as part of US Cold War policy is accurate as far as it goes: what is missing is an understanding of the extent to which birth control, concern with high female death rates due to abortion, and attempts to reduce venereal disease and improve maternal and child health have been part of the national debate in nations as diverse as Chile and Mexico, Cuba, Argentina, Uruguay and Brazil since the 1920s.[25] By analysing an international institution primarily as an instrument of US Cold War policy, the feminist political scientists replicate the old IR problem of seeing only the obvious 'players'; in this case, 'First World' policy makers.

What I would like to do in the remaining pages of this review is look at how reading feminism-sensitive, historically grounded analysis can create new understandings of feminisms and transnationalism. In her groundbreaking book *Women, Feminism and Social Change in Argentina, Chile and Uruguay 1890–1940*, Asunción Lavrin offers an immensely subtle, historically nuanced understanding of feminism as it emerged in those nations in the early twentieth century: 'the difficulty of categorising feminism speaks for its being capable of evolution and of adapting to changing political realities rather than being a fixed set of ideas'.[26] Lavrin writes that

> in the Southern Cone, the term 'feminism' came to be understood as a reevaluation of women's roles in society, encompassing a vast field of discussion: the nature of women as human beings, their mental and physical abilities, the limits of the family's and society's demands on them, and the meaning of change in their legal status for husbands and fathers, for the women themselves, for the family as an institution, for the nation as a political entity.[27]

One of the many strengths of Lavrin's book is to give agency, through meticulously documented detail, to the Argentine, Uruguayan and Chilean citizenry. In the chapters *'Puericultura*, Public Health and Motherhood', 'Feminism and Sexuality' and 'The Control of Reproduction: Gender Relations under Scrutiny', she documents how the interplay of reformists' desire to modernise the nation, the growing political power of labour, and the rise of an urban middle class, gave political space and social recognition to new groups: 'Women were one such group'.[28]

What if the history of the debates over reproduction in Argentina were incorporated into a gendered analysis of the International Planned Parenthood Federation? First, the existence of such a history immediately displaces the implication that birth-control policies were only or even primarily a 'foreign' or 'imperial' agenda imposed upon a client population. Second, knowledge of this history allows for a far more complex analysis of how gendered international institutions garner support or encounter resistance in different national settings. IPPF programmes were directly tied to United States Agency for International Development funds in the 1960s in a successful effort to encourage governments to allow clinics and programmes to be established; a knowledge of the history of the debates on reproduction in local settings illuminates who might support IPPF work and why they might do so. In her discussion of feminism and eugenics, Lavrin writes:

> Many feminists of both genders supported eugenics policies because they promised better health for future generations through attention to mothers and children, the elimination of sexually transmitted diseases, and the hope that prenuptial certificates would detect such diseases before marriage. Such an attractive promise was difficult to ignore, and many outstanding female physicians who advocated state programs for healthy mothers and babies also supported state policies that promised to change male sexual behavior.[29]

Lavrin shows us that, though far from numerous, there were spokespeople in the 1920s and 1930s who believed in a woman's need to control her own reproduction.[30]

This latter point is important. There is a tendency among many contemporary scholars to date such 'advanced' feminist ideas from the late 1960s and 'second wave' feminism; or, even more narrowly, from the 'women's lib' movements of the 1970s. Similarly, particularly in the periodical literature, there is a persistent ahistoricism which credits the United Nations Decade for Women for bringing such ideas to the attention of women world-wide. While in no way discounting the vast influence of the UN Decade for Women, it is important to know that there is a long prehistory to the issues brought forth since 1975. Lavrin writes of the Southern Cone feminist men and women of the early twentieth century, 'Whenever they looked outside for models, they did so in hope of finding viable methods to solve national problems'.[31]

In the 1990s, the examination of feminisms and transnationalism requires analysis of interactions that are at once local and global, and there is a perception that such interaction has intensified exponentially.[32] At the same time, distinctions between 'transnational' women's associations and 'international' organisations are blurred by the burgeoning of formal non-governmental organisations, or NGOs, which do have accreditations and sources of funding that differentiate them from earlier transnational women's organisations. Some contemporary NGOs have roots in pre-existing community action groups; conversely, many local community action groups owe their organisational existence to the activities of transnational institutions and networks, for example, churches, UNIFEM agencies, CLADEM (Comité Latinoamericano para la Defensa de los Derechos de la Mujer). Other NGOs receive funding from nationally based institutions such as the Swedish International Development Agency (SIDA) and the United States Agency for International Development (USAID).[33] In the 1990s the genealogies are increasingly complex.

In 1995, the Inter-American Foundation published a listing of over 20,000 non-governmental organisations active in Latin America; women's groups comprised more than half the tally and women participated in almost all NGOs listed. Preparations for the 1995 UN Conference on Women in Huairou-Beijing generated numerous congresses where ideas were shared and positions on issues hammered out. For example, in 1994 the Inter-American Development Bank (IDB) sponsored a 'Forum on Women of the Americas' which brought together 'women and men from all over Latin America and the Caribbean … representing their governments, NGOs, community groups, academic bodies and business associations, and other international institutions'.[34] One of the results of the preparatory work by local and regional women's groups, in Latin America and across the world, was that over 400 NGOs – an unprecedented number – were accredited to the formal UN meeting in Beijing .[35]

UN reports and IDB publications provide macro views of feminist work in the transnational arena. Two recent publications, *Women & Change in the Caribbean: A Pan-Caribbean Perspective*, edited by Janet Momsen, and *The Costa Rican Women's Movement: A Reader*, edited by Ilse Abshagen Leitinger, provide specific local examples of the complex contemporary interactions of feminisms and transnationalism.[36] Leitinger's reader demonstrates:

> that the development of the Costa Rican women's movement is owed to a complex interplay of domestic and international factors. Inside Costa Rica, a whole range of state institutions from the universities to government bureaucracies nourished a variety of women's groups, which in turn were influenced by Costa Ricans educated abroad and by foreign residents … NGOs and international development agencies.[37]

Momsen introduces the twenty-one analytical case studies presented in *Women & Change*: 'The Caribbean is the oldest area of European colonization in the world'.[38] Momsen and her colleagues' analyses in *Different Places, Different Voices* carry the integrity of their belief in the crucial importance of field work; the resulting book offers a dense and to date unique pan-Caribbean analysis of the 'process of change and its impact on gender roles and gender relations'. Employing a 'trans-imperial framework' to examine the multiple contemporary paradoxes of gender relations in the region, Momsen writes that the peoples of the Caribbean 'have cosmopolitan attitudes with spatial perceptions which extend their territorial boundaries to disjunct corners of New York, London, Amsterdam, Paris and Toronto'.[39]

The Caribbean and Middle America were original sites of transnational capitalist colonial practice; Momsen's and Leitinger's edited volumes document transnational, local and international woman's movement endeavours

and feminisms that present potent challenges to old patterns. Rupp noted the self-conscious effort of women internationalists to record their organisational efforts. One of the hallmarks of the contemporary women's movement in the Americas is the creation of documentation centres, incrementally establishing a base from which to build a critical, gendered analysis.[40] The wealth of information that is emerging from the presses of women's documentation centres in every country constitutes a politics of information. It is an insistence on documenting a previously unacknowledged story, inscribing public memory, and creating a new historical record.

The agenda for Beijing was forged in a thousand different women's meetings; many of the emergent issues of concern are not susceptible to 'national' solutions. They are problems that have no borders.[41] In 1995 at the United Nations Tribunal in Huairou, Frances Kissling, representing Catholics for a Free Choice, emphasised the importance of thorough, meticulous research in making women's case to governments and communities. The need for historical context is critical to this effort.

In the 1990s, the history of feminisms and transnationalism is formative. Leila Rupp's statement, 'I see my work as part of a transnational history that we are only beginning to write', is true.[42]

Notes

This essay was composed while in residence as a Visiting Fellow at the University of California Humanities Research Institute, University of California, Irvine, February 1998. I would like to thank the members of the research project 'The Culture of the Americas and Narratives of Globalization' for generously sharing their work with me: Gwen Kirkpatrick, convener; Leo Chavez; Francine Masiello; Elizabeth Marchant; Josefina Saidaiia Portillo; Roger Rouse; Sergio de la Mora; David Luis-Brown.

1. Leila J. Rupp, *Worlds of Women: The Making of an International Women's Movement* (Princeton University Press, Princeton, NJ, 1997), p. 6.

2. Francesca Miller, 'Latin American Feminism and the Transnational Arena', in *Women, Culture and Politics in Latin America. Seminar on Feminism and Culture*, ed. Emily Bergmann (University of California Press, Los Angeles and Berkeley, 1990).

3. I am grateful to Roger Rouse for this citation and for the interpretation of Boume's thesis.

4. Mary Wilhelmine Williams, *People and Politics in Latin America*, rev. ed. (Ginn, Boston, 1945); Emily Greene Balch (ed.), *Occupied Haiti* (The Writers Publishing Company, New York, 1927); Rupp, *Worlds of Women*, p. 8.

5. Rupp, *Worlds of Women*, p. 48.

6. See for example: Corinne Antezana-Pernet, 'Peace in the World and Democracy at Home: The Chilean Women's Movement in the 1940s', in *Latin America in the 1940s*, ed. David Rock (University of California Press, Berkeley, 1994); Christine Ehrick, 'Obrera, Dama, Feminista: Women's Associations and the Welfare State in Uruguay, 1900–1932', PhD dissertation, University of California Los Angeles, 1997; June E. Hahner, *Emancipating the Female Sex: The Struggle for Women's Rights in Brazil*

1885–1940 (Duke University Press, Durham, NC, 1990; Asunción Lavrin, *Women, Feminism, and Social Change in Argentina, Chile, and Uruguay, 1890–1940* (University of Nebraska Press, Lincoln, 1995); Francesca Miller, *Latin American Women and the Search for Social Justice* (University Press of New England, Hanover, NH, and London,1992); Shirlene Soto, *The Emergence of the Modern Mexican Woman: Her Participation in Revolution and Struggle for Equality* (Arden Press, Denver, 1990); K. Lynn Stoner, *From the House to the Streets: The Cuban Women's Movement for Legal Change, 1898–1940*. (Duke University Press, Durham, NC, 1991).

7. Rupp, *Worlds of* Women, pp. 48, 155, 210.

8. Rupp, *Worlds of Women*, p. 222.

9. Rupp, *Worlds of Women*, p. 222

10. Miller, 'Latin American Feminism and the Transnational Arena'.

11. Miller, 'Latin American Feminism and the Transnational Arena', pp. 118–27.

12. From 28 September 1941 to 5 April 1942, First Lady Eleanor Roosevelt made a series of radio broadcasts, sponsored by the Pan American Coffee Bureau, promoting 'the mutual desire of the nations of the Americas to build a defensive unit based on economic cooperation and cultural understanding' (transcripts of the Pan American Coffee Bureau Broadcasts, Library of Congress. Washington, DC).

13. Corrine Antezana-Pernet, 'Peace in the World and Democracy at Home', p. 167. See also Christine Ehrick, 'Obrera, Dama, Feminista: Women's Associations and the Welfare State in Uruguay, 1900–1932', PhD dissertation, University of California Los Angeles, 1997.

14. Lavrin, Asunción. 'Alicia Moreau de Justo: Feminismo y Política, 1911–1945', in *Mujer y Familia en América Latina, siglos XVIII–XX*, ed. Susana Menéndez y Barbara Potthast (Málaga, Andalucía, 1966), p. 191.

15. Miller, *Latin American Women and the Search for Social Justice*, pp. 110–35.

16. Miller, *Latin American Women and the Search. for Social Justice*, p. 124.

17. Cynthia Enloe, *Sexual Politics at the End of the Cold War: The Morning After* (University of California Press, Berkeley and Los Angeles, 1993).

18. Sylvester, Christine, *Worlds of Women and International Relations in a Post-modern Era* (Cambridge University Press, Cambridge, 1994), p. 210.

19. Sylvester, *Worlds of Women*, p. 4.

20. Sylvester, *Worlds of Women*, p. 9.

21. Sandra Whitworth, *Feminism and International Relations: Towards a Political Economy of Gender in Interstate and Non-Govemmental Institutions* (St Martins Press, New York, 1994), p. 5.

22. Whitworth, *Feminism and International Relations* , pp. 119, 144.

23. Whitworth, *Feminism and International Relations*, p. 87.

24. Whitworth, *Feminism and International Relations*, pp. 157, 11.

25. Whitworth, *Feminism and International Relations*. See also Antezana-Pernet, Ehrick, Lavrin, Stoner, Hahner, Miller, Soto. Also, Gwen Kirkpatrick, 'The Journalism of Alfonsina Stomi: A New Approach to Women's History in Argentina', in *Women, Culture and Politics in Latin America*.

26. Asunción Lavrin, *Women, Feminism, and Social Change in Argentina, Chile, and Uruguay, 1890–1940* (University of Nebraska Press, Lincoln, 1995), p. 354. Within the limits of this essay it is only possible to indicate briefly the breadth of fresh insights brought forth in Lavrin's analysis.

27. Lavrin, *Women, Feminism, and Social Change in Argentina, Chile, and Uruguay, 1890–1940*, p. 352.

28. Lavrin, *Women, Feminism, and Social Change in Argentina, Chile, and Uruguay, 1890–1940*, p. 2.

29. Lavrin, *Women, Feminism, and Social Change in Argentina, Chile, and Uruguay, 1890–1940*, p. 9.

30. See also Soto, Ehrick, Stoner.

31. Lavrin, *Women, Feminism, and Social Change in Argentina, Chile, and Uruguay, 1890–1940*, p. 355.

32. See Roger Rouse, 'Thinking through Transnationalism: Notes on the Cultural Politics of Class Relations in the Contemporary United States', *Public Culture*, 7 (1995).

33. I would argue that the struggle to introduce an understanding of gender into USAID's activities forms a proper chapter in the history of 'feminisms and transnationalism'. Credit should go to Jane Jaquette, Elsa Chaney, Martha Lewis, and the feminist scholar-activists who founded AWID (the Association of Women in International Development) in 1975 to raise gender-consciousness in the international development agencies of the United States. See *Women of the Americas: Bridging the Gender Gap* (Inter-American Development Bank, Johns Hopkins University Press, Washington, DC, 1995). Also, Jane Jaquette, Norma Stoltz Chinchilla, Maria de la Angeles Crummett, Mayra Buvinic (eds), *Women and the Transition to Democracy. the Impact of Political and Economic Reform in Latin America* (The Latin American Program, Woodrow Wilson International Center for Scholars, Washington, DC, 20560, Working Paper Series Number 211).

34. Inter-American Foundation, *A Guide to NGO Directories: How to Find Over 20,000 Nongovernmental Organizations in Latin America and the Caribbean*, 2nd ed. (Inter American Foundation, Arlington, VA, 1995).

35. As recently as the 1993 UN Conference on Population in Vienna, 'unofficial' NGOs were barred from the building where the official UN meetings were held. Rupp writes of the difficulty representatives of the transnational women's organisations experienced after the move of the League of Nations in the 1930s into a building only those with official badges could enter.

36. Janet Momsen (ed.), *Women & Change in the Caribbean: A Pan-Caribbean Perspective* (Indiana University Press, Bloomington and Indianapolis, 1993); Ilse Abshagen Leitinger (ed.), *The Costa Rican Women's Movement: A Reader* (University of Pittsburgh Press, Pittsburgh, PA, 1997).

37. Alfred Padula, 'A Reader on the Process of Organizing and Empowering Costa Rican Women', H-NET BOOK REVIEW. H-LatAm-net.mus.edu (February 1998).

38. Momsen, *Women & Change*, p. vii.

39. See Janet Momsen and Vivian Kinnaird (eds), *Different Places, Different Voices* (Routledge, London and New York, 1993): 'Generalized statistical data, as reported in the United Nations documents, provide insufficient evidence for conceptualising women's response to these crises' (quote from p. 5). See also Momsen, *Women & Change*, p. 2.

40. For example, the Center for Communication, Exchange and Human Development in Latin America (CIDHAL) founded in Cuernavaca, Mexico, in 1969, specialises in the situation of women. The *Centra Informação Mulher* (CIM) in São Paulo does similar work. In Costa Rica, the *Centra Feminista de Información y Acción* (CEFEMINA) collates information on women's legal status and uses the information to change laws. In Chile, *ISIS International* has collated information and publications on women from throughout the hemisphere for two decades; their publication *Documentas* offers monthly updates of their computerised listings. ISIS also coordinates, via computer, the *Red de Salud de las Mujeres Latinoamericanas y del Caribe* and the *Programa de*

Información y *Política sobre Violencia en contra de la Mujer*. In the Dominican Republic, the *Centro de Documentación para la Acción Femenina* (CIPAF) directly connects information to political action. In 1992, the *Facultad Latinoamericana de Ciencias Sociales* (FLACSO-Chile) began publication of a country-by-country series, *Mujeres Latinoamericanas en Cifras*: 'The first systematic, universal effort to document in numbers the situation of women in a continent of multiple hues and geographies, that also takes into account the great political, social, ethnic, cultural and economic disparities. The subordination of women, broadly debated throughout the whole world, is today an inarguable reality ... *Mujeres Latinoamericanas en Cifras* is intended to be an instrument for the transformation of this situation, which will enable an analysis of the female situation'.

41. Francesca Miller, 'Feminism and Foreign Policy in the Americas: Separate Conversations?' Latin American Studies Association, Guadalajara, April 1997.

42. Rupp, *Worlds of Women*, p. 6.

Feminisms and International Relations

V. SPIKE PETERSON

The discipline of international relations (IR) – conventionally devoted to the study of war – has been particularly reluctant to acknowledge, much less welcome, feminist interventions. Constituted as the study of ostensibly anarchical relations between (not within or across) states, IR remains dominated by Anglo- and Euro-centric male practitioners (scholars, national policy makers) and masculinist constructs (state power, national security, sovereignty, Realpolitik, military might). Dichotomies – and their attendant positivist, ahistorical and reductionist commitments – dominate the field's key assumptions and debates: war–peace, international–domestic, anarchy –order, realism–idealism, politics–economics. These parameters suggest how and why IR is difficult, even hostile terrain for feminists, especially those who decry the field's positivist premises.[1]

As in other disciplines, however, feminists have been infiltrating, expanding, and transforming the theory/practice of IR. In 1988 the London School of Economics formally initiated the study of 'gender and IR' through a seminar course and a 1988 special issue of its journal *Millennium*.[2] Conferences, panels, articles, and books followed. The Feminist Theory and Gender Studies section of the International Studies Association provided institutional visibility in 1990. I circulated a thin but rapidly growing 'gender and IR' bibliography until 1993, when the volume of relevant material exceeded my ability to track it comprehensively.[3] For this review essay, I have selected four books suggestive of the development and range of feminist IR. Following a familiar pattern, in IR we first sought to make women visible, then explored the gender of IR's concepts, methods and practices. These projects continue even as feminists move beyond critique to reconstruction: rewriting IR as theory/practice informed, indeed transformed, by feminist and other critical insights.[4]

Published in 1990, Cynthia Enloe's *Bananas, Beaches and Bases: Making Feminist Sense of International Politics* had immediate impact: it was wonderfully readable (which reduced but could not eliminate the defensiveness of non-feminist readers), it was packed with compelling images, anecdotes and analyses that made gender 'come alive' in the context of international politics, and it provided the first wide-ranging *feminist* interpretation of IR. Enloe argued that 'gender made the world go round' and demonstrated her points by asking 'where are the women?' and exposing 'how *much* power it takes to maintain the international political system in its present form'.[5] By emphasising how that which appears natural and inevitable is in fact *made*, Enloe encouraged readers to ask both who did the making and how remaking is possible.

To expose how international phenomena rely on constructions of femininity and masculinity, Enloe began with the unconventional topic of tourism cast as gendered international power relations. She explored how holiday desires are constructed (for leisure, escape, adventure), how hierarchical divisions of labour are reinforced (through feminised provision of food, comfort, and sexual pleasures), and how elite male power is enhanced (by economic profit, political clout, and international visibility of successful tourism). In short, from the images and bodies of exotica, the human 'costs' of service economies, to the politics of elite male ownership, the very big business – and international power – of tourism is sustained by gender differentiations.

Other chapters explored the gender of nationalist movements (symbolism, agents, and ideologies), foreign military bases (race and sex dynamics, geopolitics and peace actions), diplomatic wives (in support of and resistance to traditional roles), banana republics (imperial policies, producer–consumer linkages), global labour (making women's labour cheap, women organising), and domestic servants (nannies and empires, maids and states, immigration politics). In a brief conclusion, Enloe encourages us to think of the personal as not only political but also international: 'ideas about what it means to be a "respectable" woman or an "honorable" man have been shaped by colonizing policies, trading strategies and military doctrines'. Equally important, the international is personal: 'governments depend upon certain kinds of allegedly private relationships in order to conduct their foreign affairs'.[6] Enloe's emphasis here, as everywhere in her work, is to encourage *activism,* and quite literally, the dismantling of the 'wall that often separates theory from practice'.[7]

Enloe's book gave feminist IR much needed visibility, and it remains a popular classroom text. But this could only be a beginning. Enloe's disciplinary location – in geography, not IR – shaped the book's reception.[8] On the one hand, not being constrained by the rigid boundaries of conventional IR enabled Enloe to offer a fresher, livelier and richer portrayal of what feminism might mean for the study of international politics. On the other hand, insights born of an indifference to IR's conventional boundaries rendered the text less attractive to conventional IR scholars. Insofar as academe is (regrettably) structured by disciplinary divisions, 'feminist IR' required both empirical studies linking gender to IR across an increasing range of activities *and* theoretical studies more visibly integrating feminist and IR themes. In short, we needed corrective, additive *and* analytically transformative interventions that were specific to IR – if only to subvert the latter's disciplining and disciplinary claims.

Answering part of this need was J. Ann Tickner's *Gender in International Relations: Feminist Perspectives on Achieving Global Security*, the first single-authored text providing a systematic treatment of IR theory from a feminist perspective.[9] Tickner intended to expose the 'masculinist underpinnings of the field' and to examine 'what the discipline might look like if the central realities of women's day-to-day lives were included'.[10] With 'security' as its theme and dominant theories as its focus, the book had immediate appeal to an IR audience.

Beginning with Realism (the field's dominant orientation), Tickner mimics – and subverts – the discipline's three levels of analysis: individual, polity and (anarchic) system. This trio has been foundational to IR since Kenneth Waltz's *Man, The State and War* (1959) analysed each level as the source of war. Waltz concluded that the system level – of necessarily anarchic and inevitably conflictual relations among nation-states – was definitive, for in the absence of government, sovereign nations relied on self-help and ultimately war to resolve inherent conflicts.[11]

Tickner drew on feminist political theory to examine the androcentrism of 'human nature' and 'man' assumed in conventional accounts underpinning IR's model of the individual (as atomistic, competitive, aggressive, and rationally self-interested). At the next level, Tickner argued that IR theorists simply project these characteristics onto (masculinist) states, which they define as unitary, rational, competitive, and the primary actors in IR. Individuals are linked to states through citizenship that is constituted by (male only) military and property-owning qualifications, and states act as warriors in the anarchic realm of international politics where a Hobbesian 'war of everyman against everyman' is played out as a systemic condition. The latter produces a perpetual 'security dilemma' wherein increasing one's own security necessarily appears to threaten that of others, who respond by increasing their security, hence generating a spiralling dynamic constituting insecurity for all.

In arguments familiar to feminists and informing most contemporary feminist IR, Tickner exposed this self-perpetuating cycle and IR's foundational premises as based on men's experience and a masculinist model of human nature. Moreover, she argued that the field's reigning orientation, (hardheaded, resolute, rational) Realism, defines itself in opposition to (softheaded, wishful, naive) Idealism. It thereby not only claims ontological – and normative – superiority, by casting itself as uniquely *realistic,* but also evacuates the field of alternatives, which it casts as unrealisable and even dangerous. Small wonder that feminists and other critics find IR a wellfortified and aggressively defended terrain.

In her third chapter, Tickner reviews and critiques the three dominant IR approaches to the study of international political economy (IPE).[12] Liberalism's androcentrism assumes rational 'economic man' only contractually engaged in community. Its promotion of the market and free trade policies ignores how women and men are differently affected by markets, and IR scholarship ignores entirely the existing critiques of liberalism in women/ gender and development literature. Mercantilism, or economic nationalism, presumes Realism's emphasis on (sovereign) state prosperity while sharing liberalism's model of economic man. The instrumental rationality favoured for state development obscures how state policies have differential effects on women and men. In particular, it masks the state's dependence on women's biological and social reproduction and, hence, the masculinist state's regulation of women's activities to ensure that reproduction.

Marxism is itself a marginalised perspective in IR. It appears as a feature of dependency and world systems theories, which constitute the third approach to IPE. As Tickner notes, by being critical of the status quo, this approach might appear to be more hospitable to feminisms. Its reliance on class as the basic unit, however, subsumes women and their reproductive labour and replicates the gender-blindness of the first two approaches. In sum, Tickner argued that gender-sensitive theories of IPE require greater attention to how women and men are differently affected by markets and states, to contextualising rationality (acknowledging care and responsibility), and to theorising IPE from the bottom (individual level) up, hence mixing, not separating, levels of analysis.

In pursuit of alternative understandings of security, Tickner integrates two ecological discourses. Feminist critiques of nature as 'woman' (therefore to be dominated/exploited for man's use) are reviewed and brought into relation with 'common security' critiques of state-centric decision-making as definitive (therefore inadequate in regard to *trans*-national environmental crises). She considers how the dichotomies of instrumentalism and Realism intersect and enhance social hierarchies – of sexism, racism, imperialism – and reproduce an increasingly inappropriate focus on geopolitical, rather than ecopolitical, space.

In her conclusion, Tickner's move 'toward non-gendered global security' has two key components. First, the discipline must rethink its basic concepts and commit to analysis in multi-dimensional and multi-level terms. Second, IR must recognise and take seriously 'how so many of the insecurities affecting us all, women and men alike, are gendered in their historical origins, their conventional definitions, and their contemporary manifestations'.[13]

Less focused on theory but equally wide-ranging, is Spike Peterson and Anne Sisson Runyan's *Global Gender Issues*.[14] On the one hand, this book is designed as an introduction to taking gender seriously in any context. The first two chapters introduce gender as a lens: shaping not only male–female identities but also the concepts with which we think, therefore acting as a 'filter' that pervasively shapes knowledge claims as well as people, practices and institutions. Dichotomies, stereotypes and ideologies are critically reviewed for their roles in naturalising gender difference and its related hierarchies. In remaining chapters, and to emphasise the interaction of empirical and analytical gender, the authors present material as two interactive dimensions: 'women's position in world politics' (how women and men differently act within and are affected by international processes) and the 'power of gender' (how gendered lenses shape our concepts, expectations and knowledge claims).

On the other hand, the book is designed with two purposes in mind: to offer IR scholars an accessible feminist text for use in conventional IR courses, and to offer feminist scholars generally an introduction to IR themes and the importance of locating feminisms in an international/global context. As a heuristic device and organisational framework, the conventional topics of IR are recast in feminist terms as gendered divisions of power (i.e., politics), of violence (i.e., security), of labour (i.e., economics, IPE), and resources (i.e., equity and ecology). For each (overlapping) topic, the authors suggest how gendered dichotomies (public–private; reason–emotion; direct–indirect violence, soldier–protectee; paid–unpaid work, production–reproduction; culture–nature, developed–undeveloped) underpin IR thinking (about politics, security, etc.) *and* how the gender of these dichotomies both produces and is produced by gender-differentiated activities and institutions (militaries, service economies, etc.). To counter the woman-as-victim image fuelled by analysing gendered divisions and hierarchies, the authors also focus on women as key agents in political, anti-militarist, nationalist, economic, social justice, and ecological movements.

In a concluding discussion of policy recommendations, the authors articulate a non-oppositional distinction between Molyneux's practical (local, short-term, women-oriented) and strategic (system transformative, feminist-oriented) gender interests.[15] In this the authors attempt to honour – and bring into relation – both the particular needs and voices of women in the context of immediate, local struggles, and the more ambitious feminist objective of transforming systemic gender hierarchy and its structurally related oppressions (of race/ethnicity, class, sexual orientation, etc.). Inevitably, the identification of strategic gender interests involves universalising claims (e.g., to equal rights) that are cross-culturally problematic – and hotly debated in contemporary discussions of theory/practice. With Enloe and Tickner, the authors insist that gender hierarchies underpin global insecurities in such ways that IR cannot effectively address the latter until it acknowledges the former. Like Enloe's book, and unlike Tickner's, *Global Gender Issues* does not systematically engage IR theory. Yet its epistemological commitments have systemic theoretical implications. By insisting that gender is simultaneously empirical and analytical – and demonstrating this effectively in the text – *Global Gender Issues* undercuts the positivist and modernist premises that sustain conventional IR theorising.

A sophisticated exploration of IR *and* feminist theories emerges in Christine Sylvester's 1994 *Feminist Theory and International Relations in a Postmodern Era,* where empiricist, standpoint and postmodern epistemologies of contemporary feminists are brought to bear on the three gender-blind debates characterising IR's theoretical terrain. To challenge the identity politics of IR, Sylvester rewrites 'homesteading' as 'processes that reconfigure "known" subject statuses ... in ways that open up rather than fence in terrains of meaning, identity, and place'.[16] With the homesteading trope as key, and drawing on Kathy Ferguson's 'mobile subjectivities',[17] Sylvester elaborates a postmodern feminist method of 'empathetic cooperation'. The latter 'can divest IR's nostalgic gender settlements of power by infusing them with the knowledges that come from listening to and engaging canon-excluding and canon-including subjectivities ... [To shift] not to a better and more encompassing theory, a sturdier home – but to a place of mobile subjectivity where basic questions can be rephrased in many tones'.[18]

IR's first gender-blind debate pitted Realism against Idealism, with Realism the predictable winner. Sylvester argues that in their preoccupation with sovereign states and conflict, Realists deny the relevance of interdependence, households, and cooperation. Idealists acknowledge cooperation and interdependence, but deny their gendered constitution and meanings. In the discipline's second debate, positivist rationalism won the field against historical and normative methods. While (rational) neo-liberal institutionalists acknowledge interdependence and cooperation, people called 'women' can only visit these sites, offering support in service to male-identified agendas. IR's third 'post-positivist' debate ostensibly opened the field to plural voices and epistemological growth. But even as critical and postmodern theorists challenged their marginalisation by orthodox positivism/Realism, they reproduced the discipline's exclusion of feminists as author(itie)s and gender as analytically constitutive. In short, women/gender are effectively evacuated from IR and their homesteading(s) precluded.[19]

In her elaboration of feminist theories, Sylvester suggests that feminist empiricism's preferences provide homes for women within scientifically based fields. Feminist standpointers presume to offer differently invested and less distorted views and truth claims, creating spaces for women as agents of knowledge and theory. Here Sylvester develops an important theoretical point in regard to feminism and postmodernism. The latter's emphasis on the constitutiveness of (phallocentric) language inclines it toward the deconstruction of authority and destabilisation of places from which to speak/act, and hence, away from political commitment and action. In contrast, then, to feminist postmodernism, Sylvester argues for *postmodern feminism*, which inclines toward a negotiation between standpoint feminism – with its 'real' women and practical/moral implications – and postmodernism's scepticisms. So understood, postmodern feminism permits us to have meaningful identities even as we relentlessly question their political implications.

In IR, empathetic cooperation entails a shift to thinking in terms of 'relations international' – 'the myriad positions that groups assume toward one another across the many boundaries and identities that defy field-invented parameters'[20] – and to querying relations for their interlocking constraints, thus involving 'a more encompassing range of authority patterns than we have contemplated within standard IR'.[21] Homesteading IR's debates means 'tak[ing] on the gendered anarchies and reciprocities of a field, freeing prisoners from manipulated dilemmas and refusing divisive levels of analysis that have us not-seeing the lessons on cooperative relations that third world cooperatives and first world peace camps can teach'.[22]

Given its relatively recent and heavily resisted interventions, IR feminists have achieved remarkable success. In a now extensive literature, feminists have expanded and transformed IR theories as they relate to identities, sexualities, militarisms, polities, revolutions, nationalisms, social hierarchies, transnational economics, political movements, and international organisations.[23] We have institutionalised our presence at conferences and in curricula. Students have been crucial to this process: they appreciate, criticise, and contribute to our coursework, scholarship and activism. Indeed, a 'second generation' of IR feminists is already visible, pushing in new directions and further eroding disciplinary, territorial, and race/ethnic/class boundaries. Our small but growing numbers will continue to tackle an impressive array of topics.

What we do need and seek is the engagement of 'non-IR' feminists. For most of us, and especially today, IR is not simply one among other disciplinary vantage points. Global capitalism and transnational dynamics shape all of our lives – from the culture that we imbibe to the identities we embody, from the work that we do to the pains and rewards it offers, from the dreams that we have to the possibilities of a more just, less terrifying world. Hence, we urge feminists less familiar with IR to draw on our work and, in turn, to expand our understanding. In particular, we welcome historical studies. By retrieving histories of gender that shaped our international past(s), we improve the quality and likelihood of feminist futures.

Notes

1. For an early critique of gendered dichotomies and positivist premises in IR, see V. Spike Peterson, 'Transgressing Boundaries: Theories of Knowledge, Gender, and International Relations', *Millennium*, 21 (1992), pp. 183–206.

2. *Millennium*, 17, 3 (1988). The follow-up to this special issue was Rebecca Grant and Kathleen Newland (eds), *Gender and International Relations* (Indiana University Press, Bloomington and Indianapolis, 1991).

3. A 145 page bibliography (March 1994) compiled by J. D. Kenneth Boutin is available from the Centre for International and Strategic Studies at York University, Toronto. For an excellent recent overview and analysis of feminist IR, see Jacqui True, 'Feminism', in *Theories of International Relations*, ed. Scott Burchill, Richard Devetak, Andrew Linklater, Matthew Paterson, and Jacqui True (Macmillan, London, 1996), pp. 210–51.

4. Lily Ling, 'Feminist International Relations: From Critique to Reconstruction', *The Journal of International Communication,* 3 (1996), pp. 26–41.

5. Cynthia Enloe, *Bananas, Beaches and Bases: Making Feminist Sense of International Politics* (University of California Press, Berkeley, 1990), p. 3.

6. Enloe, *Bananas, Beaches and Bases,* p. 196.

7. Enloe, *Bananas, Beaches and Bases,* p. 201.

8. For a more recent effort spanning feminism, geography and international relations, see Eleonore Kofman and Gillian Youngs (eds), *Globalization: Theory and Practice* (Pinter Press, London, 1996).

9. J. Ann Tickner, *Gender in International Relations: Feminist Perspectives on Achieving Global Security* (Columbia University Press, New York, 1992). Other feminist books addressing the breadth of IR with attention to theory include V. Spike Peterson (ed.), *Gendered States: Feminist (Re)Visions of International Relations Theory* (Lynne Rienner Press, Boulder, CO, 1992); Christine Sylvester, *Feminist Theory and International Relations in a Postmodern Era* (Cambridge University Press, Cambridge, 1994); Peter Beckman and Francine D'Amico (eds), *Women, Gender, and World Politics* (Bergin and Garvey, Westport, CT, 1994); and Jill Steans, *Gender and International Relations* (Polity Press, Cambridge, 1998).

10. Tickner, *Gender in International Relations,* p. ix.

11. Kenneth Waltz, *Man, The State and War; A Theoretical Analysis* (Columbia University Press, New York, 1959)

12. In addition to the enormous literature on women/gender and development, feminist-IR critiques of IPE and globalisation include Jan Jindy Pettman, *Worlding Women: A Feminist International Politics* (Routledge, New York, 1996); V. Spike Peterson, 'The Politics of Identification in the Context of Globalization', *Women's Studies International Forum,* 19 (1996), pp. 5–15; Eileen Boris and Elisabeth Prugl (eds), *Homeworkers in Global Perspective* (Routledge, New York, 1996); Isabella Bakker (ed.), *The Strategic Silence: Gender and Economic Policy* (Zed Books, London, 1994).

13. Tickner, *Gender in International Relations,* p. 129.

14. V. Spike Peterson and Anne Sisson Runyan, *Global Gender Issues* (Westview Press, Boulder, CO, 1993). An updated, revised and expanded 2nd edition is due out in late 1998.

15. Maxine Molyneux, '"Mobilisation Without Emancipation?" Women's Interests, the State, and Revolution in Nicaragua', *Feminist Studies,* 11 (1985), pp. 227–54.

16. Christine Sylvester, *Feminist Theory and International Relations in a Postmodern Era* (Cambridge University Press, Cambridge, 1994), p. 2.

17. Kathy E. Ferguson, *The Man Question: Visions of Subjectivity and Feminist Theory* (University of California Press, Berkeley, 1993).

18. Sylvester, *Feminist Theory and International Relations,* p. 213.

19. On the continued disregard of gender in IR theorising, see for example, Sandra Whitworth, 'Gender in the Inter-Paradigm Debate', *Millennium,* 18 (1989), pp. 265–72 and 'Theory as Exclusion: Gender and International Political Economy', in *Political Economy and the Changing Global Order,* ed. Richard Stubbs and Geoffrey Underhill (McClelland and Stewart, Toronto, 1994), pp. 116–29; Susan Judith Ship, 'And What About Gender? Feminism and International Relations Theory's Third Debate', in *Beyond Positivism: Critical International Relations Theory,* ed. W. S. Cox and C. T. Sjolander (Westview Press, Boulder, CO, 1994), pp. 129–52; and Marysia Zalewski, 'Feminist Theory and International Relations', in *From Cold War to Collapse,* ed. M. Bowker and R Brown (Cambridge University Press, Cambridge, 1993), pp. 115–44.

20. Sylvester, *Feminist Theory and International Relations*, p. 219.

21. Sylvester, *Feminist Theory and International Relations*, p. 221.

22. Sylvester, *Feminist Theory and International Relations*, p. 226.

23. In addition to works cited, see for example Marysia Zalewski and Jane Parpart (eds), *The 'Man' Question in International Relations* (Westview Press, Boulder, CO, 1998; V. Spike Peterson, 'Whose Crisis? Early and Postmodern Masculinism', in *Innovation and Transformation in International Studies*, ed. Stephen Gill and James H. Mittelman (Cambridge University Press, Cambridge, 1997), pp. 185–201; Simona Sharoni, *Gender and the Israeli–Palestinian Conflict* (Syracuse University Press, Syracuse, 1995); Sandra Whitworth, *Feminism and International Relations: Towards a Political Economy of Gender in Interstate and Non-Governmental Institutions* (Macmillan, London, 1994); Mary Ann Tetreault (ed.), *Women and Revolution in Africa, Asia, and the New World* (University of South Carolina Press, Columbia, South Carolina, 1994); Deborah Stienstra, *Women's Movements and International Organizations* (St Martin's Press, New York, 1994); 'Feminists Write International Relations', Special Issue *Alternatives*, 18 (1993); and 'Gender in International Relations', Special Issue *The Fletcher Forum of World Affairs*, 17 (1993).

Feminisms and Development

VALENTINE M. MOGHADAM

Development research and policy originated in the period following World War II, but it was not until the early 1970s that international feminism began to make its mark. The body of knowledge and field of research currently known as gender and development (GAD) originated with the publication of Ester Boserup's *Women's Role in Economic Development,* which launched the field of women-in-development (WID). At the time, female development practitioners were concerned that the benefits of modernisation and economic development seemed to accrue more to men than to women, and that women were often marginalised from new productive processes and commercial enterprises. WID research and advocacy sought to ensure that development projects recognised women's roles in production and provided them with access to resources, and that new employment opportunities be available to women.[1]

In the early 1980s an alternative approach criticised the earlier WID approach for ignoring the capitalist nature of the development process, with its inherent social and gender inequities. In contrast to the liberal approach, which emphasised the need to integrate women into the development process, the socialist-feminist approach raised questions about the type of development that women were to be integrated into. This new approach, which came to be known as women and development (WAD), stressed that patriarchy and capitalism limited the options available to women.[2]

The current GAD approach combines aspects of WID and WAD but begins its analysis by examining the system of gender relations which, along with the economic system, structures the options available to both women and men. Researchers working within the GAD framework acknowledge the capitalist nature of national economies (and of the global economy) but recognise that by overcoming gender inequalities, important systemic changes may be achieved. They favour the elimination of legal, customary, and labour-market constraints on women's mobility and economic participation, while realising that these constraints are rooted in longstanding gender ideologies and asymmetrical gender relations.

In the GAD approach, the relationship between gender relations and the development process is interactive. That is, while gender roles and ideologies are part of the social structure, public policies matter and could modify gender relations. GAD researchers examine not only women's labour-force participation but also women's health, reproductive rights, female-headed households, intra-household inequalities, violence against women, women and decision-making, and women's collective action. They pay close attention to the neoliberal economic policies that have replaced the earlier statist approach to development and economic growth; and they argue that these policies are biased against women and the poor. They point out that although women's work uniquely spans the realms of production and reproduction, public policy ignores this while neoliberal economic policies intensify women's burdens. They argue that the combination of women-friendly social and economic policies will bring about an improved legal and economic status for women, while women's own capacity for mobilising and organising will result in their self-empowerment.

At present, the GAD framework is flexible and inter-disciplinary, reflecting the diversity of theoretical backgrounds and methodological approaches – including Marxism, feminism, and neoclassical economics – of the sociologists, political scientists, anthropologists and economists undertaking GAD research. Some GAD researchers highlight women's productive contributions and emphasise the losses to economic efficiency when women are marginalised. As such, they try to 'make the case for the gender variable'.[3] Others insist that gender equality and women's empowerment are legitimate objectives in and of themselves, and they are not interested in crafting persuasive arguments for economists and policy-makers.

Notwithstanding its diversity, there is a core of assumptions, concepts, and methods that may be delineated as constituting the GAD framework. The premise, of course, is that women in any society represent an unequal, disadvantaged, or oppressed social category.[4] Because of gender bias or patriarchal controls, women have had fewer rights and opportunities than men have had in the areas of literacy, reproductive control, education, salaried work, property rights, and formal politics.[5] There is also the understanding that women's positions are variable by social class; that the state and political struggles may impede or advance women's basic needs and strategic interests; and that economic policies or development objectives may have different types of outcomes for women.[6] Apart from works written by those affiliated with the World Bank, there is much agreement that the capitalist development process – the commercialisation of agriculture, industrialisation, and the recent structural adjustment policies – have had adverse effects on women in both their productive and reproductive roles.[7]

Many studies examine women's problems and prospects in the waged labour force.[8] It is understood, though, that women's roles in the spheres of production and social reproduction consist of waged employment and informal income-generating activities, domestic labour and childcare, and community-based activities.[9] These activities have tended to be undervalued by society, ignored by planners and policy-makers, and rendered invisible in national accounts.[10] Where women have been marginalised from the productive process or, conversely, where their productive and reproductive labour-time has been overstretched, the effects have been not only devastating for women, but may well have undermined the stated goals of economic development and structural change.[11]

These propositions have been tested empirically, whether through cross-national quantitative studies;[12] small-scale surveys of households in one or two countries;[13] country-case studies using ethnographic methods, including participant observation and in-depth interviews;[14] the analysis of secondary sources or data from large-scale surveys for one or more regions;[15] or some combination of research methods.[16]

Solutions to the disadvantaged position of women are varied, ranging from the passage of anti-discrimination laws to calls for greater integration of women in the development process. Although GAD theorists and researchers are extremely critical of the current neoliberal economic environment, it is perhaps a sign of the times that few explicitly call for politically organised transformation of the social structure, economic system, or political order, as did socialist-feminists and Marxists in the 1970s and 1980s. It stands to reason that because gender inequality has a systemic character, with discrimination only the end result of a complex network of social relations, it requires a systemic solution. Today there is a tendency to play down the systemic defects and to address problems and issues that may be tackled more immediately. Strategies to improve women's positions include making economists and planners more gender-aware;[17] calling on governments and employers to spread women's reproductive responsibilities equitably;[18] and calling for greater investments in women's education, access to credit, and employment.[19] It is believed that these strategies could lead to deeper transformations and the eventual economic empowerment of women in societies. It is also believed that change and especially political empowerment could come about through women's mobilisation and the activities of feminist organisations.[20]

In current GAD research, the unit of analysis may be the household, a region within the society, the female labour force, or the national economy. Increasingly, attention is being directed to the global economy. In what follows, I offer an overview of the gender dynamics of the global economy.

By gender I mean an asymmetrical social relationship between women and men based on perceived sex differences, and an ideology regarding their roles, rights, and values as workers, owners, citizens, and parents. The differential positions of women and men in the spheres of production and reproduction reflect the social relations of gender and are perpetuated by gender ideologies, while economic differences among women result from the inequalities of class and ethnicity, structured by the mode of production. By global economy I mean the increasingly integrated and interdependent system of capital-labour flows across regions, between states and through transnational corporations and international financial institutions, in the form of capital investments, technology transfer, financial exchanges, and increased trade, as well as the various forms of the deployment of labour, by which global accumulation takes place. The regions across and within which capital accumulation takes place may be understood in terms of geographic units (e.g., Latin America, Sub-Saharan Africa, Southeast Asia, North America), in terms of income levels (high-, middle-, and low-income countries); or stages of industrialisation (developing/industrialising – the South; developed/post-industrial countries – the North); or in terms of the economic zones of the world-system (core, periphery, and semi-periphery). All of these imply uneven development and unequal power relations.

Through institutions such as the transnational corporation and the state, the global economy generates capital largely through the exploitation of labour, but it is not indifferent to the gender and ethnicity of that labour. Gender and racial ideologies have been deployed to favour white male workers and exclude others, but they have also been used to integrate and exploit the labour power of women and of members of disadvantaged racial and ethnic groups in the interest of profit-making. In the current global environment of open economies, new trade regimes, and competitive export industries, global accumulation relies heavily on the work of women, both waged and unwaged, in formal sectors and in the home, in manufacturing, and in public and private services. This phenomenon has been termed the 'feminisation of labour'. Guy Standing has hypothesised that the increasing globalisation of production and the pursuit of flexible forms of labour to retain or increase competitiveness, as well as changing job structures in industrial enterprises, favour the 'feminisation of employment' in the dual sense of an increase in the numbers of women in the labour force and a deterioration of work conditions (labour standards, income, and employment status).[21] Women have been gaining an increasing share of many kinds of jobs, but in the context of a decline in the social power of labour and growing unemployment, their labour-market participation has not been accompanied by a redistribution of domestic, household, and childcare responsibilities. Moreover, women are still disadvantaged in the new labour markets, in terms of wages, training, and occupational segregation. They are also disproportionately involved in forms of employment increasingly used to maximise profits: temporary, part-time, casual, and home-based work. Generally speaking, the situation is better or worse for women depending on the type of state and the strength of the economy. Women workers in the welfare states of northern Europe fare best, followed by women in other strong Western economies. In Eastern Europe and the former Soviet Union, the economic status of working women changed dramatically for the worse following the collapse of communism. In much of the developing world, a class of women professionals and workers employed in the public sector and in the private sector has certainly emerged due to rising educational attainment, changing aspirations, economic need, and the demand for relatively cheap labour. However, vast numbers of economic-ally active women in the developing world lack formal training, work in the informal sector, have no access to social security, and live in poverty.

Women have been incorporated into the global economy as a source of relatively cheap labour. The simultaneous emergence and expansion of formal and informal employment among women can be explained in terms of labour-market segmentation, various management strategies to extract surplus-value or increase profitability, and the depressed status of unions. In the GAD perspective offered here, the global economy is maintained by *gendered* labour, with definitions of skill, allocation of resources, occupa-tional distribution, and modes of remuneration shaped by asymmetrical gender relations and by gender ideologies defining the roles and rights of men and women and the relative value of their labour. But the effects have not been uniformly negative, for there have been unintended con-sequences of women's economic participation. Tiano and Kim provide detailed accounts of how women workers in the Mexican maquilas and in a South Korean free export zone, respectively, accommodate and resist the dominating forces of global capitalism and patriarchy.[22] In my own work on the Middle East and North Africa, I show that the entry of women into the labour force in such large numbers has important implications for changes in gender relations and ideologies within the household and the larger society, and for women's gender consciousness and activism.[23]

Indeed, GAD research is attentive not only to structure (i.e., the economy, the gender system, the labour market) but also to expressions of women's agency, including the emergence of women's organisations and trans-national networks that are responding to national development problems and global economic issues. Local women's organisations and transnational feminist networks that span developing and developed countries are linked together in ways that suggest a global women's movement. These organisa-tions are increasingly networking and coordinating their activities, engag-ing in dialogue and forms of cooperation and mutual support, sending representatives to meetings in other countries and regions, and utilising a similar vocabulary to describe women's disadvantages and the desired alternatives.[24] Many were involved in the myriad preparatory activities for the world conferences of the 1990s, and they sent representatives to attend the non-governmental forums.

The mobilisation of women into feminist groups and women's non-governmental organisations has occurred on the part of women with edu-cation and work experience, and represents their response to continuing problems in the areas of literacy, education, employment, health, poverty, violence, human rights, and political participation. As such, international development may have created its most formidable and consistent critic – international feminism.

Notes

1. Ester Boserup, *Women and Economic Development* (St Martin's Press, New York, 1970); Irene Tinker, *Persistent Inequalities: Women and World Development* (Oxford University Press, New York, 1990).

2. See, for example, Lourdes Beneria and Gita Sen, 'Accumulation, Reproduction and Women's Role in Economic Development: Boserup Revisited', *Signs*, 7 (1981), pp. 279–98.

3. Rae Lesser Blumberg, *Making the Case for the Gender Variable* (Office of Women in Development, USAID, Washington, DC, 1989).

4. See Gita Sen and Caren Grown, *Development, Crises, and Alternative Visions: Third World Women's Perspectives* (Monthly Review, New York, 1987).

5. Bina Agarwal, *A Field of One's Own: Gender and Land Rights in South Asia* (Cambridge University Press, Cambridge, 1995); United Nations, *The World's Women 1995: Trends and Statistics* (United Nations, New York, 1995).

6. See, for example, Maxine Molyneux, 'Mobilization without Emancipation? Women's Interests, State, and Revolution', in *Transition and Development: Problems of Third World Socialism*, ed. Richard Fagen, Carmen Diana Deere, and José Luis Corragio (Monthly Review Press, New York, 1986), pp. 280–302; Naila Kabeer, *Reversed Realities: Gender Hierarchies in Development Thought* (Verso, London, 1994); Caroline O. N. Moser, *Gender Planning and Development: Theory, Practice and Training* (Routledge, London, 1993); Valentine M. Moghadam, 'Women in Societies', *International Social Science Journal*, no. 139 (February 1994), pp. 95–115; V. M. Moghadam (ed.), *Patriarchy and Development: Women's Positions at the End of the Twentieth Century* (Clarendon Press, Oxford, 1996).

7. See, for example, Diane Elson (ed.), *Male Bias in the Development Process* (Manchester University Press, Manchester, 1991). For critiques of structural adjustment, see especially Commonwealth Secretariat, *Engendering Adjustment for the 1990s* (Commonwealth Secretariat, London, 1989); Isabella Bakker (ed.), *The Strategic Silence: Gender and Economic Policy* (Zed Books, London, 1994); Pam Sparr (ed.), *Mortgaging Women's Lives: Feminist Critiques of Structural Adjustment* (Zed, London, 1995).

8. Studies focusing on work include Valentine M. Moghadam, *Women, Work, and Economic Reform in the Middle East and North Africa* (Lynne Rienner Publishers, Boulder, CO, 1998); Helen Safa, *The Myth of the Male Breadwinner: Women and Industrialization in the Caribbean* (Westview, Boulder, CO, 1995); Susan Tiano, *Patriarchy on the Line: Labor, Gender, and Ideology in the Mexican Maquila Industry* (Temple University Press, Philadelphia, 1994).

9. Lourdes Beneria and Martha Roldan, *The Crossroads of Class and Gender: Industrial Homework, Subcontracting, and Household Dynamics in Mexico City* (University of Chicago Press, 1987); Diane Elson, 'From Survival Strategies to Transformation Strategies: Women's Needs and Structural Adjustment', in *Unequal Burden*, ed. Lourdes Beneria and Shelley Feldman (Westview, Boulder, CO, 1992), pp. 26–48; Caroline O. N. Moser, 'Gender Planning in the Third World: Meeting Practical and Strategic Gender Needs', *World Development*, vol. 17, no. 11 (1989), 1799–1825.

10. An early examination of the non-recognition of much of women's work was in Lourdes Beneria (ed.), *Women and Development: The Sexual Division of Labor in Rural Societies* (Praeger, New York, 1982); for a more recent elaboration, see UNDP, *Human Development Report 1995* (Oxford University Press, New York, 1995).

11. For examples of this argument, see Susan Joekes, 'Gender and Macroeconomic Policy' (Association for Women in Development, Occasional Paper No. 4, Washington, DC, 1989); Ingrid Palmer, *Gender and Population in the Adjustment of African Economies* (ILO, Geneva, 1991); World Bank, *Enhancing Women's Participation in Economic Development* (The World Bank, Washington, DC, 1994).

12. See, for example, Kathryn Ward, *Women in the World-System: Its Impact on Status and Fertility* (Praeger, New York, 1984); Nilufer Catagay and Sule Ozler, 'Feminization of the Labor Force: The Effects of Long-Term Development and Structural Adjustment', *World Development*, vol. 23, no. 11 (1995), 1883–94;

13. Examples include Sylvia Chant, 'Women's Roles in Recession and Economic Restructuring in Mexico and the Philippines', in *Poverty and Global Adjustment: The Urban Experience*, ed. Alan Gilbert (Blackwell, Oxford, 1995); Brigida Garcia and Orlandina de Oliveira, 'Gender Relations in Urban Middle-Class and Working-Class Households in Mexico', in *Engendering Wealth and Well-Being: Empowerment for Global Change*, ed. Blumberg et al. (Westview, Boulder, CO, 1995), pp. 195–210; Nazneen Kanji, 'Gender and Structural Adjustment: A Case Study of Harare, Zimbabwe' (unpublished dissertation, Dept. of Geography, London School of Economics, 1994).

14. Such studies include Patricia Fernandez-Kelly, *For We Are Sold, I and My People: Women and Industry in Mexico's Frontier* (SUNY Press, Albany, 1983); Rita Gallin, 'State, Gender, and the Organization of Business in Rural Taiwan', in *Patriarchy and Economic Development: Women's Positions at the End of the Twentieth Century*, ed. V. M. Moghadam (Clarendon Press, Oxford, 1996), pp. 220–40; Helen Safa, *The Myth of the Male Breadwinner*.

15. Isabella Bakker, 'Women's Employment in Comparative Perspective', in *Feminization of the Labour Force: Paradoxes and Promises*, ed. Jane Jenson, Elisabeth Hagen and Ceallaigh Reddy (Polity Press, Cambridge, 1988), pp. 17–44; Maria Sagrario Floro, 'Economic Restructuring, Gender and the Allocation of Time', *World Development*, vol. 23, no. 11 (1995); Deniz Kandiyoti, *Women in Rural Production Systems* (UNESCO, Paris, 1985); Valentine M. Moghadam, 'The Feminization of Poverty? Notes on a Concept and Trends', Illinois State University, Women's Studies Program, Occasional Paper No. 2 (August 1997).

16. An example is Sylvia Chant, *Women-Headed Households: Diversity and Dynamics in the Developing World* (Macmillan, London, 1995). See also V. M. Moghadam, *Women, Work, and Economic Reform in the Middle East and North Africa*, and Naila Kabeer, *Reversed Realities*.

17. This approach may be found in Caroline Moser, *Gender Planning and Development*. See also Diane Elson, 'Gender Awareness in Modeling Structural Adjustment', *World Development*, vol. 23, no. 11 (1995), 1851–68; and Ruth Pearson, 'Bringing It all Back Home: Integrating Training for Gender Specialists and Economic Planners', *World Development*, vol. 23, no. 11 (1995), 1995–9.

18. This is recommended in *The Beijing Platform for Action* (United Nations, New York, 1996). For a theoretical justification, see Ingrid Palmer, 'Public Finance from a Gender Perspective', *World Development*, vol. 23, no. 11 (1995), 1981–6.

19. World Bank, *Enhancing Women's Participation in Economic Development*.

20. The role of women's movements is emphasised in Sen and Grown, *Development Crisis, and Alternative Visions*; Moser, *Gender Planning and Development*; Moghadam, 'Women in Societies', and Moghadam, *Women, Work, and Economic Reform*, ch. 9.

21. Guy Standing, 'Global Feminization Through Flexible Labour', *World Development* vol. 17, no. 7 (1989), 1077–95.

22. See Susan Tiano, *Patriarchy on the Line*; Seung-Kyung Kim, *Class Struggle or Family Struggle? The Lives of Women Factory Workers in South Korea* (Cambridge University Press, Cambridge, UK, 1997).

23. See, in particular, ch. 9 in Moghadam, *Women, Work, and Economic Reform*.

24. For an elaboration, see Marilee Karl, *Women and Empowerment: Participation and Decision-Making*, (Zed Books, London, 1995); Valentine M. Moghadam, 'Feminist Networks North and South', *Journal of International Communication*, 3 (1996), pp. 111–21; Geertje Lycklama À Nijeholt, Virginia Vargas and Saskia Wieringa (eds), *Women's Movements and Public Policy in Europe, Latin America, and the Caribbean* (Garland Publishing, Inc., New York, 1998).

NOTES ON CONTRIBUTORS

Margot Badran is affiliated with the Center for Middle Eastern Studies at the University of Chicago. She was recently a visiting professor at the Women's Studies Center at the University of Sana`a. The author of *Feminists, Islam, and Nation: Gender and the Making of Modern Egypt* and co-editor of *Opening the Gates: A Century of Arab Feminist Writing*, she is now working on a comparative study of Islamic feminism.

Heloise Brown is completing a DPhil on women pacifists and internationalists, 1870–1902, at the Centre for Women's Studies, University of York, UK. She is co-editor with Ann Kaloski and Ruth Symes of *Celebrating Women's Friendship: Past, Present and Future* (UCL, in press).

Antoinette Burton is Senior Lecturer in History and the Associate Director of the Women's Studies Program at the Johns Hopkins University. She is the author of two books – *Burdens of History: British Feminists, Indian Women and Imperial Culture 1865–1915* (North Carolina, 1994) and *At the Heart of the Empire: Indians and the Colonial Encounter in Late-Victorian Britain* (California, 1998) – as well as numerous articles on race, nation, empire, feminism, and colonialism. She is currently at work on a book-length project about Indian women writers and the architectural idioms of memory and home.

Christine Ehrick is an Assistant Professor of History at the University of Northern Iowa. Her research looks at the different types of 'feminisms' that existed in Uruguay in the years prior to women's suffrage, as well as the specific interaction between liberal feminism and the emerging Uruguayan welfare state in the early twentieth century.

Donna J. Guy is Professor of History at the University of Arizona. Author of *Sex and Danger in Buenos Aires: Prostitution, Family and Nation in Argentina* (1991) and co-editor with Daniel Balderston of *Sex and Sexuality in Latin America* (1997), she has also published many articles on the history of women in Argentina and Latin America. Currently she is researching the history of state policies toward street children and orphans in Argentina and their impact on the construction of modern notions of mothering and fathering.

Ping-Chun Hsiung is an Associate Professor of Sociology at the University of Toronto at Scarborough. Her areas of interest are feminist theories, methodology and epistemology. She has done extensive field work in Taiwan and China. She is author of *Living rooms as Factories: Class, Gender and Satellite Factory Systems in Taiwan*.

Jayne O. Ifekwunigwe lectures in Anthropology and Sociology at the University of East London in Britain. She has just finished writing her book *Scattered Belongings: Cultural Paradoxes of 'Race', Nation and Gender* (forthcoming 1998). She is also a self-taught visual artist and a poet.

Mary E. John is Senior Fellow at the Centre for Women's Development Studies, New Delhi, India. She is the author of *Discrepant Dislocation: Feminism, Theory and Post Colonial Histories*, (1996) and editor with Janaki Nair of *A Question of Silence? The Sexual Economics of Modern India* (forthcoming). She is currently researching the history of the women's movement and women's studies in India and is especially interested in questions of globalism and international feminism.

Insook Kwon is a doctoral candidate in Women's Studies at Clark University. She is writing a dissertation about 'Militarism in My Heart: Militarization of Women's

Consciousness and Culture in South Korea'. She has published her autobiography, *Beyond a Wall* (Gureum Press, 1989) and three books of *Labor Human Rights Annual Report* (Yeoksa Bipyung Press, 1990, 1991, 1992).

Asunción Lavrin is Professor of History at Arizona State University. She has written extensively in English and in Spanish, on the history and the historiography of women in Latin America between the sixteenth and the late twentieth century. She is the editor and co-author of *Latin American Women: Historical Perspectives* (1978); *Sexuality and Marriage in Colonial Latin America* (1989), and author of *Women, Feminism, and Social Change: Argentina, Chile and Uruguay, 1890–1940* (1995). The latter won the 1996 Arthur P. Whitaker Prize conferred by the Middle-Atlantic Council of Latin American Studies.

Francesca Miller is a visiting fellow at the University of California Humanities Research Institute at Irvine and an affiliate of the Department of History, University of California, Davis. She is the author of *Latin American Women and the Search for Social Justice* (University Press of New England, 1991), and co-author of *Women, Culture and Politics in Latin America* (University of California Press, 1990).

Valentine M. Moghadam was born in Tehran, Iran and received her higher education in Canada and the US. After obtaining her PhD in sociology from the American University in Washington DC in 1986, she taught the sociology of development and women in development at New York University. From 1990 until January 1996 she was Senior Researcher and Coordinator of the Research Program on Women and Development at the WIDER Institute of the United Nations University (UNU), and was based in Helsinki, Finland. She was a member of the UNU delegation to the Social Summit in Copenhagen (March 1995) and the Fourth World Conference on Women in Beijing (September 1995). Dr Moghadam has published numerous articles and has edited six books. She is also the author of *Modernizing Women: Gender and Social Change in the Middle East* (1993), and *Women, Work and Economic Reform in the Middle East and North Africa* (1998). She is currently Director of Women's Studies and Associate Professor of Sociology at Illinois State University.

V. Spike Peterson is Associate Professor of Political Science at the University of Arizona. She is contributor to and editor of *Gendered States: Feminist (Re)Visions of International Relations Theory* and co-author of *Global Gender Issues*. Her current research focuses on sexing the state and 'rewriting political economy as reproductive, productive and symbolic economies'.

Shahnaz Rouse is an Associate Professor in the Sociology Faculty at Sarah Lawrence College, New York. Her research interests include gender and nationalism, women, religion and the state, and the politics of representation. She is currently working on a project of comparative women's struggles in colonial Egypt and India.

Leila J. Rupp teaches women's history at Ohio State University. She is the author, most recently, of *Worlds of Women: The Making of an International Women's Movement* (Princeton University Press, 1998). She is also the editor of the *Journal of Women's History*.

Mrinalini Sinha is Associate Professor of History at Southern Illinois University at Carbondale and is the North American co-editor for *Gender & History*. She is the author of *Colonial Masculinity: The 'manly Englishman' and the 'effeminate Bengali' in the late nineteenth century* (1995), and has edited and introduced a new edition of Katherine Mayo's *Mother India*, which was first published in 1927 (forthcoming 1998). She is currently completing a monograph on the implications of the massive international controversy generated by Mayo's *Mother India*.

Angela Woollacott is an Associate Professor of History and teaches in the Women's Studies program at Case Western Reserve University in Cleveland, Ohio, USA. Her publications include *On Her Their Lives Depend: Munitions Workers in the Great War* (1994) and, co-edited with Miriam Cooke, *Gendering War Talk* (1993). She is currently working on a book tentatively titled 'White Colonials, Modernity and the Metropolis: Australian Women in London 1870–1940'.

Yuk-Lin Renita Wong is a PhD candidate of Sociology and Equity Studies at the Ontario Institute for Studies in Education of the University of Toronto. Her forthcoming dissertation is on Hong Kong people's pursuit of developing China in launching poverty eradication and mass education projects in China. It is part of her larger research interests in gender, development, nation-building (post)colonialism and questions of identity.

Index